CONCISE DICTIONARY OF SCIENCE

A Perfect Reference for Aspirants of IAS, IIT-JEE, AIEEE, CBSE-PMT, and Students of All Age Groups

Editorial Board

Published by:

F-2/16, Ansari road, Daryaganj, New Delhi-110002
☎ 23240026, 23240027 •Fax: 011-23240028
Email: info@vspublishers.com

Branch : Hyderabad
5-1-707/1, Brij Bhawan (Beside Central Bank of India Lane)
Bank Street, Koti, Hyderabad - 500 095
☎ 040-24737290
E-mail: vspublishershyd@gmail.com

Follow us on:

All books available at **www.vspublishers.com**

© Copyright: V&S PUBLISHERS
ISBN 978-93-815886-4-2
Edition: 2012

The Copyright of this book, as well as all matter contained herein (including illustrations) rests with the Publishers. No person shall copy the name of the book, its title design, matter and illustrations in any form and in any language, totally or partially or in any distorted form. Anybody doing so shall face legal action and will be responsible for damages.

Printed at: Param Offsetters, Okhla, New Delhi

Contents

Publisher's Note	5
Introduction	7
A	13
B	34
C	45
D	83
E	97
F	113
G	123
H	136
I	151
J	163
K	164
L	166
M	176
N	196
O	211
P	219
Q	249
R	251
S	273
T	304
U	320
V	324
W	330
X	335
Y	339
Z	342
Appendices	
Appendix – I	345
Appendix – II	348
Appendix – III	349
Appendix – IV	350
Appendix – V	352
Appendix – VI	354
Appendix – VII	355
Appendix – VIII	357
Appendix – IX	358

Publisher's Note

Innumerable books are available in the market on science and its allied branches, like, physics, chemistry, and biology et al, both as textbook and reference manual. Written for different age-groups and class, quite a number of these books come replete with jargon-filled terms; and just fail to connect with readers' inclination and curiosity level. On top of that, new words keep finding their way into the books every other day. Every new addition contributes to difficulty in comprehending the matter.

An average reader is interested only in knowing what a specific word means without getting lost with heavy sounding inputs.

Following an open-ended discussion with a cross-section of students and other stakeholders we realised that many books on science (physics, chemistry and biology) take readers' understanding of scientific terms for granted and make short passing references while alluding to the term in the text. Presentations of this nature in no way assist readers in understanding the subject properly.

You need to suffer no longer.

V&S Publishers has come out with four dictionaries of terms; in science, physics, chemistry and biology. These have been compiled to help readers grasp the meaning of popular scientific terms. For easy reference terms have been arranged alphabetically. Terms that have come into the reckoning even in the early 2012 have been incorporated and suitably explained in such a way that an average secondary and senior secondary student can grasp them easily. High resolution images, illustrations and examples, where appropriate, have been added for reader's convenience. For all readers, who have not made a special study of any science subject, explanations of terms will be found to be easily comprehensible.

An attempt has been made to include important scientific charts, tables, constants, conversion tables as appendices to make this dictionary more useful. A glossary of Nobel Prize winners and their contributions is an added attraction.

We would be happy to have your views and comments about the book.

Introduction

Why Study Science?
Let's look at why we must have a working knowledge of science in everyday life.

Science is the study of the world around us - we learn all about the world that we live in - how things work, what living things there are, how things happen, etc. Science is the study supported by logic and reasoning. Learning science is all about examining properties of a thing in a systematic manner, endorsed by validation of the theoretical knowledge through the scientific experimentation and research, etc.

Science helps us, so to say, to separate grain from the chaff - there are a lot of misrepresentations on the television, the internet, and by word of mouth. If we arrive at the truth by learning science, we won't fall for all those inaccuracies!

Scope
Studying science equips us with the essential skills that make us employable, be that in a scientific or non-scientific arena. Science enables us to become more confident, gain proficiency with figures and calculations that prove invaluable when it comes to future employment. The 'mathematical application within science' is more than just putting numbers into formulae; it involves analysing data and understanding trends in the same way that businessmen might examine market data or sales figures. Problem solving is another key skill that needs to be mastered within science.

How is Science Classified?
Science can be classified in the following broad categories:

Biology - Biology is the study of anything that is alive; there are many sub-categories like microbiology, botany, and zoology.
- Learning how living things work helps us to understand our own body and our health
- Learning how living things survive helps us to understand why people act the way they do
- Learning how living things are connected helps us to see why we should preserve our planet

Physical Science - Physical Science includes those sciences that study living and non-living things. These sciences are physics, chemistry, earth sciences (geology, meteorology, oceanography, etc), and astronomy (studying the stars and other planets).

- Learning how the universe works helps us to understand why things happen
- Learning how the earth came into existence helps us to understand why the world is the way it is
- Learning how the earth works helps us to survive earthquakes, tornadoes, and tsunamis
- Learning how the universe works helps us to see connections between all things

Social Science - These are sciences dealing with human beings. Some examples of social sciences include anthropology, geography, economics, and history.

- Learning how people interact helps us to get along with others better
- Learning how the world works helps us to be more successful
- Learning what people have done in the past helps us to avoid making the same mistakes
- Learning how people in different cultures live helps us to understand them and avoid conflicts

Application

Everything around us concerns about science...

Cooking involves process like condensation, evaporation, boiling... Inner metabolism of our body can be understood through study of biology which is part of science... The transportation, navigation, constructions and many others involves calculations, physics, logical and critical thinking - part of science. Geologists study about the ages of our World and fossils, shifting of continental shelves, occurrences of natural phenomenon all related to Science. Science starts with observation and most ends with a theory, prediction, anything which improves our daily lives.

Employability

The skills acquired by studying science are versatile and are applicable to any profession; a foundation in science can lead to a huge variety of career options in all sectors. Study of science is obviously relevant to many science-related jobs, such as engineering, information technology, medicine, psychology, sports science, biotechnology, animal health, forensics or astronomy, but they are also significant to working in banking, journalism, teaching, television, marketing, law, photography, art restoration, media and film production, and so on.

Benefits

In addition to providing students with useful skills and making them highly employable, it has been shown that achieving further qualifications in science brings greater rewards in monetary terms in future employment when compared to other subjects. The research carried out by PricewaterhouseCoopers in 2005 showed that students of chemistry and physics earn on average 30% more than those studied other subjects.

Without science we wouldn't have all the great inventions that we have amongst us today.

It makes one understand nature and how they exist.

Scientific conclusions are arrived through trials and errors. By trials and errors we make new inventions. Those precious cell phones to teenagers, those cars we rely on, the understanding of animals, the rainforests we study, the understanding of our need for trees to create oxygen, that's all science.

Science helps our understanding of nature and needs. Our cutting of rainforests might have continued at a higher rate than it is now if it wasn't for science discovering how we need those trees for oxygen or for animals. Our understanding of the world we live in is important for our survival and our knowledge of what is to come.

Scientific understanding has taken the world out of the dark ages and turned humanity into a culture that can control its own destiny.

Medical science has extended the human life expectancy nearly four times in the last 300 years.

Physics perpetuates the ground works understanding of the world and universe as a whole.

Chemistry is responsible for every industrial material you can name.

Biology has vastly improved all understanding of the way life was created, perpetuates and thrives; thus fuelling all medical and life research.

Engineering has brought everything from bridges, buildings, roads, planes to computers, satellites, space stations and nanotechnology from the grasp of the ever inquisitive scientist and into the home of the common person.

Astronomy has been the foreground of every great discovery in fundamental physics since the dawn of civilisation.

The most elementary advantage of studying science is that we can satisfy ourselves by getting answers to all the questions coming in our mind such as why it works like this... What is this..??? How it works..??? And many other different questions.

Great Physicists of All Time

1. Archimedes (Greek) - Archimedes described concept of buoyancy and developed formulae for the areas and volumes of spheres, cylinders, parabolas, and several other solids. He worked extensively with levers. He also invented the Archimedes screw to raise water. In warfare he developed several siege engines that served to hamper the Roman invasion of his home city of Syracuse.
2. Galileo Galilei (Italian) - Galileo discovered the law of uniformly accelerated motion. He improved on the refracting telescope and discovered the four largest satellites of Jupiter. He also described projectile motion and the concept of weight. He is however best known for his championing of the

Copernican theory of heliocentricity against church opposition.
3. Michael Faraday (English) - Faraday showed how a changing magnetic field can be used to generate an electric current. He also described the principles of electrolysis. Faraday is the early pioneer in the field of low temperature study.
4. Johannes Kepler (German) - Kepler outlined three fundamental laws of planetary motion and described elliptical motion of planets around the sun. His work served as the precursor to that of Newton's.
5. Isaac Newton (English) - Newton described laws of motion and gravity. He explained the concept of light dispersion and co-invented the Calculus. He also invented the reflecting telescope.
6. Albert Einstein (German/Swiss/American) - Einstein developed Theories of Special and General Relativity. He worked on the photoelectric effect and described mass-energy equivalence.

Great Chemists of All-time
1. Dmitri Mendeleyev (Russian) - Mendeleyev devised the Periodic table of elements and predicted that several more elements would be discovered.
2. Antoine Lavoisier (French) - Lavoisier showed that air is a mixture of oxygen (O) and nitrogen (N). He disproved the old Theory of phlogiston and determined the nature of combustion. Lavoisier wrote the first modern book on chemistry and explained the law of conservation of matter.
3. Henry Cavendish (English) - Cavendish showed that water could be produced from two gases and discovered hydrogen (H).
4. Amedeo Avogadro (Italian) - Avogadro was the first to distinguish molecules from atoms he developed Avogadro's Constant (The number of particles of a substance in a mole) and studied the effect of combining volumes.
5. Jons Jakob Berzelius (Swedish) - Berzelius developed the symbols for many of the chemicals. He also calculated the atomic weights accurately of many of them and discovered Selenium, Silicon and Thorium.
6. John Dalton (English) - Developed an atomic theory of matter and explained the laws of partial pressure.
7. Robert Boyle (Irish) - Boyle studied gases and showed how pressure and volume at a constant mass were indirectly proportional to one another.

Great Biologists of All-time
1. Aristotle - Greek philosopher and scientist. He is sometimes called the father of biology. He was able to describe plant and animal specimens received from all parts of the far-flung Alexandrian empire. Out of 400 treatises that Aristotle wrote only 30 survive. Of these, most important in connection with biology are his Enquiry into Animals, Motion of Animals, Gait of Animals, Parts of Animals and Generation of Animals.
2. Charles Robert Darwin - An English naturalist. He established that all

species of life have descended over time from common ancestors, and proposed the scientific theory that this branching pattern of evolution resulted from a process that he called natural selection. Darwin published his theory with compelling evidence for evolution in his 1859 book On the Origin of Species, overcoming scientific rejection of earlier concepts of transmutation of species.
3. Walther Flemming - German biologist and a founder of cytogenetics. Flemming investigated the process of cell division and the distribution of chromosomes to the daughter nuclei, a process he called mitosis. His discovery of mitosis and chromosomes is considered one of the 100 most important scientific discoveries of all times.
4. Oswald Avery - an American physician and medical researcher. He was one of the first molecular biologists and a pioneer in immunochemistry, but he is best known for his discovery in 1944, with his co-workers Colin MacLeod and Maclyn McCarty, that DNA is the material of which genes and chromosomes are made.
5. Gregor Mendel - An Austrian scientist who gained fame as the founder of the new science of genetics. Mendel demonstrated that the inheritance of certain traits in pea plants follows particular patterns. This theory is now referred to as the laws of Mendelian inheritance. Although the significance of Mendel's work was not recognised until the turn of the 20th century, the independent rediscovery of these laws formed the foundation of the modern science of genetics.
6. Louis Pasteur - French chemist and microbiologist. He is remembered for his remarkable breakthroughs in the causes and preventions of diseases. He created the first vaccines for rabies and anthrax. He is best known for inventing a method to stop milk from causing sickness, a process that came to be called pasteurisation. He is regarded as one of the founders of microbiology. Pasteur also made many discoveries in the field of chemistry, most notably the molecular basis for the asymmetry of certain crystals
7. Linus Carl Pauling - An American chemist, biochemist, peace activist. He was one of the most influential chemists in history and among the first scientists to work in the fields of quantum chemistry and molecular biology. He is one of only two people awarded Nobel Prizes in different fields (chemistry and peace prizes). Besides being the greatest architect of chemistry, Pauling was a founder of molecular biology and a pioneer in quantum mechanics. Pauling combined chemistry and physics to solve various puzzles related to the nature of chemical bonding which now are fundamental to modern theories of molecular structure. Pauling determined crystal structure by X-ray crystallography and the structure of gas molecules by electron diffraction.

Future of Science

Science is omnipresent in modern society. Due to the unsustainable demands we make on the world's resources and the impact we have on our environment, the contribution of science is vital to ensure the survival of our planet by developing new or alternative solutions for everything we do from fuel production to waste disposal. With current issues such as gene therapy, nuclear power, oil exploration, genetically modified foods, bird flu and global warming, future scientists have a fascinating and crucial role to play, be it developing new communications solutions or contributing to make the world a better place. Studying science provides an excellent foundation, keeps options open and offers a good progression route either directly into employment or to higher education to study them or other related subjects further. By opting for science, students could find themselves contributing to ensuring the future of the planet as well as safeguarding their own secure future in the world of employment.

Aberration
Property of an optical system that causes an image to have certain easily recognisable flaws. Aberrations are caused by geometrical factors such as the shapes of surfaces, their spacing, and alignments. Image problems caused by factors such as scratches or contamination are not called aberrations.

Abiotic
Pertaining to nonliving properties, including light, air, water, nutrients and other physical and chemical properties of an environment.

Absolute date
An estimate of the true age of a mineral or rock based on the rate of decay of radioactive minerals.

Absolute pressure
The measurement of pressure relative to the pressure in a vacuum. It is equal to the sum of the pressure shown on a pressure gauge and atmospheric pressure.

Absolute pressure transducer
A transducer which measures pressure in relation to zero pressure (a vacuum on one side of the diaphragm).

Absolute risk
The probability that an individual will develop a particular condition, based on family history and/or test results.

Absolute zero
The lowest temperature ever reached in the Universe: 0 Kelvin (0K), equivalent to minus 273 degrees Celsius (-273 °C). In laboratories on Earth physicists can get very close to that temperature, but have not been able to achieve the absolute zero.

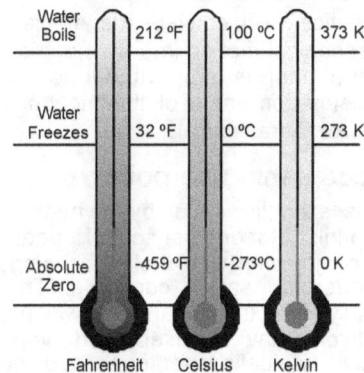

Absolute Zero
Thermometers compare Fahrenheit Celsius and Kelvin scales

Absorption
Decrease in intensity of radiation, when it crosses a material medium, as a consequence of an interaction between the radiation and the material medium.

Abundance
Relative number of atoms of a particular element, or isotope of an element, in the chemical composition of a single substance or object.

Abundant centre distribution
The highest population densities are observed in the range core, but the species becomes increasingly rare towards its range margin.

AC
Alternating current; an electric current that reverses its direction at regularly recurring intervals.

Acarology
Branch of Zoology dealing with ticks & mites.

Acceleration
A change in the velocity of a body or particle with respect to time. The parameter that an accelerometer measures (dv/dt). Units expressed in "g".

Accelerometer
A device which converts the effects of mechanical motion into an electrical signal that is proportional to the acceleration value of the motion. A sensor. A transducer.

Acceptable use policy
This is a policy set up by the network administrator or other school leaders in conjunction with their technology needs and safety concerns. This policy restricts the manner in which a network may be used, and helps provide guidelines for teachers using technology in the classroom.

Acceptor arm
The arm in tRNA to which an amino acid attaches.

Accessory chromosome
Any extra chromosome in the karyotype of an organism.

Accretion (disk, zone)
Process whereby small particles of matter accumulate and create larger bodies under the influence of their mutual gravitational attraction or as a result of chance collisions.

Accumulators
Plants containing intermediate concentrations of certain chemical elements (frequently metals or metallic compounds).

Accuracy
The closeness of an indication or reading of a measurement device to the actual value of the quantity being measured. Usually expressed as ± percent of full scale output or reading.

Acentric chromatid
Lacks a centromere; produced when crossing over takes place within a paracentric inversion. The acentric chromatid does not attach to a spindle fiber and does not segregate in meiosis or mitosis, so it is usually lost after one or more rounds of cell division.

Acequia
acequias are gravity driven waterways, similar in concept to a flume. Most are simple ditches with dirt banks, but they can be lined with concrete. They were important forms of irrigation in the development of agriculture in the American Southwest. The proliferation of cotton, pecans and green chile as major agricultural staples owe their progress to the acequia system.

Acetylation
An enzymatic reaction that results in the addition of an acetyl group to a biochemical.

Acid
a substance that has a pH of less than 7, which is neutral. Specifically, an acid has more free hydrogen ions (H^+) than hydroxyl ions (OH^-).

Acidic activation domain
Commonly found in some transcriptional activator proteins, a domain that contains multiple amino acids with negative charges and stimulates the transcription of certain genes.

Acoustics
The degree of sound. The nature, cause, and phenomena of the vibrations of elastic bodies; which vibrations create compressional waves or wave fronts which are transmitted through various media, such as air, water, wood, steel, etc.

Acre-foot (acre-ft)
the volume of water required to cover 1 acre of land (43,560 square feet) to a depth of 1 foot. Equal to 325,851 gallons or 1,233 cubic metres.

Acrobatics
The art of performing acrobatic feats (gymnastics)

Acrocentric chromosome
1. Chromosome in which the centromere is near one end, producing a long arm at one end and a knob, or satellite, at the other end.
2. A chromosome in which the centromere is located close to one end.

Across the flats
Measurement between 2 parallel faces on a nut. Indicates the size of spanner or socket required to tighten or loosen the nut.

Action potential
An electrical signal that carries information from the sensory organ to the brain via the nervous system.

Activation domain
Part of a transcription factor that is modular and independent from the DNA-binding activity. An activation domain stimulates activity at the locus.

Activation energy
The energy required to initiate a chemical reaction.

Activator
Protein in eukaryotic cells that binds to consensus sequences in regulatory promoters or enhancers and affects transcription initiation by stimulating or inhibiting the assembly of the basal transcription apparatus.

Active galactic nucleus (AGN)
Central region of a galaxy in which considerable energy is generated by processes other than those present in normal stars. The energy generated by the nucleus may outshine all the other stars in the galaxy. Most astronomers believe that at the centre of an AGN lies a supermassive black hole.

Active galaxy
A galaxy which releases large amounts of energy from its centre, the active galactic nucleus. The central engine of an active galaxy probably is a supermassive black hole. Seyfert galaxies, quasars and blazars are active galaxies.

Active restoration
Accelerating the process or attempting to change the trajectory of succession. For example, mine tailings would take so long to recover passively that active restoration is usually appropriate.

Active volcano
A volcano that is erupting; or one that, while not erupting at the present, has erupted within (geologically) recent time and is considered likely to do so in the (geologically) near future.

Activity (AI)
A thermodynamic term for the apparent or active concentration of a free ion in solution. It is related to concentration by the activity coefficient.

Activity coefficient (FI)
A ratio of the activity of species $i(a_i)$ to its molality (C). It is a correction factor which makes the thermodynamic calculations correct. This factor is dependent on ionic strength, temperature, and other parameters. Individual ionic activity coefficients, $f+$ for cation and $f-$ for an anion, cannot be derived thermodynamically. They can be calculated only by using the Debye-Huckel law for low concentration solutions in which the interionic forces depend primarily on charge, radius, and distribution of the ions and on the dielectric constant of the medium rather than on the chemical properties of the ions. Mean ionic activity coefficient $(f\pm)$ or the activity of a salt, on the other hand, can be measured by a variety of techniques such as freezing point depression and vapour pressure as well as paired sensing electrodes. It is the geometric mean of the individual ionic activity coefficients:
$$f \pm = (f + n + f - n-)\ 1/n$$

Adaptation
1. A process of genetic change in a population whereby, as a result of natural selection, the average state of a character becomes improved with reference to a specific function, or whereby a population is thought to have become better suited to some feature of its environment. Also, a feature that has become prevalent in a population because of a selective advantage conveyed by that feature in the improvement in some function.
2. A phenotypic trait that has evolved to help an organism cope with an environmental challenge or to increase its mating success.

Adapter
A mechanism or device for attaching non-mating parts.

Adaptive
A behaviour or trait that contributes either directly or indirectly to an individual.s fitness.

Adaptive evolution
The adjustment of an organism to its environment, or the process by which it enhances such fitness.

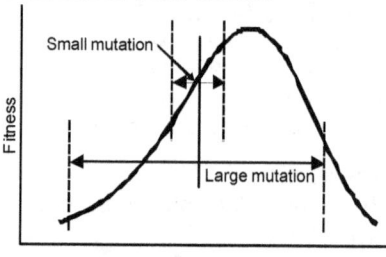

Adaptive immunity
A slow, specific immune response that develops after exposure to a foreign antigen.

Adaptive landscape
A three-dimensional depiction of population mean fitness as a function of genotype or phenotype, in which the horizontal axes are allele frequencies at two loci or two phenotypic traits, and the vertical axis is population mean fitness.

Adaptive mutation
Process by which a specific environment induces mutations that enable organisms to adapt to the environment.

Adaptive peak
1. A population mean fitness maximum, defined by values of

allele frequencies or phenotypic traits.
2. That allele frequency, or combination of allele frequencies at two or more loci, at which the mean fitness of a population has a (local) maximum. Also, the mean phenotype (for one or more characters) that maximizes mean fitness.

Adaptive radiation
Evolutionary divergence of members of a single phylogenetic lineage into a variety of different adaptive forms; usually the taxa differ in the use of resources or habitats, and have diverged over a relatively short interval of geological time. The term "evolutionary radiation" describes a pattern of rapid diversification without assuming that the differences are adaptive.

Adaptive topography
A three-dimensional depiction of population mean fitness as a function of genotype or phenotype, in which the horizontal axes are allele frequencies at two loci or two phenotypic traits, and the vertical axis is population mean fitness (synonym: adaptive topography).

Adaptive valley
A set of allele frequencies at which mean fitness has a minimum.

Adaptive zone
A set of similar ecological niches occupied by a group of (usually) related species, often constituting a higher taxon.

Adc
Analogue-to-Digital Converter: an electronic device which converts analog signals to an equivalent digital form, in either a binary code or a binary-coded-decimal code. When used for dynamic waveforms, the sampling rate must be high to prevent aliasing errors from occurring.

Addition rule
States that the probability of any of two or more mutually exclusive events occurring is calculated by adding the probabilities of the individual events.

Additive effect
The magnitude of the effect of an allele on a character, measured as half the phenotypic difference between homozygotes for that allele compared with homozygotes for a different allele.

Additive genetic correlation
A measure of the degree to which two traits are affected by the same genes (pleiotropy) or pairs of genes (linkage disequilibrium). Selection on one trait produces an evolutionary change in all traits that have an additive genetic correlation with the selected trait.

Additive genetic variance
1. That component of the genetic variance in a character that is attributable to additive effects of alleles.
2. The magnitude of the phenotypic (and genotypic) variance that is due to additive effects of genes and that determines the degree to which the average phenotype of the parents is reflected in the average phenotype of their progeny.

Additive genetic variance-covariance matrix
A square matrix with additive genetic variances for the traits on the diagonal and additive genetic covariances on the off-diagonal.

Additivity
The type of gene action in which the alleles at a locus do not affect each

other's expression or the expression of alleles at other loci; in other words, gene action with no dominance or epistasis.

Address
The label or number identifying the memory location where a unit of information is stored.

Adenine
A purine base in DNA and RNA.

Adenine (A)

Adenosine-3',5'-cyclic monophosphate
Modified nucleotide that functions in catabolite repression. Low levels of glucose stimulate high levels of cAMP; cAMP then attaches to CAP, which binds to the promoter of certain operons and stimulates transcription.

Adiabatic rate
The rate of temperature change in the atmosphere due to the raising or lowering of an air mass. The "dry adiabatic rate" is 5.5 deg. F. per 1000 feet, while the "wet" rate is 3.5 deg. F. per 1000 feet.

Adiabatic system
A system that neither gains or looses heat.

Adjacent-1 segregation
Type of segregation that takes place in a heterozygote for a translocation. If the original, nontranslocated chromosomes are N1 and N2 and the chromosomes containing the translocated segments are T1 and T2, then adjacent-1 segregation takes place when N1 and T2 move toward one pole and T1 and N2 move toward the opposite pole.

Adjacent-2 segregation
Type of segregation that takes place in a heterozygote for a translocation. If the original, nontranslocated chromosomes are N1 and N2 and the chromosomes containing the translocated segments are T1 and T2, then adjacent-2 segregation takes place when N1 and T1 move toward one pole and T2 and N2 move toward the opposite pole.

A-DNA
Right-handed helical structure of DNA that exists when little water is present.

Adult-onset
Describes a condition in which the phenotype does not manifest itself until later in life. The physical manifestation of such a condition is not present until after puberty.

Aerodynamics
1. The branch of mechanics that deals with the motion of air and other gases.
2. The study of the motion and control of solid bodies like aircraft, missiles, etc. in air.

Aeronautics
The science or art of flight.

Aeronomy
The study of the atmosphere of a planet, with particular attention to the composition, properties and motion of atmosphere constituents.

Aerosol
A gaseous suspension of ultramicroscopic particles of a liquid or a solid.

Aerosol collector
An instrument that collects aerosols and analyzes their composition.

Aerostatics
The branch of statics that deals with gases in equilibrium and with gases and bodies in them.

Aesthetics
The philosophy of fine arts.

Aetiology
The science of causation.

Affinity chromatography
A method of separating biochemical components based on specific interactions between the components of the biochemical mixture and other molecules (e.g., antigen-antibody or receptor-ligand).

AFLP
Genetic markers detected by cleaving DNA with one or more restriction enzymes and then amplifying some of these fragments by PCR using primers with random nucleotide sequences.

African sleeping sickness
A vector-borne disease caused by parasites from the genus Trypanosoma.

Ageing
The decline in organismal fitness that occurs with increasing age.

Agrobiology
The science of plant life and plant nutrition.

Agronomic
The science of managing land or crops.

Agronomy
The science of soil management & production of field crops.

Agrostology
The study of grasses.

Alara
Most often used in reference to chemical or radiation exposure levels.

Alarp
It is applied to the reduction of risk by taking measures to reduce risk until the cost of further measures is grossly disproportionate to the benefits they would deliver.

Alchemy
Chemistry in ancient times.

Alcohol
Organic compound used in gums, resins, dyes and perfumes. Fermentation produces ethanol not alcohol.

Alder
A common flowering plant along the successional chain of species for a forest.

Algol
Best known variable star, varying in brightness from about 2.2 to 3.5 magnitudes over a period of approximately 69 hours. It is in fact a binary system in which the two stars regularly cross in front of each other as viewed from Earth.

Alias
A file that points to another item, such as a programme, document, folder, or disk. When an alias is opened, the original item that the alias points to is opened. This helps in the organizing and accessing of files. Alias is purely a Mac term. The equivalent term for Windows-based computers is a shortcut.

Aliasing
If the sample rate of a function (fs) is less than two times the highest frequency value of the function, the frequency is ambiguously presented. The frequencies above (fs/2) will be folded back into the lower frequencies producing erroneous data.

Alignment
Process of mounting optical elements and adjusting their positions and orientations so that light follows exactly the desired path through the instrument and each optical element performs its function as planned.

Alkali
A base that is soluble in water.

Alkaline
Sometimes water or soils contain an amount of alkali (strongly basic) substances sufficient to raise the pH value above 7.0 and be harmful to the growth of crops.

Alkalinity
the capacity of water for neutralizing an acid solution.

Alkaptonuria
A single-gene disorder identified by Archibald Garrod that is characterized by dark urine. Garrod first coined the term "inborn error in metabolism" to describe this and other congenital, inherited disorders that affect metabolic pathways.

Allele
Alleles are alternate forms of a gene.

Allele frequency
The allele frequency represents the incidence of a gene variant in a population.

Alleles
Alternative versions of genes that are located at a specific position on a specific chromosome.

Allelopathy
Biochemical production by a plant which alters growth and survival of other plants or itself.

Alliance contract
A contract that generally relates to a specific and discrete set of services such as design or maintenance.

Allometric coeffient
(a) in the linear equation, $\log y = a \log x + \log b$, the slope of the line.

Allometric equations
An equation to aid in the calculation of the change in proportion of various parts of an organism as a consequence of growth.

Allometric growth
Growth of a feature during ontogeny at a rate different from that of another feature with which it is compared.

Allometry
Biological scaling relationships, be it for morphological traits, physiological traits or ecological traits; the study of the relationship between size and shape.

Allopatric
Of a population or species, occupying a geographic region different from that of another population or species.

Allopatric speciation
An evolutionary process in which one species becomes two usually due to a physical barrier.

Allopolyploid
A polyploid in which the several chromosome sets are derived from more than one species.

Allosteric protein
Protein that changes its conformation on binding with another molecule.

Allotrope
Element with more than one natural form.

Alloy
A substance formed by the combination of two or more elements, at least one of which must be a metal.

Alloy 11
A compensating alloy used in conjunction with pure copper as the negative leg to form extension wire for platinum-platinum rhodium thermocouples Types R and S.

Alloy 200/226
The combination of compensating alloys used with tungsten vs. tungsten 26% rhenium thermocouples as extension cable for applications under 200°C.

Alloy 203/225
The combination of compensating alloys used with tungsten 3% rhenium vs. tungsten 150 rhenium thermocouples as extension cable for applications under 200°C.

Alloy 405/426
The combination of compensating alloys used with tungsten 5% rhenium vs. tungsten 26% rhenium thermocouples as extension cable for applications under 870°C.

Alluvium
deposits of clay, silt, sand, gravel, or other particulate material that has been deposited by a stream or other body of running water in a streambed, on a flood plain, on a delta, or at the base of a mountain.

Alpha diversity
Within-habitat diversity.

Alphanumeric
A character set that contains both letters and digits.

Alternate segregation
Type of segregation that takes place in a heterozygote for a translocation. If the original, nontranslocated chromosomes are N1 and N2 and the chromosomes containing the translocated segments are T1 and T2, then alternate segregation takes place when N1 and N2 move toward one pole and T1 and T2 move toward the opposite pole.

Alternation of generations
Complex life cycle in plants that alternates between the diploid sporophyte stage and the haploid gametophyte stage.

Alternative processing pathway
One of several pathways by which a single pre-mRNA can be processed in different ways to produce alternative types of mRNA.

Alternative splicing
1 Process by which a single pre-mRNA can be spliced in more than one way to produce different types of mRNA.
2 Splicing of different sets of exons from mRNA to form mature transcripts that are translated into different proteins (thus allowing the same gene to encode different proteins).

Altitude
Height in space of an object or point relative to sea level or ground level.

Altruism
Conferral of a benefit on other individuals at an apparent cost to the donor.

Altruistic
Behaviour by an individual that may reduce its immediate direct fitness but increases the fitness of another.

ALU
Arithmetic Logic Unit. The part of a CPU where binary data is acted upon with mathematical operations.

ALU
Part of a family of short, interspersed repeats, these are the most abundant sequence repeats in the human genome (making up 5%.10% of the total). Alu sequences can be propagated by retrotransposition, although most are sterile, or DNA "fossils."

Alumel
An aluminum nickel alloy used in the negative leg of a Type K thermocouple (Trade name of Hoskins Manufacturing Company).

Amanitin
A highly poisonous polypeptide that selectively inhibits the activity of mammalian RNA polymerase.

Ambient compensation
The design of an instrument such that changes in ambient temperature do not affect the readings of the instrument.

Ambient conditions
The conditions around the transducer (pressure, temperature, etc.).

Ambient pressure
Pressure of the air surrounding a transducer.

Ambient temperature
The average or mean temperature of the surrounding air which comes in contact with the equipment and instruments under test.

American national standards institute
A private non-profit organization that administers and coordinates the U.S. voluntary standardisation and conformity assessment system.

American wire gauge
A standarised method for specifying the properties - including diameter - of electrical and electronic wire.

Ames test
Test in which special strains of bacteria are used to evaluate the potential of chemicals to cause cancer.

Amino acids
Carbon, hydrogen, oxygen and nitrogen compounds the composition of which are determined by genes.

Aminoacyl (A) site
One of three sites in a ribosome occupied by a tRNA in translation. All charged tRNAs (with the exception of the initiator tRNA) first enter the A site in translation.

Aminoacyl-trna synthetase
Enzyme that attaches an amino acid to a tRNA. Each aminoacyl-tRNA synthetase is specific for a particular amino acid.

Ammeter
An instrument used to measure current.

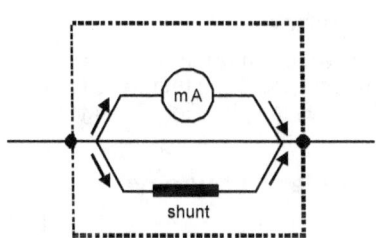

Amniocentesis
Procedure used for prenatal genetic testing to obtain a sample of amniotic fluid from a pregnant woman. A long sterile needle is inserted through the abdominal wall into the amniotic sac to obtain the fluid.

Ampere (amp)
A unit used to define the rate of flow of electricity (current) in a circuit; units are one coulomb (6.28×10^{18} electronics) per second.

Amphibian
Animal with smooth, moist skin; it has gills when young and then develops lungs when older. Frogs, toads, and salamanders are amphibians.

Amplifier
A device which draws power from a source other than the input signal and which produces as an output an enlarged reproduction of the essential features of its input.

Amplitude
A measurement of the distance from the highest to the lowest excursion of motion, as in the case of mechanical body in oscillation or the peak-to-peak swing of an electrical waveform.

Amplitude span
The Y-axis range of a graphic display of data in either the time or frequency domain. Usually a log display (dB) but can also be linear.

Anagenesis
Evolution of a feature within a lineage over an arbitrary period of time.

Analogue output
A voltage or current signal that is a continuous function of the measured parameter.

Analogue-to-Digital Converter (A/D or ADC)
A device or circuit that outputs a binary number corresponding to an analogue signal level at the input.

Analysis of variance
Statistical technique for testing for differences among the means of several groups with respect to a continuous variable.

Analytical model
A model in which the relationships among variables are defined using equations.

Anaphase
Anaphase is the fourth phase of mitosis, which is a process that separates the duplicated genetic material carried in the nucleus of a parent cell into two, identical daughter cells.

Anaphase I
Stage of meiosis I. In anaphase I, homologous chromosomes separate and move toward the spindle poles.

Anaphase II
Stage of meiosis II. In anaphase II, chromatids separate and move toward the spindle poles.

Anatomy
The science dealing with the structure of animals, plants or human body.

Ancestral species
A species at the root of a clade of related organisms.

Andesite
Intermediate volcanic rocks containing 54 to 62 percent silica and moderate amounts of iron and magnesium. Andesite minerals commonly include plagioclase and hornblende, with lesser amounts of mica, pyroxene, and various accessory minerals. Andesites are aphanitic in texture and are usually medium dark in colour. They occur with composite volcanic cones associated with convergent plate margins.

Anemology
The science of wind.

Anemometer
An instrument for measuring and/or indicating the velocity of air flow.

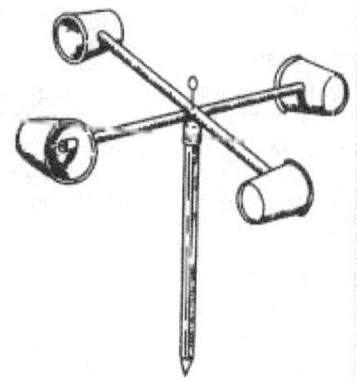

Aneuploidy
Change from the wild type in the number of chromosomes; most often an increase or decrease of one or two chromosomes.

Angiology
The science of blood & lymph vessels.

Angstrom
Ten to the minus tenth metres (10^{-10}) or one millimicron, a unit used to define the wave length of light. Designated by the symbol ‰.

Angular frequency
The motion of a body or a point moving circularly, referred to as the circular frequency O which is the frequency in cycles per second (cps) multiplied by the term (2) and expressed in radians per second (2pf).

Animal
A living thing that can move from place to place, has a body covering, and eats other animals or plants for food. Monkeys and ocelots are two kinds of animals found in a tropical rain forest.

Animal development
The process whereby a fertilized egg undergoes cell division and cellular differentiation to generate the different tissue types of a fully functional complex organism.

Animal production
A subcategory of secondary production, the production of an animal population.

Anion
A negatively charged ion (Cl-, NO3-, S2- etc.)

Anisotropy, Inhomogeneity (in the cosmic microwave background)
Very small patches in the sky where the temperature of the cosmic microwave background is slightly different to the average; these temperature variations are of the order of microkelvin.

Anneal
The process of using heating and slow cooling to toughen steel (or glass) by reducing its brittleness and internal stresses.

Annubar
A device that uses Pitot tubes to measure the gas flow rate within a pipeline.

Ansi
American National Standards Institute.

Antagonistic interaction
An interaction between two organisms that benefits one to the detriment of the other.

Antagonistic relationships
Relationships in which organisms compete for resources, spread disease to their neighbors, or consume each other.

Antagonistic selection
A source of natural selection that opposes another source of selection on a trait.

Antenna (high gain, low gain)
An aerial for receiving or transmitting radio signals. A high gain antenna is highly focused, whereas a low gain antenna receives or transmits over a wide angle.

Antennapedia complex
Cluster of five homeotic genes in fruit flies that affects development of the adult fly's head and anterior thoracic segments.

Antennapedia homeodomain
A sequence-specific transcription factor from Drosophila melanogaster. The wild-type Antennapedia homeodomain complex works to initiate a series of transcription events that results in anterior-posterior polarity in the organism.

Anthropogenic
Processes or materials derived from human activities, in contrast to those produced by natural processes

Anthropology
The science that deals with the origin and physical and cultural development of mankind.

Antibiotic resistance
Heritable changes in bacteria that allow them to withstand antibiotic treatments that would normally kill them.

Antibody
Produced by a B cell, a protein that circulates in the blood and other body fluids. An antibody binds to a specific antigen and marks it for destruction by making it easier for a phagocytic cell to ingest the antigen.

Anticipation
Increasing severity or earlier age of onset of a genetic trait in succeeding generations. For example, symptoms of a genetic disease may become more severe as the trait is passed from generation to generation.

Anticodon
Sequence of three nucleotides in tRNA that pairs with the corresponding codon in mRNA in translation.

Antifeedants
A substance that inhibits normal feeding behaviour.

Antigen
Substance that is recognized by the immune system and elicits an immune response.

Antigenic drift
A process by which circulating influenza viruses are constantly changing, which allows the viruses to cause annual epidemics of illness. Antigenic drift occurs when mutations accumulate in the hemagglutinin and neuraminidase genes that alter the antigenicity of these proteins such that the "drifted" strains are no longer neutralized by antibodies that were specific for previously circulating strains.

Antigenic shift
A process by which a new influenza A virus hemagglutinin subtype (with or without an accompanying new neuraminidase subtype) is introduced into the human population, which lacks prior experience of and immunity to the subtype. Antigenic shift can occur as a result of the direct introduction of an influenza virus from an animal or avian host into humans, or by the exchange or reassortment of gene segments between human and non-human influenza viruses when they co-infect animals or humans.

Antimatter
The 'opposite' to ordinary matter. For every particle of ordinary matter there is an almost identical antiparticle of antimatter: protons and antiprotons; electrons and positrons...the particle's mass is exactly the same as its antiparticle's mass, but their electrical charges and other fundamental properties are opposite. When a particle meets its antiparticle, they annihilate each other.

Antiparallel
Refers to a characteristic of the DNA double helix in which the two polynucleotide strands run in opposite directions.

Anti-reset windup
This is a feature in a three-mode PID controller which prevents the integral (auto reset) circuit from functioning when the temperature is outside the proportional band.

Antisense RNA
Small RNA molecule that base pairs with a complementary DNA or RNA sequence and affects its functioning.

Antiterminator
Protein or DNA sequence that inhibits the termination of transcription.

Aperture
Opening that allows light to fall onto an instrument's optics.

Aphelion
The point on a planet's elliptical orbit at which it is furthest from the Sun.

Apocentre
The point on a spacecraft's orbit at which it is furthest away from the body it is orbiting.

Apogee
The most distant point from Earth on a satellite's orbit.

Apomixis
Parthenogenetic reproduction in which an individual develops from one or more mitotically produced cells that have not experienced recombination or syngamy.

Apomorphic
Having a derived character or state, with reference to another character or state. See also synapomorphy.

Apoptosis
Programmed cell death, in which a cell degrades its own DNA, the nucleus and cytoplasm shrink, and

the cell undergoes phagocytosis by other cells without leakage of its contents.

Aposematic
Coloration or other features that advertise noxious properties; warning coloration.

Aposematic coloration
Antipredator adaptation in which conspicuous markings on an animal that is poisonous or unpalatable serve to discourage potential predators.

Application
A software programme that lets you complete a task, such as writing a paper, creating a poster, designing an image, or viewing a Web page.

Application programme
A computer programme that accomplishes specific tasks, such as word processing.

Applied restoration
A multi-step process, which may include some or all of these stages: assessing the site, formulating project goals, removing sources of disturbance, restoring processes/ disturbance cycles, rehabilitating substrates, restoring vegetation, and monitoring and maintenance.

Appropriation doctrine
The system for allocating water to private individuals used in most Western states. The doctrine of Prior Appropriation was in common use throughout the arid west as early settlers and miners began to develop the land. The prior appropriation doctrine is based on the concept of "First in Time, First in Right." The first person to take a quantity of water and put it to Beneficial Use has a higher priority of right than a subsequent user. Under drought conditions, higher priority users are satisfied before junior users receive water. Appropriative rights can be lost through nonuse; they can also be sold or transferred apart from the land.

Aptamer
Nucleic acid that binds to a specific target molecule.

Aquaculture
farming of plants and animals that live in water, such as fish, shellfish, and algae.

Aqueduct
a pipe, conduit, or channel designed to transport water from a remote source, usually by gravity.

Aquiclude
An impermeable geologic formation or stratum which will not hold or transmit fluid.

Aquifer
a geologic formation(s) that is water bearing. A geological formation or structure that stores and/or transmits water, such as to wells and springs. Use of the term is usually restricted to those water-bearing formations capable of yielding water in sufficient quantity to constitute a usable supply for people's uses.

Aquifer (confined)
Soil or rock below the land surface that is saturated with water. There are layers of impermeable material both above and below it and it is under pressure so that when the aquifer is penetrated by a well, the water will rise above the top of the aquifer.

Aquifer (unconfined)
An aquifer whose upper water surface (water table) is at atmospheric pressure, and thus is able to rise and fall.

Aquifer, confined (or Artesian)
An aquifer overlain by a non-permeable layer or layers, in which pressure will force water to rise above the aquifer.

Aquifer, perched
An aquifer containing unconfined groundwater separated from an underlying body of groundwater by an unsaturated zone.

Aquifer, principal
The aquifer or combination of related aquifers in a given area that is the important economic source of water to wells.

Aquifer, secondary
Any aquifer that is not the main source of water to wells in a given area.

Aquifer, unconfined (or Water Table)
An aquifer in which the upper surface is the water table.

Aquitard
A geologic formation or stratum that significantly retards fluid movement.

Arboriculture
Cultivation of trees & vegetables.

Archaea
One of the three primary divisions of life. Archaea consist of unicellular organisms with prokaryotic cells.

Archaeology
The study of antiquities.

Arcmin, arcsec
The size of an object in the sky can be measured by the angle that it covers when viewed from Earth. The full circle has 360 degrees. An arcmin is 1/60 of a degree; an arcsec is 1/60 of an arcmin or 1/3600 of a degree. The diameter of the full Moon is about one-half of a degree or 30 arcmin.

Area effect
The larger a place is, the more species it can support.

Argon
A chemical element, (symbol Ar, atomic number 18).

Ariane (4, 5) rockets
European launcher family (Ariane 4 and Ariane 5) developed by the European Space Agency. Launched from Kourou, French Guiana, flights are commercialised and operated by the Arianespace company.

Armour
A type of protective covering for the body. A hard covering of armor could protect a dinosaur from sharp teeth.

Array comparative genomic hybridization
Similar to conventional comparative genomic hybridization (CGH), but during hybridization, cloned chromosomal DNA fragments (about 200 kb in size) replace the metaphase chromosomes. This method offers greater sensitivity and resolution than conventional CGH in detecting copy number changes.

Artesian water
Ground water that is under pressure when tapped by a well and is able to rise above the level at which it is first encountered. It may or may not flow out at ground level. The pressure in such an aquifer commonly is called artesian pressure, and the formation containing artesian water is an artesian aquifer or confined aquifer.

Artesian well
A well in an aquifer where the groundwater is confined under pressure and the water level will rise above the top of the confined aquifer.

Artificial recharge
The unnatural addition of surface waters to groundwater. Recharge could result from reservoirs, storage basins, leaky canals, direct injection of water into an aquifer, or by spreading water over a large land surface.

Artificial selection
1. The process of selective breeding of organisms by humans to produce domesticated animals with more desirable traits; also used by evolutionary biologists to test for genetic variation and covariation.
2. Selection by humans of a deliberately chosen trait or combination of traits in a (usually captive) population; differing from natural selection in that the criterion for survival and reproduction is the trait chosen, rather than fitness as determined by the entire genotype.

ASCII
American Standard Code for Information Interchange. This international standard contains 128 codes that correspond to all upper and lower-case Latin characters, numbers, and punctuation marks. Each code is represented by a seven-digit binary number: 0000000 through 1111111.

Asexual
Pertaining to reproduction that does not entail meiosis and syngamy.

Ash
Fine particles of rock material ejected during an explosive volcanic eruption (commonly intermediate to felsic events). Ash may be either solid or molten when first erupted, and generally measures less than 0.10 inch in size (larger particles have other names).

Ash flow
A turbulent mixture of gas and rock fragments, most of which are ash-sized particles, ejected violently from a crater or fissure. The mass of pyroclastics is normally of very high temperature and moves rapidly down the slopes, or even along a level surface.

Ashfall (subaerial)
Volcanic ash that has fallen through the air. The resulting deposit is usually well sorted and exhibits a finely layered structure.

Asme
American Society of Mechanical Engineers. The professional organisation focused on technical; educational and research issues of the engineering and technology community.

Aspect
Whether north or south facing.

Assemblages
Species that share an attribute of habitat or taxonomic similarity.

Assembler
A programme that translates assembly language instructions into machine language instructions.

Assembly language
A machine oriented language in which mnemonics are used to represent each machine language instruction.

Each CPU has its own specific assembly language.

Assisted reproductive technologies
Procedures that replace a gamete or the uterus to help people with fertility problems have children.

Association study
A case-control study in which genetic variation, often measured as single-nucleotide polymorphisms that form haplotypes, is compared between people with a particular condition and unaffected individuals.

Assortative mating
Nonrandom mating on the basis of phenotype; usually refers to positive assortative mating, the propensity to mate with others of like phenotype.

Asteroid
One of billions of rocky objects, less than 1000 km in diameter, which orbit the Sun. Also known as minor planets. Thought to be planetesimals leftover from the formation of the planets. The first asteroid (Ceres) was discovered by Giuseppe Piazzi in 1801. More than 10 000 asteroids have so far been discovered and given permanent identification numbers. The largest asteroid is 2001 KX76 with a diameter of at least 1200 km.

Asteroid belt
Region between the orbits of Mars and Jupiter which is populated by billions of asteroids.

Astigmatism
Failure of an optical system, such as a lens or a mirror, to image a point source of light as a single point.

Astm
American Society for Testing and Materials.

Astrology
The ancient art of predicting the course of human destinies with the help of indications deduced from the position and movement of heavenly bodies.

Astrometry
The branch of astronomy concerned with measuring the positions of celestial bodies, such as stars and galaxies, and their real and apparent motions.

Astronautics
The science of space travel.

Astronomical unit (au)
1 Astronomical Unit corresponds to the distance separating the Earth from the Sun. 1AU = 150 million km.

Astronomy
The study of space and the heavenly bodies. Galileo's study of Earth's orbit around the sun is astronomy.

Astrophysics
Study of the physical nature of the Universe, its objects and the composition of the space between them.

Asymmetrical response
A common result in artificial selection experiments in which there is a greater response to selection in one direction than there is in the opposite direction for the same trait.

Asymmetry potential
The potential developed across the glass membrane with identical solutions on both sides. Also a term used when comparing glass electrode potential in pH 7 buffer.

Asynchronous
A communication method where data is sent when it is ready without being

referenced to a timing clock, rather than waiting until the receiver signals that it is ready to receive.

Atavism
The reappearance in an organism of characteristics that are present in the organism's remote ancestors.

ATC
Automatic temperature compensation.

Atmosphere
Layer of gases surrounding a star or planet.

Atomic number
The number of protons in an atom.

Atomic symbol
The letters representing each of the elements.

Atomic weight
The average weight of an atom.

Atoms
Composite particles of protons, neutrons and electrons. The smallest part of a substance that can take part in a chemical reaction.

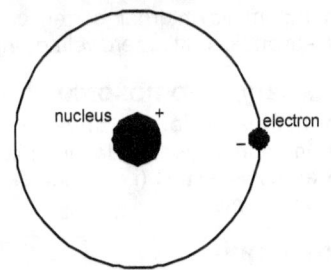

ATP
Adenosine 5-triphosphate, or ATP, is the principal molecule for storing and transferring energy in cells.

Attached-X
A pair of X chromosomes in Drosophila melanogaster that are connected together at one end and inherited jointly.

Attachment site
Special site on a bacterial chromosome where a prophage may insert itself.

Attenuation
Type of gene regulation in some bacterial operons, in which transcription is initiated but terminates prematurely before transcription of the structural genes.

Attenuator
Secondary structure that forms in the 5' untranslated region of some operons and causes the premature termination of transcription.

Attitude
Orientation of the spacecraft's axes relative to Earth.

Aurora
Illumination of the night sky, caused when electrons and protons from space collide with atoms and molecules of air in the Earth's upper atmosphere. Satellite observations usually show them as rings centred on the planet's magnetic poles. Popularly known as the Northern and Southern Lights. Various types of aurora are also found on Jupiter, its moon Ganymede, and Saturn.

Autoantibodies
Antibodies that attack the body's own cells.

Autoimmune disease
Characterized by an abnormal immune response to a person's own (self) antigen.

Automatic reset
1. A feature on a limit controller that automatically resets the controller

when the controlled temperature returns to within the limit bandwidth set.
2. The integral function on a PID controller which adjusts the proportional bandwidth with respect to the set point to compensate for droop in the circuit, i.e., adjusts the controlled temperature to a set point after the system stabilizes.

Autonomous element
Transposable element that is fully functional and able to transpose on its own. DNA sequence that confers the ability to replicate; contains an origin of replication.

Autopolyploidy
Condition in which all the sets of chromosomes of a polyploid individual possessing more than two haploid sets are derived from a single species.

Autoradiography
Method for visualizing DNA or RNA molecules labeled with radioactive substances. A piece of X-ray film is placed on top of a slide, gel, or other substance that contains DNA labeled with radioactive chemicals. Radiation from the labeled DNA exposes the film, providing a picture of the labeled molecules.

Autosomal
A chromosome that is not a sex chromosome; there are equal numbers of copies of autosomes in males and females of a given species.

Autosomal dominant
The inheritance pattern of a dominant allele on an autosome. The phenotype can affect males and females and does not skip generations.

Autosomal inheritance
Genetic transmission of genes on autosomes (nonsex chromosomes).

Autosomal recessive
The inheritance pattern of a recessive allele on an autosome. The phenotype can affect males and females and can skip generations.

Autosome
An autosome is a chromosome that is not a sex chromosome, or allosome; that is to say, there is an equal number of copies of the chromosome in males and females.[1] For example, in humans, there are 22 pairs of autosomes. In addition to autosomes, there are sex chromosomes, to be specific: X and Y. So, humans have 23 pairs of chromosomes.

Autotrophs
Organisms that obtain energy from the sun or from the oxidation of inorganic substance and convert it into their food through a series of chemical reactions.

Auto-zero
An automatic internal correction for offsets and/or drift at zero voltage input.

Auxillary chromosome
Former name for an unpaired sex chromosome. Used today to indicate an artificial "extra" (i.e., engineered) chromosome.

Auxotroph
Bacterium or fungus that possesses a nutritional mutation that disrupts its ability to synthesize an essential biological molecule; cannot grow on minimal medium but can grow on minimal medium to which has been added the biological molecule that it cannot synthesize.

Avalanche

A large mass of material falling or sliding rapidly due to the force of gravity. In many cases, water acts as a catalyst and/or lubricant. Avalanches often are classified by what is moving, such as a snow, ice, soil, or rock avalanche. A mixture of these materials is commonly called a debris flow.

Axis of rotation (spin axis)

The axis of rotation (spin axis) is that straight line about which a body rotates.

B

B1
A cross in which an F1 or F1' individual is mated to one of its parents (P1) or to another individual that is genetically identical to one of its parents.

B2
A cross in which an F1 or F1' individual is mated to one of its parents (P2) or to another individual that is genetically identical to one of its parents.

Backbone
Part of an oligo that holds the nucleic acid bases together; in DNA, this is the part of the molecule composed of deoxyribose sugars and phosphate linkages.

Backcross
A mating between an F1 or F1' individual to one of its parents (P1 or P2) or to another individual that is genetically identical to one of its parents. The term "backcross" may be used as a verb (describing the process of setting up the required mating) or as a noun to describe the mating or to describe the progeny that result from such a hybrid cross.

Backcross 1
Cross of an F1 or F1' individual to a P1 individual.

Backcross 2
Cross of an F1 or F1' individual to a P2 individual.

Background extinction
A long-prevailing rate at which taxa become extinct, in contrast to the highly elevated rates that characterize mass extinction.

Background noise
The total noise floor from all sources of interference in a measurement system, independent of the presence of a data signal.

Background selection
Elimination of deleterious mutations in a region of the genome; may explain low levels of neutral sequence variation.

Backup
A system, device, file or facility that can be used as an alternative in case of a malfunction or loss of data.

Bacteria
Single celled organisms non-green (except the blue-green bacteria {algae}) which have cell wall compositions different than other living organisms.

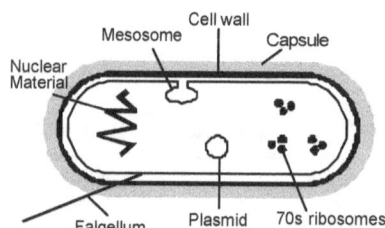

Bacterial artificial chromosome
Cloning vector used in bacteria that is capable of carrying DNA fragments as large as 500 kb.

Bacterial colony
Clump of genetically identical bacteria derived from a single bacterial cell that undergoes repeated rounds of division.

Bacteriology
The study of bacteria.

Bacteriophage
A bacteriophage is a type of virus that infects bacteria.

Baffle
A device used to prevent stray light.

Bag cell hormones
Hormones that control the onset of egg-laying behaviour.

Balance hypothesis
Proposes that much of the molecular variation seen in natural populations is maintained by balancing selection that favors genetic variation.

Balanced lethals
The arrangement of two recessive lethal alleles such that the alleles lie in repulsion; here, it is essentially as if the organism was a heterozygote for the lethal allele. Homozygosity would result in death of the organism.

Balanced polymorphism
Maintenance of a harmful recessive allele in a population because the heterozygote has a reproductive advantage.

Balanced translocation
When pieces of chromosomes are rearranged but no genetic material is gained or lost in the cell.

Balancing selection
A form of natural selection that maintains polymorphism at a locus within a population.

Bandwidth
The amount of information that one can send through a connection, measures in bits-per-second (Bps). A standard page of English text contains about 16,000 bits.

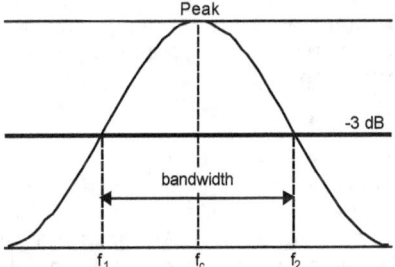

Barr body
Condensed, darkly staining structure that is found in most cells of female placental mammals and is an inactivated X chromosome.

Barrel
A volumetric unit of measure for crude oil and petroleum products. Derived by the original use of spent whiskey barrels to hold oil in the 1800s. One barrel equals 42 U.S. gallons, equivalent to 158.978 litres.

Barrel of oil equivalent
A measure of gas. A BoE has similar energy content as a barrel of Oil. Approx 167 MMscf depending on calorific value of the gas.

Barrels of oil per day
The unit of measurement of crude oil produced by a well or a field. The volume of a barrel is equivalent to 42 US gallons (0.16 metres cubed).

Baryons
The class of subatomic particles in which protons and neutrons are included. The baryons form the atomic nucleus, along with another class of particles - the mesons. We, and everything we can see around us, are made of baryonic matter.

Basal transcription apparatus
Complex of transcription factors, RNA polymerase, and other proteins that assemble on the promoter and are capable of initiating minimal levels of transcription.

Basalt
Volcanic rock (or magma) that is generally dark in colour, contains 45 to 54 percent silica, and is rich in iron and magnesium. An eruption of basaltic magma is generally quiet, and results in flows (both vesicular and non-vesicular) and breccias. Undersea eruptions commonly result in the formation of "pillow lavas." Basalt represents the initial differentiated material erupted by the earth at spreading centres, and is considered by GeoMan to be the "blood of the earth."

Base
A substance that has a pH of more than 7, which is neutral. A base has less free hydrogen ions (H^+) than hydroxyl ions (OH^-).

Base analogue
Chemical substance that has a structure similar to that of one of the four standard bases of DNA and may be incorporated into newly synthesized DNA molecules in replication.

Base flow
Sustained flow of a stream in the absence of direct runoff. It includes natural and human-induced streamflows. Natural base flow is sustained largely by ground-water discharges.

Base substitution
1. Mutation in which a single pair of bases in DNA is altered.
2. A mutation that occurs when one nucleotide base is substituted for another in a DNA sequence.

Base-excision repair
DNA repair that first excises modified bases and then replaces the entire nucleotide.

Basic
A high-level programming language designed at Dartmouth College as a learning tool. Acronym for Beginner's All-purpose Symbolic Instruction Code.

Basic transportation reference
The basic transportation section of the U.S. Government Test Specification MIL-STD-810D, Method 514.3, Paragraph I-3.2.1, Page 514.3-5. Basic transportation defines the test profiles that have been defined for equipment that is shipped as secured cargo; by land, by sea or by air. The test levels are based upon land transport stress levels because these are higher than stresses imposed by air or sea transportation environments.

Bateman's principle
Female reproduction is primarily limited by their access to resources to nourish and produce large gametes, whereas male reproduction is mainly limited by access to females.

Batesian mimicry
A situation in which a harmless species has evolved to imitate the

warning signals of a harmful or distasteful species directed at a common predator. It is named after the English naturalist Henry Walter Bates, after his work in the rainforests of Brazil.

Eastern Coral Snake (venomous)
Scarlet King Snake (non-venomous)

Battery limits
The perimeter surrounding the processing area and included process equipment of a process plant.

Baud
A unit of data transmission speed equal to the number of bits (or signal events) per second; 300 baud = 300 bits per second.

Baud rate
The serial communications data transmission rate expressed in bits per second.

BCC
Blind Courtesy Copy or Blind Carbon Copy. A way to send an e-mail message to more than one recipient, without the parties knowing that an identical message was sent to others. Using the BCC is a good way to avoid the long list of recipients that your correspondents usually have to wade through in the header of a mass-mailing.

BCD, buffered
Binary-coded decimal output with output drivers, to increase line-drive capability.

BCD, parallel
A digital data output format where every decimal digit is represented by binary signals on four lines and all digits are presented in parallel. The total number of lines is 4 times the number of decimal digits.

BCD, serial
A digital data output format where every decimal digit is represented by binary signals on four lines and up to five decimal digits are presented sequentially. The total number of lines is four data lines plus one strobe line per digit.

BCD, three-state
An implementation of parallel BCD, which has 0, 1 and high-impedance output states. The high-impedance state is used when the BCD output is not addressed in parallel connect applications.

B-cell
Particular type of lymphocyte that produces humoral immunity; matures in the bone marrow and produces antibodies.

B-DNA
Right-handed helical structure of DNA that exists when water is abundant; the secondary structure described by Watson and Crick and probably the most common DNA structure in cells.

Bearing
A part which supports a journal and in which a journal revolves.

Beat frequency
Beat frequencies are periodic vibrations that result from the addition and subtraction of two or more sinusoids. For example, in the case of two turbine aircraft engines that are rotating at nearly the same frequency

but not precisely at the same frequency; Four frequencies are generated: (f1) the rotational frequency of turbine one, (f2) the rotational frequency of turbine two, (f1 + f2) the sum of turbine rotational frequencies one and two, and (f1 - f2) which is the difference or "beat" frequency of turbines one and two. The difference of the two frequencies is the lower frequency and is the one that is "felt" as a beat or "wow" in this case.

Beaver dam
A wall built by a beaver to hold back flowing water. A beaver dam is made with cut trees, stones, and mud.

Beckwith-wiedemann syndrome
Syndrome of unknown etiology characterized by the presence of macroglossia (large tongue), visceromegaly (large organs), macrosomia (large body size), and hypoglycemia. Patients show an increased susceptibility to tumor development.

Bedrock
the solid rock beneath the soil and superficial rock. A general term for solid rock that lies beneath soil, loose sediments, or other unconsolidated material.

Behavioral homeostasis
Perceptions of need that usually link directly to physiological control systems.

Benthic
Inhabiting the bottom, or substrate, of a body of water.

Bentonite
A clay material composed principally of the mineral montmorillonite. It has a great affinity for fresh water and when hydrated will increase its volume more than seven times. Water/bentoninte suspensions are essentially impermeable. Commonly used as a sealant for ponds.

Bepposax satellite
An Italian-Dutch X-ray astronomy satellite launched in 1996.

Beryllia
BeO (Beryllium Oxide) A high-temperature mineral insulation material; toxic when in powder form.

Best fit straight line (bfsl)
A line midway between two parallel straight lines enclosing all output vs. pressure values.

Beta ratio
The ratio of the diameter of a pipeline constriction to the unconstricted pipe diameter.

Bias current
A very low-level DC current generated by the panel metre and superimposed on the signal. This current may introduce a measurable offset across a very high source impedance.

Bicoid homeodomain
The maternally transcribed gene bicoid organizes anterior development in Drosophila. Bicoid encodes a homeodomain-containing transcriptional factor, its gradient acting to position the transcription of gap and pair rule genes along the anterior-posterior axis.

Bidirectional replication
Replication at both ends of a replication bubble.

Big bang
The Big Bang theory is the most accepted theory so far to describe the

origin and evolution of the Universe. According to it, all the matter and energy in the Universe was originally contained in a very small 'point' - technically called a 'singularity' - at an almost infinite temperature and density. About 10 to 20 billion years ago this tiny Universe started to expand, and has not stopped expanding since. This theory was first drafted by Russian physicist George Gamow in the late forties, although only when the cosmic microwave background was discovered in 1964 did the astronomical community start to take it seriously. As of today, apart from the cosmic microwave background, two other pillars support the Big Bang theory: the current expansion of the Universe and the measured abundance of light elements.

Bill of materials
A listing of materials for a job. The result of a Material Take Off.

Billion
One billion equals one thousand million.

Binary
Refers to base 2 numbering system, in which the only allowable digits are 0 and 1. Pertaining to a condition that has only two possible values or states.

Binary coded decimal (bcd)
The representation of a decimal number (base 10, 0 through 9) by means of a 4 bit binary nibble.

Binary star
Pair of stars bound together by mutual gravitation and orbiting their common centre of mass.

Binomial expansion
Describes a statistical method of examining characteristics in a population. Hardy-Weinberg used this technique to provide a mathematical model of population genetics.

Biochemistry
The study of chemical processes of living things.

Biodiversity
Genetic and phenotypic variation both within and among species, plus the variety of ecosystems created by these species.

Bioethics
The study of the ethical, moral, and societal implications of biological research and discovery.

Biogeography
The study of the geographic distribution of organisms.

Bioinformatics
Synthesis of molecular biology and computer science that develops databases and computational tools to store, retrieve, and analyze nucleic acid and protein sequence data.

Biological oxygen demand
The amount of oxygen used for biochemical oxidation by a unit volume of water at a given temperature and for a given time.

Biological species
A population or group of populations within which genes are actually or potentially exchanged by interbreeding, and which are reproductively isolated from other such groups. See also species, phylogenetic species concept.

Biomass
Living material.

Biomes
Regions of similar climate and dominant plant types.

Biometry
The application of mathematics to the study of living things.

Biomimicry
The study of natural products that provide solutions to human needs. For example, shark skin provided the model for hydrodynamic swimming suits.

Bionics
The study of functions, characteristics and phenomena observed in the living world and the application of this knowledge to the world of machines.

Bionomics
The study of the relation of an organism to its environment.

Bionomy
The science of the laws of life.

Biophysics
The physics of vital processes (living things).

Bios
Acronym for basic input/output system. The commands used to tell a CPU how it will communicate with the rest of the computer.

Biostratigraphy
The study and classification of rocks and their history based on their fossil content.

Biotechnology
Use of biological processes, particularly molecular genetics and recombinant DNA technology, to produce products of commercial value.

Biotic
Pertaining to living organisms in an environment.

Bipolar
The ability of a panel metre to display both positive and negative readings.

Bird
A two-legged animal with feathers and wings. A bird is the only animal that has feathers covering its body.

Birth defects
Any malformations or defects of development found at birth.

Bit
Binary DigIT. A single digit number in base-2 (either a one or a zero). This is the smallest unit of computerized data.

Bithorax complex
Cluster of three homeotic genes in fruit flies that influences the adult fly's posterior thoracic and abdominal segments.

Bivalent
Refers to a synapsed pair of homologous chromosomes.

Black hole
An object with so much mass concentrated in it, and therefore such a strong gravitational pull that nothing, not even light can escape from it. One way in which black holes are believed to form is when massive stars collapse at the end of their lives.

Blackbody
A theoretical object that radiates the maximum amount of energy at a given temperature, and absorbs all the energy incident upon it. A blackbody is not necessarily black. (The name blackbody was chosen because the colour black is defined as the total absorption of light energy.)

Blast
Basic Local Alignment Search Tool; a sequence comparison algorithm, optimized for speed, used to search sequence databases for regions of local similarity between sequences. The programme compares nucleotide or protein sequences to sequence databases and calculates the statistical significance of matches.

Blastocyst
A hollow ball of cells descended from a fertilized ovum.

Blastomere
A cell of a blastocyst.

Blazar
Type of active galaxy named after an object in the constellation of Lacerta, the BL Lacertae object. They form a subset of the quasar population. The emission of blazars is highly variable. The activity may be caused by jets of gas being expelled from the central region of the active galaxy, i.e. the supermassive black hole in the active galactic nucleus.

Blending inheritance
Early concept of heredity proposing that offspring possess a mixture of the traits from both parents.

Block
Angular chunk of solid rock ejected during a volcanic eruption.

Blow out preventor
The hydraulically or mechanically actuated valve installed at the wellhead to control pressure within the well.

Blowout
The uncontrolled flow of gas and/or oil or other well fluids from a well during drilling.

Blueshift
When a distant object moves toward the observer the lines in its spectrum shift to shorter (bluer) wavelengths. This is because of the apparent compression of the wave of light. As a result of this compression the wavelength shortens and thus shifts towards the blue side of the electromagnetic spectrum. The blueshift of an astronomical object is an indication of the speed at which this object is approaching the observer.

BNC
A quick disconnect electrical connector used to inter-connect and/or terminate coaxial cables.

Boiling point
The temperature at which a substance in the liquid phase transforms to the gaseous phase; commonly refers to the boiling point of water which is 100°C (212°F) at sea level.

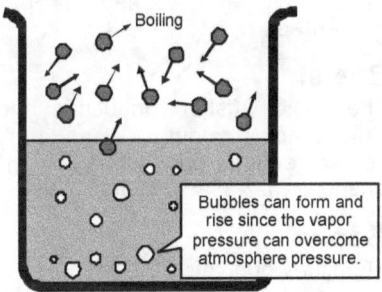

Boiling Point

Bolometer
A kind of detector mainly used to measure infrared radiation. A bolometer works by heating up as it absorbs the radiation that reaches it. The increase in temperature is measured by an internal electrical resistance, and is a measure of the amount of radiation absorbed.

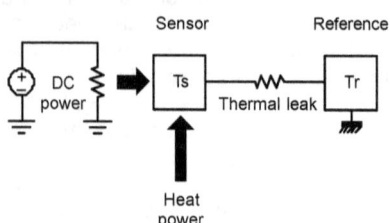

Bolometer

Bomb
Fragments of molten or semi-molten rock, several inches to several feet in diameter, which are blown out during an explosive volcanic eruption. Because of their semi-plastic condition, bombs are often modified in shape during their flight or upon impact.

Bond
A chemical link between atoms.

Boreal
Area located in northern latitudes, between the tundra and the temperate forest, mostly from 52 degrees N to 66 degrees N.

Bosiet
The basic Offshore Induction and Emergency Training - mandatory course required prior to visiting UK offshore Oil & Gas installations.

Botany
The study of plants.

Bottleneck
A severe, temporary reduction in population size.

Bottom up control
Control of a population by available nutrients or food.

Bottom-up forces
Forces within a community that influence the community from lower to higher trophic.

Bounce
To rebound from a surface. A ping pong ball will bounce higher than a baseball.

BPS
Bits per second.

BPSD
Barrels per Stream Day - A unit of flow measurement used on refineries.

Branch
Evolutionary connections between organisms in a phylogenetic tree.

Branch migration
Movement of a cross bridge along two DNA molecules.

Branch point
Adenine nucleotide in nuclear pre-mRNA introns that lies from 18 to 40 nucleotides upstream of the 3' splice site.

Breakdown voltage rating
The dc or ac voltage which can be applied across insulation portions of a transducer without arcing or conduction above a specific current value.

Breccia
Angular fragments of material, commonly formed by physical weathering processes or explosive volcanic activity.

Breeding value
The effect of an individual's genes on the value of a given trait in its offspring; sometimes called the additive genotype. It is equal to two times the deviation of the mean of the individual's offspring from the overall population mean.

Bremsstrahlung
The German word 'Bremsstrahlung' means 'braking radiation'. A fast,

charged particle, for example an electron, is slowed down when it passes through matter. The energy lost by the particle is emitted as electromagnetic radiation, or Bremsstrahlung.

Bridge resistance
See Input impedance and Output impedance.

British thermal unit
A unit of energy i.e. the amount of energy required to raise the temperature of 1 pound of water 1 degree Fahrenheit when the water is near 39.2 degrees Fahrenheit.

Brittle-ductile transition zone
The location at depth within the earth's crust where the temperature and pressure have risen to such a high level that directed stress results in plastic deformation as opposed to fracturing and faulting.

Broad-sense heritability
Proportion of the phenotypic variance that can be attributed to genetic variance.

Brown dwarf
A kind of 'failed' star: a small and opaque object whose mass is not sufficient to start, in its core, the nuclear reaction to transform hydrogen into helium. A brown dwarf cannot therefore produce enough energy to shine as a star. A brown dwarf's mass is not more than 0.08 solar masses.

Browser
The software application that allows you to view Internet pages.

Browser-safe colours
Although there are millions of colours in the computer world, there are only 216 colours that are browser-safe, or are able to be read by any Web browser. These colours will remain true no matter what platform or browser you use, and their hexadecimal codes (numerical names for colours) are made up by using any combination of 00 33 66 99 CC or FF.

BTU
British thermal units. The quantity of thermal energy required to raise one pound of water at its maximum density, 1 degree F. One BTU is equivalent to .293 watt hours, or 252 calories. One kilowatt hour is equivalent to 3412 BTU.

BTW
An acronym often used in e-mail messages and chat sessions to mean: "by the way."

Buffer
1. A storage area for data that is used to compensate for a speed difference, when transferring data from one device to another. Usually refers to an area reserved for I/O operations, into which data is read, or from which data is written.
2. Any substance or combination of substances which, when dissolved in water, produces a solution which resists a change in its hydrogen ion concentration on the addition of an acid or alkali.

Buffer capacity (b)
A measure of the ability of the solution to resist pH change when a strong acid or base is added.

Bulb (liquid-in-glass thermometer)
The area at the tip of a liquid-in-glass thermometer containing the liquid reservoir.

Burn-in
A long term screening test (either vibration, temperature or combined test) that is effective in weeding out infant mortalities because it simulates actual or worst case operation of the device, accelerated through a time, power, and temperature relationship.

Burst pressure
The maximum pressure applied to a transducer sensing element or case without causing leakage.

Burst proportioning
A fast-cycling output form on a time proportioning controller (typically adjustable from 2 to 4 seconds) used in conjunction with a solid state relay to prolong the life of heaters by minimizing thermal stress.

Bus
Parallel lines used to transfer signals between devices or components. Computers are often described by their bus structure (i.e., S-100, IBM PC).

Bus bar
A conducting bar that carries heavy current to supply several electric circuits.

Byte
A set of 8 bits that means something to the computer, like a letter, number, or punctuation mark. For example, the byte 01001000 signifies the character *H*. The three-letter word 'hat' requires 3 bytes.

C

C value
Amount of DNA found in a cell of an organism.

C3 plant
A C3 plant is one that produces phosphoglyceric acid, (a molecule that has three carbon atoms) as a stable intermediary in the first step in photosynthesis (the Calvin Cycle). Most plants on Earth (over 95 percent) are C3 plants.

C4 plant
A C4 plant is one that produces oxaloacetic acid (a molecule that has four carbon atoms) as a stable intermediary in the first step in photosynthesis. Very few plants on Earth (less than 1 percent) are C4 plants (including corn and sugarcane). Photorespiration in C4 plants is more efficient in strong light. The processes in C4 biochemistry were studied by M. D. Hatch and C. R. Slack.

Cacao
The cacao plant (Theobroma cacao) is a evergreen flowering tree native to wet, warm forests of South and Central America. This tree grows to 40 feet (12 m) in height. After flowering, 10 to 14-inch long red fruit pods develop. In each pod are almond-shaped cacao beans and pulp. Chocolate is made from the beans in the pods of the cacao plant. Also known as COCOa.

Cache
Stores of food made by many species of animals for future consumption.

Cactus
A cactus (the plural is cacti) is a succulent plant that can live in dry areas. It has a structure that minimizes water loss. The stems are photosynthetic, green, and fleshy. The leaves are reduced to spines or are absent. Classification: Division Magnoliophyta (angioperms), Class Magnoliopsida (dicots), Subclass Caryophyllidae, Order Caryophyllales, Family Cactaceae (Cactus).

Caenorhabditis elegans
A model eukaryotic, multicellular organism. C. elegans is a nematode that serves as a valuable model to study basic developmental processes,

neurological function, and cell communication.

Calcitonin
An example of multiple different polypeptides being generated by alternative splicing from the same gene. Different tissues express the different transcripts. For example, calcitonin is more prevalent in the thyroid, while CGRP is highly expressed in brain tissue.

Caldera
The Spanish word for cauldron, a basin-shaped volcanic depression; by definition, at least a mile in diameter. Such large depressions are typically formed by the subsidence of volcanoes. Crater Lake occupies the best-known caldera in the Cascades.

Calender-van Dusen Equation
An equation that defines the resistance-temperature value of any pure metal that takes the form of $RT = RO(1 + AT + BT2)$ for values between the ice point (0°C) and the freezing point of antimony (630.7°C) and the form $RT = RO[1 + AT + BT2 + C(T-100)T2]$ between the oxygen point (-183.0°C) and the ice point (0°C).

Calibration
The process of adjusting an instrument or compiling a deviation chart so that its reading can be correlated to the actual value being measured.

California poppy
A golden poppy (Eschscholzia californica) from western North America. It has finely-divided foliage and cup-shaped flowers.

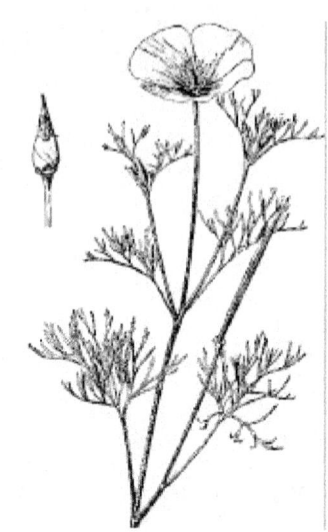

Calisthenics
The systematic exercises for attaining strength & gracefulness.

Calorie
A unit of heat energy. The amount of heat required to raise the temperature of 1 gram (cubic Centimeter) of water 1 degree Celsius. Also, the substance which gives food its flavor.

Calvin cycle
The second stage in the process of phtosynthesis is called the Calvin Cycle (it is also called the Calvin-Benson Cycle or the Carbon Fixation Cycle. In the Calvin Cycle, carbon molecules from carbon dioxide, CO_2, are fixed into the sugar glucose, ($C_6H_{12}O_2$) (in six repeats of the cycle). The Calvin Cycle takes place in the stroma of eucaryotic chloroplasts. The major enzyme that mediates the Calvin Cycle is Rubisco (ribulose-1-5-biphosphate carboxylase). The Calvin Cycle was first investigated in the late 1940s and early 1950s by the Nobel Prize winning chemist Melvin Calvin (1911-1997).

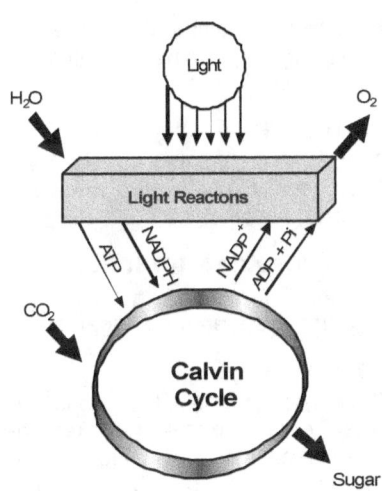

Calyx
The calyx is the sepals of a flower.

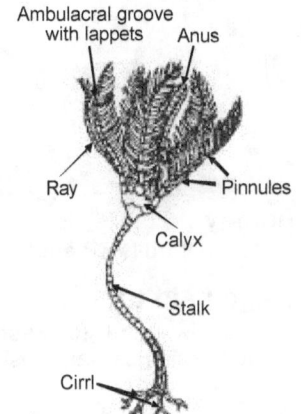

Cambium
Cambium is a layer of dividing cells found in the stems of plants. The cambium forms the specialized xylem and phloem cells and causes the stem to increase in thickness.

Canalization
The evolution of internal factors during development that reduce the effect of perturbing environmental and genetic influences, thereby constraining variation and consistently producing a particular (usually wild-type) phenotype.

Cancer
A group of disorders resulting from a loss of cell cycle control.

Candidate gene
A gene thought to be involved in the evolution of a particular trait based on its mutant phenotype or the function of the protein it encodes.

Candidate gene approach
A technique which attempts to determine if genes of known function affect complex phenotypic traits.

Canopy
The canopy consists of the upper parts of the trees of a rainforest (about 65 to 130 feet or 20 to 40 m above the ground). The canopy is the part of a forest in which the branches of the trees spread out and block sunlight from reaching the forest floor. This leafy environment is full of life in a tropical rainforest and includes insects, birds, reptiles, mammals, and more.

Capacitance
The ability to store an electric charge.

Capillary action
Capillary action is the movement of water as it is pulled upwards through tubes (xylem) within a plant's roots, stems, and leaves. The water (containing minerals and dissolved nutrients) is driven against gravity by adhesion of the water molecules (they stick to the sides of the tubes), cohesion of those molecules (the water molecules sticking together), and surface tension (the forces of the molecules on surface of the upward-moving water).

Capsule
A capsule is a seed pod that opens when it is dry and the seeds are mature.

Capture orbit
The first orbit of a spacecraft after it has been captured by the gravitational attraction of a celestial body. The capture is achieved by reducing the speed of the spacecraft.

Carbohydrates
The major energy source within plants and animals: sugars, starches and glucose polymers.

Carbon
The basic element in all organic compounds.

Carbon abatement technology
It includes improving the efficiency of and co-firing of power plant with low carbon alternatives such as biomass.

Carbon dioxide
Carbon dioxide, CO_2, is a molecule that has one carbon atom and two oxygen atoms; it is a gas at standard temperature and pressure. Plants use carbon dioxide gas in the photosynthetic process.

Carbonaceous compounds
Material containing carbon or carbon compounds.

Carcinogen
A substance that causes cancer.

Cardiology
The science that deals with heart functions and diseases.

Caretaker
Tumor suppressor genes or proteins that act to protect the genome from damage or mutations. Many caretaker genes encode proteins that recognize or repair DNA damage.

Carnivore
Carnivores are animals that eat meat. They usually have sharp teeth and powerful jaws.

Carnivorous interactions
Species interactions in which one organism eats another organism.

Carpel
The carpel is the female reproductive organ of a flower - it makes the seeds. It consists of the stigma, style and ovary. There may be more than one carpel in a flower.

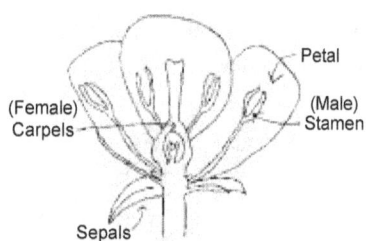

Carpology
The science of fruits & seeds.

Carriage paid to
The incoterm used to describe responsibilities for carriage; risk and cost.

Carrier
An individual organism that carries two different alternative forms, or alleles, of a gene. Carriers are often heterozygous for a mutant, deleterious allele whose effect does not manifest because of the presence of a dominant allele.

Carrying capacity
The maximum population of a species that a particular ecosystem can sustain.

Cartography
The science of map-making.

Case-control study
An epidemiological method in which people with a particular condition are compared to individuals as much like them as possible, but without the disease.

Casparian strip
The Casparian strip is waxy layer (a band of suberin, a waterproofing material) that is located in the walls of plant root cells. This barrier strip stops the transport of water and minerals into the main vascular system of the root.

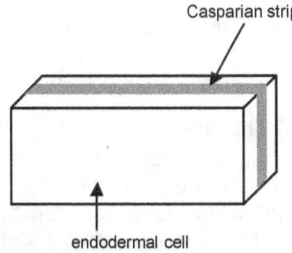
Casparian strip
endodermal cell

Caspase
Enzyme that cleaves other proteins and regulates apoptosis. Each caspase is synthesized as a large, inactive precursor (a procaspase) that is activated by cleavage, often by another caspase.

Cassegrain telescope
Popular design for large, two-mirror reflecting telescopes in which the primary mirror has a concave parabolic shape and the secondary mirror has a convex hyperbolic shape. A hole in the primary allows the image plane to be located behind the large mirror.

Cassini division
A gap in Saturn's rings that divides the outer set from the inner set of rings.

Cassini-Huygens mission
The joint NASA/ESA spacecraft, intended to study Saturn and its moons, carrying onboard ESA's Huygens Probe. Named after Jean Dominique Cassini (1625-1712), the Italian-French astronomer who discovered several Saturnian satellites and the magnificent rings of Saturn, and Christiaan Huygens (1629-1695), who discovered Titan in 1655.

Cat cracker
A refinery unit used to break up large hydrocarbon molecules into smaller ones. The conversion operation takes place at very high temperatures (500 degrees Celsius) in the presence of a catalyst.

Catabolite activator protein
Protein that functions in catabolite repression. When bound with cAMP, CAP binds to the promoter of certain operons and stimulates transcription.

Catabolite repression
System of gene control in some bacterial operons in which glucose is used preferentially and the metabolism of other sugars is repressed in the presence of glucose.

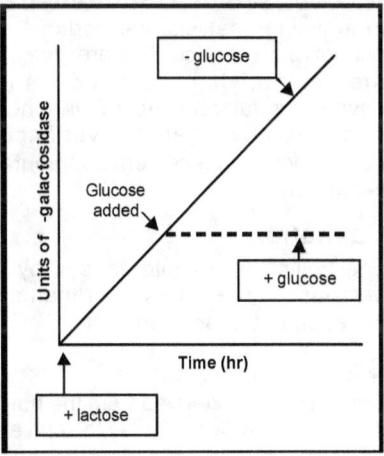

Cataclysmic variable
A binary star system containing a white dwarf that exhibits sudden outbursts of energy.

Catalyst
A substance that reduces the activation energy of a reaction.

Category
In taxonomy, one of the ranks of classification (e.g., genus, family).

Cation
A positively charged ion (Na+, H+).

Catkins
Small inconspicuous strings of reproductive parts.

Caudex
The caudex is an enlarged, woody base of the stem or trunk (located just below the gound) on some plants - it is used for water storage. Many desert plants have a caudex, an adaptation to dry conditions. Some palms, cycads, and succulents have a caudex.

Caudiciform
Caudiciform means having a caudex.

Causal variance components
In a sibling analysis, the portions of phenotypic variance that are due to the underlying genetic and environmental sources of variance (e.g., additive genetic variance, dominance variance, environmental variance).

Cavitation
The boiling of a liquid caused by a decrease in pressure rather than an increase in temperature.

Cc
Courtesy Copy, derived from the non-digital Carbon Copy. A way to send an e-mail message to a person other than the main recipient or recipients. The CC'ed party can see that they are not the main recipient of the letter.

CCCTC binding factor
A transcriptional regulator that plays important roles in epigenetic control of gene expression. CTCF is a zinc finger protein that is known for transcriptional insulation.

CCS
Three methods of capture used are pre combustion; post combustion and oxy-firing. The storage of captured CO_2 usually in depleted oil reservoirs.

CDNA
A DNA molecule that is the complement of an mRNA, copied using reverse transcriptase.

Cdna library
Collection of bacterial colonies or phage colonies containing DNA fragments that have been produced by reverse transcription of cellular mRNA.

Cedar
Cedar trees (genus Cedrus) are large evergreen coniferous trees (up to about 80 feet tall) that have dense clusters of needles held in wide, woody peg-like structures.

Cell   Cellulose

The barrel-shaped cones are held upright above a branch. Some cedars include: Cedar of Lebanon (Cedrus libani); Atlas cedar (Cedrus atlantica) - with blue-green foliage; Deodar cedar (Cedrus deodara) - with drooping branches.

Cell
The cell is the basic structural unit of all organisms. Plant cells have a tough outer cell wall, a cell membrane, genetic material (DNA), cytoplasm, and many organelles.

Cell culture
Cells removed from complex organisms and grown in nutrient solutions, usually at a defined temperature and sometimes with supplemental carbon dioxide.

Cell cycle
Stages through which a cell passes from one cell division to the next.

Cell line
Genetically identical cells that divide indefinitely and can be cultured in the laboratory.

Cell membrane
The cell membrane or plasma membrane is a biological membrane that separates the interior of all cells from the outside environment. The cell membrane is selectively permeable to ions and organic molecules and controls the movement of substances in and out of cells.

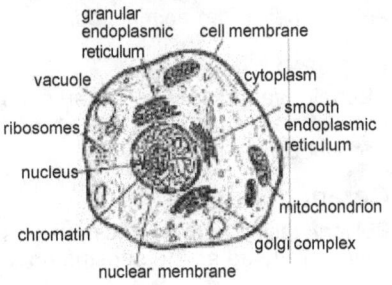

Cell theory
States that all life is composed of cells, that cells arise only from other cells, and that the cell is the fundamental unit of structure and function in living organisms.

Cell wall
Plant cells have a thick, rigid cell wall located outside the cell membrane. The cell wall is made of cellulose (a polysaccharide carbohydrate), proteins, and sometimes lignin. The cell wall gives the cell most of its support and structure. The cell wall also bonds with other cell walls to form the structure of the plant.

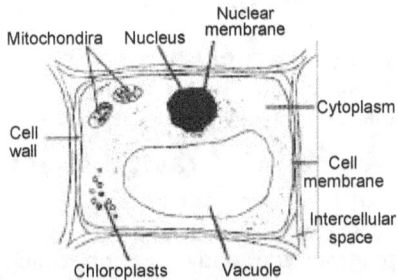

Cellular immunity
Type of immunity resulting from T cells, which recognize antigens found on the surfaces of self cells.

Cellular respiration
Cellular respiration is a process in which energy is produced from various molecules (like glucose), producing ATP (adenosine triphosphate). During cellular respiration, oxygen is used and carbon dioxide is produced Cellular respiration occurs in the mitochondria of eukaryotes, and in the cytoplasm of prokaryotes.

Cellulose
Cellulose is a carbohydrate that comprises much of a plant's cell, especially the cell wall.

Celsius (centrigrade)
A temperature scale defined by 0°C at the ice point and 100°C at boiling point of water at sea level.

Celsius (°c)
Scale of temperature for which water freezes at 0 degrees and boils at 100 degrees (under standard conditions).

Cenozoic era
The "Age of Mammals" (65 million years ago to today), saw the emergence of familiar life forms, humans, the modern look of the continents, and a cooling climate. The Cenozoic (meaning "recent life") followed the Mesozoic Era.

Centaur (rocket)
A launcher; the rocket used to launch the Cassini-Huygens spacecraft.

Centre of Gravity (Mass Centre)
The centre of gravity of a body is that point in the body through which passes the resultant of weights of its component particles for all oriontations of the body with respect to a uniform gravitational field.

Centimorgan
1. The usual unit for measuring distance on a genetic map. One cM is equivalent to a rate of recombination of 1% (i.e., c = 0.01).
2. Another name for map unit.

Central dogma
Concept that genetic information passes from DNA to RNA to protein in a one-way information pathway.

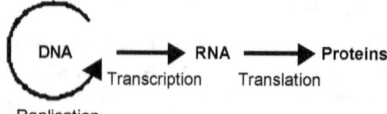

Centriole
Cytoplasmic organelle consisting of microtubules; present at each pole of the spindle apparatus in animal cells.

Centripetal force
A force exerted on an object moving in a circular path which is exerted inward toward the centre of rotation.

Centromere
Constricted region on a chromosome that stains less strongly than the rest of the chromosome; region where spindle microtubules attach to a chromosome.

Centromeric sequence
DNA sequence found in functional centromeres.

Centrosome
A centrosome (also called the "microtubule organizing centre") is a small body located near the nucleus - it has a dense centre and radiating tubules. The centrosome is where microtubules are made. During cell division (mitosis), the centrosome divides and the two parts move to opposite sides of the dividing cell. Unlike centrosomes in animal cells, plant cell centrosomes do not have centrioles.

Cephalization
The concentration of the coordinating parts of the nervous systems and some of the sensory systems in the anterior part of an animals body.

Cepheid variable
Cepheid variables are a particular class of star which vary regularly and continuously in luminosity.

Ceramic
Polycrystalline ferroelectric materials which are used as the sensing units

Ceramic insulation

in piezoelectric accelerometers. There are many different grades, all of which can be made in various configurations to satisfy different design requirements.

Ceramic insulation

High-temperature compositions of metal oxides used to insulate a pair of thermocouple wires The most common are Alumina (Al_2O_3), Beryllia (BeO), and Magnesia (MgO). Their application depends upon temperature and type of thermocouple. High-purity alumina is required for platinum alloy thermocouples. Ceramic insulators are available as single and multihole tubes or as beads.

Cereal

A cereal is a grain that is used for human food. Some cereals include rice, oats, wheat, and barley.

Cerrado

The cerrado is a grassy, treeless plain that surrounds the Brazilian rainforest.

Cesi

It also provide power system studies and consultancy to power producers; electrical utilities; large-scale users of electricity and Financial Institutions.

Cessation of Production

One of the first significant mile stones in platform decommissioning.

Cetology

The science of aquatic mammals, especially whales.

Cf.

Cf. is an abbreviation for "compare" or "compare with."

Cfm

The volumetric flow rate of a liquid or gas in cubic feet per minute.

C-Fos

A cellular proto-oncogene that is often transcribed as a result of signal transduction pathways initiated by growth factors.

Chain reaction

Polymerisation initiated by the bonding of a free radical with a monomer.

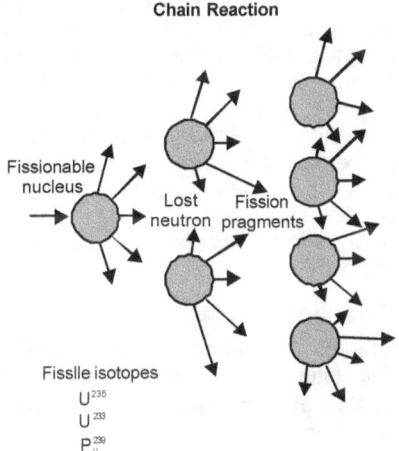

Chain Reaction

Chalk

Chalk is a soft, white type of limestone (a sedimentary rock). It consists mostly of calcium carbonate ($CaCO_3$) from ancient, microscopic, single-celled marine invertebrate shells. This type of rock is very porous, soft (a hardness of 3 on the Mohs scale), and crumbly. The chalk used to draw with is actually gypsum (calcium sulphate, $CaSO_4\text{-}2H_2O$)

Chaos theory

The study of iterative non-linear systems in which arbitrarily small variations in initial conditions become magnified over time.

Chaperone protein

A protein that binds a polypeptide as it begins to fold, directing the folding.

Character
A character is a inherited trait of an organism. Characters are usually described in terms of a state, for example: "blue eyes" vs. "brown eyes," where "eyes" is the character, and "blue" and "brown" are its states.

Character displacement
Usually refers to a pattern of geographic variation in which a character differs more greatly between sympatric than between allopatric populations of two species; sometimes used for the evolutionary process of accentuation of differences between sympatric populations of two species as a result of the reproductive or ecological interactions between them.

Character state
One of the variant conditions of a character (e.g., yellow versus brown as state of the character .colour of snail shell.).

Chargaff's rules
Rules developed by Erwin Chargaff and his colleagues concerning the ratios of bases in DNA.

Charge
The amount of unbalanced electricity in a system. Either positive or negative.

Charge sensitivity
For accelerometers that are rated in terms of charge sensitivity, the output voltage (V) is proportional to the charge (Q) divided by the shunt capacitance (C). This type of accelerometer is characterized by a high output impedance. The sensitivity is given in terms of charge; picocoulombs per unit of acceleration (g).

Charged particles
Particles with positive or negative charge, for example electrons, protons or ions.

Chatter
The rapid cycling on and off of a relay in a control process due to insufficient bandwidth in the controller.

Chattermarks
Erosional features associated with alpine glaciers.

Checkout
A test procedure needed to assess the correct functioning of a spacecraft's performances.

Checkpoint
A key transition point at which progression to the next stage in the cell cycle is regulated.

Chemical (empirical) formula
The ratio of elements in a substance. For example: the chemical formula of common salt is NaCl, sodium and chlorine in a ratio of 1:1.

Chemical equation
The mathematical representation of a chemical reaction.

Chemical oxygen demand
The quantity of oxygen used in biological and non-biological oxidation of materials in water.It is used as a measure of water quality.

Chemical reaction
The transformation of substances by the rearrangement of their atoms.

Chemistry
Chemistry is the science of matter, especially its chemical reactions, but also its composition, structure and properties. Chemistry is concerned with atoms and their interactions with other atoms, and particularly with the properties of chemical bonds. Chemistry is sometimes called "the central science" because it connects

Chemoautotrophs
Organisms that obtain energy through chemical reactions and build biomass directly from inorganic carbon.

Chemosynthetic
The synthesis of organic compounds within an organism, with chemical reactions providing the energy source.

Chemotherapy
The treatment of disease by using chemical substances.

Chiasma
Point of attachment between homologous chromosomes at which crossing over took place.

Chicxulub crater
The Chicxulub crater at the tip of the Yucatán Peninsula is an impact crater that dates from 65 million years ago. It is 120 miles wide and 1 mile deep. It is probably the site of the K-T meteorite impact that caused the extinction of the dinosaurs and many other groups of organisms.

Chimeric oligo
An oligo with a backbone that is composed of subunits with different backbone structures.

Chip on chip assay
A method that combines chromatin immunoprecipitation and DNA microarray analysis to analyze protein-DNA interactions across the genome.

Chi-square test
A statistical test that allows one to determine whether observed quantities of a specific characteristic differed from the expected value purely by chance.

Chloramphenicol acetyl transferase
An enzyme in bacteria that acetylates chloramphenicol, rendering it inactive in bacterial cells. In molecular biology, it is often used as a reporter to measure gene expression.

Chlorophyll
Chlorophyll is a molecule that can use light enrgy from sunlight to turn water and carbon dioxide gas into sugar and oxygen (this process is called photosynthesis). Chlorophyll is magnesium based and is usually green.

Chloroplast
Chloroplasts are small green structures in plants that contain chlorophyll. Leaves have many chloroplasts.

Chloroplast DNA
DNA in chloroplasts; has many characteristics in common with eubacterial DNA and typically consists of a circular molecule that lacks histone proteins and encodes some of the rRNAs, tRNAs, and proteins found in chloroplasts.

Chondritic meteor
Chondritic meteors are stony meteors with chondrules, tiny glass spheres. These meteors are unchanged since their formation, shortly after the formation of the sun. These meteors consist of elements also common in the Earth's core.

Choreography
The science of dance & composing ballet.

Chorionic villus sampling
Procedure used for prenatal genetic testing in which a small piece of the

chorion (the outer layer of the placenta) is removed from a pregnant woman. A catheter is inserted through the vagina and cervix into the uterus. Suction is then applied to remove the sample.

Chorography
The science of geographical regions; plant & animal distribution.

Chromatid
A single, long DNA molecule and its associated proteins, forming half of a replicated chromosome.

Chromatin
Chromatin is a complex of DNA and proteins that forms chromosomes within the nucleus of eukaryotic cells.

Chromatin immunoprecipitation
An assay used in biology to identify proteins, such as transcription factors, that bind to a specific piece of chromatin in vivo.

Chromatin remodeling
Adding or removing chemical groups to or from histones, which can alter gene expression.

Chromatin-remodeling complex
Complex of proteins that alters chromatin structure without acetylating histone proteins.

Chromatin-remodeling protein
Binds to a DNA sequence and disrupts chromatin structure, causing the DNA to become more accessible to RNA polymerase and other proteins.

Chromega®
A chromium-nickel alloy which makes up the positive leg of type K and type E thermocouples (registered trademarks of OMEGA ENGINEERING, INC.).

Chromosomal abnormality
Any change in the total number of chromosomes or the physical structure of a chromosome.

Chromosomal puff
Localized swelling of a polytene chromosome; a region of chromatin in which DNA has unwound and is undergoing transcription.

Chromosomal rearrangements
A class of mutations in which whole segments of chromosomes are involved, including inversions and translocations.

Chromosomal scaffold protein
Protein that plays a role in the folding and packing of the chromosome, revealed when chromatin is treated with a concentrated salt solution, which removes histones and some other chromosomal proteins.

Chromosome
A chromosome is an organized structure of DNA and protein found in cells. It is a single piece of coiled DNA containing many genes, regulatory elements and other nucleotide sequences. Chromosomes also contain DNA-bound proteins, which serve to package the DNA and control its functions. Chromosomes vary widely between different organisms. The DNA molecule may be circular or linear, and can be composed of 100,000 to 10,000,000,000 nucleotides in a long chain. Typically, eukaryotic cells (cells with nuclei) have large linear chromosomes and prokaryotic cells (cells without defined

nuclei) have smaller circular chromosomes, although there are many exceptions to this rule. Also, cells may contain more than one type of chromosome; for example, mitochondria in most eukaryotes and chloroplasts in plants have their own small chromosomes.

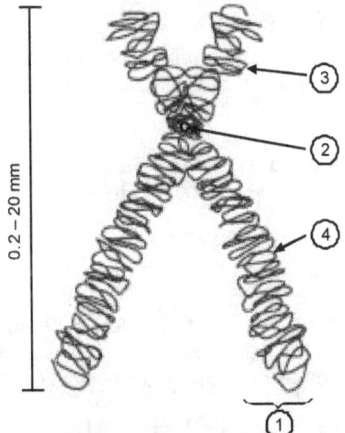

Chromosome deletion
Loss of a chromosome segment.

Chromosome duplication
Mutation that doubles a segment of a chromosome.

Chromosome inversion
Rearrangement in which a segment of a chromosome has been inverted 180 degrees.

Chromosome map
Representation of the physical location of genes on a chromosome, generally derived from studies looking at recombination rates between known loci.

Chromosome mutation
Difference from the wild type in the number or structure of one or more chromosomes; often affects many genes and has large phenotypic effects.

Chromosome painting
Visualization of individual, whole chromosomes by fluorescence in situ hybridization (FISH).

Chromosome rearrangement
Change from the wild type in the structure of one or more chromosomes.

Chromosome territories
The areas of the nucleus in which particular chromosomes reside.

Chromosome theory of heredity
States that genes are located on chromosomes.

Chromosome walking
Method of locating a gene by using partly overlapping genomic clones to move in steps from a previously cloned, linked gene to the gene of interest.

Chromosphere
Layer of the Sun's atmosphere located above the photosphere and below the corona. It is about 10 000 km deep and consists mainly of ionised hydrogen, helium and calcium. Its temperature ranges from 6000 °C at the photosphere boundary to 100 000 °C at the boundary with the corona. Its low density means it is usually only visible during a total solar eclipse.

Chronobiology
The study of duration of life.

Chronology
The science of arranging time in periods and ascertaining the dates and historical order of past events.

Chronosequence
Predictable change of vegetation over time.

Chronosequence method
Used to infer succession by replacing a successional stage by spatial differences in time since an initial community state.

Chronospecies
A segment of an evolving lineage preserved in the fossil record that differs enough from earlier or later members of the lineage to be given a different binomial (name). Not equivalent to biological species.

Chrysalis
A pupa (the stage between a larva and an adult) enclosed in a firm case or cocoon. The chrysalis was pale gray and about an inch long.

Cinchona tree
The cinchona tree is a tropical tree that is the primary source of the anit-malarial drug quinine. Quinine is found in the bark of the cinchona tree. Quinine is a chemical that cures malaria, a deadly tropical disease carried by mosquitoes. There are many species of cinchona; they range from about 15 to 20 metres tall.

The cinchona tree is native to rainforests of the eastern slope of the Amazonian Andes of South America, where it is called the "fever tree." Classification: Family Rubiaceae, Genus Cinchona, Species C. officinalis, C. ledgeriana, C. uccirubra, C. calisaya, and others.

Cinder cone
A volcanic cone built entirely of loose fragmented material (pyroclastics.)

CIS
CIS-acting elements affect only loci on the same strand of DNA.

CIS configuration
Arrangement in which two or more wild-type genes are on one chromosome and their mutant alleles are on the homologous chromosome; also called coupling configuration.

CIS-regulatory element
A noncoding DNA sequence in or near a gene required for proper spatiotemporal expression of that gene, often containing binding sites for transcription factors. Often used interchangeably with enhancer.

Clade
A clade is a group of all the organisms that share a particular common ancestor (and therefore have similar features). The members of a clade are related to each other. A clade is monophyletic.

Cladistics
Cladistics is a method of classifying organisms based on common ancestry and the branching of the evolutionary family tree. Organisms that share common ancestors (and therefore have similar features) are grouped into taxonomic groups called clades. Cladistics can also be used

to predict properties of yet-to-be discovered organisms.

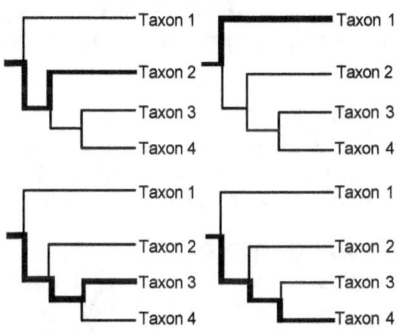

Cladode
A cladode is a stem that looks like a leaf.

Cladogenesis
Branching of lineages during phylogeny.

Cladogram
Cladograms are branching diagrams that depict species divergence from common ancestors. They show the distribution and origins of shared characteristics. Cladograms are testable hypotheses of phylogenetic relationships.

Class
In classification (taxonomy), a class is a group of related or similar organisms. A class contains one or more orders. A group of similar classes forms a phylum.

Classification
The classification of organisms helps in their study. Cladistics is a method based on common ancestry; the Linnean system is based on a simple hierarchical structure.

Clear
To restore a device to a prescribed initial state, usually the zero state.

Cleavage
A series of rapid mitotic cell divisions after fertilization.

Cleft
A cleft (also called parted) leaf is one in which the margins between the irregular teeth go more than halfway to the midrib.

Client/server
A term denoting the technology relationship between two types of computers, the client (normally your Mac or PC) and the server (a computer that stores and delivers information or files to you). When surfing the Internet, you are the client, and the pages you are reading come from the server, such as the www4teachers server.

Climate
The long-term prevailing weather in an area that is largely determined by temperature and precipitation.

Climate change
Changes in intensity and distribution of solar radiation reaching Earth.s surface.

Climatology
The study of climate - the prevailing atmospheric conditions of humidity, temperature, winds etc.

Climax
A state for communities which represents the final, or permanent end-stage of succession.

Climax community
A community composed of species that represents the final stage of colonization of a habitat.

Climax vegetation
Climax vegetation is the final stage in the development of an area.

Cline
A gradual change in an allele frequency or in the mean of a character over a geographic transect.

Clinical trial
The process by which new drugs are tested in humans in hopes of winning Food and Drug Administration approval so that the drugs can be sold in the United States.

Clipping
The term applied to the phenomenon which occurs when an output signal is limited in some way by the full range of an amplifier, ADC or other device. When this occurs, the signal is flattened at the peak values, the signal approaches the shape of a square wave, and high frequency components are introduced. Clipping may be hard, as is the case when the signal is strictly limited at some level; or it may be soft, in which case the clipping signal continues to follow the input at some reduced gain.

Clock
The device that generates periodic signals for synchronization.

Clonal evolution
Process by which mutations that enhance the ability of cells to proliferate predominate in a clone of cells, allowing the clone to become increasingly rapid in growth and increasingly aggressive in proliferation properties.

Clone
A genetically identical copy of an individual, cell or fragment of DNA produced by an individual or cell.

Cloning strategy
Particular set of methods used to clone a gene or DNA fragment.

Cloning vector
Stable, replicating DNA molecule to which a foreign DNA fragment can be attached and transferred to a host cell.

Closeness of Control
Total temperature variation from a desired set point of system. Expressed as "closeness of control" is ±2°C or a system bandwidth with 4°C, also referred to as amplitude of deviation.

Cloud
A mass of tiny droplets of water that condensed from the air. A dark cloud blocked the sunlight.

Cloud forest
A cloud forest is a rainforest that is on a mountainside. It is usually misty and cloudy.

Cloverleaf structure
Secondary structure common to all tRNAs.

Club mosses

Club mosses (Lycopsids) are primitive, vascular plants (pteridophytes) that evolved over 375 million years ago (during the Devonian). Huge club mosses went extinct during the Permian mass extinction; smaller ones lived during the time of the dinosaurs. These plants live near moisture (in order for their spores to germinate). These fast-growing, resilient plants propagate with rhizomes (underground stems). Classification: Division Lycopodiophyta, Class Lycopodiopsida, Order Lycopodiales, Family Lycopodiaceae (Club-mosses).

Cluster mission

ESA cornerstone mission to explore the interaction between the Sun and the Earth's magnetosphere. Launched in July (Salsa and Samba) and August (Rumba and Tango) 2000. The four spacecraft fly in tetrahedral formation in order to study electrical and magnetic phenomena both inside the magnetosphere and in the solar wind 'upstream' of the Earth.

CMR (common-mode rejection)

The ability of a panel metre to eliminate the effect of AC or DC noise between signal and ground. Normally expressed in dB at dc to 60 Hz. One type of CMR is specified between SIG LO and PWR GND. In differential metres, a second type of CMR is specified between SIG LO and ANA GND (METRE GND).

CMV (common-mode voltage)

The AC or DC voltage which is tolerable between signal and ground. One type of CMV is specified between SIG LO and PWR GND. In differential metres, a second type of CMV is specified between SIG HI or LO and ANA GND (METRE GND).

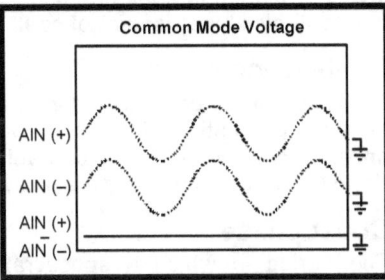

Co-accumulation

Simultaneous accumulation of more than one element by plants.

Coactivator

Protein that cooperates with an activator of transcription. In eukaryotic transcriptional control, coactivators often physically interact with transcriptional activators and the basal transcription apparatus.

Coadapted gene pool

A population or set of populations in which prevalent genotypes are composed of alleles at two or more loci that confer high fitness in combination with each other, but not with alleles that are prevalent in other such populations.

Coal

Coal is a combustible mineral formed from organic matter (mostly plant material) that lived about 300 million years ago (during the Pennsylvanian Period). During the Pennsylvanian Period, the earth was covered with huge swampy forests of giant ferns, horsetails, and club mosses. As layer upon layer of these plants died, they were compressed and covered with soil, stopping the decomposition process, forming peat. Heat and pressure chemically forced out oxygen and hydrogen, leaving carbon-rich deposits, called coal. A 20-foot-thick layer of plant material produces a one-foot-thick layer (seam) of coal.

Coalescence
Derivation of the gene copies in one or more populations from a single ancestral copy, viewed retrospectively (from the present back into the past).

Coast phase
The period in which a spacecraft starts approaching its target.

Coded mask
Mask made for example of lead, tungsten, aluminium etc. with a pattern of opaque and transparent elements. Coded masks are used for gathering powerful gamma radiation that cannot be focused by lenses or mirrors. A coded mask telescope is a pinhole camera but with many holes. The coded mask is placed above a detector. The gamma rays project the shadow of the mask onto the detector plane. By analysing the detected pattern of light and shadow an image of the sky can be obtained.

Coding exons of genes
A sequence of DNA that is transcribed to messenger RNA and codes information for protein synthesis.

Coding strand
The side of the double helix for a particular gene from which RNA is not transcribed.

Codominance
Type of allelic interaction in which the heterozygote simultaneously expresses traits of both homozygotes.

Codominant marker
A genetic marker in which the heterozygotes can be distinguished from both homozygotes.

Codon
1. A codon is a sequence of three DNA or RNA nucleotides that corresponds with a specific amino acid or a stop signal during protein synthesis.
2. Sequence of three nucleotides that codes for one amino acid in a protein.

Coefficient of coincidence
Ratio of observed double crossovers to expected double crossovers.

Coefficient of relatedness
The proportion of genes identical by descent (IBD) among two individuals I and J.

Coevolution
Strictly, the joint evolution of two (or more) ecologically interacting species, each of which evolves in response to selection imposed by the other. Sometimes used loosely to refer to evolution of one species caused by its interaction with another, or simply to a history of joint divergence of ecologically associated species.

Cognition
The ability of an animal to separate itself from the immediacy of its environment and to reflect on the past in order to solve future problems. Cognition involves the ability to make novel associations.

Coherence function
A frequency domain function computed to show the degree of a linear, noise-free relationship between a system's input and output. The value of the coherence function ranges between zero and one, where a value of zero indicates there is no causal relationship between the input and the output. A value of one indicates

the existence of linear noise-free frequency response between the input and the output.

Cohesin
Molecule that holds the two sister chromatids of a chromosome together. The breakdown of cohesin at the centromeres enables the chromatids to separate in anaphase of mitosis and anaphase II of meiosis.

Cohesive end
Short, single-stranded overhanging end on a DNA molecule produced when the DNA is cut by certain restriction enzymes. Cohesive ends are complementary and can spontaneously pair to rejoin DNA fragments that have been cut with the same restriction enzyme.

Cointegrate structure
Produced in replicative transposition, an intermediate structure in which two DNA molecules with two copies of the transposable element are fused.

Coisogenic
Two strains that are genetically identical (i.e., isogenic), except for a single locus. This occurs most often by a spontaneous mutation by many generations of backcrossing. Coisogenic strains are also becoming available due to target mutagenesis (knockouts) in embryonic stem (ES) cells.

Cold work
The carrying out of any task or the use of any tool or equipment which will not produce a source of ignition.

Coleoptile
A coleoptile is a protective sheath that surrounds the shoot tip and the embryonic leaves of the young shoot of grasses.

Colinearity
Concept that there is a direct correspondence between the nucleotide sequence of a gene and the continuous sequence of amino acids in a protein.

Collection
The accumulation of precipitation into surface and underground areas, including lakes, rivers, and aquifers.

Colour code
The ANSI established colour code for thermocouple wires in the negative lead is always red. Colour Code for base metal thermocouples is yellow for Type K, black for Type J, purple for Type E and blue for Type T.

Coma
(1) Cloud of gas and dust surrounding a comet nucleus. Caused by vapourisation of the nucleus and emission of jets containing gas and dust. It grows in size as the comet approaches the Sun and may be up to one million kilometres across soon after the comet reaches perihelion.
(2) Lens aberration that gives an image a 'tail'.

Comah
The control of Major Accidents and Hazards - Onshore equivalent of the offshore safety case document.

Combined dna index system
In the United States, CODIS is a distributed database that is organized into three hierarchical levels: local, state, and national. All three levels store indexed and searchable digitized representations of typed DNA samples. The hierarchical design allows state and local laboratories to configure CODIS to meet their specific needs.

Comcept of dominance
Principle of heredity discovered by Mendel stating that, when two different alleles are present in a genotype, only one allele may be expressed in the phenotype. The dominant allele is the allele that is expressed, and the recessive allele is the allele that is not expressed.

Comet
Icy body which orbits the Sun. Thought to be leftover planetesimals from the formation of planets in the outer Solar System. The small, solid nucleus consists of water and other ices coated with dark organic compounds. As the nucleus approaches the Sun, it vapourises, creating a coma and two main tails. These tails one made of gas and one of dust may stream million of kilometres into space, and almost always point away from the Sun. Some 'dead' comets, which no longer display a coma or tails, resemble asteroids.

Commensalism
Commensalism is a situation in which two organisms are associated in a relationship in which one benefits from the relationship and the other is not affected much. The two animals are called commensals. An example pf commensalism is bromeliads (plants living on trees in rainforests) and frogs; the frogs get shelter and water from the bromeliad but the bromeliad is unaffected. Commensalism is a type of symbiosis.

Commercial water use
water used for motels, hotels, restaurants, office buildings, other commercial facilities, and institutions. Water for commercial uses comes both from public-supplied sources, such as a county water department, and self-supplied sources, such as local wells.

Commitment to differentiation
The notion that a cell has irreversibly initiated a series of transcriptional events that results in a change in various aspects of cell physiology, such as size, shape, polarity, metabolism, signal transduction, and gene expression profiles.

Common garden
A place in which (usually conspecific) organisms, perhaps from different geographic populations, are reared together, enabling the investigator to ascribe variation among them to genetic rather than environmental differences. Originally applied to plants, but now more generally used to describe any experiment of this design.

Common garden experiment
An experimental design in which individuals from multiple populations are raised together in the same environment in order to test for genetic differentiation in phenotypic traits.

Common mode
The output form or type of control action used by a temperature controller to control temperature, i.e. on/off, time proportioning, PID.

Common mode rejection ratio
The ability of an instrument to reject interference from a common voltage at its input terminals with relation to ground. Usually expressed in db (decibels).

Communication
Transmission and reception of data among data processing equipment and related peripherals.

Community
A group of interacting species that inhabit a particular location at a particular time.

Community assembly
How species are added to and lost from communities, and how communities change over time.

Community assembly theory
Theory suggesting that similar sites can develop different biological communities depending on order of arrival of different species.

Community ecology
The study of how resource availability influences ecosystem characteristics, including the number and types of species present.

Companion cell
A companion cell is a type of cell that pumps nutrients (sugars) into phloem cells.

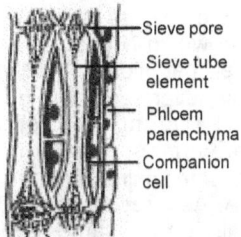

- Sieve pore
- Sieve tube element
- Phloem parenchyma
- Companion cell

Comparative genomic hybridization
A molecular cytogenetic method of screening cells for DNA gains and losses at a chromosomal level. Differentially labelled test and reference DNA are hybridized simultaneously to metaphase chromosomes to generate a map of DNA copy number changes.

Comparative genomics
Comparative studies of the genomes of different organisms.

Comparative method
A procedure for inferring the adaptive function of a character by correlating its states in various taxa with one or more variables, such as ecological factors hypothesized to affect its evolution.

Compartment
A contiguous group of cells, descended from the same progenitor cell, that form a spatially discrete part of a developing organ or structure and often act as a discrete developmental unit. Cells from one compartment typically do not intermix with cells from other compartments.

Compensated connector
A connector made of thermocouple alloys used to connect thermocouple probes and wires.

Compensating alloys
Alloys used to connect thermocouples to instrumentation. These alloys are selected to have similar thermal electric properties as the thermocouple alloys (however, only over a very limited temperature range).

Compensating loop
Lead wire resistance compensation for RTD elements where an extra length of wire is run from the instrument to the RTD and back to the instrument, with no connection to the RTD.

Compensation
An addition of specific materials or devices to counteract a known error.

Compensatory mutations
A mutation that ameliorates the deleterious fitness effects of another mutation.

Competent cell
Capable of taking up DNA from its environment (capable of being transformed).

Competition
An interaction between individuals of the same species or different species whereby resources used by one are made unavailable to others.

Competition exclusion principles
Principle stating that no two species competing for the same resource can coexist indefinitely.

Competitive exclusion
Extinction of a population due to competition with another species.

Compiler
A programme that translates a high-level language, such as Basic, into machine language.

Complementary
Refers to the relation between the two nucleotide strands of DNA in which each purine on one strand pairs with a specific pyrimidine on the opposite strand (A pairs with T, and G pairs with C).

Complementation
Two different mutations in the heterozygous condition are exhibited as the wild-type phenotype; indicates that the mutations are at different loci.

Complementation test
Test designed to determine whether two dfferent mutations are at the same locus (are allelic) or at different loci (are nonallelic). Two individuals that are homozygous for two independently derived mutations are crossed, producing F1 progeny that are heterozygous for the mutations. If the mutations are at the same locus, the F1 will have a mutant phenotype. If the mutations are at different loci, the F1 will have a wild-type phenotype.

Complete dominance
Exists when the phenotype of a heterozygote is identical to that of a homozygous dominant individual.

Complete flower
A complete flower has a stamen, a pistil, petals, and sepals.

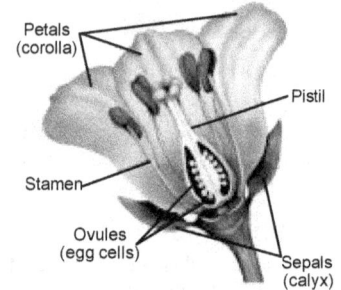

Complete linkage
Complete linkage is defined as the state in which two loci are so close together that alleles of these loci are virtually never separated by crossing over. During reproduction, chromosomes on the same chromosome pair, exchange sections of DNA. As a result, genes that were originally on the same chromosome can finish up on different chromosomes - genetic recombination. The closer the physical location of two genes on the DNA, the less likely they are to be separated.

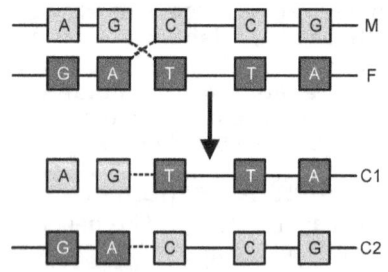

Complete medium
Used to culture bacteria or some other microorganism; contains all the

nutrients required for growth and synthesis, including those normally synthesized by the organism. Nutritional mutants can grow on complete medium.

Complex disease
A pathological condition of the body that is the result of defects in a number of genetic and environmental factors. These conditions do not follow Mendelian inheritance patterns.

Complex life cycle
Life cycle of a parasite which involves two hosts where the parasite must spend time in both to complete its life cycle.

Complex wave
The resultant form of a number of sinusoidal waves that are summed together forming a periodic wave. Such waves may be analyzed in the frequency domain to readily determine their component parts.

Composite flower
A composite flower (like the sunflower) has a many individual flowers (called florets) on a wide, flat receptacle, that look like a single flower. The flowers in the central disk are called disk flowers; the flowers on the periphery are called ray flowers. This group is called Asteraceae (Compositae).

Composite transposon
Type of transposable element in bacteria that consists of two insertion sequences flanking a segment of DNA.

Composite volcano
A steep volcanic cone built by both lava flows and pyroclastic eruptions.

Composition
The relative proportion of habitat types in the landscape, regardless of spatial distribution.

Compound
A substance containing more than one element.

Compound chromosome
Fusion of two separate chromosomes.

Compound heterozygote
An individual organism that possesses two different mutant alleles at a locus.

Compound leaf
A compound leaf is a leaf that is divided into many separate parts (leaflets) along a midrib (the rachis). All the leaflets of a compound leaf are oriented in the same plane. When a compound leaf falls from the tree, it falls as a unit. A double compound leaf is one in which each leaflet of a compound leaf is also made up of secondary leaflets.

Compound leaf

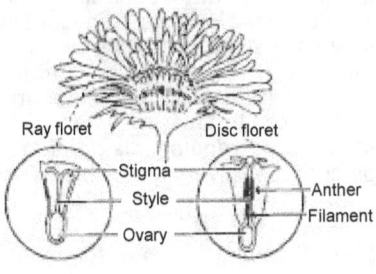

Compton scattering (and inverse compton scattering)
If a photon encounters a charged particle it may transfer some of its momentum to the electron and is then scattered away with reduced energy, i.e. a longer wavelength. The inverse process may happen if a photon encounters a very fast electron. It may then gain energy and can be boosted to shorter wavelengths.

Concave
Curved inwards (as opposed to convex), as in certain mirrors.

Concerted evolution
Maintenance of a homogeneous nucleotide sequence among the members of a gene family, which evolves over time.

Conchology
The branch of Zoology dealing with the shells of molluscs.

Concordance
Percentage of twin pairs in which both twins have a particular trait.

Concordant
Refers to a pair of twins both of whom have the trait under consideration.

Condensate
A term used to describe light liquid hydrocarbons separated from crude oil after production and sold separately.

Condensation
The process of water vapour in the air turning into liquid water. Water drops on the outside of a cold glass of water are condensed water. Condensation is the opposite process of evaporation.

Conditional mutation
Expressed only under certain conditions.

Conductance
The measure of the ability of a solution to carry an electrical current. (See Equivalent Conductance)

Conduction
Heat or electricity transfer through molecular interaction, eg: heat passing along a metal bar.

Conductivity, thermal
A measure of the ability of a body to conduct heat.

Cone
A cone (strobilus) is the reproductive fruiting structure of many tracheophytes. It is a group of scales that are joined to a central stalk; the seeds are borne on the surface of the cone scales. A cone scale contains either ovules or spores (depending on whether it is female or male).

Confidence level
The range (with a specified value of uncertainty, usually expressed in percent) within which the true value of a measured quantity exists.

Confidentiality
The idea that private information about an individual will not be shared with others.

Configuration
Refers to almost limitless aspects of landscape heterogeneity, especially the physical and spatial distribution of landscape elements. Configuration metrics that apply across an entire landscape would include characteristics such as the dendritic pattern of streams in a watershed, random or regular distribution of patches, and diversity of habitat types.

Conformation
The three-dimensional shape of a molecule.

Conformity error
For thermocouples and RTDs, the difference between the actual reading and the temperature shown in published tables for a specific voltage input.

Congenic
Organisms that are almost genetically identical; ideally, they differ at only one locus.

Congenic strain
An inbred strain of animals that are continually interbred. Generally, it takes 10 generations of crossing two inbred lines to create a congenic line that differs in only one locus.

Congenital
A condition that is present at birth.

Congenital disorder
A congenital disorder, or congenital disease, is a condition existing at birth and often before birth, or that develops during the first month of life (neonatal disease), regardless of causation. Of these diseases, those characterized by structural deformities are termed "congenital anomalies"; that is a different concept (MeSH) which involves defects in or damage to a developing fetus.

Conifer
Most conifers are evergreen trees and shrubs that bear naked seeds in cones (a woody strobilus). Examples of modern-day conifers include pine, fir, larch, redwood, and spruce trees. Mesozoic Era conifers included redwoods, yews, pines, the monkey puzzle tree (Araucaria), cypress, and Pseudofrenelopsis (a Cheirolepidiacean). Towards the end of the Mesozoic, flowering plants flourished and began to overtake conifers as the dominant flora.

Conjugation
Mechanism by which genetic material may be exchanged between bacterial cells. During conjugation, two bacteria lie close together and a cytoplasmic connection forms between them. A plasmid or sometimes a part of the bacterial chromosome passes through this connection from one cell to the other.

Connate water
Water included in the groundwater which is derrived from the rock itself, as opposed to water which has percolated down from the surface.

Connection head
An enclosure attached to the end of a thermocouple which can be cast iron, aluminum or plastic within which the electrical connections are made.

Connective tissue
Connective tissue is the material inside your body that supports many of its parts. It is the .cellular glue. that gives your tissues their shape and helps keep them strong. It also helps some of your tissues do their work. Cartilage and fat are examples of connective tissue.

Connectives
Strains of organisms developed by backcrossing the nuclear genome from one strain into the cytoplasm of another; the mitochondrial parent is always the female parent during the backcrossing programme.

Consanguinity
Relation by descent from a common ancestor.

Consensus sequence
Comprises the most commonly encountered nucleotides found at a specific location in DNA or RNA.

Conservation biology
A multidisciplinary science that has developed to address the loss of biological diversity. Conservation biology has two central goals: to evaluate human impacts on biological diversity, and to develop practical approaches to prevent the extinction of species.

Conservation
Conservation is the wise use of natural resources (plants, animals, minerals, water, etc.) so that they are not damaged and will be in good condition in the future.

Conserve
To keep and protect from harm, loss, or change. Let's conserve our drinking water so that we don't run out.

Consomic strain
Organisms that are produced by repeated backcrossing of a whole chromosome such as the X or Y chromosome onto an inbred strain. As with congenic strains, a minimum of 10 backcross generations is required.

Conspecific
Belonging to the same species.

Constantan
A copper-nickel alloy used as the negative lead in Type E, Type J, and Type T thermocouples.

Constitutive mutation
Causes the continuous transcription of one or more structural genes.

Consumer
A consumer is a living thing that eats other living things to survive. It cannot make its own food (unlike most plants, which are producers). Primary consumers eat producers, secondary consumers eat primary consumers, and so on. There are always many more primary consumers than secondary consumers, etc.

Consumptive use
that part of water withdrawn that is evaporated, transpired by plants, incorporated into products or crops, consumed by humans or livestock, or otherwise removed from the immediate water environment. Also referred to as water consumed.

Contig
Set of overlapping DNA fragments that have been assembled in the correct order to form a continuous stretch of DNA sequence.

Continental crust
Solid, outer layers of the earth, including the rocks of the continents.

Continental drift
Continental drift is the movement of the Earth's continents. The land masses are hunks of Earth's crust that float on the molten core. The ideas of continental drift and the supercontinent of Pangaea were presented by A. Wegener in 1015.

Continental islands
Islands which have broken off from a mainland.

Continental shelf
Portions of the continental land masses covered by sea water. Extend varying distances outward from the exposed continental margins. Usually, the continental shelf will be wider along a passive continental margin, and narrower along an active margin. Continued professional development The planned acquisition of knowledge; experience; skills and the development of personal qualities necessary for the execution of

professional duties throughout the working life.

Continuous characteristic
Displays a large number of possible phenotypes that are not easily distinguished, such as human height.

Continuous replication
Replication of the leading strand in the same direction as that of unwinding, allowing new nucleotides to be added continuously to the 3' end of the new strand as the template is exposed.

Continuous spectrum
A frequency spectrum that is characterized by non-periodic data The spectrum is continuous in the frequency domain and is characterized by an infinite number of frequency components.

Contractile root
A contractile root is a root that contracts (gets smaller) and pulls down the crown of the plant below the surface of the soil.

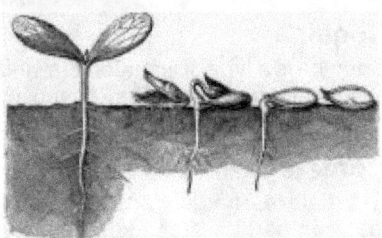

Control character
A character whose occurrence in a particular context starts, modifies or stops an operation that effects the recording, processing, transmission or interpretation of data.

Control key (CTRL)
A key used to access commands through the keyboard rather than the menus. CTRL commands are commonly shortcuts.

Control mode
The output form or type of control action used by a temperature controller to control temperature, i.e., on/off, time proportioning, PID.

Control panel
A window you can open to adjust various aspects of your computer, such as the volume, fonts, desktop background, mouse speed, and clock.

Control point
The temperature at which a system is to be maintained.

Convection
1. The circulatory motion that occurs in a fluid at a non-uniform temperature owing to the variation of its density and the action of gravity.
2. The transfer of heat by this automatic circulation of fluid.

Convection model
A heat transport model based on convection, in which the energy is transported by means of motion.

Convergent evolution
Convergent evolution (convergence) is when a trait develops independently in two or more groups of organisms. An example of convergence is the wings of Pterodactyls and bats.

Convex
Surface curved like the outside of a circle.

Conveyance loss
Water that is lost in transit from a pipe, canal, or ditch by leakage or evaporation. Generally, the water is not available for further use; however,

leakage from an irrigation ditch, for example, may percolate to a groundwater source and be available for further use.

Cooksonia
Cooksonia is the oldest-known land plant. This primitive plant dates from Silurian period, about 428 million years ago Cooksonia was an erect plant with dichotomous branches and terminal sporangia (sacs that produce reproductive spores). Cooksonia fosils have been found in the USA, Canada, and Czechoslovakia.

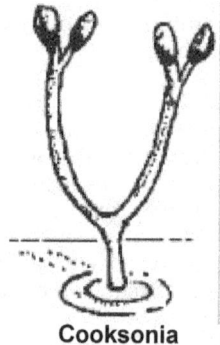

Cooksonia
(The oldest vascular land plant)

Cool down
Movements done to slow the heart and relax the muscles after exercising. The runner walked to cool down after the race.

Cooperation
An association in which all members benefit.

Cooperative breeding
When (typically) non-breeding auxiliaries, or helpers, raise others. offspring.

Co-option
The evolution of a function for a gene, tissue, or structure other than the one it was originally adapted for. At the gene level, used interchangeably with recruitment and, occasionally, exaptation.

Coordinate induction
Simultaneous synthesis of several enzymes that is stimulated by a single environmental factor.

Coppice shoot
A coppice shoot (also called a epicormic shoot, sap shoot, water shoot, or water sprout) is a shoot (new growth) that arises from an adventitious or dormant bud on a branch or a stem of a plant (usually near the base of the plant). This fast-growing shoot often starts to grow when part of a forest canopy is removed or thinned (allowing light in).

Coppice stand
A coppice stand is an area of coppice shoots.

Copy number variation
When the number of copies of a particular genetic sequence is different between individuals.

Coquina
Coquina is a type of limestone (a kind of sedimentary rock) that is mostly made of shells and shell fragments.

Cordate leaf
A cordate leaf has a heart shape, with the wide part towards the petiole.

Core
The central region of a star, planet or galaxy. In the case of a star or planet, it is usually the hottest, most dense part e.g. the iron-rich core at the centre of the Earth. In galaxies, it is the most luminous region which contains the largest concentration of matter - often with a black hole at the centre.

Core element
Consensus sequence in eukaryotic RNA polymerase I promoters that extends from -45 to -20 and is needed to initiate transcription; rich in guanine and cytosine nucleotides.

Core enzyme
Part of bacterial RNA polymerase that, during transcription, catalyzes the elongation of the RNA molecule by the addition of RNA nucleotides; consists of four subunits: two copies of alpha (.), a single copy of beta (.), and a single copy of beta prime (.').

Core promoter
Located immediately upstream of eukaryotic promoter, DNA sequences to which the basal transcription apparatus binds.

Corepressor
Substance that inhibits transcription in a repressible system of gene regulation; usually a small molecule that binds to a repressor protein and alters it so that the repressor is able to bind to DNA and inhibit transcription.

Coriolis force
A result of centripetal force on a mass moving with a velocity radially outward in a rotating plane.

Cork
Cork (also called periderm) is the soft, light-weight bark of the cork oak tree. This low-density material floats in water. Cork cells are made by cork cambium cells. Cork contains suberin, a waxy, water-proof material. Cork protects the tree from water loss and from insects and infections.

Corm
A corm is a fleshy underground stem of some plants. It looks like a bulb, but is solid (it is not formed in layers).

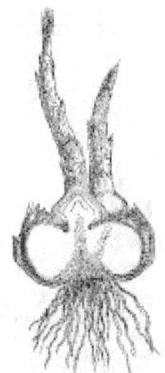

Corn
Corn (Zea mays), also called maize, is a type of cereal grass; it is an edible grain. This tall, annual plant has long, alternately-spaced blade-like leaves, and a strong, solid stem. A flowering plant, staminate (male) flowers grow on the tassels at the end of the main axis of the stem. The pistillate (female) inflorescence grows into the ear of corn, and is a spike having a thick axis paired spikelets in rows (each row of paired spikelets produces two rows of grain). The ear is covered by modified leaves, called husks or shucks. Corn evolved in the Americas, but has been brought all around the world by people; it is the second-largest food crop (behind wheat). Classification: Division Magnoliophyta (angioperms), Class Magnoliopsida (dicots), Class Liliopsida (monocots), Subclass Commelinidae (grasses,

sedges and rushes), Order Cyperales, Family Poaceae (Gramineae) (grasses).

Cornerstone
Category name given to the European Space Agency's key missions in its long-term space science programmes Horizon 2000 and Horizon 2000+.

Corolla
The corolla consists of the petals of a flower.

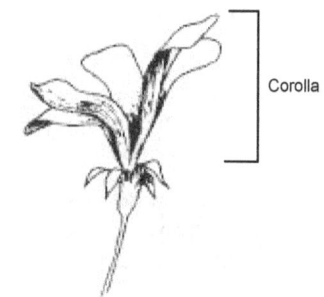

Corolla

Corona
The outermost part of the Sun's atmosphere. It extends outwards for several times the Sun's radius and consists of extremely hot plasma which may exceed one million degrees Celsius. Normally only visible as a white halo during a total solar eclipse. Usually seen as streamers or filaments flowing away from the Sun, but sometimes it almost disappears in regions known as coronal holes.

Coronagraph
Device that allows the corona to be viewed.

Coronal mass ejection (CME)
An outward eruption of billions of tonnes of material thrown into space from the Sun's corona. Caused by magnetic storms on the Sun. The most energetic of all solar explosions, they send material at high speed (200 - 400 km/s) into space, and have a great influence on the magnetosphere. They are most frequent around the time of solar maximum.

Corpse flower
The "corpse flower" is the world's largest flower. This giant bloom is found in rainforests of Indonesia. It's scientific name is Rafflesia arnoldi. Rafflesia gives off a putrid smell that reminds people of rotting meat (this odor attracts its pollinators, beetles and flies), hence its nickname. Rafflesia's enormous flower is about 3 feet (1 m) across and weighs about 20 pounds (9 kilograms). The flower takes about a year to develop, then it blooms for about a week before dying. The flower has five wide orange petals (with pale dots) surrounding a spiked cup. Rafflesia has no stem, no roots, and no leaves. The flower is supported by fungus-like tissue that lives in another plant - the Tetrastigma vine.

Correction (balancing) plane
A plane perpendicular to the shaft axis of a rotor in which correction for unbalance is made.

Correlated response to selection
An evolutionary change in an unselected trait caused by an additive genetic correlation between the unselected trait and a trait under selection.

Correlation
Degree of association between two or more variables.

Correlation coefficient
Statistic that measures the degree of association between two or more

variables. A correlation coefficient can range from -1 to +1. A positive value indicates a direct relation between the variables; a negative correlation indicates an inverse relation. The absolute value of the correlation coefficient provides information about the strength of association between the variables.

Correlational selection
A type of selection in which two traits interact nonadditively to determine fitness, characterized by the finding that certain combinations of trait values have higher fitness than other combinations.

Corridors
Relatively narrow, linear strips of habitat between otherwise isolated habitat patches.

Cosmic background explorer (COBE) satellite
A NASA satellite launched in 1989 to observe the cosmic microwave background. In 1992, COBE detected for the first time minute variations of temperature (the anisotropies) in the cosmic microwave background.

Cosmic microwave background radiation
Diffuse electromagnetic radiation that fills the entire Universe. Believed to be the remnant radiation from the Big Bang, which created the Universe 12-15 billion years ago. Its temperature has now cooled to 2.73 degrees above absolute zero (2.73 K). Discovered in 1964 by Arno Penzias and Robert Wilson. Space and ground-based observations show ripples in the radiation which are believed to be the first signs of structure emerging in the early Universe.

Cosmic rays
Highly energetic nuclei and particles, generally electrically charged, with energies ranging from 100 million eV to 10 million billion eV. Part of this radiation comes from the Sun, interstellar space, and intergalactic space. When a cosmic ray collides with our atmosphere a shower of secondary particles is created in the upper atmosphere. This air shower triggers a cascade of particle reactions and interactions which propagate to the ground.

Cosmid
Cloning vector that combines the properties of plasmids and phage vectors and is used to clone large pieces of DNA in bacteria. Cosmids are small plasmids that carry cos sites, allowing the plasmid to be packaged into viral coats.

Cosmogony
The science of the nature of heavenly bodies.

Cosmography
The science that describes & maps the main features of universe.

Cosmology
Cosmology is the study of the Universe as a whole. Cosmological models are usually based on the cosmological principle which states that any observer in any galaxy sees the same general features of the Universe as any other. Based upon the concepts of homogeneity (matter is uniformly spread throughout space), isotropy (the Universe looks the same no matter in which direction one looks), and universality (the laws of physics that work on Earth work the same in every part of the Universe).

Cost
A reduction in fitness caused by a correlated effect of a feature that provides an increment in fitness (i.e., a benefit).

Cost benefit ratio
The ratio of the cost of an act to its benefit, measured in terms of evolutionary fitness.

Cost of resistance
The fitness effects of an allele that confers resistance to a pesticide or antibiotic in the absence of the pesticide or antibiotic.

Cost to Company
It is used in relation to employment - Includes holidays; training; salary; sickness pay etc.

Cotransduction
Process in which two or more genes are transferred together from one bacterial cell to another. Only genes located close together on a bacterial chromosome will be cotransduced.

Cotransformation
Process in which two or more genes are transferred together during cell transformation.

Cotyledon
The cotyledon is the embryonic leaf within a seed.

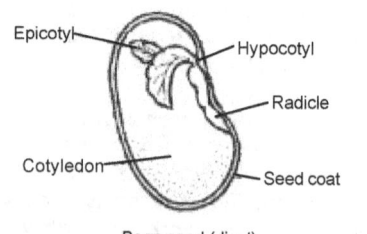

Bean seed (dicot)

When a seed germinates, the cotyledon is the first leaf to grow.

Monocots have one cotyledon; dicots have two cotyledons.

Coulomb
A measurement of the quantity of electrical charge, usually expressed as pico coulomb (10^{-12} coulombs).

Coulomb attraction
Electrostatic attraction between bodies of opposite charge

Coulomb sensitivity
Charge/unit acceleration, expressed in Pc/g (charge sensitivity).

Counter weight
A weight added to a body so as to reduce a calculated unbalance at a desired place.

Counts
The number of time intervals counted by the dual-slope A/D converter and displayed as the reading of the panel metre, before addition of the decimal point.

Covalent bond
A bond formed between atoms that share electrons.

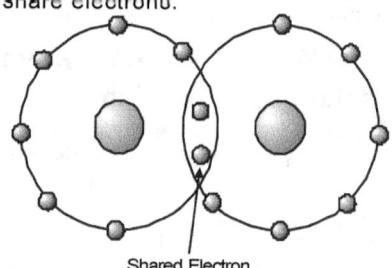

Shared Electron

Covariance
A measure of how much two variables change together.

CPG island
DNA region that contains many copies of a cytosine base followed by a guanine base; often found near

transcription start sites in eukaryotic DNA. The cytosine bases in CpG islands are commonly methylated when genes are inactive but are demethylated before the initiation of transcription.

CPS
Cycles per second; the rate or number of periodic events in one second, expressed in Hertz (Hz).

CPU
Central Processing Unit. The CPU is the hardware that most people consider the "brain" of the computer. It takes instructions from software, makes calculations, and helps run the show!

Crainology
The science that deals with skull.

Crater
Basin-shaped depression in the surface of a planet or moon. May be caused by a comet or asteroid impact, or by a volcanic eruption. Usually circular as seen from above, impact craters often have a raised rim formed from material (ejecta) thrown out by the collision. Larger impact craters have central mountain peaks. Volcanic craters may contain lava which is supplied from subsurface magma. They are surrounded by material produced during previous volcanic eruptions.

Creationism
The doctrine that each species (or perhaps higher taxon) was created separately, essentially in its present form, by a supernatural creator.

Crenate
A crenate leaf has edges (margins) shaped like rounded teeth.

Crenolate
A crenolate leaf margin has edges that are shallow-toothed.

Cretaceous period
Dinosaurs were at their height during the Cretaceous period, 146-65 million years ago, and flowering plants spread and flourished. There was a mass extinction (the K-T mass extinction) at the end of the Cretaceous, marking the end of the dinosaurs and many other species of animals and plants.

Cri du chat syndrome
A group of symptoms that result from missing a piece of chromosome 5. The syndrome's name is based on the cry of affected infants, which is high pitched and sounds catlike.

Criminology
The study of crime & criminals.

Crisped
Crisped leaves have a tighly curled margin. Parsley and kale leaves are crisped.

Cristae
(singular crista) The multiply-folded inner membrane of a cell's mitochondrion that are finger-like

projections. The walls of the cristae are the site of the cell's energy production (it is where ATP is generated).

Critical damping
Critical damping is the smallest amount of damping at which a given system is able to respond to a step function without overshoot.

Critical density
The current expansion of the Universe will be stopped in the future if the density of all the existing matter amounts to a particular value. That precise value for the total density of the Universe is called the 'critical density'. If the Universe has precisely the critical density it is a 'flat universe' (also called 'Euclidean universe'). The critical density is calculated to be about $(1-2) \times 10^{-26}$ kg/m^3. This is about 100 times larger than the average density inferred to be present in visible matter, such as stars and galaxies. Many scientists believe that the Universe should have the critical density and so there is a dark matter problem, in the sense that there should be much more mass present in the Universe in forms we have not yet detected.

Critical period
The time during prenatal development when a structure is sensitive to damanage from a mutation or an environmental intervention.

Critical speed
The rotational speed of the rotor or rotating element at which resonance occurs in the system. The shaft speed at which at least one of the "critical" or natural frequencies of a shaft is excited.

Cross bridge
In a heteroduplex DNA molecule, the point at which each nucleotide strand passes from one DNA molecule to the other.

Cross resistance
The condition in which resistance to one pesticide or antibiotic confers increased resistance to a second pesticide or antibiotic.

Cross-fostering
An experimental technique in which offspring are reared (fostered) by animals other than their genetic parents; cross-fostering is designed to reduce parental effects.

Crossing over
1. Exchange of genetic material between homologous but nonsister chromatids.
2. During meiosis, the process in which portions of homologous chromosomes undergo physical exchange.

Cross-pollination
Cross-pollination is the transfer of pollen from the anther to the stigma of a flower on a different plant

Crown
The crown of a plant is the area from which new shoots arise or the point at which the roots meet the stem. Also, the upper area of the tree that has a lot of branching and leaves.

Crozier
The crozier is the spirally coiled "fiddlehead" of a young fern leaf.

Cruciform
Structure formed by the pairing of inverted repeats on both strands of double-stranded DNA.

Crude unit
The refinery processing unit where initial crude oil distillation takes place.

The crude unit makes the first rough distillation cut. The lighter products produced in this process are further refined in the cat cracker or the reforming unit. Heavier products which cannot be vaporised and separated in this process are distilled still further in the vacuum distillation unit or the coker.

Cruise phase
The phase of a spacecraft's journey needed to reach its target.

Crust
The solid surface layer of a planet or moon. In the inner Solar System, it is usually made of rock, while in the outer Solar System it is usually water-ice. The crust formed early in the planet's history, when it was still completely molten. Lighter materials 'floated' to the surface and formed the crust, leaving denser elements to form the core.

Cryogenics
The science dealing with the production, control and application of very low temperatures.

Cryostat
Container used to isolate thermally a fluid from its environment and maintain it at low temperatures.

Crypsis
Defence of prey species through a shape or coloration that provides camouflage from predators.

Cryptic choice
Post-copulatory female choice is the ability of females to affect the likelihood that sperm from a particular male fertilizes their eggs, and their decision to invest in offspring based on the identity of the male with whom they mate; this choice is made via morphological, chemical and behavioral adaptations that happens inside the female reproductive tract and cannot be detected from behavioral studies alone.

Cryptogam
Cryptogams are plants and plant-like organisms that do not reproduce with seeds and do not produce flowers. Many cryptogams reproduce using spores. Ferns, mosses, fungi, and algae are cryptogams.

Cryptography
The study of ciphers.

Cryptology
The science dealing with codes and ciphers.

Crystal
Solid substance with a regular geometirc arrangement of atoms.

Crystallography
The study of structures, forms & properties of crystals.

Crystals
A crystal or crystalline solid is a solid material whose constituent atoms, molecules, or ions are arranged in an orderly, repeating pattern extending in all three spatial dimensions. In addition to their microscopic structure, large crystals are usually identifiable by their macroscopic geometrical shape, consisting of flat faces with specific, characteristic orientations.

CSA
Canadian Standards Administration.

Cubic feet per second (cfs)
A rate of the flow, in streams and rivers, for example. It is equal to a volume of water one foot high and one foot wide flowing a distance of one foot in one second. One "cfs" is equal to 7.48 gallons of water flowing each

second. As an example, if your car's gas tank is 2 feet by 1 foot by 1 foot (2 cubic feet), then gas flowing at a rate of 1 cubic foot/second would fill the tank in two seconds.

Culm
A culm is the elongated straw or hollow stem of grasses. The culm usually supportes the inflorescence.

Cultivar
A cultivar is a plant that is a cultivated (bred) variety.

Cuneate
Cuneate means wedge-shaped.

Cure point
The temperature at which a normally magnetic material goes through a magnetic transformation and becomes non-magnetic.

Current
The rate of flow of electricity. The unit of the ampere (A) defined as 1 ampere = 1 coulomb per second.

Current proportioning
An output form of a temperature controller which provides a current proportional to the amount of control required. Normally is a 4 to 20 milliamp current proportioning band.

Curve fitting
Curve fitting is the process of computing the coefficients of a function to approximate the values of a given data set within that function. The approximation is called a "fit". A mathematical function, such as a least squares regression, is used to judge the accuracy of the fit.

Cuticle
The cuticle is the fatty or waxy outer layer of epidermal cells that are above ground.

C-value paradox
The lack of correlation between the DNA content of eukaryotic genomes and a given organism's phenotypic complexity (i.e., the genome of a less complex eukaryotic organism, such as a plant, may contain far more DNA than that of a more complex organism, such as a human being). The paradox is explained by the amount of noncoding repetitive DNA sequences in a genome.

Cyanobacteria
Cyanobacteria Blue-green algae (also called blue-green algae) are simple, (usually) one-celled photosynthetic organisms that lack a membrane-bound nucleus (they are prokaryotic). They belong to the kingdom Monera.

Cyanobacterial
Relating to or caused by cyanobacteria, photosynthetic bacterial.

Cycad
Cycads (Cycadophyta) are primitive seed plants that dominated the Jurassic period (cycads comprised 20% of the world flora). Cycads are palm like trees that live in warm climates. Separate male and female plants exist (they are dioecious). These gymnosperms have long, divided leaves and produce large cones. Cycads evolved during the Pennsylvanian, had their heyday during the Mesozoic, and only about 185 species (in 11 genera) still exist today. Leptocycas (shown above) and Ptilophyllum were Mesozoic Era cycads. Later cycads had a more rounded, barrel-like base. Classifcation: Division Pinophyta (Gymnosperms), Subdivision Cycadicae, Class Cycadopsida, Order Cycadales, Family Cycadaceae (Cycads).

Cycadeoid
Cycadeoids (Bennettitales) were plants with woody stems (some erect, some spherical) and very tough leaves. Cycadeoids do not always have separate male and female plants. Cycadeoids are now extinct. Some Mesozoic Cycadeoids included: Cycadeoidea, Vardekloeftia, Williamsonia (shown above), Williamsoniella, Westersheimia, and Leguminanthus.

Cycadophytes
Cycadophytes included the Cycads and Cycadeoids (Bennettitales), plants with woody stems (some erect, some spherical) and very tough leaves. These two groups differ mainly in the way they reproduce: Cycads have separate male and female plants; Cycadeoids do not always. Cycadeoids are now extinct but there are still a few cycads. Some Mesozoic Era Cycads included: Leptocycas, Cycas, Zamia, Dioon, Bowenia, Stangeria, and Microcyas. Some Mesozoic Cycadeoids included: Cycadeoidea, Vardekloeftia, Williamsonia, Williamsoniella, Westersheimia, and Leguminanthus.

Cycle time
The time usually expressed in seconds for a controller to complete one on/off cycle.

Cyclic AMP
A second messenger formed from ATP that is involved in signal transduction, generally translating hormonal signals to the nucleus.

Cyclic AMP response element
An element, or sequence, in DNA found in genes whose transcription is induced by cAMP.

Cyclic AMP response element binding transcription factor
A protein that is activated by cAMP and subsequently phosphorylated by protein kinase A. It then binds to cAMP response elements in certain genes to initiate their transcription.

Cyclin
A key protein in the control of the cell cycle; combines with a cyclin-dependent kinase (CDK). The levels of cyclin rise and fall in the course of the cell cycle.

Cyclin-dependent kinase
A key protein in the control of the cell cycle; combines with cyclin.

Cygnus X-1
Source of intense X-ray radiation, discovered in 1965 in the Cygnus constellation. It is believed to be a black hole system.

Cygnus X-3
Source of intense X-ray radiation in the Cygnus constellation which is associated with a compact binary system in which two stars revolve around each other in less than 5 hours.

Cyme
A cyme is an inflorescence where the central flower opens first.

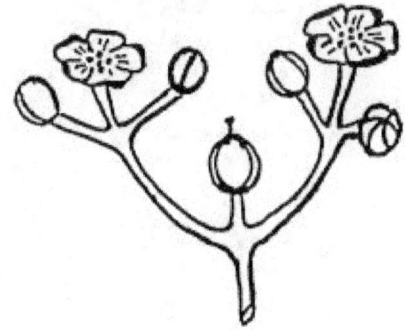

Cytochemistry
The branch of cytology dealing with the chemistry of cells.

Cytogenetics
The branch of biology dealing with the study of heredity from the point of view of cytology & genetics.

Cytokine
A biochemical that a T cell secretes which controls immune function.

Cytokinesis
Cytokinesis is the physical process of cell division that divides the cytoplasm of a parent cell into two daughter cells.

Cytology
The study of cells, especially their formation, structure & functions.

Cytoplasm
Cytoplasm is the jelly-like material outside the cell nucleus in which the organelles are located (the entire contents of the cell located inside the plasma membrane, but excluding the nucleus).

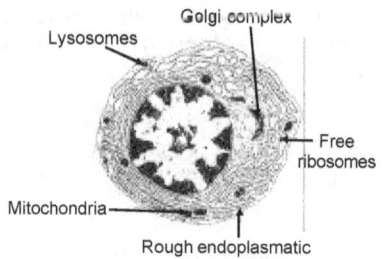

Cytoplasmic inheritance
Inheritance of characteristics encoded by genes located in the cytoplasm. Because the cytoplasm is usually contributed entirely by only one parent, cytoplasmically inherited characteristics are usually inherited from a single parent.

Cytoplasmic trait
A trait encoded by a gene found in a cytoplasmic organelle.

Cytosine
Pyrimidine in DNA and RNA.

Cytosine methylation
The addition of methyl groups to cytosine nucleotides in a DNA molecule.

Cytoskeleton
The cytoskeleton is a network of protein filaments and microtubules that are located in the cytoplasm of eukaryotic cell, just under the cell membrane. The cytoskeleton acts as a support for the cell, as a spatial organizer, and as a channel for some chemical transport.

Cytosol
Cytoplasm is the jelly-like material in cells, excluding the cell nucleus and all organelles (the entire contents of the cell located inside the plasma membrane, but excluding the nucleus and other organelles).

D

D loop
Region of mitochondrial DNA that contains an origin of replication and promoters; is displaced during initiation of replication, leading to the name displacement, or D, loop.

Dacite
Volcanic rock (or lava) that characteristically is light in colour and contains 62 to 69 percent silica and moderate amounts of sodium and potassium.

Dactyliology
The technique of communication by signs made with the fingers. It is generally used by the deaf.

Dactylography
The study of finger prints for the purpose of identification.

Dam methylase
An enzyme that adds methyl groups to specific sites in DNA, inhibiting transcription from these sites.

Damping
The reduction of vibratory movement through dissipation of energy. Types include viscous, coulomb, and solid.

Dams
The female parents in a quantitative genetic breeding experiment.

Danio rerio
The Latin name for zebrafish, a commonly used model organism.

Dark matter
Matter that cannot be detected by current instruments, although its existence can be inferred by its gravitational interactions. For instance, by studying the speed at which the 'arms' in the spiral galaxies rotate, astronomers know that they must be more massive than what can be estimated based on the light that a telescope measures. It has been proposed that part of this matter might be in the form of non-baryonic matter.

Darwin mission
The Darwin mission is an ESA scientific mission currently under study. The scientific goal of Darwin is to detect Earth-like planets circling nearby stars and to set constraints on the possibility of life in the Universe as we know it.

Data
Facts (in the form of values, quantities given by an instrument) from which other information may be inferred. Plural term commonly treated as singular.

Data base
A large amount of data stored in a well-organized manner. A data base

management system (DBMS) is a programme that allows access to the information.

DB (Decibel)
The decibal scale measures sound based on human hearing. It is also used in measurement of acoustics, electronics & control systems, such as gains of amplifiers, attenuation of signals and signal-to-noise ratios. The decibel is a logrithmic unit that indicates the ratio of a physical quantity (usually power or intensity) relative to a specified reference level.

DC
Direct current; an electric current flowing in one direction only and substantially constant in value.

Dead band
1. For chart records: the minimum change of input signal required to cause a deflection in the pen position.
2. For temperature controllers: the temperature band where heat is turned off upon rising temperature and turned on upon falling temperature expressed in degrees. The area where no heating (or cooling) takes place.

Dead volume
The volume of the pressure port of a transducer at room temperature and ambient barometric pressure.

Deamination
Loss of an amino group (NH_2) from a base.

Debris avalanche
A flow of unsorted masses of rock and other material downslope under the influence of gravity. Water is commonly involved as a catalyst and/or lubricant. For example a rapid mass movement that included fragmented cold and hot volcanic rock, water, snow, glacial ice, trees and other debris, and hot pyroclastic material was associated with the May 18, 1980 eruption of Mt. St. Helens. Most of the deposits in the upper valley of the North Fork Toutle River and in the vicinity of Spirit Lake are from the debris avalanche resulting from the eruption.

Debug
To find and correct mistakes in a programme.

Decaying orbit
An unstable orbit from which the orbiting object will gradually spiral into the body it is orbiting.

Decimal
Refers to a base ten number system using the characters 0 through 9 to represent values.

Dedifferentiated
A cell less specialized than the cell it descended from, such as a cancer cell.

Deep space network (dsn)
NASA network of radio telescopes used to communicate with spacecraft operating far from the Earth. It includes three 70 m antennas located at Goldstone (California), near Madrid (Spain) and near Canberra (Australia).

Default
The value(s) or option(s) that are assumed during operation when not specified.

Degenerate code
Refers to the fact that the genetic code contains more information than is needed to specify all 20 common amino acids.

Degree
An incremental value in the temperature scale, i.e., there are 100

degrees between the ice point and the boiling point of water in the Celsius scale and 180°F between the same two points in the Fahrenheit scale.

Deletion
1. A mutation in which one or more base pairs is removed from a DNA sequence.
2. Mutation in which one or more nucleotides are deleted from a DNA sequence.

Deletion mapping
Technique for determining the chromosomal location of a gene by studying the association of its phenotype or product with particular chromosome deletions.

Deletion stock
A line of Drosophila that has a piece of a chromosome missing from its genome.

Delivered duty paid
Incoterm used to describe responsibilities for carriage; risk and cost.

Delivered duty unpaid
Incoterm used to describe responsibilities for carriage; risk and cost.

Delivered ex ship
Incoterm used to describe responsibilities for carriage; risk and cost.

Delta sequence
Long terminal repeat in Ty elements of yeast.

Deme
A local interbreeding unit within a metapopulation.

Demographic
Pertaining to processes that change the size of a population.

Demography
The study of statistics relating to birth and deaths in populations.

Denaturation
Process that separates the strands of doublestranded DNA when DNA is heated.

Dendrology
The study of trees.

Denitrification
A process facilitated by bacteria, in which nitrates (NO_3) break down to molecular nitrogen (N2).

Denotology
The study of moral responsibilities.

Density
A measure of how tightly packed the atoms of a substance are. Measured in grams per cubic centimetre. Varies by the mineral or substance. For example, gold has a high density, while quartz has a low density. See also "specific gravity."

Density dependence
The performance of individuals in a population depends on how many individuals are in that population.

Density-dependent
Affected by population density.

Density-dependent selection
Selection that differs according to population density.

Deoxyribocleotide
Basic building block of DNA, consisting of a deoxyribose sugar, a phosphate, and a nitrogenous base.

Deoxyribonuclease I
An enzyme that makes single-stranded nicks in DNA.

Deoxyribonucleic acid
The genetic material; the biochemical that forms genes.

Deoxyribose sugar
Five-carbon sugar in DNA; lacks a hydroxyl group on the 2'-carbon atom.

Depurination
Break in the covalent bond connecting a purine base to the 1'-carbon atom of the deoxyribose sugar, resulting in the loss of the purine base. The resulting apurinic site cannot provide a template in replication, and a nucleotide with another base may be incorporated into the newly synthesized DNA strand opposite the apurinic site.

Derivative
The derivative function senses the rate of rise or fall of the system temperature and automatically adjusts the cycle time of the controller to minimize overshoot or undershoot.

Derived character
A character (or character state) that has evolved from an antecedent (ancestral) character or state.

Derrick
Metal tower erected vertically above a well for the purpose of lifting and lowering tubes and tools into the well.

Desalination
the removal of salts from saline water to provide freshwater. This method is becoming a more popular way of providing freshwater to populations.

Descent phase
The phase during which a spacecraft is dropped onto a celestial body, such as a planet or a moon.

Desktop
The background behind all your windows, menus, and dialogue boxes: your virtual desk. You can change the look of your desktop by applying different properties to it through your control panel.

Detachment plane
The surface along which a landslide disconnects from its original position.

Determination
Process by which a cell becomes committed to developing into a particular cell type.

Deterministic
Causing a fixed outcome, given initial conditions.

Deterrence
The degree to which a plant defence is able to reduce damage during a choice test (in which a natural enemy is able to choose between defended and undefended plants).

Deviation
The difference between the value of the controlled variable and the value at which it is being controlled.

Dew point
The dew point is the temperature to which a given parcel of humid air must be cooled, at constant barometric pressure, for water vapour to condense into liquid water. The condensed water is called dew when it forms on a solid surface. The dew point is a saturation temperature.

Diakinesis
Fifth substage of prophase I in meiosis. In diakinesis, chromosomes contract, the nuclear membrane breaks down, and the spindle forms.

Diaphragm
The sensing element consisting of a membrane which is deformed by the pressure differential applied across it.

Dicentric bridge
Structure produced when the two centromeres of a dicentric chromatid are pulled toward opposite poles, stretching the dicentric chromosome across the centre of the nucleus. Eventually, the dicentric bridge breaks as the two centromeres are pulled apart.

Dicentric chromatid
Chromatid that has two centromeres; produced when crossing over takes place within a paracentric inversion. The two centromeres of the dicentric chromatid are frequently pulled toward opposite poles in mitosis or meiosis, breaking the chromosome.

Dicer
A ribonuclease that cleaves double-stranded RNA molecules into fragments approximately 20 to 25 nucleotides long that ultimately interfere with the expression of the corresponding gene.

Dideoxyribonucleoside triphosphate
Special substrate for DNA synthesis used in the Sanger dideoxy sequencing method; identical with dNTP (the usual substrate for DNA synthesis) except that it lacks a 3'-OH group. The incorporation of a ddNTP into DNA terminates DNA synthesis.

Dielectric constant
Related to the force of attraction between two opposite charges separated by a distance in a uniform medium.

Diethylstilbestrol
A synthetic nonsteroidal estrogen that was found to cause birth defects in pregnant women.

Differential
For an on/off controller, it refers to the temperature difference between the temperature at which the controller turns heat off and the temperature at which the heat is turned back on. It is expressed in degrees.

Differential gene expression
Differences in the time, location, and/or quantitative level at which a gene expresses the protein it encodes. Differential gene expression involves differences between species, developmental stages, or physiological states in the specific cells, tissues, structures, or body segments that express a given gene; it is believed to be a significant agent of morphological change over evolutionary time.

Differential input
A signal-input circuit where SIG LO and SIG HI are electrically floating with respect to ANALOGUE GND (METRE GND, which is normally tied to DIG GND). This allows the measurement of the voltage difference between two signals tied to the same ground and provides superior common-mode noise rejection.

Differential pressure
The difference in static pressure between two identical pressure taps at the same elevation located in two different locations in a primary device.

Differential rotation
(1) The variable rotation rate of a gaseous body, such as a star or Jupiter-type planet according to latitude (distance from its equator).

This results in gas near the equator rotating more quickly than gas near the poles.
(2) The variable rotation in a disc-shaped structure, such as a galaxy, according to distance from its centre. Stars near the centre take less time to complete one rotation than those further away.

Differentiation
Cell specialization, reflecting differential gene expression.

Diffraction
The deviation in the path of a wave that encounters the edge of an obstacle.

Diffraction grating
Grating device that splits light into a spectrum of the component wavelengths.

Diffuse X-ray background
An X-ray emission not associated with known individual sources. Part of this emission, particularly at soft X-ray energies, arises from hot gas within the Galaxy.

Diffusion
The random movement of molecules within a fluid.

Digit
A measure of the display span of a panel metre. By convention, a full digit can assume any value from 0 through 9, a 1/2-digit will display a 1 and overload at 2, a 3/4-digit will display digits up to 3 and overload at 4, etc. For example, a metre with a display span of ±3999 counts is said to be a 3-3/4 digit metre.

Digital output
An output signal which represents the size of an input in the form of a series of discrete quantities.

Digital-to-analogue converter (D/A or DAC)
A device or circuit to convert a digital value to an analogue signal level.

Dihybrid cross
A dihybrid cross describes a mating experiment between two organisms that are identically hybrid for two traits.

DIN (deutsche industrial norm)
A set of German standards recognized throughout the world. The 1/8 DIN standard for panel metres specifies an outer bezel dimension of 96 x 48 mm and a panel cutout of 92 x 45 mm.

DIN 43760
The standard that defines the characteristics of a 100 ohm platinum RTD having a resistance vs. temperature curve specified by a = 0.00385 ohms per degree.

Dinosaur
One of a large group of reptiles that lived millions of years ago. All dinosaurs lived on land.

Diode
Semiconductor electronic component. Ideally, a diode conducts electricity in one direction and does not allow the current to flow in the opposite direction. Thanks to this property diodes are used to rectify alternating currents, i.e., to convert alternating current (AC) to direct current (DC).

Dioecious
Refers to species whose members have either male or female reproductive structures.

Diploid
1. Diploid cells are cells that contain two copies of each chromosome.

2. Organisms that have two copies of each chromosome (except for the sex chromosomes), and therefore two copies of each gene, one from each parent. The diploid chromosome number is denoted by 2n.

Diploid cell
Cell containing two copies (one from each parent) of chromosomes.

Diplotene
Fourth substage of prophase I in meiosis. In diplotene, centromeres of homologous chromosomes move apart, but the homologs remain attached at chiasmata.

Di-polar
The arrangement of the hydrogen atoms of a water molecule at 105 deg. across the oxygen results in a slight electrical charge to the molecule. It also results in water molecules looking like Mickey Mouse instead of Alfred E. Newman.

Direct benefits
Benefits gained by females from their choice of mate and that directly affect her survival and/or fecundity.

Direct development
A life history in which the intermediate larval stage is omitted and development proceeds directly from an embryonic form to an adult-like form.

Direct fitness
Reproductive success through ones own offspring.

Direct repair
DNA repair in which modified bases are changed back to their original structures.

Direct selection
The type of selection in which there is a causal relationship between a phenotypic trait and fitness, which can result in adaptation.

Direct to consumer
The marketing or selling any item directly to consumers, bypassing clinicians.

Direct transmission
Movement of a parasite from one host to another of the same species without an intermediate organism.

Direction
The course taken by a moving body. Putting the car in reverse will change its direction.

Directional selection
1. Selection for a value of a character that is higher or lower than its current mean value.
2. The form of selection characterized by a linear fitness function, with fitness increasing or decreasing in proportion to phenotypic value.

Discharge
the volume of water that passes a given location within a given period of time. Usually expressed in cubic feet per second.

Discharge time constant
The time required for the output-voltage from a sensor or system to discharge 37% of its original value in response to a zero rise time step function input. This parameter determines a low frequency response.

Discontinuous characteristic
Exhibits only a few, easily distinguished phenotypes. An example is seed shape in which seeds are either round or wrinkled.

Discontinuous replication
Replication of the lagging strand in the direction opposite that of unwinding, which means that DNA must be synthesized in short stretches.

Discordant
Refers to a pair of twins of whom one twin has the trait under consideration and the other does not.

Discrete generations
A life history, like that of an annual plant, in which the parental generation has died by the time the offspring generation reproduces.

Discrete polymorphism
A phenotypic trait that exhibits only a few (usually two or three) distinct types or morphs.

Disease
A pathological condition of the body that results in abnormal functioning of an organ or organ system.

Disk operating system (dos)
Programme used to control the transfer of information to and from a disk, such as MS DOS.

Disomy
Describes the state of cell that has two members of a pair of homologous chromosomes.

Dispersal
In population biology, movement of individual organisms to different localities; in biogeography, extension of the geographic range of a species by movement of individuals.

Dispersion
Scattering of an electromagnetic wave as light is split into its constituent colours by a prism or diffraction grating.

Displaced chromosome duplication
Duplication of a chromosome segment in which the duplicated segment is some distance from the original segment.

Displacement
The measured distance traveled by a point from its position at rest. Peak to peak displacement is the total measured movement of a vibrating point between its positive and negative extremes. Measurement units expressed as inches or millinches.

Displacement behaviour
Grooming, touching, or scratching which occurs when an animal is faced with conflicting behavioral needs, or is placed in a circumstance where it cannot express the behaviour it is motivated to perform.

Disruptive selection
1. The form of selection in which fitness is lowest at some intermediate phenotype and higher at each phenotypic extreme.
2. Selection in favor of two or more modal phenotypes and against those intermediate between them; also called diversifying selection.

Dissipation constant
The ratio for a thermistor which relates a change in internal power dissipation to a resultant change of body temperature.

Dissociation constant (k)
A value which quantitatively expresses the extent to which a substance dissociates in solution. The smaller the value of K, the less dissociation of the species in solution. This value varies with temperature, ionic strength, and the nature of the solvent.

Distributed control system
A control system with multiple processors connected by a network.

Disturbance
Any process that removes biomass from the community; an abiotic event, natural or human-caused such as fires and storms, that kills or damages some organisms and thereby creates opportunities for other organisms to grow and reproduce.

Disturbance events
Variation in climate, variation in flooding frequency or drought frequency, or frequencies of storm events characterized by their frequency and impact.

Disturbed habitat species
Species that often live where avalanches, mud slides, and fires occur frequently.

Diurnal
An animal who is active during the day and sleeps at night.

Divergence
The evolution of increasing difference between lineages in one or more characters.

Diversification
An evolutionary increase in the number of species in a clade, usually accompanied by divergence in phenotypic characters.

Diving support vessel
A dedicated vessel for assistance of subsea diving and installation work.

Dizygotic twins
Nonidentical twins that arise when two different eggs are fertilized by two different sperm; also called fraternal twins.

DMA
Acronym direct memory access. A high speed data storage mode of the IBM PC.

DNA (deoxyribonucleic acid)
A chemical chain of linked nucleotides. Two such chains in double helical form represent the basic molecules of which genes are composed.

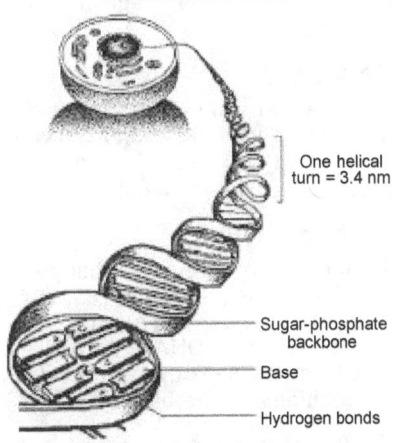

The Structure of DNA

One helical turn = 3.4 nm

Sugar-phosphate backbone
Base
Hydrogen bonds

DNA binding domain
A general term for a single- or double-stranded region of DNA for which a specific protein has an affinity to bind.

DNA fingerprinting
Technique used to identify individuals by examining their DNA sequences.

DNA footprinting
Technique used to determine which DNA sequences are bound by a protein.

DNA forensics
A field of science that uses DNA evidence to assist in the solving of crimes.

DNA gyrase
E. coli topoisomerase enzyme that relieves torsional strain that builds up ahead of the replication fork.

DNA helicase
Protein that unwinds double-stranded DNA by breaking hydrogen bonds.

DNA library
Collection of bacterial colonies containing all the DNA fragments from one source.

DNA ligase
Enzyme that catalyzes the formation of a phosphodiester bond between adjacent 3_-OH and 5_-phosphate groups in a DNA molecule.

DNA methylation
1. A heritable, chemical change to DNA that is part of the epigenetic control of gene expression.
2. Modification of DNA by the addition of methyl groups to certain positions on the bases.

DNA polymerase
Eukaryotic DNA polymerase that replicates the leading strand and continues replication of the lagging strand after initiation by DNA polymerase.

DNA polymerase I
Bacterial DNA polymerase that removes and replaces RNA primers with DNA nucleotides.

DNA polymerase II
Bacterial DNA polymerase that takes part in DNA repair; restarts replication after synthesis has halted because of DNA damage.

DNA polymerase III
Bacterial DNA polymerase that synthesizes new nucleotide strands off the primers.

DNA polymerase IV
Bacterial DNA polymerase; probably takes part in DNA repair.

DNA polymerase V
Bacterial DNA polymerase; probably takes part in DNA repair.

DNA probe
A labeled short sequence of DNA that, when applied to a biological sample, binds its complement, revealing its locus.

DNA repair
Any one of many cellular processes that attempts to correct errors in cellular DNA introduced via the environment or during cell division.

DNA sequencing
Process of determining the sequence of bases along a DNA molecule.

Dnase I hypersensitive site
Chromatin region that becomes sensitive to digestion by the enzyme DNase I.

Dnase I sensitivity
A method that detects DNA sites in chromosomes that show increased sensitivity to digestion by DNAse I. These sites probably represent regions of the chromosome that are nucleosome-free, and often correspond to gene-control regions.

DNS
Domain Name System. This is a service that stores, translates, and retrieves the numerical address equivalents of familiar host names that you use everyday. Each host name corresponds to a numerical address required by standard Internet protocol that the DNS retrieves in order to allow you to remember addresses with names, not numbers. DNS entries are

housed on numerous servers worldwide.

Doghouse
Small house located on the floor of a drill rig used as an office by the driller.

DoI
Direct On Line - A type of motor starter for induction motors. This is the simplest form of starter comprising a switch (typically an electromagnetic contactor) and an overload protection relay.

Domain
1. A relatively small protein segment or module (100 amino acids or less) that can fold into a specific three-dimensional structure independently of other domains.
2. Functional part of a protein.

Domain name
The unique address name for an Internet site. The part on the left is the most specific, and the part on the right is the most general. Each domain name is associated with one and only one Internet Protocol Number, which is translated by a Domain Name System (DNS).

Dome
A steep-sided mass of viscous (doughy) lava extruded from a volcanic vent, often circular in plane view and spiny, rounded, or flat on top. Its surface is often rough and blocky as a result of fragmentation of the cooler, outer crust during growth of the dome.

Domestic water use
Water used for household purposes, such as drinking, food preparation, bathing, washing clothes, dishes, and dogs, flushing toilets, and watering lawns and gardens. About 85% of domestic water is delivered to homes by a public-supply facility, such as a county water department. About 15% of the Nation's population supply their own water, mainly from wells.

Dominance
Of an allele, the extent to which it produces when heterozygous the same phenotype as when homozygous. Of a species, the extent to which it is numerically (or otherwise) predominant in a community.

Dominance genetic variance
Component of the genetic variance that can be attributed to dominance (interaction between genes at the same locus).

Dominance variance
The magnitude of the phenotypic (and genotypic) variance that is due to dominance, that is, the interaction between alleles at the same locus.

Dominant
It refers to a trait that is expressed even if only one copy of that allele is present; heterozygotes are phenotypically dominant.

Dominant marker
A known DNA sequence that generally characterizes an example of variation in a genome, like a mutation, single nucleotide polymorphism, or variable number of tandem repeats. Dominant markers allow for analyzing the DNA in multiple parts across an entire genome.

Dominant species
The most abundant species in a community, exerting a strong influence over the occurrence and distribution of other species.

Doppler shift
The change in observed frequency due to relative motion between source and observer.

Dormant volcano
This term is used to describe a volcano which is presently inactive but which may erupt again. The major volcanic cones of the Cascade Mountains (in Washington, Oregon, and California) are believed to be dormant rather than extinct.

Dosage compensation
Equalization in males and females of the amount of protein produced by X-linked genes. In placental mammals, dosage compensation is accomplished by the random inactivation of one X chromosome in the cells of females.

Double fertilization
Fertilization in plants; includes the fusion of a sperm cell with an egg cell to form a zygote and the fusion of a second sperm cell with the polar nuclei to form an endosperm.

Double helix
The double helix is a description of the molecular shape of a double-stranded DNA molecule.

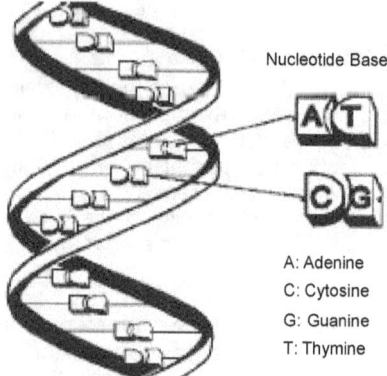

Nucleotide Bases

A: Adenine
C: Cytosine
G: Guanine
T: Thymine

Double precision
The degree of accuracy that requires two computer words to represent a number. Numbers are stored with 17 digits of accuracy and printed with up to 16 digits.

Double-strand-break model
Model of homologous recombination in which a DNA molecule undergoes doublestrand breaks.

Down
Toward the ground. The bicycle rolled down the hill.

Down mutation
Decreases the rate of transcription.

Down syndrome
Characterized by variable degrees of mental retardation, characteristic facial features, some retardation of growth and development, and an increased incidence of heart defects, leukemia, and other abnormalities; caused by the duplication of all or part of chromosome 21.

Download
To save a file onto your computer from another source, like the Internet. People often download files, such as free-ware, share-ware, for installations, and sounds, movie clips, text files, or news streams onto their computer for viewing or listening.

Downstream
Generic term that includes oil refining; petrochemicals; synthetic gas and fertilizer production facilities.

Downstream core promoter element
Consensus sequence [RG(A or T)CGTG] found in some eukaryotic RNA polymerase II core promoters; usually located approximately 30 bp downstream of the transcription start site.

Drag
Effect of an atmosphere that slows a spacecraft and forces its orbit to decay.

Drainage basin
land area where precipitation runs off into streams, rivers, lakes, and reservoirs. It is a land feature that can be identified by tracing a line along the highest elevations between two areas on a map, often a ridge. Large drainage basins, like the area that drains into the Mississippi River contain thousands of smaller drainage basins. Also called a "watershed."

Drawdown
A lowering of the ground-water surface caused by pumping.

Drift
A change of a reading or a set point value over long periods due to several factors including change in ambient temperature, time, and line voltage.

Drip irrigation
a common irrigation method where pipes or tubes filled with water slowly drip onto crops. Drip irrigation is a low-pressure method of irrigation and less water is lost to evaporation than high-pressure spray irrigation.

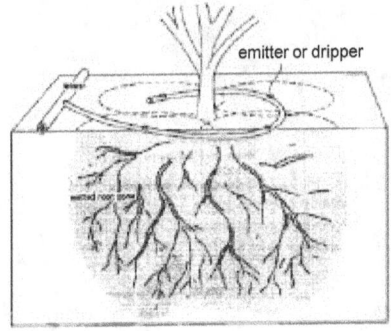
emitter or dripper

Droop
A common occurrence in time-proportional controllers. It refers to the difference in temperature between the set point and where the system temperature actually stabilizes due to the time-proportioning action of the controller.

Drosophila melanogaster
A commonly used model organism.

Drug
A substance that is used in the treatment of disease.

Dryas
A common plant along the successional chain of species for forests.

Dual element sensor
A sensor assembly with two independent sensing elements.

Dual-slope A/D converter
An analogue-to-digital converter which integrates the signal for a specific time, then counts time intervals for a reference voltage to bring the integrated signal back to zero. Such converters provide high resolution at low cost, excellent normal-mode noise rejection, and minimal dependence on circuit elements.

Dulotic
A practice of ants in which they force ants of another species to work for their colony; slave-making ants.

Duplex
The name given to a family of stainless steels which have a near equal mix of austenite and ferrite. Duplex stainless steels exhibit high strength and excellent corrosion resistance.

Duplex wire
A pair of wires insulated from each other and with an outer jacket of insulation around the inner insulated pair.

Duplication
The production of another copy of a locus (or other sequence) that is

inherited as an addition to the genome.

Dust (cosmic, interstellar)

Tiny particles in space (in the Solar System, around and among the stars...). Typically a few angstroms in size. Dust is produced in many diverse processes, such as supernovae explosions or asteroid collisions. The dust hampers the view of optical telescopes - to which it is opaque - but can be detected with infrared telescopes. The dust around a star absorbs the star's light and re-emits it as infrared light; therefore, dusty regions (e.g., star-forming regions) are best studied with infrared telescopes.

Duty cycle

The total time to one on/off cycle. Usually refers to the on/off cycle time of a temperature controller.

Dynamic (two-plane) balancing machine

A dynamic balancing machine is a centrifugal balancing machine that furnishes information for performing two-plane balancing.

Dynamic calibration

Calibration in which the input varies over a specific length of time and the output is recorded vs. time.

Dynamic mosaic paradigm

In this paradigm landscapes are viewed as heterogeneous with more continuous variation rather than divided into discrete and distinct habitats. The conceptual emphasis is viewed from the perspective of a particular ecological process or organism. in contrast to the patch-corridor-matrix.

Dynamic pressure

The difference in pressure levels from static pressure to stagnation pressure caused by an increase in velocity. Dynamic pressure increases by the square of the velocity.

Dynamic unbalance

Dynamic unbalance is that condition in which the central principal axis is not coincident with the shaft axis.

E

Earth
The third of the four terrestrial planets counting out from the Sun. The distance between the Earth and the Sun is 1 astronomical unit (about 150 million km).

Echo
To reflect received data to the sender. For example, keys depressed on a keyboard are usually echoed as characters displayed on the screen.

Eclipse, lunar
When the Moon enters the Earth's shadow as the Earth moves between the Sun and the Moon.

Eclipse, solar
When the Earth enters the Moon's shadow as the Moon moves wholly (total eclipse) or partially (partial eclipse) in front of the Sun as seen from Earth.

Ecliptic plane
The plane of Earth's orbit and the planets' orbit around the Sun. Projected onto the celestial sphere it is the path the Sun takes across the sky and because it is the plane of the Solar System, the planets always stay close to it in their passages across the sky.

Eclose
When an adult insect emerges from pupal or a larvae emerge from an egg.

Ecological drift
Random change in species abundance over time.

Ecological levels
The organizational levels at which ecologists study the interactions between organisms and their environment. These levels include individuals, populations, communities, and ecosystems.

Ecological niche
The range of combinations of all relevant environmental variables under which a species or population can persist; often more loosely used to describe the role of a species, or the resources it utilizes.

Ecological release
The expansion of a population's niche (e.g., range of habitats or resources used) where competition with other species is alleviated.

Ecological restoration
Efforts to recreate, initiate, or accelerate the recovery of an ecosystem that has been disturbed.

Ecological succession
The process by which biological community composition (the number and proportion of different species in an ecosystem) recover over time following a disturbance event.

Ecology
The study of the relation of animals and plants to their surroundings, animate & inanimate.

Econometrics
The application of mathematics in testing economic theories.

Economic threshold
The population density of the potential pest below which the damage to the crop is insignificant (i.e. it is not really necessary to spray).

Economics
The science dealing with the production, distribution and consumption of goods & services.

Ecosystem ecology
The study of all organisms living in a particular area as well as the nonliving, physical components with which they interact such as air, soil, water and sunlight.

Ecosystem services
Resources and processes provided to humankind by natural ecosystems.

Ecosytem
Interacting systems of organisms living in a particular area and the physical environment with which they interact such as air, soil, water and sunlight.

Ecosytem engineer
An organism that creates or modifies habitats in landscape, for example beaver which create ponds and modify wetlands. Plants are important ecosystem engineers, for example altering shading or providing habitat for other organisms. Humans are the most influential ecosystem engineers.

Ecotones
Transitional zones between two different parts of an ecosystem which often have important influences on ecological processes. An example might be the transitional structure between forest and grassland patches.

Ecotourism
Travel with the desire to view, sustain, and support natural ecosystems and local cultures.

Ecotype
A genetically determined phenotype of a species that is found as a local variant associated with certain ecological conditions.

Ectoderm
The outermost primary germ layer.

Ectoparasite
Parasite that lives and feeds on the outside of body of its host.

Ectotherms
Organisms that control body temperature through external means.

Edge effects
Impacts of one habitat on an adjacent habitat.

Edward syndrome
Characterized by severe retardation, low-set ears, a short neck, deformed feet, clenched fingers, heart problems, and other disabilities; results from the presence of three copies of chromosome 18.

Effective area
The unrestricted collecting area of a telescope after obstructions in the optical path have been taken into account.

Effective population size
The effective size of a real population is equal to the number of individuals in an ideal population (i.e., a population in which all individuals reproduce equally) that produces the rate of genetic drift seen in the real population.

Effluent
Water that flows from a sewage treatment plant after it has been treated.

Egg
Female gamete.

Egg-polarity gene
Determines the major axes of development in an early fruit fly embryo. One set of egg-polarity genes determines the anterior-posterior axis and another determines the dorsalventral axis.

Einstein Cosmological Constant (lambda)
The value of a supposed repulsion force that would contribute to the expansion of the Universe. It was first predicted by Einstein in 1917 to avoid one of the results of his own equations, which implied that the Universe would collapse one day under its own gravity. At that time the Universe was thought to be static. When the observations proved that the Universe is actually expanding, Einstein said that the cosmological constant had been his biggest error. However, some physicists believe today that there is indeed such a repulsion force in the Universe.

Ejecta
Material that is thrown out by a volcano, including pyroclastic material (tephra) and, from some volcanoes, lava bombs.

El Nina's southern oscillation
A climate pattern that occurs across the tropical Pacific Ocean on average every three to seven years and affects trade winds and ocean currents due to a redistribution of heat.

Elasticity
The ability of a body to regain its original shape after deformation.

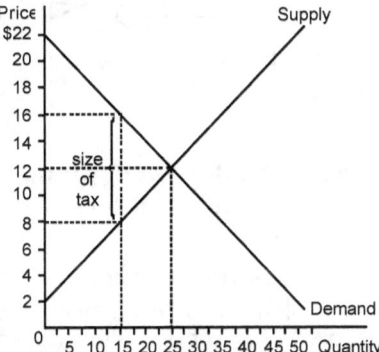

Electric current
Electric current is a flow of electric charge through a medium. This charge is typically carried by moving electrons in a conductor such as wire. It can also be carried by ions in an electrolyte, or by both ions and electrons in a plasma. The SI unit for measuring the rate of flow of electric charge is the ampere, which is charge flowing through some surface at the rate of one coulomb per second. Electric current is measured using an ammeter.

Electric propulsion
Advanced propulsion system, as used on certain satellites (SMART-1), employing solar electric power to ionise and expel a propellant (such as Xenon gas) at high speed, causing it to move forwards. Compared with conventional chemical propulsion systems, electric propulsion requires less propellant to perform similar operations.

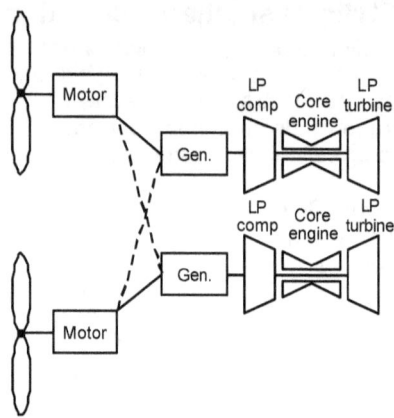

Electric submersible pump
The sub sea pump using electricity as its primary power.

Electrical interference
Electrical noise induced upon the signal wires that obscures the wanted information signal.

Electrode potential (e)
The difference in potential established between an electrode and a solution when the electrode is immersed in the solution.

Electrolyte
Any substance which, when in solution will conduct an electric current. Acids, bases, and salts are common electrolytes.

Electromagnetic radiation
Electromagnetic radiation, or light, can be considered to be composed of particles (photons) or waves. Its properties depend on its wavelength: longer waves are less energetic than shorter waves photons with long wavelength have less energy than short-wavelength photons. Electromagnetic radiation is usually described as bands of radiation of similar wavelength, e.g., infrared, radio waves, microwaves, gamma rays, X-rays. (These bands of radiation roughly correspond to the range of wavelengths which can be detected by different instruments.) Only a small fraction of the entire range of electromagnetic radiation can be detected by the human eye: visible light, or what in everyday-life is referred to simply as light. The human eye cannot detect wavelengths longer than those of the visible light, such as those of infrared light, microwaves (wavelengths of centimetres), or radio waves (wavelengths of metres). Wavelengths shorter than visible light cannot be seen either: ultraviolet light, X-rays, gamma rays (the most energetic). Electromagnetic radiation can be described in terms of wavelength (L), measured in metres (m), or frequency (f), measured in hertz (Hz). The relationship between these two is given by:

$f = L/c$ where $c=$ speed of light.

Electromagnetic spectrum
The electromagnetic spectrum is the complete range of wavelengths of the electromagnetic radiation.

Electromagnetic waves
Waves with both an electric and magnetic component. They are: radio, micro, infra-red, visible light, ultraviolet, X and gamma rays.

Electromotive Force (emf)
The potential difference between the two electrodes in a cell. The cell emf is the cell voltage measured when no current is flowing through the cell. It can be measured by means of a pH metre with high input impedance.

Electron
A fundamental physical particle with negative charge. A component of atoms.

Electronic industries association (EIA)
A standards organization specializing in the electrical and functional characteristics of interface equipment.

Electron-positron annihilation
When an electron and its anti-particle, a positron, collide, they annihilate emitting a pair of gamma-ray photons each with an energy of 511 keV.

Electronvolt (EV)
Unit of energy defined as the energy acquired by an electron in falling through a potential difference of one volt. Electronvolts are used as a measure of the energy of cosmic rays and high-energy photons. For example, X-rays can have energies of 1000 eV (1 keV) or more.

Electrophoresis
A technique for separating macromolecules (proteins, RNA, DNA) on a gel using an electric field.
Electrophoretic mobility shift assay
A method that examines whether a specific protein binds to a specific piece of DNA. After allowing the DNA and protein to interact in vitro, the complex is electrophoresed, analyzed, and compared to DNA alone versus DNA plus protein. If the protein has bound, the complex will not move as far into the gel due to its larger size.

Element
Set of stable atoms from which all known molecules are made out. These atoms are organised as a function of their chemical properties in the so-called 'Periodic Table of the Elements'.

Elevational gradient
As one travels to higher elevations, the number of species peaks at mid-elevations or declines.

Elimination sample
A DNA sample collected from an individual not thought to be a suspect in a crime (such as the partner of a rape victim) to help investigators to analyze the evidence.

Elliptical orbit
An orbit which describes an ellipse or oval shape.

Elongation factor for translation
Protein that facilitates the extension of a growing polypeptide.

Elongation factor G (EF-G)
Protein that combines with GTP and is required for movement of the ribosome along the mRNA during translation.

Elongation factor Ts
Protein that regenerates elongation factor Tu in the elongation stage of protein synthesis.

Elongation factor Tu
Protein taking part in the elongation stage of protein synthesis; forms a complex with GTP and a charged amino acid and then delivers the charged tRNA to the ribosome.

Embryo

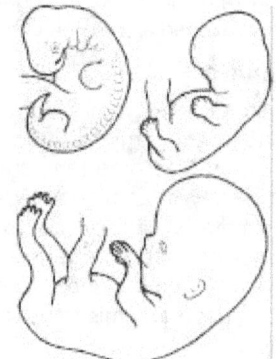

In humans, prenatal development until the end of the eighth week. Embryo cells can be distinguished from each other, but all basic structures are not yet present.

Embryology
The study of development of embryos.

Embryonic stem cell
A cell from a preimplantation embryo and then cultured from that; can give rise to all differentiated cell types.

Emergency shutdown system
An automatic system for shutting down plant in a prescribed orderly manner to prevent escalation of a potentially hazardous situation.

Emery's rule
Social parasites and their hosts share common ancestry and hence are closely related to each other.

Emf
Electromotive force. A rise in (electrical) potential energy. The principal unit is the volt.

Emi
Electromagnetic interference.

Emission
The release of electromagnetic radiation (e.g., light, X-rays, gamma rays) from excited atoms or molecules.

Emissivity
The ratio of energy emitted by an object to the energy emitted by a blackbody at the same temperature. The emissivity of an object depends upon its material and surface texture; a polished metal surface can have an emissivity around 0.2 and a piece of wood can have an emissivity around 0.95.

Empiric risk
Probability that a trait will recur based on its incidence in a population.

End labeling
Method for adding a radioactive or chemical label to the ends of DNA molecules.

End point (potentiometric)
The apparent equivalence point of a titration at which a relatively large potential change is observed.

Endangered species
A species that is likely to become extinct in all or a major portion of its range.

Endemic
Of a species, restricted to a specified region or locality.

Endocrine system
A system of glands and organs that secrete hormones into the bloodstream to regulate behavioral responses, seasonal changes in behaviour, mating and parental care.

Endoderm
The innermost primary germ layor of the primordial embryo.

Endonuclease
An enzyme that cleaves a nucleic acid.

Endoparasite
Parasite that lives inside the body of its host.

Endoplasmic reticulum
A labyrinth of membranous intracellular tubules on which proteins, lipids, and sugars are synthesized.

Endosymbiotic theory
The states that some membrane-bounded organelles, such as

mitochondria and chloroplasts, in eukaryotic cells originated as free-living eubacterial cells that entered into an endosymbiotic relation with a eukaryotic host cell and evolved into the present-day organelles; supported by a number of similarities in structure and sequence between organelle and eubacterial DNAs.

Endothermic
Absorbs heat. A process is said to be endothermic when it absorbs heat.

Endothermic reaction
A reaction in which heat is absorbed ie: melting or boiling.

Endotherms
Organisms that control body temperature internally.

Energetic war of attrition
A model that assumes that each individual does not have access to information on its opponent.s RHP. Instead, each individual keeps fighting until an individual threshold of costs, which could build up either as a result of performing non-injurious agonistic behaviours or receiving injuries, is reached. The weaker individual should reach its threshold first.

Energy
The capacity of a body or system to do work. In the metric measurement system, the unit of energy is the Joule, which is the work produced by a force of 1 Newton moving over a distance of 1 metre.

Energy equivalence rule
Rule posing that the energy spent by a population is independent of the body mass of its individuals (a population of mice uses roughly the same energy as one of mice).

Energy flow
In an ecological context, the flow of energy through trophic levels or major functional groups of organisms in an ecosystem; typically includes production, consumption, assimilation, non-assimilation losses (feces), and respiration (maintenance costs).

Engrailed
A homeodomain containing protein that is expressed in the anterior region of 14 evenly spaced "stripes" during early Drosophila embryonic development.

Enhancer
1. A segment of DNA that binds to trans-acting factors in order to increase gene transcription of a specific gene; sequence that stimulates maximal transcription of distant genes. Affects only genes on the same DNA molecule (is cis acting), contains short consensus sequences, is not fixed in relation to the transcription start site, can stimulate almost any promoter in its vicinity, and may be upstream or downstream of the gene. The function of an enhancer is independent of sequence orientation.
2. A DNA sequence that, when acted on by transcription factors, controls transcription of an associated gene.

Enhancer trap
A system that allows investigators to find endogenous enhancers in a genome. The reporter gene in an enhancer trap is often based on a transposable element that can easily insert into the genome at random locations. This reporter gene has minimal promoter sequence so it is only expressed when it inserts near an endogeous sequence that results in

gene transcription.

Enthalpy
The sum of the internal energy of a body and the product of its volume multiplied by the pressure.

Entomology
The study of insects.

Entropy
The state of disorder in a thermodynamic system: the more energy the higher the entropy.

Environment
The complex of external physical, chemical, and biotic factors that may affect a population, an organism, or the expression of an organism's genes; more generally, anything external to the object of interest (e.g., a gene, an organism, a population) that may influence its function or activity. Thus, other genes within an organism may be part of a gene's environment, or other individuals in a population may be part of an organism's environment.

Environmental conditions
All conditions in which a transducer may be exposed during shipping, storage, handling, and operation.

Environmental correlation
A measure of the degree to which two traits respond to variation in the same environmental factors.

Environmental deviation
The difference between the phenotypic and genotypic values caused by the environment.

Environmental protection agency
A US government agency that issues emissions standards and monitoring policies for environmental pollutants in air; water and soil.

Environmental variance
1. Component of the phenotypic variance that is due to environmental differences among individual members of a population.
2. Variation among individuals in a phenotypic trait that is caused by variation in the environment rather than by genetic differences.

Enzymatic
Describes a process mediated by an enzyme.

Enzyme
A type of protein that speeds the rate of a specific biochemical reaction, making it fast enough to be compatible with life.

Enzymes
Biological catalysts, proteins that control specific processes within the body.

Epic
Engineering Procurement Installation and Construction. It is usually in reference to a contract e.g. an EPIC contract.

Epicormic
A shoot arising spontaneously from an adventitious or dormant bud on the stem or branch of a woody plant often following exposure to increased light levels or fire.

Epidemiology
The branch of medicine dealing with incidence & risks of diseases.

Epidemiology
The study of the frequency and determinants of disease across populations.

Epigenetic process
A process that affects the expression of genes; often a process that brings about genetic alterations that can be reversed, such as the methylation of DNA.

Epigenomic
Epigenomics is the study of the complete set of epigenetic modifications on the genetic material of a cell, known as the epigenome. The field is analogous to genomics and proteomics, which are the study of the genome and proteome of a cell. Epigenetic modifications are reversible modifications on a cell's DNA or histones that affect gene expression without altering the DNA sequence. Two of the most characterized epigenetic modifications are DNA methylation and histone modification.

Epigraphy
Epigraphy is the study of inscriptions or epigraphs as writing; it is the science of identifying graphemes, clarifying their meanings, classifying their uses according to dates and cultural contexts, and drawing conclusions about the writing and the writers. Specifically excluded from epigraphy are the historical significance of an epigraph as a document and the artistic value of a literary composition.

Episome
Plasmid capable of integrating into a bacterial chromosome.

Epistasis
1. Type of gene interaction in which a gene at one locus masks or suppresses the effects of a gene at a different locus.
2. A form of gene action in which two or more loci interact nonadditively with each other to determine the phenotype; when epistasis is present, the phenotype associated with a particular genotype depends on which alleles are present at another locus.

Epistatic gene
Masks or suppresses the effect of a gene at a different locus.

Epistatic selection
The type of selection in which fitness depends upon nonadditive interactions between alleles at different loci.

Epistatic variance
The portion of the phenotypic (and genotypic) variance that is due to epistasis, that is, interactions among gene loci.

Epitope
Part of a protein that is recognized by an antibody.

Eprom
Erasable Programmable Read-Only Memory. The PROM can be erased by ultraviolet light or electricity.

Equational division
The second meiotic division, producing four cells from two.

Equilibrium
An unchanging condition, as of population size or genetic composition. Also, the value (e.g., of population size, allele frequency) at which this condition occurs. An equilibrium need not be stable. See also stability, unstable equilibrium.

Equilibrium concept
Especially with regard to models of ecosystems, the concept attaches fundamental significance to the idea that there is a steady state toward which populations return when disturbed or toward which communities evolve, even when disturbed. The conceptual framework focuses attention on average and long-term states, as opposed to transient dynamics and variation.

Equilibrium constant
The product of the concentrations (or activities) of the substances produced at equilibrium in a chemical reaction divided by the product of concentrations of the reacting substances, each concentration raised to that power which is the coefficient of the substance in the chemical equation.

Equilibrium density gradient centrifugation
Method used to separate molecules or organelles of different density by centrifugation.

Equitransference
Equal diffusion rates of the positively and negatively charged ions of an electrolyte across a liquid junction without charge separation.

Equivalent conductance (l)
Equivalent conductance of an electrolyte is defined as the conductance of a volume of solution containing one equivalent weight of dissolved substances when placed between two parallel electrodes 1 cm apart, and large enough to contain between them all of the solution. l is never determined directly, but is calculated from the specific conductance (Ls). If C is the concentration of a solution in gram equivalents per litre, then the concentration per cubic centimetre is C/1000, and the volume containing one equivalent of the solute, is, therefore, 1000/C.

Erosion
The movement of weathered material downslope under the influence of gravity. Water acts as a catalyst and as a lubricant. Some common types of erosion includes landslides, rockfalls, creep, etc. Erosion takes weathered material and puts it in a river so it can be transported to the beach.

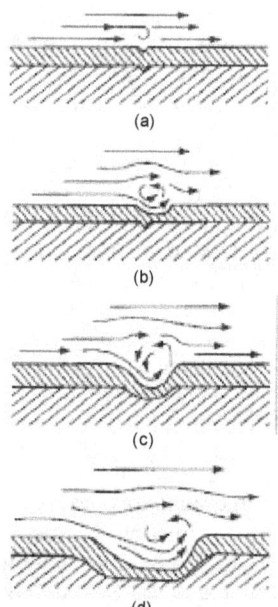

Erratic (glacial)
Large rocks or other debris deposited by a glacier, usually in an area far removed from its source. Commonly used to indicate a big chunk of debris which is clearly out of place and shouldn't even be where it is.

Error
The difference between the value indicated by the transducer and the true value of the measurand being sensed. Usually expressed in percent of full scale output.

Error band
The allowable deviations to output from a specific reference norm. Usually expressed as a percentage of full scale.

Eruption
The process by which solid, liquid, and gaseous materials are ejected into the earth's atmosphere and onto the earth's surface by volcanic activity. Eruptions range from the quiet overflow of liquid rock to the tremendously violent expulsion of pyroclastics.

Eruption cloud
The column of gases, ash, and larger rock fragments rising from a crater or other vent. If it is of sufficient volume and velocity, this gaseous column may reach many miles into the stratosphere, where high winds will carry it long distances.

Eruptive vent
The opening through which volcanic material is emitted.

Erythroblast
An erythroblast is a type of red blood cell which still retains a cell nucleus. It is the immediate precursor of a normal erythrocyte.

Erythrocyte
Red blood cells are the most common type of blood cell and the vertebrate organism's principal means of delivering oxygen (O2) to the body tissues via the blood flow through the circulatory system. They take up oxygen in the lungs or gills and release it while squeezing through the body's capillaries.

Erythroid cell
The progenitor cell of erythrocytes.

Escape velocity
The minimum speed needed to escape the gravitational attraction of a celestial body and enter space. The Earth's escape velocity is 11.2 km/s.

Eschatology
The study of death, destiny.

Essentialism
The philosophical view that all members of a class of objects (such as a species) share certain invariant, unchanging properties that distinguish them from other classes.

Estrogen
A steroid hormone produced by the ovaries.

Estuary
a place where fresh and salt water mix, such as a bay, salt marsh, or where a river enters an ocean.

Ethane
A colourless and odorless gas that belongs to the alkane series of the hydrocarbons.

Ethernet
A common method of networking computers in a Local Area Network (LAN). Ethernet can handle from 10,000,000-100,000,000 bits-per-second (or 10-100 megabits-per-second) and can be used with almost any kind of computer.

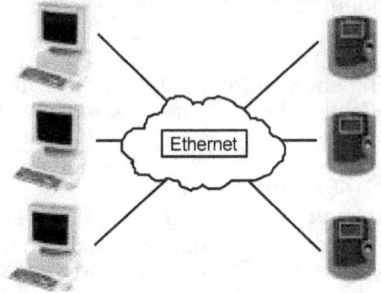

Ethics
Psychological study of moral principles.

Ethnography
A branch of anthropology dealing with the scientific description of individual cultures.

Ethnology
A branch of anthropology that deals with the origin, distribution and distinguishing characteristics of the race of mankind.

Ethologists
Scientists who study animal behaviour.

Ethology
The study of animal behaviour.

Etymology
The study of origin and history of words.

Eubacteria
One of the three primary divisions of life. Eubacteria consist of unicellular organisms with prokaryotic cells and include most of the common bacteria.

Eucalypts
Woody plants belonging to three closely related genera: Eucalyptus, Corymbia and Angophora.

Euchromatin
Chromatin that undergoes condensation and decondensation in the course of the cell cycle.

Eugenics
The study of the production of better offspring by the careful selection of parents.

Eukaryote
Eukaryotes are organisms whose cells contain a nucleus and other organelles. There is a wide range eukaryotic organisms, including all animals, plants, fungi, protists and most algae, and eukaryotes may be either single-celled or multicellular.

Eukaryotic
Describing a characteristic of a eukaryote.

Euler's constant
An important mathematical constant; numbers that arise naturally in a number of mathematical contexts.

Euploid
A somatic cell with the normal number of chromosomes for that species.

European space agency (esa)
An intergovernmental organisation with a mission to provide and promote for exclusively peaceful purposes the exploitation of space science, research & technology, and space applications. The 15 ESA Member States are: Austria, Belgium, Denmark, Finland, France, Germany, Ireland, Italy, Norway, the Netherlands, Portugal, Spain, Sweden, Switzerland and the United Kingdom.

Eusocial
Groups that display each of the following three traits: cooperative care of young; non-reproducing worker castes; and an overlap of at least two generations of life stages capable of contributing to colony labor.

Eutectic temperature
The lowest possible melting point of a mixture of alloys.

Eutherian
A taxon that includes placental mammals (including humans).

Evaporates
The change in form that water goes through when it turns from a liquid to a gas. As you boil water, it evaporates

and becomes a gas.

Evaporation
The process of liquid water becoming water vapour, including vaporization from water surfaces, land surfaces, and snow fields, but not from leaf surfaces.

Evapotranspiration
Water used by plants and animals and subsequently returned directly to the atmosphere.

Evolution
Natural selection, the survival of the fittest, is the driving force behind evolution and is measured by a species viability and fecundity. Governed by Darwin's theory of evolution by natural selection:
1. The distinguishing features (characters) of an organism may affect it fitness.
2. The design of an species (its morphology) differs within a population and may improve its fitness.
3. An organism may be susceptible to a lack of vital resources, predation and disease reducing its fitness.
4. The characters that improve fitness must be inherited. Individuals that inherit these characters will survive at the expense of those who do not.
5. Mutation is essential for evolution: the inheritance of non-standard genes that improve fitness.

Evolutionarily significant units
Populations of threatened or endangered organisms that need to be saved from extinction.

Evolutionarily stable strategy
A phenotype such that, if almost all individuals in a population have that phenotype, no alternative phenotype can invade the population or replace it.

Evolutionary allometry
The relationship of x and y that are traits measured in different species.

Evolutionary arms race
An evolutionary struggle between organisms with co-evolving traits that develop adaptations and counter-adaptations against each other, resembling an arms race.

Evolutionary constraint
Any biological factor that slows the rate of adaptive evolution.

Evolutionary fitness
The number of offspring contributed by an individual relative to the number of offspring produced by other members of the population. Ultimately defined as the relative genetic contribution of an individual or individuals to future generations.

Evolutionary reversal
The evolution of a character from a derived state back toward a condition that resembles an earlier state.

Evolutionary synthesis
The reconciliation of Darwin's theory with the findings of modern genetics, which gave rise to a theory that emphasized the coaction of random mutation, selection, genetic drift, and gene flow; also called the modern synthesis.

Evolutionary trajectories
Pathways that populations traverse across adaptive landscapes during evolution, tracing the ways that the joint allele frequencies or mean phenotypes might evolve.

Ex vivo gene therapy
Genetic alteration of cells removed from a patient, then reinfused or implanted back.

Exaptation
The evolution of a function of a gene, tissue, or structure other than the one it was originally adapted for; can also refer to the adaptive use of a previously nonadaptive trait.

Excision repair
Enzyme-catalyzed removal of pyrimidine dimers in DNA.

Excitation
The external application of electrical voltage current applied to a transducer for normal operation.

Exercise
Moving the body. Walking fast is good exercise.

Exhabitational
Organisms who are relatively independent physically, but interact directly.

Exia
The explosion protection by means of the concept of Intrinsic Safety where protection is maintained with up to 2 component or other faults.

Exib
The explosion protection by means of the concept of Intrinsic Safety where protection is maintained with up to 1 component or other fault.

Exit site
One of three sites in a ribosome occupied by a tRNA. In the elongation stage of translation, the tRNA moves from the peptidyl (P) site to the E site from which it then exits the ribosome.

Exobiology
A branch of biology that deals with the search for extraterrestrial life, especially intelligent life, outside our solar system. Exobiology is sometimes called xenobiology or astrobiology.

Exon
1. Exons are coding sections of an RNA transcript, or the DNA encoding it, which are translated into a protein.
2. That part of a gene that is translated into a polypeptide (protein).

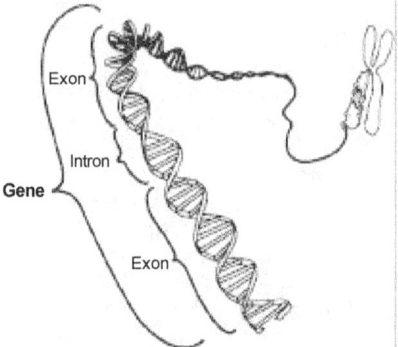

Exon shuffling
The formation of new genes by assembly of exons from two or more preexisting genes. The classical model of exon shuffling generates new combinations of exons mediated via recombination of intervening introns; however, exon shuffling can also come about by retrotransposition of exons into preexisting genes.

Exonic splicing enhancer
Sequences located in exons adjacent to 5' and 3' splice sites that are required for proper recognition of the splice sites by the spliceosome. These enhancers are position dependent.

Exonuclease
An enzyme that cleaves one nucleotide at a time in the 3' → 5' direction.

Exothermic
Gives off heat. A process is said to be exothermic when it releases heat.

Exothermic reaction
A reaction from which heat is lost eg: combustion.

Expanding trinucleotide repeat
Mutation in which the number of copies of a trinucleotide (or some multiple of three nucleotides) increases in succeeding generations.

Expansion factor
Correction factor for the change in density between two pressure measurement areas in a constricted flow.

Expected heterozygosity
Proportion of individuals that are expected to be heterozygous at a locus when the Hardy-Weinberg assumptions are met.

Expected outcome
The predicted outcome of observable events in an experiment.

Explosion-proof enclosure
An enclosure that can withstand an explosion of gases within it and prevent the explosion of gases surrounding it due to sparks, flashes or the explosion of the container itself, and maintain an external temperature which will not ignite the surrounding gases.

Explosive decompression
The phenomenon whereby seals of a valve (or similar) absorb high pressure gas and when the system is depressurised the seals release their pressure causing failure.

Exponential population growth
Unlimited growth of a population in an unlimited environment. Represented by a J-shaped curve when population size is plotted over time.

Exposed junction
A form of construction of a thermocouple probe where the hot or measuring junction protrudes beyond the sheath material so as to be fully exposed to the medium being measured. This form of construction usually gives the fastest response time.

Expressed-sequence tag
Unique fragment of DNA from the coding region of a gene, produced by the reverse transcription of cellular RNA. Parts of the fragments are sequenced so that they can be identified.

Expression vector
The cloning vector containing DNA sequences such as a promoter, a ribosome-binding site, and transcription initiation and termination sites that allow DNA fragments inserted into the vector to be transcribed and translated.

Expressivity
The degree to which a trait is expressed.

Extent
The extended range of study, or the area included within the landscape boundary, such as a national park or state.

Extinct
When all animals of one kind die; no longer existing as a species. There are no dinosaurs today because these animals are extinct.

Extinct volcano
A volcano that is not presently erupting and is not likely to do so for a very long time in the future.

Extinction
Reduction in the intensity of electromagnetic radiation received from a celestial body (e.g. a star) as a result of scattering and absorption by intervening material (e.g. dust).

Extravehicular
Outside the spacecraft; activity in space conducted by astronauts (EVA = extravehicular activity).

Extreme ultraviolet (EUV)
Region of the spectrum between the ultraviolet and X-ray regions covering wavelengths between 10-100 nm.

Extremophiles
The organisms that live in an environment where conditions are so extreme that few other species can survive there.

Extrinsic hypothesis
Prediction of the number of observed individuals with specific characteristics based on calculations performed before the experiment is completed.

F

F factor
Episome of E. coli that controls conjugation and gene exchange between E. coli cells. The F factor contains an origin of replication and genes that enable the bacterium to undergo conjugation.

F1 cross
A cross between two pure-breeding or homozygous lines. Such homozygous lines are also called parental lines. Parental lines differ in a pair of contrasting traits (e.g, red eyes or white eyes in Drosophila, or tall or short pea plants). Females from one of the parental lines (Parental Line 1 or P1) are mated to males from the other parental line (Parental Line 2 or P2). The mating is called the F1 cross, and the progeny resulting from this mating are the F1 progeny or F1 generation.

F1 generation
Offspring of the initial parents (P) in a genetic cross.

F1 reciprocal
The reverse of an F1 cross. If females from one line (Parental Line 1) are crossed with males from Parental Line 2 for an F1 cross, the reciprocal cross would use males from Parental Line 1 and females from Parental Line 2. P2 females can be mated with P1 males. Progeny from this mating are the reciprocal F1 progeny or the reciprocal F1 generation.

F2
The F2 cross is the quintessential segregating generation. For a single autosomal gene, the F2 generation is the first generation in which both parental phenotypes occur. For two or more genes, it is the first generation in which all new combinations of phenotypes can occur at the same time. These new phenotypes reflect independent assortment among the allele genes that formed the gametes of the F1 generation.

F2 generation
Offspring of the F1 generation in a genetic cross; the third generation of a genetic cross.

Facilitation
When one species, or a group of species, colonizes a disturbed area, and subsequently alters the environment of that area (by altering soil nutrients, light accessibility, or water availability), making it more habitable for later successional species.

Facilitation succession model
Where species modify the environment in a way that allows other species to colonize.

Factory acceptance test
A test of equipment carried out at supplier's factory prior to shipment of equipment - usually witnessed by purchaser.

Factory mutual
North American insurance company who provide certification of industrial and commercial products.

Facula
(1) Bright region of the Sun's photosphere. Faculae can occur anywhere on the Sun, but the largest faculae are found near sunspots.
(2) A bright spot on a planet or moon.

Facultative slave-makers
A type of social parasitism in ants where colonies can survive with or without slave ants.

Fahrenheit (°F)
Temperature scale on which water freezes at 32 °F and water boils at 212°F. The conversion between the Fahrenheit temperature scale (F) and the Celsius temperature scale (C) is: F = 32 + 1.8 x C.

Failure Modes and Effects Analysis
Identifies failure modes - their causes and effects - the safeguards already incorporated and the potential additional measures that could be considered.

Familial Down syndrome
Caused by a Robertsonian translocation in which the long arm of chromosome 21 is translocated to another chromosome; tends to run in families.

Father
Male parent of an offspring.

Fats
Molecules of fatty acids or glycerol. Used as a food store, insulation and for shock absorption.

Fault
A crack or fracture in the earth's surface in which there has been movement of one or both sides relative to the other. Movement along the fault can cause earthquakes or, in the process of mountain-building, can release underlying magma and permit it to rise to the surface as a volcanic eruption.

Fault tree analysis
A method of calculating the probability of an event from the probabilities or frequencies of its causal events.

Feather
Body covering of birds. Feathers keep a bird warm.

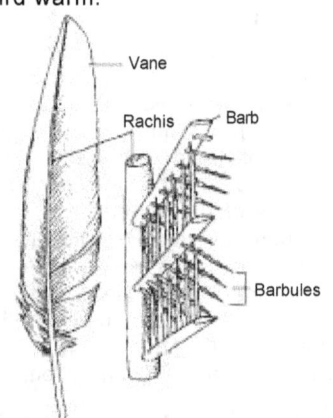

Fecundity
The quantity of gametes (usually eggs) produced by an individual.

Feral
An organism that has escaped domestication and returned to a wild state.

Ferrule
A compressible tubular fitting that is compressed onto a probe inside a compression fitting to form a gas-tight seal.

Fertilization
Fusion of gametes, or sex cells, to form a zygote.

Fetal cell sorting
Separation of fetal cells from maternal blood. Genetic testing on the fetal cells can provide information about genetic diseases and disorders in the fetus.

Fetus
The prenatal human after the eighth week of development, when structures grow and specialize.

Field
A region in space that is defined by a vector function. Common fields are: gravitational, electric and magnetic.

Field balancing equipment
An assembly of measuring instruments for performing balancing operations on assembled machinery which is not mounted in a balancing machine.

Field of View
A volume in space defined by an angular cone extending from the focal plane of an instrument.

Fieldbus
A communications protocol often used with SCADA systems.

Filament
A solar prominence which is seen as a dark streak against the bright disc of the Sun, and appears as bright streams of plasma in the solar corona which appear to radiate away from the Sun when seen off the solar limb.

File
A set of related records or data treated as a unit.

Filling solution
A solution of defined composition to make contact between an internal element and a membrane or sample. The solution sealed inside a pH glass bulb is called an internal filling solution. This solution normally contains a buffered chloride solution to provide a stable potential and a designated zero potential point. The solution which surrounds the reference electrode internal and periodically requires replenishing is called the reference filling solution. It provides contact between the reference electrode internal and sample through a junction.

Filter (wheel)
Accessory used with an optical instrument or detector of electromagnetic radiation to either narrow down the wavelength band or to reduce the total intensity passing into the instrument.

Finder
The Finder is the default open application on a Macintosh, and it's represented by a little, purple, happy face icon in the top right-hand corner of the screen. Most people think of it as the desktop, however, or as the utility that lets you navigate quickly among open programmes. When you click on the Finder, you can designate which of your open applications will be the *active* one.

Fire regime
The characteristic pattern of fire in a particular place.

Firewall
Hardware and/or software that separates a Local Area Network (LAN) into two or more parts for security purposes.

Firn
The intermediate "granular" stage which occurs during the conversion of snow to glacial ice.

First filial cross
Crossing of two parental lines.

First point assessment ltd
Oil and gas industry steered company with objective to identify opportunities for cost reduction and performance improvement throughout the supply chain.

First polar body
One of the products of meiosis I in oogenesis; contains half the chromosomes but little of the cytoplasm.

Fish
An animal that lives in water that has gills for breathing and fins for swimming. Many fish have scales as a body covering.

Fission
Splitting the nucleus of an atom into smaller units.

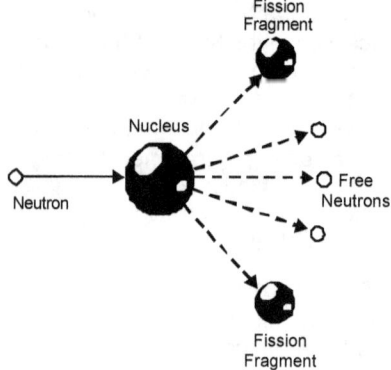

Fissures
Elongated fractures or cracks on the slopes of a volcano. Fissure eruptions typically produce liquid flows, but pyroclastics may also be ejected.

Fitness
The success of an entity in reproducing; hence, the average contribution of an allele or genotype to the next generation or to succeeding generations.

Fitness function
The curve that describes the relationship between fitness and a phenotypic trait.

Fitness surface
A three-dimensional representation of the relationship between two phenotypic traits and individual fitness.

Fixation
1. Attainment of a frequency of 1 (i.e., 100%) by an allele in a population, which thereby becomes monomorphic for the allele.
2. Point at which one allele reaches a frequency of 1. At this point, all members of the population are homozygous for the same allele.

Fixation index
Wright's measure of population differentiation.

Fixed
A population in which all members are homozygous for the same allele at a given locus.

Flag
Any of various types of indicators used for identification of a condition or event; for example, a character that signals the termination of a transmission.

Flameproof
The common name for hazardous area protection type EExd.

Flank eruption
An eruption from the side of a volcano (in contrast to a summit eruption.)

Flanking direct repeat
Short, directly repeated sequence produced on either side of a transposable element when the element inserts into DNA.

Flash point
Flash Point Temperature is the lowest temperature at which a liquid releases sufficient vapour that can be ignited by an energy source.

Flat teeth
Teeth that are good for grinding food. Most plant-eating dinosaurs had flat teeth.

Flexible hose assembly
A complete hose with end fittings and any associated accessories.

Floatel
A vessel moored alongside a platform to provide accommodation for platform workers - a floating hotel.

Flood
An overflow of water onto lands that are used or usable by man and not normally covered by water. Floods have two essential characteristics: The inundation of land is temporary; and the land is adjacent to and inundated by overflow from a river, stream, lake, or ocean.

Flood plain
A floodplain, or flood plain, is a flat or nearly flat land adjacent a stream or river that stretches from the banks of its channel to the base of the enclosing valley walls and experiences flooding during periods of high discharge. It includes the floodway, which consists of the stream channel and adjacent areas that carry flood flows, and the flood fringe, which are areas covered by the flood, but which do not experience a strong current. In other words, a floodplain is an area near a river or a stream which floods easily.

Flood stage
The elevation at which overflow of the natural banks of a stream or body of water begins in the reach or area in which the elevation is measured.

Flood, 100-year
A 100-year flood does not refer to a flood that occurs once every 100 years, but to a flood level with a 1 percent chance of being equaled or exceeded in any given year.

Floodplain
The low relief lands bordering a stream or river, common to the mature and old age stages of stream development. Floodplains store excess water in times of high water, and excess sediments in times of low water. Beware of building your dream house on a floodplain - they tend to get rather wet at irregular intervals.

Floodway
The channel of a river or stream and the parts of the floodplain adjoining the channel that are reasonably required to efficiently carry and discharge the flood water or flood flow of a river or stream.

Floppy disk
A small, flexible disk carrying a magnetic medium in which digital data is stored for later retrieval and use.

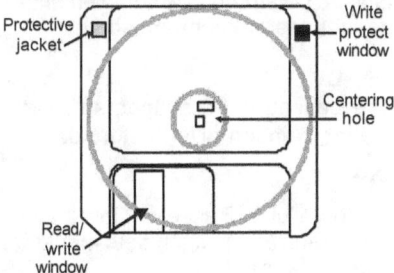

Flow
Travel of liquids or gases in response to a force (i.e. pressure or gravity).

Flow rate
Actual speed or velocity of fluid movement.

Flower
The part of a plant from which seeds can develop. This flower has a bright red blossom and a sweet smell.

Flowing well/spring
A well or spring that taps ground water under pressure so that water rises without pumping. If the water rises above the surface, it is known as a flowing well.

Flowline
Pipeline carrying reservoir fluid on the seabed from a well to a riser.

Flowmeter
A device used for measuring the flow or quantity of a moving fluid.

Fluid
A liquid or gas.

Fluorescence assay
A method that tags a biological sample with a fluorophore in order to monitor that sample.

Fluorescence in situ hybridization
A technique that binds fluorescently labeled DNA probes to complementary sequences on a chromosome.

Fly-by
The passage of a spacecraft near a planet, a moon or an asteroid.

Fm
Factory Mutual Research Corporation. An organization which sets industrial safety standards.

Fm approved
An instrument that meets a specific set of specifications established by Factory Mutual Research Corporation.

Focal plane
Axis or geometric plane where incoming light is focused by the telescope.

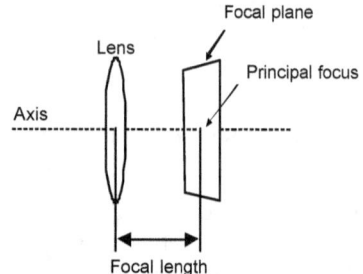

Focus
Point at which converging rays meet and at which a clearly defined image can be obtained.

Food web
Feeding relationships or organisms within an ecosystem or community.

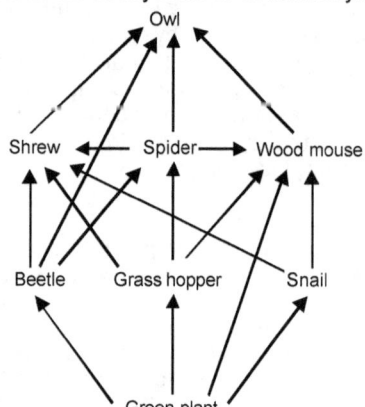

Footprinting
A technique in biology that attempts to map protein binding sites on DNA by examining the areas on a DNA molecule that are protected from

nuclease activity due to protein binding.

Foraging behavour
Predicts that foraging options that deliver the highest payoff should be favoured by foraging animals because it will have the highest fitness payoff.

Forbs
Broad-leaved herbaceous plants.

Force
An action (transfer of energy) that will accelerate a body in the direction of the applied force.

Forced vibration
Vibration of a system caused by an imposed force. Steady-state vibration is an unchanging condition of periodic or random motion.

Formicine ants
Ants of the subfamily Formicinae.

Fortran
Formula Translation language. A widely used high-level programming language well suited to problems that can be expressed in terms of algebraic formulas. It is generally used in scientific applications.

Forward mutation
Alters a wild-type phenotype.

Fossil
Evidence of past life on earth. Can include the preserved hard and soft parts of plants and animals, tracks and burrows, whole organisms preserved intact in amber or tar, and fossilized dung. Any evidence of life constitutes a fossil.

Fossil remains
What is left of a plant or an animal that lived long ago. Scientists study fossil remains to learn more about dinosaurs.

Foundation species
The species that exert influence on a community not through their trophic interactions, but by causing physical changes in the environment. These organisms alter the environment through their behaviour or their large collective biomass.

Founder effect
The principle that the founders of a new population carry only a fraction of the total genetic variation in the source population.

Founder event
A type of bottleneck, defined as the creation of a new population by a small number of colonists.

FPM
Flow velocity in feet per minute.

FPS
Flow velocity in feet per second.

FPSO
Floating Production Storage and Offloading vessel - a floating facility installed above or close to an offshore oil and gas field to receive; process; store and export hydrocarbons.

Fractionation
The separation of crude oil into its more valuable and usable components through distillation.

Fragile site
The constriction or gap that appears at a particular location on a chromosome when cells are cultured under special conditions. One fragile site on the human X chromosome is associated with mental retardation (fragile-X syndrome) and results from an expanding trinucleotide repeat.

Fragmentation
The process of breaking a natural landscape into fewer, smaller and more disjointed areas of habitat. Loss of total area and variety of habitats is called change in composition. Change in the variety, spatial arrangement, shape and size of habitats is change in configuration.

Frameshift mutation
1. A frameshift mutation is a genetic mutation caused by a deletion or insertion in a DNA sequence, which shifts the way the sequence is read.
2. An insertion or deletion of base pairs in a translated DNA sequence that alters the reading frame, resulting in multiple downstream changes in the gene product.

Fraternal twins
Fraternal or dizygotic (DZ) twins (also referred to as "non-identical twins", "dissimilar twins", "biovular twins", and, in cases of females, sororal twins) usually occur when two fertilized eggs are implanted in the uterus wall at the same time. When two eggs are independently fertilized by two different sperm cells, fraternal twins result. The two eggs, or ova, form two zygotes, hence the terms dizygotic and biovular.

Free carrier
Incoterm used to describe responsibilities for carriage; risk and cost.

Free on board
Incoterm used to describe responsibilities for carriage; risk and cost.

Free radical
A highly reactive molecule that has at least one unpaired, or free, electron.

Freezing point
The temperature at which the substance goes from the liquid phase to the solid phase.

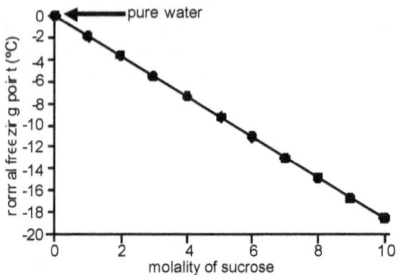

French guiana
French overseas territory on the northeast coast of the South American continent where the European Spaceport of Kourou is located.

Frequency
Usually used to mean proportion (e.g., the frequency of an allele is the proportion of gene copies having that allelic state).

Frequency dependent selection
A type of natural selection in which the fitness of each genotype or phenotype depends on its frequency in the population. In positive frequency dependence, fitness increases as the genotype or phenotype becomes more common, and in negative frequency dependence, fitness increases as the genotype or phenotype becomes rarer.

Frequency distribution
Graphical way of representing values. In genetics, usually the phenotypes found in a group of individuals are displayed as a frequency distribution. Typically, the phenotypes are plotted on the horizontal (x) axis and the numbers (or proportions) of individuals with each phenotype are plotted on the vertical (y) axis.

Frequency modulated output
A transducer output which is obtained in the form of a deviation from a centre frequency, where the deviation is proportional to the applied stimulus.

Frequency of Vibration
The number of cycles occurring in a given unit of time. RPM - revolutions per minute. CPM- cycles per minute.

Frequency output
An output in the form of frequency which varies as a function of the applied input.

Frequency, natural
The frequency of free (not forced) oscillations of the sensing element of a fully assembled transducer.

Freshwater, freshwater
water that contains less than 1,000 milligrams per litre (mg/L) of dissolved solids; generally, more than 500 mg/L of dissolved solids is undesirable for drinking and many industrial uses.

Friction
The interaction between surfaces: a measure of the resistance felt when sliding one body over another.

Front end engineering and design
A study used to analyse the various technical options for new developments with the objective to define the facilities required.

FTP
File Transfer Protocol. A set of rules that allows two computers to "talk" to one another while transferring files from one to another. This is the protocol used when you transfer a file from one computer to another across the Internet. Many Internet sites have publicly accessible repositories of information that can be obtained using FTP, by logging in using the account name "anonymous." These sites are called "anonymous ftp servers."

Fugitive emmissions
Emissions (air pollutants) released to the air other than those from stacks or vents. They are often due to equipment leaks; evaporative processes and windblown disturbances.

Full bridge
A Wheatstone bridge configuration utilizing four active elements or strain gages.

Full scale output
The algebraic difference between the minimum output and maximum output.

Fumarole
A vent or opening through which issue steam, hydrogen sulfide, or other gases. The craters of many dormant volcanoes contain active fumaroles.

Function
The way in which a character contributes to the fitness of an organism.

Functional dna
Segments of DNA that code for proteins and essential RNA molecules, as well as sequences that help turn genes on and off.

Functional genomics
Area of genomics that studies the functions of genetic information contained within genomes.

Functions
Three mode PID controller. A timeproportioning controller with integral and derivative functions. The integral function automatically adjusts

the system temperature to the set point temperature to eliminate droop due to the time proportioning function.

Fundamental particles
Those particles that are not known to contain any smaller components: leptons, quarks and gauge bosons.

Fusion
1. Change of state of a substance from a solid to a liquid.
2. The joining together of two atomic nuclei.

Fusion pattern
Method of using protein fusion to infer gene function. If two proteins that are separate in one species exist as a fused protein in another species, the two separate proteins in the first species may be functionally related.

Fusion protein
A protein that forms from transcription of two genes as a unit and then translation. Can cause cancer.

Futurology
The study of the future.

G

G
The force of acceleration due to gravity equal to 32.1739 ft/sec^2 or 386 in./sec^2.

G0
Nondividing stage of the cell cycle.

G1
Stage in interphase of the cell cycle in which the cell grows and develops.

G1/S checkpoint
Important point in the cell cycle. After the G1/S checkpoint has been passed, DNA replicates and the cell is committed to dividing.

G2
Stage of interphase in the cell cycle that follows DNA replication. In G2, the cell prepares for division.

G2/M checkpoint
Important point in the cell cycle near the end of G2. After this checkpoint has been passed, the cell undergoes mitosis.

Gage factor
A measure of the ratio of the relative change of resistance to the relative change in length of a piezoresistive strain gage.

Gage height
The height of the water surface above the gage datum (zero point). Gage height is often used interchangeably with the more general term, stage, although gage height is more appropriate when used with a gage reading.

Gage length
The distance between two points where the measurement of strain occurs.

Gage pressure
Absolute pressure minus local atmospheric pressure.

Gage pressure transducer
A transducer which measures pressure in relation to the ambient pressure.

Gaging station
A site on a stream, lake, reservoir or other body of water where observations and hydrologic data are obtained. The U.S. Geological Survey measures stream discharge at gaging stations.

Gaia mission
Gaia is an ESA scientific mission related to astrometry. The aim of Gaia is to perform three-dimensional mapping of the stars in our Galaxy. This mission will build upon the scientific and technical expertise gained from ESA's Hipparcos space astrometry mission.

Gain
The amount of amplification used in an electrical circuit.

Gain-of-function mutation
Produces a new trait or causes a trait to appear in inappropriate tissues or at inappropriate times in development.

Galaxy
The structure formed by as assembly of thousands of millions of stars together with gas and dust. Our Galaxy, the Milky Way, is a spiral galaxy. Galaxies may be described as elliptical, irregular or spiral. Our Galaxy is just one among many millions.

Galaxy clusters
Groups of galaxies that may contain up to a few thousand galaxies.

Galvanometer
An instrument that measures small electrical currents by means of deflecting magnetic coils.

Game theory
A branch of economic theory devoted to modeling interactions between competing individuals or organizations. In biology, "evolutionary game theory" is used to model "competition" in evolutionary time between alternative behavioral strategies. The aim is to determine which strategy, out of a set of alternatives, would be favored by natural selection. Evolutionary game theory has been applied to a wide range of problems in animal behaviour but fighting behaviour was the first application. The Hawk-Dove game is an example of a model based on evolutionary game theory.

Gamete
1. Gametes are an organisms reproductive cells.
2. Haploid reproductive cell (sperm or egg).

Gamete intrafallopian transfer
An infertility treatment in which sperm and oocytes are placed in a woman's uterine tube.

Gametes
Egg and sperm; the reproductive cells. In diploid organisms (2n) they are haploid cells (n) that, as sperm and egg, will combine at fertilization to form a diploid zygote.

Gametic array
A method of describing in mathematical terms that the sum of the proportion of gametes that carries a specific allele is equal to 1. For example, a heterozygote embryo of genotype Aa has the gametic array of $1/2A + 1/2a = 1$.

Gametic phase disequilibrium
A nonrandom relationship between the alleles present at two or more loci, which can cause a genetic correlation.

Gametophyte
Haploid phase of the life cycle in plants.

Gamma diversity
Combines alpha diversity and beta diversity. Also called large-scale landscape diversity.

Gamma ray
The most powerful form of electromagnetic radiation. A typical

gamma ray is a photon with an energy greater than 100 keV.

Gamma-ray astronomy
Field of astronomy which studies very energetic processes. Gamma-ray astronomers observe the formation of new elements in space (nucleosynthesis), very dense objects such as neutron stars or black holes, active galaxies, supernovae and the most powerful explosions in the Universe. Because gamma rays are absorbed by the Earth's atmosphere, gamma-ray astronomy has to be done from space.

Gamma-ray burst (GRB)
A burst of gamma rays from space. GRBs are registered about twice a day by satellites in orbit. The bursts may last from as little as a hundredth of a second up to 90 minutes. GRBs are extremely far away and must be caused by tremendous explosions. They probably are hypernovae exceptionally violent supernovae, or mergers of neutron stars or black holes.

Ganymede
The largest of Jupiter's moons and the largest moon in the entire Solar System.

Gap genes
In fruit flies, set of segmentation genes that define large sections of the embryo. Mutations in these genes usually eliminate whole groups of adjacent segments.

Gas
A form of matter that can move about freely and does not have a definite shape. Water vapour is a gas and can move through Earth's atmosphere.

Gastrula
A three-layered embryo.

Gatekeeper
Tumor suppressor genes or proteins that regulate cellular responses that prevent the survival or proliferation of potential cancer cells.

Gauge bosons
Particles that mediate the transfer of energy between other particles: protons, gravitons, W and Z particles.

G-banding
A staining protocol for chromosomes. Chromosomes are generally pretreated with an enzyme that facilitates staining with Giemsa dye. Each chromosome has a unique staining pattern that allows it to be distinguished from other chromosomes.

Gel electrophoresis
Gel electrophoresis is a laboratory method used to separate mixtures of DNA, RNA, or proteins according to their sizes.

Gene
A region of DNA (deoxyribonucleic acid) coding either for the messenger RNA encoding the amino acid sequence in a polypeptide chain or for a functional RNA molecule.

Gene action
The manner in which genotype affects phenotype, including additivity, dominance, pleiotropy, and epistasis.

Gene array
A technology that allows investigators to measure the relative abundance of transcripts of specific genes by binding labeled cDNA probes from cells to a microchip with covalently attached microscopic spots of DNA, with each spot representing a single gene.

Gene cloning
Inserting DNA fragments into bacteria in such a way that the fragments will be stable and copied by the bacteria.

Gene complex
A group of two or more genes that are members of the same family and in most cases are located in close proximity to one another in the genome, often in tandem separated by various amounts of intergenic, noncoding DNA.

Gene conversion
A process involving the unidirectional transfer of DNA information from one gene to another. In a typical conversion event, a gene or part of a gene acquires the same sequence as the other allele at that locus (intralocus or intraallelic conversion), or the same sequences as a different, usually paralogous, locus (interlocus conversion). One consequence of gene conversion may be the homogenization of sequences among members of a gene family.

Gene doping
Modifying the genetic makeup of an individual with the specific purpose of improving athletic performance.

Gene duplication
When new genes arise as copies of preexisting gene sequences. The result can be a gene family.

Gene expression
1. Transcription of a gene.
2. The process of creating RNA transcripts and proteins from the genetic information contained in DNA.

Gene expression profiling
Use of DNA microarrays to detect the types and amounts of cDNAs reverse transcribed from the mRNAs in a particular cell source.

Gene family
Two or more loci with similar nucleotide sequences that have been derived from a common ancestral sequence.

Gene flow
1. Movement of genes between populations caused by migration and subsequent mating.
2. The incorporation of genes into the gene pool of one population from one or more other populations.

Gene interaction
Interactions between genes at different loci that affect the same characteristic.

Gene knockdown
Temporary decrease in gene expression caused by an experimental technique, often an antisense oligo.

Gene knockout
The permanent change in DNA leading to the loss of function of a gene, caused by a manipulation of the organism's DNA in a laboratory followed by breeding to produce a population of organisms that are homozygotes for the changed gene.

Gene mutation
Affects a single gene or locus.

Gene neighbor analysis
Analysis of the locations of genes in different species to infer gene function. If two genes are consistently linked in different species, they may be functionally related.

Gene ontology
A hierarchical organization of concepts (ontology) with three organizing

principles: molecular function, the tasks done by individual gene products, an example of which is 'transcription factor'; biological process, broad biological goals, such as mitosis, that are accomplished by ordered assemblies of molecular functions; cellular component, subcellular structures, locations and macromolecular complexes (examples include the nucleus and the telomere).

Gene pool
The totality of the genes of a given sexual population.

Gene regulation
Mechanisms and processes that control the phenotypic expression of genes.

Gene regulatory sites
A segment of DNA where regulatory proteins such as transcription factors bind preferentially. In this way, they control gene expression and thus protein expression.

Gene sequencing
The determining the complete sequence of a molecule or molecules of DNA, often through highly automated procedures.

Gene targeting
A biotechnology in which an introduced gene exchanges places with its counterpart on a host cell's chromosome by homologous recombination.

Gene therapy
Use of recombinant DNA to treat a disease or disorder by altering the genetic makeup of the patient's cells.

Gene tree
1. A diagram representing the history by which gene copies have been derived from ancestral gene copies in previous generations.
2. Phylogenetic tree representing the evolutionary relationships among a set of genes.

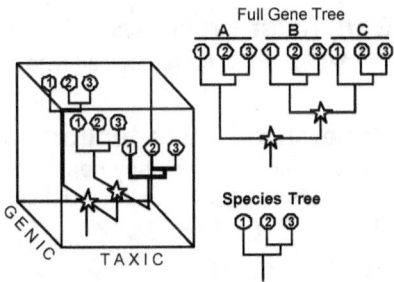

Genealogy
The study of family ancestries & histories.

Genecology
The study of genetical composition of plant population in relation to their habitats.

Gene-environment interaction
1. Phenotypic variation arising from the difference in the effect of the environment on the expression of different genotypes.
2. The phenomenon in which different genotypes respond differently to environmental variation; represents genetic variation for phenotypic plasticity.

General relativity
Theory of gravitation developed by Albert Einstein. Its fundamental principle is the equivalence of gravitational and inertial forces. General relativity is a geometric theory which states that gravity causes space-time to curve. This curvature affects the motion of objects in space-time. General relativity explains the bending of light by massive objects or the nature of black holes.

General transcription factor
The protein that binds to eukaryotic promoters near the start site and is a part of the basal transcription apparatus that initiates transcription.

Generalist preadators
Predators that consume alternate prey.

Generalized transduction
Transduction in which any gene may be transferred from one bacterial cell to another by a virus.

Generic drug
A copy of a drug that is introduced after the patent expires.

Genes
The basic unit of heredity consisting of a specific nucleotide sequence in DNA (or RNA, in some viruses).

Genesiology
The science of generation.

Genetic bottleneck
Sampling error that arises when a population undergoes a drastic reduction in population size; leads to genetic drift.

Genetic code
The genetic code is a set of rules that defines how the four-letter code of DNA is translated into the 20-letter code of amino acids, which are the building blocks of proteins.

Genetic conflict
The antagonistic fitness relationships between alleles at different loci in a genome.

Genetic correlation
The phenotypic correlation due to the same genes affecting two or more characteristics.

Genetic counseling
The educational process that attempts to help patients and family members deal with all aspects of a genetic condition.

Genetic differentiation
The differences between populations in allele frequencies at one or more loci, or in mean phenotypes in a common environment.

Genetic distance
Any of several measures of the degree of genetic difference between populations, based on differences in allele frequencies.

Genetic drift
The change in frequency of alleles in a population due to sampling error inherent in the transmission of gametes by individuals in a finite population.

Genetic engineering
Genetic engineering, also called genetic modification, is the direct human manipulation of an organism's genome using modern DNA technology. It involves the introduction of foreign DNA or synthetic genes into the organism of interest. The introduction of new DNA does not require the use of classical genetic methods, however traditional breeding methods are typically used for the propagation of recombinant organisms.

Genetic load
Any reduction of the mean fitness of a population resulting from the existence of genotypes with a fitness lower than that of the most fit genotype.

Genetic map
1. A linear representation of the positions of loci (especially marker

loci) along chromosomes, based on the frequency of recombination between the loci.
2. Map of the relative distances between genetic loci, markers, or other chromosome regions determined by rates of recombination; measured in percent recombination or map units.

Genetic marker
Any gene or DNA sequence used to identify a location on a genetic or physical map.

Genetic maternal effect
The phenotype of an offspring. With genetic maternal effect, an offspring inherits genes for the characteristics from both parents, but the offspring's phenotype is determined not by its own genotype but by the nuclear genotype of its mother.

Genetic screen
An experiment in which mutant organisms are generated in the laboratory and isolated based on a specific, desired phenotype.

Genetic screening
Analyzing DNA to determine the presence of a genetic variation that is responsible for an inherited disease.

Genetic testing
A medical test, using blood or tissue from a patient, that can definitively determine if a mutation in the genome of the patient is causing a specific disease.

Genetic variance
1. Component of the phenotypic variance that is due to genetic differences among individual members of a population.
2. Variation in a trait within a population, as measured by the variance that is due to genetic differences among individuals.

Genetic variation
Naturally occurring genetic differences among organisms in the same species.

Genetically engineered organism
An animal or plant that has genes from a different species (i.e., transgenes).

Genetically modified foods
Foods from genetically modified organisms, organisms that have acquired one or more genes from related or non-related species through the use of gene technology.

Genetically modified organisms
Organisms that have acquired has acquired one or more genes from related or non-related species through the use of gene technology.

Genetic-environmental interaction variance
Component of the phenotypic variance that results from an interaction between genotype and environment. Genotypes are expressed differently in different environments.

Genetics
The branch of biology dealing with the phenomena of heredity and the laws governing it.

Genic balance system
The sex-determining system in which sexual phenotype is controlled by a balance between genes on the X chromosome and genes on the autosomes.

Genic interaction variance
Component of the genetic variance that can be attributed to genic interaction (interaction between genes at different loci).

Genic selection
A form of selection in which the single gene is the unit of selection, such that the outcome is determined by fitness values assigned to different alleles.

Genic sex determination
The sex determination in which the sexual phenotype is specified by genes at one or more loci, but there are no obvious differences in the chromosomes of males and females.

Genome
A genome is the complete set of genetic information in an organism. It provides all of the information required by an organism to function.

Genome sequence
The order of nucleotides of a particular genome.

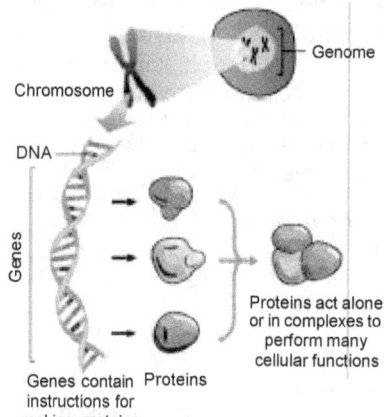

Genome size
The total number of DNA base pairs contained within one copy of a genome.

Genome wide association study
A case-control study in which genetic variation, often measured as SNPs that form haplotypes across the entire genome, is compared between people with a particular condition and unaffected individuals.

Genomic imprinting
The differential expression of a gene that depends on the sex of the parent that transmitted the gene. If the gene is inherited from the father, its expression is different than if it is inherited from the mother.

Genomic library
The collection of bacterial or phage colonies containing DNA fragments that consist of the entire genome of an organism.

Genomics
Genomics is the large-scale study of all the genes in an organism.

Genotype
1. A genotype is the particular the combination of alleles for a particular gene or locus.
2. The set of genes possessed by an individual organism; often, its genetic composition at a specific locus or set of loci singled out for discussion.

Genotypic array
A prediction of the possible genotypic combinations in an offspring based on the genotypes of two parents.

Genotypic frequencies
The proportion of each of the various genotypes present in a population or sample of a population.

Genotypic frequency
Proportion of a particular genotype.

Genotypic value
The phenotype produced by a given genotype averaged across environments.

Genotypic variance
The magnitude of the phenotypic variance that is due to all genetic causes, corresponding to the sum of the additive, dominance, and epistatic variances.

Geobiology
The biology of terrestrial life.

Geobotany
The branch of Botany dealing with all aspects of relations between plants & the earth's surface.

Geochemistry
The study of the chemical composition of the earth's crust and the changes which takes place within it.

Geographic variation
Differences among spatially distributed populations of a species.

Geography
The science of the earth's surface, physical features, climate, population, etc.

Geology
The science that deals with the physical history of the earth.

Geoman
Your's truly, and a real GeoGeek.

Geomedicine
The branch of medicine dealing with the influence of climate and environmental conditions on health.

Geomorphology
The study of the characteristics, origin and development of land forms.

Geomorphology
The study of landforms and the geological processes that shape them.

Geophysics
The physics of the earth.

Geothermal energy
Energy derived from the internal heat of the earth.

Geothermal power
Power generated by using the heat energy of the earth.

Germanium detector
Instrument for detecting powerful radiation such as gamma rays. Germanium is a semiconductor material and is used in detectors for the most sensitive gamma-ray line spectroscopy.

Germ-line mutation
Mutation in a germ-line cell (one that gives rise to gametes).

Germ-plasm theory
States that cells in the reproductive organs carry a complete set of genetic information.

Gerontology
The study of old age, its phenomena, diseases, etc.

Geyser
A geothermal feature of the Earth where there is an opening in the surface that contains superheated water that periodically erupts in a shower of water and steam.

Giardiasis
A disease that results from an infection by the protozoan parasite Giardia Intestinalis, caused by drinking water that is either not filtered or not

chlorinated. The disorder is more prevalent in children than in adults and is characterized by abdominal discomfort, nausea, and alternating constipation and diarrhea.

GIF
Graphics Interchange Format. An efficient method of storing graphics developed for CompuServe in the early 1980s. GIF files take up a small amount of disk space and can be transmitted quickly over phone lines. GIFs can be viewed on any computer platform and are best for illustrations, cartoons, logos, or similar non-photographic graphics.

Giotto mission
ESA's first deep space probe. Made close fly-bys of comets Halley (1986) and Grigg-Skjellerup (1992) and obtained the first close range pictures of a comet nucleus. Other experiments measured the magnetic field, charged particle distribution, dust and gas composition and concentration.

Glacial abrasion
A copmmon mechanical weathering process where rock and debris frozen into the sides and bottom of a glacier act like sandpaper and wear down the bedrock the glacier is mocing across.

Glacial ice
Naturally occurring ice which exhibits internal plastic flow and deformation.

Glacial polish
Polished bedrock surfaces left behind after melting of glacial ice. The polishing is probably due to very fine grained rock flour carried at the base of the ice.

Glacial quarrying (plucking)
A common mechanical weathering process in alpine glaciated terrain where glacial ice frozen into cracks in the bedrock literally "pluck" rock material from the valley floor.

Glacier
A huge mass of ice, formed on land by the compaction and recrystallization of snow, that moves very slowly downslope or outward due to its own weight.

Global climate change
A change in the statistical distribution of weather over periods of time that can range from decades to millions of years.

Globin
The protein that carries the oxygen in red blood cells.

Glottochronlogy
The study of the history of language.

Glycolipid
A molecule that consists of a sugar bonded to a lipid.

Glycoprotein
A molecule that consists of a sugar bonded to a protein.

G-matrix
A square matrix with additive genetic variances for the traits on the diagonal and additive genetic covariances on the off-diagonal.

Good health habits
Habits that help a person to stay well. Getting enough rest and exercise are good health habits.

GPH
Volumetric flow rate in gallons per hour.

GPM
Volumetric flow rate in gallons per minute.

Graben
An elongate crustal block that is relatively depressed (downdropped) between two fault systems.

Grade
A group of species that have evolved the same state in one or more characters and typically constitute a paraphyletic group relative to other species that have evolved further in the same direction.

Gradualism
The proposition that large differences in phenotypic characters have evolved through many slightly different intermediate states.

Granulation
A mottled cellular pattern visible on the Sun's photosphere. It is caused by the convective motion of hot gas rising from the Sun's interior.

Grating (transmission, reflection)
Optical device which has a fine regular pattern used to disperse electromagnetic radiation into a spectrum. A transmission grating consists of a large number of narrow, closely spaced bars. A reflection grating consists of narrowly spaced saw-teeth or steps ruled on a polished surface such as glass or metal.

Gravitational (arc, lens)
Light cannot escape the pull of gravity; the light from astronomical objects therefore gets deformed - bent, curved or even amplified - if it passes close to a massive body. The massive body causing the effect, a galaxy cluster, for instance, plays the role of a lens. If the lens is spherical then the image appears as an Einstein ring (the image appears as a ring of light), if the lens is elongated then the image is an Einstein cross (it appears split into four distinct images) and if the lens is a galaxy cluster then arcs and arclets of light are formed.

Gravitational field
The area influenced by an object's gravity.

Gravitational wave
Ripple in the structure of space-time which may occur individually or as continuous radiation. According to Einstein's Theory of General Relativity, they are emitted when extremely massive objects experience sudden accelerations or changes of shape. They travel through space at the speed of light. Gravitational waves remain undetected.

Gravity
A physical force that appears to exert a mutual attraction between all masses. It is proportional to the mass of the object. In Einstein's Theory of General Relativity, it is explained as a curvature of space-time.

Gravity assist
Natural 'slingshot' effect which increases a spacecraft's speed and changes its direction of flight. It occurs when a spacecraft gains energy as it flies close to a planet or moon. At the same time, the planet loses a tiny amount of momentum, which causes its orbital speed to be fractionally reduced.

Grazing incidence
Describes the low angle of incidence of incoming electromagnetic waves on a reflecting surface. X-rays can only be reflected off a super-smooth surface at very shallow angles of the order of half a degree. In other words, they only reflect if they 'graze' the surface.

Green fluorescent protein
A protein originally isolated from the jellyfish (Aequorea victoria) that retains the property of fluorescing green when exposed to blue light and when fused to other cellular proteins.

Greywater
Wastewater from clothes washing machines, showers, bathtubs, hand washing, lavatories and sinks.

Grigg-Skjellerup (comet)
Periodic comet which orbits the Sun once every 5.1 years. Named after New Zealander John Grigg, who first saw it on 23 July 1902, and Australian James Francis Skjellerup, who rediscovered the comet on 17 May 1922. It travels around the Sun in the same direction as the planets and its orbit ranges from just inside the orbit of Jupiter to the orbit of the Earth.

Ground
1. The electrical neutral line having the same potential as the surrounding earth.
2. The negative side of DC power supply.
3. Reference point for an electrical system.

Ground segment
All the facilities and systems required on Earth to control and operate a space mission.

Ground water
1. Water that flows or seeps downward and saturates soil or rock, supplying springs and wells. The upper surface of the saturate zone is called the water table.
2. Water stored underground in rock crevices and in the pores of geologic materials that make up the Earth's crust.

Ground water recharge
Inflow of water to a ground-water reservoir from the surface. Infiltration of precipitation and its movement to the water table is one form of natural recharge. Also, the volume of water added by this process.

Ground water, confined
Ground water under pressure significantly greater than atmospheric, with its upper limit the bottom of a bed with hydraulic conductivity distinctly lower than that of the material in which the confined water occurs.

Ground water, unconfined
Water in an aquifer that has a water table that is exposed to the atmosphere.

Grounded junction
A form of construction of a thermocouple probe where the hot or measuring junction is in electrical contact with the sheath material so that the sheath and thermocouple will have the same electrical potential.

Group I intron
Belongs to a class of introns in some ribosomal RNA genes that are capable of self-splicing.

Group II intron
Belongs to a class of introns in some protein-encoding genes that are capable of self-splicing and are found in mitochondria, chloroplasts, and a few eubacteria.

Group predation
Carnivorous interactions involving many small individuals consuming a larger one.

Group selection
The differential rate of origination or extinction of whole populations (or

species, if the term is used broadly) on the basis of differences among them in one or more characteristics.

Guanine
Purine in DNA and RNA.

Guaranteed time
Proportion of a science mission's operational time that is allocated to priority users such as the principal investigators of its science instruments.

Guide RNA
RNA molecule that serves as a template for an alteration made in mRNA during RNA editing.

Gynandromorph
Individual organism that is a mosaic for the sex chromosomes, possessing tissues with different sex-chromosome constitutions.

Gyroscope
A disc with a heavy rim mounted in such a way that its axis of rotation can adopt any position. Once the disc is spinning, the rotation axis remains fixed with reference to fixed stars, which makes the gyroscope useful for determining movement away from a fixed course. Three gyroscopes rotating about perpendicular axes help to maintain the orientation of a spacecraft in space by detecting rotation about any of the axes and initiating a mechanism to correct it.

Habitat
A place in which a plant or an animal lives. A living thing gets all the things it needs to stay alive from its habitat.

Habitat enhancement
The process of increasing the suitability of a site as habitat for some desired species.

Habitat fragmentation
It occurs when continuous areas of habitat become disconnected by natural or human causes (e.g., building roads through a forest).

Habitat patchiness
Landscape spatial heterogeneity caused by spatial and temporal variation in the distribution and abundance of vital resources, as well as in geological and ecological processes.

Habitat selection
The capacity of an organism (usually an animal) to choose a habitat in which to perform its activities. Habitat selection is not a form of natural selection.

Hadrons
Quark composites: mesons and baryons. Protons and neutrons are the most common hadrons.

Haematology
The study of blood.

Hair
Body covering of mammals. Hair helps mammals stay warm and protects their skin.

Hairpin
The secondary structure formed when sequences of nucleotides on the same strand are complementary and pair with each other.

Hairpin loop (mrna)
A hairpin loop is an unpaired loop of messenger RNA (mRNA) that is created when an mRNA strand folds and forms base pairs with another section of itself. Hairpins are a common type of secondary structure in RNA molecules.

Hale-Bopp (comet)
The brightest comet to appear in the night sky for many decades. Discovered by Alan Hale and Thomas Bopp on 22 July 1995, it reached perihelion on 1 April 1997 and was a naked eye object for many months. Its nucleus appears to be very large, about 40 km across.

Half bridge
Two active elements or strain gages.

Half-duplex
One way at a time data communication; both devices can transmit and receive data, but only one at a time.

Half-energy width
The angle within which half of the electromagnetic radiation (e.g. X-rays) coming from a point source is focused by an X-ray optic.

Half-life
The time taken for the level of radioactivity in an element to halve.

Halley (comet)
The most famous periodic comet. Its aphelion is beyond the orbit of Neptune, but it returns to the inner Solar System every 76 years. Named after the 17th century British scientist, Edmond Halley, who first recognised its regular pattern of reappearances. Studied by a fleet of spacecraft during its 1986 apparition, including ESA's Giotto.

Halogen
Highly reactive gases forming group 7 of the periodic table.

Hamilton's RULE
A general model that details the conditions under which altruistic behaviour should evolve.

Hand arm vibration syndrome
A potentially debilitating disorder resulting from prolonged exposure to vibration - specifically to the hands and forearms while using vibrating tools.

Handshake
An interface procedure that is based on status/data signals that assure orderly data transfer as opposed to asynchronous exchange.

Haplodiploid
A genetic system in which an individual.s sex is determined not by the presence or absence of a sex chromosome, but instead by the number of copies of the genome in an individual.s cells.

Haploid
1. Haploid cells are cells that contain a single set of chromosomes.
2. Of a cell or organism, possessing a single chromosome complement, hence a single gene copy at each locus.

Haploid cell
Cells containing only one set of chromosomes.

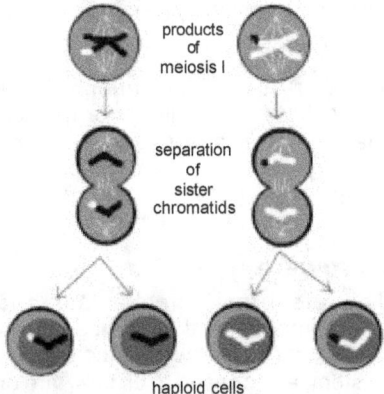

Haploinsufficiency
The appearance of a mutant phenotype in an individual cell or organism that is heterozygous for a normally recessive trait.

Haploinsufficient gene
It must be present in two copies for normal function. If one copy of the gene is missing, a mutant phenotype is produced.

Haplotype
A haplotype is a group of genes, which is inherited together by an organism from a single parent

Hapmap project
An international consortium of scientists working together to catalog

the genetic variation in the human genome.

Hard drive
A device for storing information in a fixed location within your computer. The equivalent of a filing cabinet in an office, the hard drive is used for storing programmes and documents that are not being used.

Hardcopy
Output in a permanent form (usually a printout) rather than in temporary form, as on disk or display terminal.

Hardness
A water-quality indication of the concentration of alkaline salts in water, mainly calcium and magnesium. If the water you use is "hard" then more soap, detergent or shampoo is necessary to raise a lather.

Hardware
The electrical, mechanical and electromechanical equipment and parts associated with a computing system, as opposed to its firmware or software.

Hardy-Weinberg equation
The Hardy-Weinberg equation is a mathematical expression that can be used to calculate the genetic variation of a population at equilibrium.

Hardy-Weinberg equilibrium
1. The Hardy-Weinberg equilibrium is a principle stating that the genetic variation in a population will remain constant from one generation to the next in the absence of disturbing factors.
2. The population condition characterized by the genotypic frequencies produced under random mating; for two alleles the genotype frequencies are given by p2, 2pq, and q2.

Hardy-Weinberg law
Important principle of population genetics stating that, in a large, randomly mating population not affected by mutation, migration, or natural selection, allelic frequencies will not change and genotypic frequencies stabilize after one generation in the proportions p2 (the frequency of AA), 2pq (the frequency of Aa), and q2 (the frequency of aa), where p equals the frequency of allele A and q equals the frequency of allele a.

Hardy-weinberg models
Allele frequencies will remain constant over time if there are no forces to change them.

Harem
An aggregation of females that can be monopolized by a single male for the purpose of mating.

Harmonic tremor
A continuous release of seismic energy typically associated with the underground movement of magma. It contrasts distinctly with the sudden release and rapid decrease of seismic energy associated with the more common type of earthquake caused by slippage along a fault.

Hastelloy
A widely used nickel-molybdenum-chromium alloy. Offers excellent resistance to wet chlorine, hypochlorite bleach, ferric chloride and nitric acid.

Hawk-dove game
This particular model pits a Hawk strategy (i.e., always try to injure your opponent and only withdraw from the contest if an injury is received) against a Dove strategy (i.e., always use a non-injurious display if the rival is another Dove and always withdraw if the rival is a Hawk).

Hazid - hazard identification
The process of identifying credible hazards for a Quantified Risk Assessment (QRA).

Head loss
The loss of pressure in a flow system measured using a length parameter (i.e., inches of water, inches of mercury).

Head pressure
Pressure in terms of the height of fluid, $P = yrg$, where r = fluid density and y = the fluid column heights. Expression of a pressure in terms of the height of fluid, $r = yrg$, where r is fluid density and y = the fluid column height. g = the acceleration of gravity.

Headwater(s)
1. The source and upper reaches of a stream; also the upper reaches of a reservoir.
2. The water upstream from a structure or point on a stream.
3. The small streams that come together to form a river. Also may be thought of as any and all parts of a river basin except the mainstream river and main tributaries.

Health and safety executive
The authority responsible for the regulation of almost all the risks to health and safety arising from work activity in Britain.

Heart
The heart is a myogenic muscular organ found in all animals with a circulatory system (including all vertebrates), that is responsible for pumping blood throughout the blood vessels by repeated, rhythmic contractions. The term cardiac (as in cardiology) means "related to the heart" and comes from he Greek kardia, for "heart".

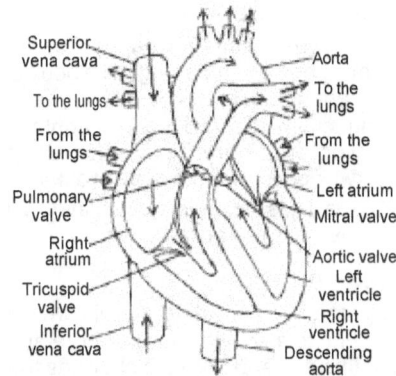

Heat
Thermal energy. Heat is expressed in units of calories or BTU's.

Heat capacity
Also known also as thermal capacity. The energy submitted to a body in order to increase its temperature by one degree.

Heat shield
A thick layer that protects from heat.

Heat shock element
A DNA sequence to which heat shock transcription factors bind when activated.

Heat shock transcription factor
A transcription factor that becomes activated upon cellular stress, resulting in its trimerization, binding to heat shock elements, and induction of transcription of a number of proteins.

Heat sink
1. Thermodynamic. A body which can absorb thermal energy.
2. Practical. A finned piece of metal used to dissipate the heat of solid state components mounted on it.

Heat transfer
The process of thermal energy flowing from a body of high energy to a body of low energy. Means of transfer are: conduction; the two bodies contact. Convection; a form of conduction where the two bodies in contact are of different phases, i.e. solid and gas. Radiation: all bodies emit infrared radiation.

Heat treating
A process for treating metals where heating to a specific temperature and cooling at a specific rate changes the properties of the metal.

Heat-shock protein
Produced by many cells in response to extreme heat and other stresses; helps cells prevent damage from such stressing agents.

Hela cell
An immortalized human cell line frequently used in biological research.

Helicase
Helicase is an enzyme that unwinds and separates the two strands of the DNA double helix.

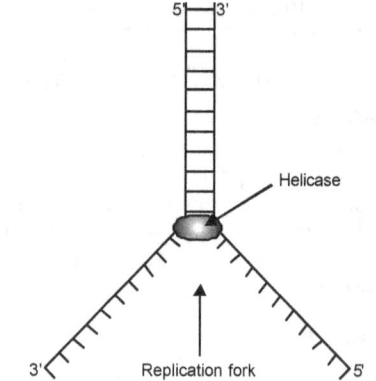

Helicopter underwater escape training
Part of the Basic Offshore Induction and Emergency Training course where participants swim from an inverted helicopter submerged in a swimming pool.

Heliocentric
With the Sun in the centre. Our Solar System is heliocentric.

Helioseismology
The study of the Sun's interior by measuring oscillations (ripples) as they appear at the surface. The oscillations are caused by sound waves that originate at different depths inside the Sun. By measuring their travel times and the distance they travel, scientists can study conditions in the Sun's interior.

Heliosphere
The volume of space around the Sun which contains the charged particles and magnetic field carried in the solar wind. Its outer boundary (which has never been crossed) is called the heliopause and marks the beginning of interstellar space. This is thought to be 50 - 100 AU from the Sun.

Heliotherapy
The sun cure.

Helix-loop-helix
An area of a protein that folds in a predictable way and characterizes a group of transcription factors. Specifically, helix-loop-helix is a polypeptide that has a structure of two alpha-helices connected by a loop.

Helix-turn-helix
A common protein motif characterized by two adjacent alpha helices that make contact with DNA and regulate gene transcription.

Helminthology
The study of worms, especially parasitic worms.

Hemagglutinin
A type I integral membrane glycoprotein that binds to cell-surface receptors and facilitates fusion between the viral envelope and endosomal membrane. It is the main target antigen of the humoral immune response to influenza viruses.

Hemicryptophytes
Plants with their perennating buds at or near the soil surface (e.g. many grasses).

Hemizygote
An organism that has only one allele at a given locus.

Hemizygous
Possessing a single allele at a locus. Males of organisms with XX-XY sex determination are hemizygous for X-linked loci, because their cells possess a single X chromosome.

Herbivore
Animal adapted to eat plants.

Heritability
1. The proportion of the variance in a trait among individuals that is attributable to differences in genotype. Heritability in the narrow sense is the ratio of additive genetic variance to phenotypic variance.
2. The proportion of the total phenotypic variance that is due to genetic causes; in other words, heritability measures the relative importance of genetic variance in determining phenotypic variance. Narrow-sense heritability is the additive genetic variance divided by the phenotypic variance (VA/VP), whereas broad-sense heritability is the genotypic variance divided by the phenotypic variance (VG/VP).

Hermaphroditism
Condition in which an individual organism possesses both male and female reproductive structures. True hermaphrodites produce both male and female gametes.

Herpetology
The study of reptiles & amphibians.

Herschel (formerly FIRST) mission
Herschel is an ESA scientific mission dealing with cosmology. Herschel will study the formation of the first stars and galaxies which formed in our Universe.

Hertz (hz)
A measure of frequency. It is the number of oscillations per second of a vibrating system.

Hertzsprung-Russell (HR) diagram
A diagram in which the luminosities of stars are plotted against their colours or spectral types. In the conventional way in which this diagram is plotted, luminosity increases logarithmically up the vertical axis and temperature increases from right to left along the horizontal axis. Stars do not occupy all regions of the H-R diagram but form various sequences, the most important being the main sequence, the giant branch and the horizontal branch.

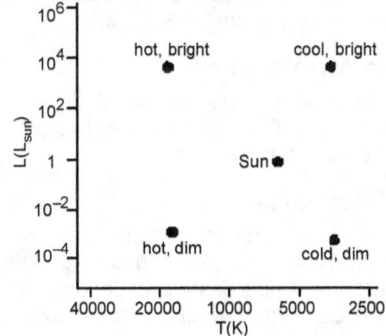

Heterochromatin
Chromatin that remains in a highly condensed state throughout the cell cycle, found at the centromeres and telomeres of most chromosomes.

Heterochrony
An evolutionary change in phenotype caused by an alteration of timing of developmental events.

Heteroduplex DNA
DNA consisting of two strands, each of which is from a different chromosome.

Heterogametic sex
The sex (male or female) that produces two types of gametes with respect to sex chromosomes. For example, in the XX-XY sex-determining system, the male produces both X-bearing and Y-bearing gametes.

Heterokaryon
The cell possessing two nuclei derived from different cells through cell fusion.

Heterokaryotype
A genome or individual that is heterozygous for a chromosomal rearrangement such as an inversion.

Heteromorphic chromosomes
A pair of chromosomes that share some genetic homology but differ in physical characteristics like size, shape, or staining patterns.

Heteroplasmy
Presence of two or more distinct variants of DNA within the cytoplasm of a single cell.

Heterosis
Phenomenon in which the F1 generation has higher fitness than the parental strains or subpopulations that were crossed (mated) to produce them.

Heterotroph
Organisms that obtain their food by eating other organisms or substances derived from them; organisms that cannot synthesize its own organic material and must obtain energy from other organisms.

Heterozygosity
In a population, the proportion of loci at which a randomly chosen individual is heterozygous, on average.

Heterozygotes
Individuals who have two different alleles at a locus (e.g., at a locus with two alleles, A and a, the heterozygote has genotype Aa).

Heterozygote advantage
Phenomenon in which the heterozygous genotype has a higher phenotypic value (especially for fitness) than either homozygous genotype.

Heterozygote screening
Testing members of a population to identify heterozygous carriers of a disease-causing allele who are healthy but have the potential to produce children with the disease.

Heterozygous
Refers to an individual organism that possesses two different alleles at a locus.

Heterozygous advantage
The manifestation of higher fitness by heterozygotes than by homozygotes at a specific locus.

Hexadecimal
Refers to a base sixteen number system using the characters 0 through 9 and A through F to represent the values. Machine language programmes are often written in hexadecimal notation.

Hexadecimal code
Also called Hex codes. In HTML, colours are identified by a six-character string of numbers and letters (0,1,2,3,4,5,6,A,B,C,D,E,F) derived from base-16 mathematics. The codes are used to convert RGB (red, red, and red) values into something HTML can understand. Pure red would be FF0000.

Hhv
Heating Value is defined as the amount of energy released when a fuel is burned completely in a steady-flow process and the products are returned to the state of the reactants. The heating value is dependent on the phase of water/steam in the combustion products. If H2O is in liquid form the heating value is called HHV (Higher Heating Value).

High integrity protective system
High Integrity Protective System or sometimes High Integrity Protection System. An automatic safety system with a SIL level of 3 or more.

High pressure
It is often used with reference to a utility or vent line e.g. HP air supply.

Highly repetitive DNA
DNA that consists of short sequences that are present in hundreds of thousands to millions of copies; clustered in certain regions of chromosomes.

High-mobility group
Small, highly-charged proteins that vary in amount and composition in different tissues and different stages of the cell cycle; may play an important role in chromatin structure.

Hinged jaws
Jaws joined with a hinge-like joint so they open wide. Hinged jaws let some dinosaurs swallow huge chunks of meat.

Hipaa
A U.S. federal law that requires improved efficiency in health care delivery by standardized electronic data interchange and protection of confidentiality and security of health data.

Hipparcos mission
ESA scientific mission related to astrometry whose goal was to accurately measure the distance of stars within our Galaxy.

Histology
The study of tissues.

Histone
1. Histones are a family of basic proteins, which associate with DNA in the nucleus and help to condense the DNA into a smaller volume.
2. Low-molecular weight protein found in eukaryotes that complexes with DNA to form chromosomes.

Histone acetyl transferase
A family of proteins that is responsible for catalyzing the bonding of an acetyl group to specific lysines on histones, generally resulting in increased transcription at that locus.

Histone code
The combination of all the different modifications that can occur on histones.

Histone deacetylase
A protein that catalyzes the removal of an acetyl group from histones.

Histone demethylase
A protein that catalyzes the removal of a methyl group from histones.

Histone methyltransferase
The proteins that catalyze the addition of methyl groups to lysines or arginines in histone proteins, causing the DNA to be less available for transcriptional machinery.

Hitchhiking
The change in the frequency of an allele due to linkage with a selected allele at another locus.

HMG nuclear protein
A protein component of chromatin that was named based on its mobility in polyacrilimide gels.

Holandric
It refers to a trait that is encoded by a gene on the Y chromosome.

Hold
Metre HOLD is an external input which is used to stop the A/D process and freeze the display. BCD HOLD is an external input used to freeze the BCD output while allowing the A/D process to continue operation.

Holliday intermediate
Structure that forms in homologous recombination; consists of two duplex molecules connected by a cross bridge.

Holliday junction
Model of homologous recombination that is initiated by single-strand breaks in a DNA molecule.

Hollow tube
A tube with an empty space within it. Some dinosaurs may have used the hollow tubes on their heads to make sounds.

Holoblastic cleavage
Describes a cell division event during development that results in complete cleavage between the two daughter cells. Often this type of cleavage is evident in animals in which the zygotic stage does not have a large amount of yolk.

Holoenzyme
Complex of enzyme and other protein factors necessary for complete function.

Homeobox
Conserved subset of nucleotides in homeotic genes. In Drosophila, it consists of 180 nucleotides that encode 60 amino acids of a DNA-binding domain related to the helix-turn-helix motif.

Homeobox genes
A large family of eukaryotic genes that contains a DNA sequence known as the homeobox. The homeobox sequence encodes a protein homeodomain about 60 amino acids in length that binds DNA. Most homeobox genes are transcriptional regulators.

Homeodomain
The region of a homeobox protein that can bind DNA.

Homeostasis
Homeostasis is the property of a system that regulates its internal environment and tends to maintain a stable, constant condition of properties like temperature or pH. It can be either an open or closed system.

Homeotic complex
The major cluster of homeotic genes in fruit flies; consists of the Antennapedia complex, which affects development of the adult fly's head and anterior segments, and the bithorax complex, which affects the adult fly's posterior thoracic and abdominal segments.

Homeotic genes
The genes that determine the developmental fate of entire segments of an animal.

Homeotic mutation
A mutation that causes a transformation of one structure into another of the organism's structures.

Homepage
The page on the Internet which most often gives users access to the rest of the Web site. A site is a collection of pages.

Homogametic sex
The sex (male or female) that produces gametes that are all alike with regard to sex chromosomes. For example, in the XX-XY sex-determining system, the female produces only X-bearing gametes.

Homokaryotype
A genome or individual that is homozygous for a chromosomal rearrangement such as an inversion.

Homologous
The similar in position, structure, function, or characteristics.

Homologous dna
DNA derived from a common evolutionary ancestor.

Homologous genes
Evolutionarily related genes, having descended from a gene in a common ancestor.

Homologous pair of chromosomes
Two chromosomes that are alike in structure and size and that carry genetic information for the same set of hereditary characteristics. One chromosome of a homologous pair is inherited from the male parent and the other is inherited from the female parent.

Homologous recombination
Homologous recombination is a type of genetic recombination in which nucleotide sequences are exchanged between two similar or identical molecules of DNA. It is most widely used by cells to accurately repair harmful breaks that occur on both strands of DNA, known as double-strand breaks. Homologous recombination also produces new combinations of DNA sequences during meiosis, the process by which eukaryotes make gamete cells, like sperm and egg cells in animals. These new combinations of DNA represent genetic variation in offspring, which in turn enables populations to adapt during the course of evolution. Homologous recombination is also used in horizontal gene transfer to exchange genetic material between different strains and species of bacteria and viruses.

Homologous recombination repair
A relatively error-free pathway that repairs DNA double-strand breaks using an undamaged sister chromatid or homologous chromosome as a template.

Homology
The possession by two or more species of a character state derived, with or without modification, from their common ancestor. Homologous chromosomes are those members of a chromosome complement that bear the same genes.

Homomorphic chromosomes
Homologous chromosomes that are morphologically identical.

Homonymous
It pertaining to biological structures that occur repeatedly within one segment of the organism, such as teeth or bristles.

Homoplasmy
The presence of only one version of DNA within the cytoplasm of a single cell.

Homoplasy
The possession by two or more species of a similar or identical character state that has not been derived by both species from their common ancestor; embraces convergence, parallel evolution, and evolutionary reversal.

Homotzygotes
Individuals who have two copies of the same allele at a locus (e.g., at a locus with two alleles, A and a, the homozygotes have genotypes AA and aa).

Homozygosity
The frequency of homozygous genotypes, often symbolized as P or Q.

Homozygote
An individual organism that has the same allele at each of its copies of a genetic locus.

Homozygous
A diploid genotype or individual with two indistinguishable alleles at a given locus.

Homozygous line
Another name for a "pure-breeding" line; a strain of organisms that are homozygous for the alleles associated with a particular phenotype.

Hooke's law
Defines the basis for the measurement of mechanical stresses via the strain measurement. The gradient of Hooke's line is defined by the ratio of which is equivalent to the Modulus of Elasticity E (Young's Modulus).

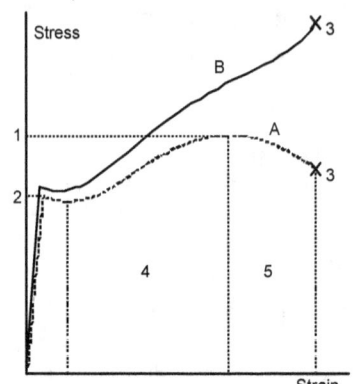

Horizontal blast
An explosive eruption in which the resultant cloud of hot ash and other material moves laterally rather than upward.

Horizontal gene exchange
Transfer of genes from one organism to another by a mechanism other than reproduction.

Horizontal gene transfer
Transfer of genetic information from one species to another in ways other than common descent.

Horizontal transfer
The movement of genes between species.

Horizontal transmission
The movement of genes or symbionts (such as parasites) between individual organisms other than by transmission from parents to their offspring (which is vertical transmission). Horizontal transmission of genes is also called lateral gene transfer.

Horticulture
The cultivation of flowers, fruits, vegetables and ornamental plants.

Host
The name given to any computer directly connected to the Internet. Host computers are usually associated with running computer networks, online services, or bulletin board systems. A host computer on the Internet could be anything from a mainframe to a personal computer.

Hot work
This includes welding or the use of any flame or electric arc or the use of any equipment likely to cause heat or flame or spark.

Hot-spot volcanoes
volcanoes related to a persistent heat source in the mantle.

Hox genes
1. Genes that contain a homeobox.
2. A subfamily of homeobox genes, conserved in all metazoan animals, that controls anterior-posterior segment identity by regulating the transcription of many genes during development.

Hpa II endonuclease
A methyltransferase that recognizes the sequence CCGG and is responsible for methylating the second cysteine.

Html
Hypertext Markup Language. This is the coding language used to create sites on the World Wide Web.

Hubble constant
A measure of the rate at which the Universe is expanding. The Hubble Constant relates the apparent recession velocity of a galaxy to its distance from the Milky Way. The precise value of the Hubble Constant is unknown, although independent measurements have established the value of this constant to be between 50 and 80 kilometres per second per megaparsec (in other words, for every megaparsec, the object's velocity of recession increases by 50 to 80 km/s).

Hubble law
In 1929 US astronomer Edwin T. Hubble discovered that galaxies were moving away from each other, and that the farther they were, the faster they separated. Their velocities increased proportionally to their distances. This is the Hubble Law. The Hubble Constant is the proportionality factor in this law.

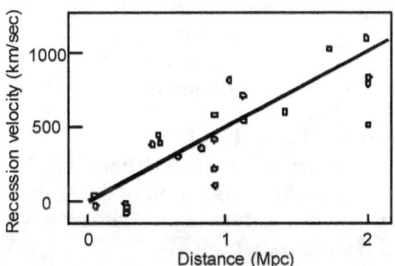

Hubble's Data

Hubble space telescope (HST) mission
ESA/NASA astronomy mission dedicated to the observation of the Universe in wavelengths going from the ultraviolet to the infrared. This broad spectrum of observation can be achieved because the telescope is located outside the Earth's atmosphere.

Human genome project
The Human Genome Project was an international research project that sequenced all of the genes in humans.

Human machine interface
A dated term superseded by SCADA.

Humoral immunity
The humoral immune response (HIR) is the aspect of immunity that is mediated by secreted antibodies (as opposed to cell-mediated immunity, which involves T lymphocytes) produced in the cells of the B lymphocyte lineage (B cell). B Cells (with co-stimulation) transform into plasma cells which secrete antibodies. The co-stimulation of the B cell can come from another antigen presenting cell, like a dendritic cell. This entire process is aided by CD4+ T-helper 2 cells, which provide co-stimulation. Secreted antibodies bind to antigens on the surfaces of invading microbes (such as viruses or bacteria), which flags them for destruction. Humoral immunity is so named because it involves substances found in the humours, or body fluids.

Huygens mission
ESA's probe to study Titan, named after the Dutch astronomer Christiaan Huygens. It is carried on board NASA's Cassini spacecraft.

Hybrid
An individual formed by mating between unlike forms, usually genetically differentiated populations or species.

Hybrid dysgenesis
The sudden appearance of numerous mutations, chromosome aberrations, and sterility in the offspring of a cross between a male fly that possesses P elements and a female fly that lacks them.

Hybrid vigour
The phenomenon in which the F1 generation has higher fitness than the parental strains or subpopulations that were crossed (mated) to produce them.

Hybrid zone
A region in which genetically distinct populations come into contact and produce at least some offspring of mixed ancestry.

Hybridization
The pairing of two partly or fully complementary single-stranded nucleotide chains. The nucleotide chains may come from the same species or different species.

Hydrazine
Storable liquid propellant used on spacecraft. Combination of hydrogen and nitrogen (N_2H_4).

Hydrocarbon
A chemical compound that consists only of hydrogen (H) and carbon (C).

Hydrodynamics
The mathematical study of the forces, energy and pressure of liquid in motion.

Hydroelectric power water use
The use of water in the generation of electricity at plants where the turbine generators are driven by falling water.

Hydrogen bond
A weak electrostatic bond which arises from the attraction between the slight positive charge on a hydrogen atom and a slight negative charge on a nearby oxygen or nitrogen atom.

Hydrogen ion activity (ah+)
Activity of the hydrogen ion in solution. Related to hydrogen ion concentration (CH+) by the activity coefficient for hydrogen (f H+).

Hydrography
The science of water measurements of the earth with special reference to their use for navigation.

Hydrologic cycle
The cyclic transfer of water vapour from the Earth's surface via evapotranspiration into the atmosphere, from the atmosphere via precipitation back to earth, and through runoff into streams, rivers, and lakes, and ultimately into the oceans.

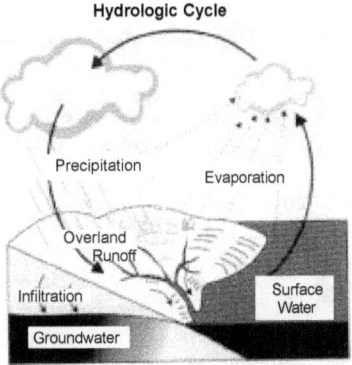

Hydrologic Cycle

Hydrology
The study of water with reference to its occurrence and properties in the hydrosphere and atmosphere.

Hydrometallurgy
The process of extracting metals at ordinary temperature by leaching ore with liquids.

Hydropathy
The cure of disease by the internal and external use of water.

Hydroponics
The cultivation of plants by placing the roots in nutrient solution rather than in soil.

Hydrostatics
The mathematical study of forces and pressures in liquids.

Hydrotest
A pressure test of piping; pressure vessels or pressure-containing parts; usually performed by pressurising the internal volume with water.

Hydrothermal reservoir
An underground zone of porous rock containing hot water.

Hygiene
The science of health and its preservation.

Hyperaccumulators
The plants containing extremely large amounts of certain chemical elements (frequently metals or metallic compounds).

Hyperallometry
For ontogenetic allometry, when the organ has a higher growth rate than the body as whole, a > 1; for static/evolutionary allometry, when an organ is proportionally larger in larger individuals/species.

Hyperbolic
Having the shape of a hyperbola, a particular form of curve whose two 'arms' diverge and never rejoin.

Hypermorphosis
An evolutionary increase in the duration of ontogenetic development, resulting in features that are exaggerated compared to those of the ancestor.

Hypertext
Generally any text in a file that contains words, phrases, or graphics that, when clicked, cause another document to be retrieved and displayed. Hypertext most often appears blue and underlined in Web pages.

Hypnology
The study of sleep.

Hypostatic gene
Gene that is masked or suppressed by the action of a gene at a different locus.

Hypoxia
An environmental condition in which the concentration of oxygen is lower than normally found in the environment.

Hyprotech systems process modeling software by aspentech
It is used for steady state simulation; design; performance monitoring; optimization and business planning for oil & gas production; gas processing and petroleum refining industries.

Hysteresis
The difference in output when the measurand value is first approached with increasing and then with decreasing values. Expressed in percent of full scale during any one calibration cycle. See also Deadband.

Hysteresis (electrode memory)
When an electrode system is returned to a solution, equilibrium is usually not immediate. This phenomenon is often observed in electrodes that have been exposed to the other influences such as temperature, light, or polarization.

I kappa B transcription inhibitor
A protein that interacts with NF-kappaB in the cytoplasm, ensuring its partner does not homodimerize. When phosphorylated, I-kappaB releases NF-kappaB, which can then homodimerize and initiate downstream transcriptional events.

I/o - input output
Term used for signals entering (Inputs) and exiting (Outputs) a control system.

Ichthyology
The study of fish.

Icon
A graphic functional symbol display. A graphic representation of a function or functions to be performed by the computer.

Iconography
Teaching with aid of pictures & models.

Iconology
The study of symbolic representations.

Icp
Integrated Circuit Piezoelectric; term sometimes used to describe an accelerometer with built-in electronics.

Id protein
A helix-loop-helix containing protein that can inhibit differentiation of muscle. Id proteins lack the DNA binding domain common to this class of proteins. Thus, when they heterodimerize to other transcription factors, they do not allow for interaction with DNA and inhibit subsequent transcription.

Ideal gas
One which obeys the ideal gas law. At low pressures, real gases behave like ideas gases.

Identical by descent
Of two or more gene copies, being derived from a single gene copy in a specified common ancestor of the organisms that carry the copies.

Identical twins
Twins that arise when a single egg fertilized by a single sperm splits into two separate embryos.

Identity
When two (or more) genetic sequences are exactly the same.

Idiogram
A diagram of chromosomal morphology, particularly depicting the banding patterns of specific chromosomes.

Igneous rock
Rock that has crystallised from a molten state (magma).

Illuminated (back/front)
Describes a type of electromagnetic wave detector. In solid-state detectors such as CCD silicon chips, the electrodes are all laid on one face of the chip. The incoming X-rays, for example, can enter the silicon detector either on the electrode (front-illuminated) side or the rear (back-illuminated) surface of the detector.

Image
(1) Figure formed by rays of light or other electromagnetic radiation at a mirror's focal plane.
(2) A picture obtained by a telescope, camera, or other imaging device.

Imager
A device for producing an image.

Imaging
Making an image.

Immigration
The movement of individuals into a population or population area.

Immunogenicity
The capacity to elicit an immune response, such as the production of specific antibodies.

Immunoglobulin gene
A gene that encodes the basic functional unit of an antibody, an immunoglobulin.

Immunoglobulins
A class of proteins, with a characteristic structure, active as receptors and effectors in the immune system.

Immunohistochemistry
A set of methods for using an antibody to detect the presence and distribution of a protein in a tissue.

Impedance
The total opposition to electrical flow (resistive plus reactive).

Impermeable layer
A layer of solid material, such as rock or clay, which does not allow water to pass through.

Imprinting
In genetics, the differential modification of a gene depending on whether it is present in a male or a female. In animal behaviour, a rapid form of learning in which an animal comes to make a particular response, which is maintained for life, to some object or other organism.

In situ hybridization
Method used to determine the chromocomal loocation of a gene or other specific DNA fragment or the tissue distribution of an mRNA by using a labeled probe that is complementary to the sequence of interest.

In vitro fertilization
The process in which an oocyte is fertilized by sperm in a laboratory setting.

Inborn error of metabolism
Heritable disorder of an organism's biochemistry.

Inbred strain
A group of organisms that are homozygous at every locus.

Inbreeding
The mating of closely related individuals.

Inbreeding coefficient
Measure of inbreeding; the probability (ranging from 0 to 1) that two alleles are identical by descent.

Inbreeding depression
Decreased fitness arising from inbreeding; often due to the increased expression of lethal and deleterious recessive traits.

Inclination angle
The angle between the rotation axis of a planet and the perpendicular to the ecliptic plane.

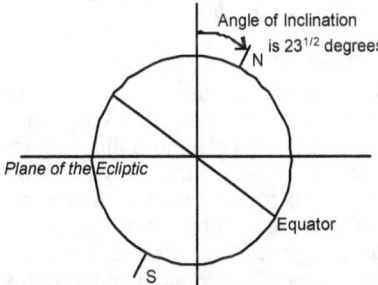

Inclusive fitness
The fitness of a gene or genotype as measured by its effect on the survival or reproduction of both the organism bearing it and the genes, identical by descent, borne by the organism's relatives.

Incoloy
A nickel-chromium alloy. It is noted for good strength and excellent resistance to oxidation and carburisation in high-temperature atmospheres.

Incomplete dominance
It refers to the phenotype of a heterozygote that is intermediate between the phenotypes of the two homozygotes.

Incomplete linkage
Linkage between genes that exhibit some crossing over; intermediate in its effects between independent assortment and complete linkage.

Incomplete penetrance
Refers to a genotype that does not always express the expected phenotype. Some individuals possess the genotype for a trait but do not express the phenotype.

Inconel
A nickel-chromium-iron alloy. It is noted for having high temperature strength while maintaining excellent corrosion resistance.

Incorporated error
Incorporation of a damaged nucleotide or mismatched base pair into a DNA molecule.

Independent assortment
Independent separation of chromosome pairs in anaphase I of meiosis; contributes to genetic variation.

Indigenous species
A species that is native to a give area if its presence was obtained by natural processes.

Indirect benefits
Benefits gained by females from their choice of mate and affect the female through the fitness of her progeny.

Indirect development
A life history consisting of a larval stage between embryo and adult stages.

Indirect fitness
Gene copies contributed by an individual to the next generation in the form of non-offspring, usually kin (e.g., siblings, nieces).

Indirect selection
A covariance between a trait and fitness within a generation that is caused by a phenotypic correlation between that trait and another trait that experiences direct selection.

Individual selection
A form of natural selection consisting of nonrandom differences among different genotypes (or phenotypes) within a population in their contribution to subsequent generations.

Induced mutation
The results from environmental agents, such as chemicals or radiation.

Inducer
The substance that stimulates transcription in an inducible system of gene regulation; usually a small molecule that binds to a repressor protein and alters that repressor so that it can no longer bind to DNA and inhibit transcription.

Inducible operon
Operon or other system of gene regulation in which transcription is normally off. Something must happen for transcription to be induced, or turned on.

Induction
Stimulation of the synthesis of an enzyme by an environmental factor, often the presence of a particular substrate.

Industrial melanism
The increase in frequency of dark (melanic) pigmentation in insects as an adaptation to remain inconspicuous on surfaces darkened by soot from air pollution.

Industrial water use
Water used for industrial purposes in such industries as steel, chemical, paper, and petroleum refining. Nationally, water for industrial uses comes mainly (80%) from self-supplied sources, such as a local wells or withdrawal points in a river, but some water comes from public-supplied sources, such as the county/city water department.

Inertia
Tendency of a body to remain at rest or move in straight line.

Infectious disease
An illness that can be passed from one individual to another.

Infiltration
Flow of water from the land surface into the subsurface.

Inflationary universe
A model of the early evolution of the Universe involving its exponential expansion. This hypothetical phase in the evolution of the early Universe has been introduced to account for the observed isotropy of the Universe on a large scale and the fact that its density is within a factor of ten of the critical density. In the most popular version of the theory, the exponential expansion is associated with a phase change which occurred about 10^{-34} seconds after the beginning of the Big Bang. According to grand unified theories of elementary particles, the strong force decoupled from the electroweak force (a force which unifies the electromagnetic and weak nuclear forces) at this time. This event released enormous energy, stored until then in the vacuum of space-time. This scenario can account for the present vast extent of the Universe and its uniformity.

Inflorescences
A group or cluster of flowers arranged on a stem that is composed of a main

In-frame deletion
Deletion of some multiple of three nucleotides, which does not alter the reading frame of the gene.

In-frame insertion
Insertion of some multiple of three nucleotides, which does not alter the reading frame of the gene.

Infrared
An area in the electromagnetic spectrum extending beyond red light from 760 nanometers to 1000 microns (106 nm). It is the form of radiation used for making non-contact temperature measurements.

Infrared astronomical satellite (IRAS)
A UK-Dutch-US infrared satellite launched in 1983. It had a lifetime of 10 months and is considered to be the first infrared satellite.

Infrared light
Infrared radiation (or infrared light) is invisible to the human eye, but can be sensed as 'heat', or thermal radiation. Even cold objects emit infrared radiation. It has a wavelength between 7000 Angstroms (less than a micron) and several hundred microns. Only a small fraction of the infrared light coming from astronomical objects can go through the Earth's atmosphere: to detect the full range of infrared wavelengths a space telescope is needed. Cold and dusty astronomical objects - such as planets, asteroids or star forming regions - are best observed with infrared telescopes. ESA's Infrared Space Observatory (ISO), operating at wavelengths from 2.5 to 240 microns, could observe objects that remain hidden for optical telescopes. The next ESA infrared space telescope, Herschel, will peer even deeper into these objects.

Infrared Space Observatory (ISO) mission
ESA scientific mission focusing on infrared astronomy.

Inhabitational
One organisms living wholly or partly inside the other.

Inherit
The process by which offspring acquire genetic material from their parents.

Inheritance
The features of an organism are determined by a set of chromosomes. These originate in the parents and are passed on to an offspring during fertilisation. It follows then that since chromosomes are inherited, all the features of an organism must be inherited.

Inheritance of acquired characteristics
Early notion of gene transmission proposing that acquired traits are passed to descendants.

Inhibition
When one species, or a group of species colonizes a disturbed area, and subsequently alters the environment of that area (by altering soil nutrients, light accessibility, or water availability), making it less habitable for later successional species.

Inhibition succession model
Where the species that arrive first dominate until a disturbance removes them.

Initial unbalance
Initial unbalance is that unbalance of any kind that exists in the rotor before balancing.

Initiation codon
The codon in mRNA that specifies the first amino acid (fMet in bacterial cells; Met in eukaryotic cells) of a protein; most commonly AUG.

Initiation factor 1
Protein required for the initiation of translation in bacterial cells; enhances the dissociation of the large and small subunits of the ribosome.

Initiation factor 2
Protein required for the initiation of translation in bacterial cells; forms a complex with GTP and the charged initiator protein and then delivers the charged tRNA to the initiation complex.

Initiation factor 3
Protein required for the initiation of translation in bacterial cells; binds to the small subunit of the ribosome and prevents the large subunit from binding during initiation.

Initiator protein
Binds to an origin of replication and unwinds a short stretch of DNA, allowing helicase and other single-strand binding proteins to bind and initiate replication.

Injection (into orbit)
The placing of a satellite into its required orbit or trajectory.

Injection well
refers to a well constructed for the purpose of injecting treated wastewater directly into the ground. Wastewater is generally forced (pumped) into the well for dispersal or storage into a designated aquifer. Injection wells are generally drilled into aquifers that don't deliver drinking water, unused aquifers, or below freshwater levels.

Input impedance
The resistance of a panel metre as seen from the source. In the case of a voltmeter, this resistance has to be taken into account when the source impedance is high; in the case of an ammeter, when the source impedance is low.

Input resistance (impedance)
The input resistance of a pH metre is the resistance between the glass electrode terminal and the reference electrode terminal. The potential of a pH-measuring electrode chain is always subject to a voltage division between the total electrode resistance and the input resistance.

Insect
An animal with three main body parts and six legs. Ants are one kind of insect found in the rain forest.

Insertion
A mutation that occurs when one or more base pairs is added to a DNA sequence.

Insertion sequence
Simple type of transposable element found in bacteria and their plasmids that contains only the information necessary for its own movement.

Instrument
Apparatus capable of registering information with a precise objective. A science spacecraft can carry several instruments such as cameras, spectrographs, magnetometers, gas analysers, etc.

Insulation resistance

Ipts-68

International Practical Temperature Scale of 1968. Fixed points in thermometry set by the 1968 General Conference of Weights and Measures.

Ir 35

Term given to UK legislation which aims to remove opportunities for the avoidance of tax and Class 1 National Insurance Contributions by the use of intermediaries in circumstances where an individual worker would otherwise be an employee of the client.

Iron-response element

A short region found in mRNAs that forms a stem-loop structure and is bound by iron-response proteins. The presence of iron can mediate changes in mRNA stability and therefore increase (high iron) or decrease (low iron) translation from IRE containing mRNAs.

Irrigation

the controlled application of water for agricultural purposes through manmade systems to supply water requirements not satisfied by rainfall.

Irrigation water use

water application on lands to assist in the growing of crops and pastures or to maintain vegetative growth in recreational lands, such as parks and golf courses.

Island model

The simplest model of gene flow, in which a proportion of migrants are exchanged between discrete subpopulations in each generation.

Iso 9001

A quality assurance standard issued by the International Organization for Standards. Standard is titled; Quality systems - Model for quality assurance in design/development, production, installation and servicing.

Isoaccepting trnas

Different tRNAs with different anticodons that specify the same amino acid.

Isolating barrier

A genetically determined difference between populations that restricts or prevents gene flow between them. The term does not include spatial segregation by extrinsic geographic or topographic barriers.

Isolation

The reduction of the capacity of a system to respond to an external force by use of resilient isolating materials.

Isomer

Chemical compounds with the same composition but different shapes.

Isomeric structure

The shape of a molecule. The isomeric structure is determined by the order in which the atoms are bonded together.

Isometry for ontogenetic allometry

When an organ grows at the same rate as the rest of the body, a = 1, such an organ maintains a constant proportionate size (but not absolute size) throughout development; for static/evolutionary allometry, when an organ is proportionally the same size in larger and small individuals/species.

Isopotential point

A potential which is not affected by temperature changes. It is the pH value at which dE/dt for a given electrode pair is zero. Normally, for a glass electrode and SCE reference, this potential is obtained approximately when immersed in pH 7 buffer.

Isostasy
The vertical readjustment of the surface of the earth due to the addition or removal of weight. Commonly associated with the advance and retreat of glacial ice.

Isothermal
A process or area that is a constant temperature.

Isotope
A chemical element is characterised by the number of protons in its atomic nucleus. Isotopes are atoms of the same element, i.e. with the same number of protons, but with different numbers of neutrons. Isotopes have the same atomic number but differ in their mass number.

Isotopic labeling
Use of radioisotopes to label biomolecules, enabling scientists to investigate them in cells or tissue.

Isotropy
Having the same value of some physical property (e.g., density) when measured in any direction.

Isozymes
Different forms of the same enzyme. Commonly used as genetic markers, especially between 1970 and 1990. The term isozyme is often used interchangeably with allozyme.

Iteroparity/polycarpy
Life histories characterized by reproducing repeatedly.

Iteroparous
Pertaining to a life history in which individuals reproduce more than once.

Insulator
DNA sequence that blocks or insulates the effect of an enhancer; must be located between the enhancer and the promoter to have blocking activity; also may limit the spread of changes in chromatin structure.

Insulin
The gene that encodes a hormone synthesized in islet cells of the pancreas that promotes the conversion of glucose into the storage material, glycogen.

Insurance hypothesis
If more species are present (i.e., diversity is higher), then there is a greater chance that at least one of the species will maintain functioning during disturbance or stress, compensating for other species that experience declines.

Integral
A form of temperature control.

Integral mission
International Gamma-Ray Astrophysics Laboratory. ESA's gamma-ray observatory due for launch in October 2002.

Integrase
Enzyme that inserts prophage, or proviral, DNA into a chromosome.

Integrated pollution prevention and control
EU directive 96/61/EC of 1996 which aims to minimise pollution from various point sources throughout the European Union.

Integrated safe system of work
An electronic system designed to improve and enhance paper-based Permit to Work (PTW) systems. Widely used in the UK North Sea.

Integrated service contract
A contract likely to include design and project services; maintenance; upgrades as well as reliability and integrity management.

Integration (satellite, instrument)
Construction phase for a satellite, instrument or piece of equipment, when its constituent parts are assembled.

Integrative levels of organization
The idea that matter is arrayed in orders of increasing complexity, and that at each level, there are emergent properties such that the higher level cannot be reduced to the lower.

Interaction
Strictly, the dependence of an outcome on a combination of causal factors, such that the outcome is not predictable from the average effects of the factors taken separately. More loosely, an interplay between entities that affects one or more of them (as in interactions between species).

Intercalated
Inserted between two other things.

Intercalating agent
The chemical substance that is about the same size as a nucleotide and may become sandwiched between adjacent bases in DNA, distorting the three-dimensional structure of the helix and causing single-nucleotide insertions and deletions in replication.

Interchangeability error
A measurement error that can occur if two or more probes are used to make the same measurement. It is caused by a slight variation in characteristics of different probes.

Interchromosomal recombination
The recombination among genes on different chromosomes.

Interdemic selection
The third phase of the shifting balance theory, in which subpopulations (demes) at higher adaptive peaks export migrants to subpopulations at lower adaptive peaks, causing the lower-fitness subpopulations to evolve toward the higher peak.

Interface
The means by which two systems or devices are connected and interact with each other.

Interference
The degree to which one crossover interferes with additional crossovers.

Interferometer
Measurement device in which a beam of electromagnetic radiation is split and subsequently recombined after travelling different pathlengths so that the beams interfere and produce an interference pattern. This pattern can be used to measure a wide variety of physical parameters.

Interferometry
Experimental technique making use of an interferometer to measure a physical parameter.

Intergenic suppressor mutation
It occurs in a gene (locus) that is different from the gene containing the original mutation.

Interkinesis
The period between meiosis I and meiosis II.

Intermediate disturbance hypothesis
It predicts that intermediate frequency or intensity of disturbance will maximize diversity.

Internal promoter
It is located within the sequences of DNA that are transcribed into RNA.

Internal reference electrode (Element)
The reference electrode placed internally in a glass electrode.

International atomic energy agency
It works for the safe secure and peaceful uses of nuclear science and technology.

International electrotechnical commission
The body composed of 60 plus countries that issues standards for all electrical electronic and related technology.

International ultraviolet explorer (IUE) emission
ESA scientific mission focusing on ultraviolet astronomy.

Interphase
The period in the cell cycle between the cell divisions. In interphase, the cell grows, develops, and prepares for cell division.

Interplanetary voyage
The journey of a spacecraft through the planets of the Solar System.

Interpreter
A system programme that converts and executes each instruction of a high-level language programme into machine code as it runs, before going onto the next instruction.

Interrupt
To stop a process in such a way that it can be resumed.

Interspecific interactions
The competition between members of different species.

Interspersed repeat sequences
Repeated sequences at multiple locations throughout the genome.

Interstellar
Between celestial objects; often refers to matter in space that is not a star, such as clouds of dust and gas.

Intrachromosomal recombination
Recombination among genes located on the same chromosome.

Intragenic mapping
Mapping the locations of mutations within a single locus.

Intragenic suppressor mutation
It occurs in the same gene (locus) as the mutation that it suppresses.

Intrasexual selection
Competition between members of the same sex (usually males) for access to mates.

Intraspecific competition
Competition for resources between individuals of two or more species.

Intrinsic hypothesis
When expected proportions of individuals with the observed characteristics are calculated after the experiment is done using a specific piece of required data.

Intrinsic rate of natural increase
The number of births minus the number of deaths per generation time.

Intrinsic rate of natural increase
The potential per capita rate of increase of a population with a stable age distribution whose growth is not depressed by the negative effects of density.

Intrinsic safety
Method of explosion prevention by limiting the energy stored in electrical circuits.

Intrinsically safe
An instrument which will not produce any spark or thermal effects under normal or abnormal conditions that will ignite a specified gas mixture.

Introduced species
A species that originated in a different region that becomes established in a new region, often due to deliberate or accidental release by humans.

Introgression
1. The permanent incorporation of genes from one set of differentiated populations (species, subspecies, races and so on) into another.
2. Movement of genes from one species or population into another by hybridization and backcrossing; carries the implication that some genes in a genome undergo such movement, but others do not.

Intron
Introns are non-coding sections of an RNA transcript, or the DNA encoding it, which are spliced out, or removed, before the RNA molecule is translated into a protein.

Invasion biology
The study of species that become invasive in a system and their impacts on the system they have invaded, as well as the remediation of such invasions.

Invasive species
Non-native species that increase rapidly in numbers and that have negative impacts on native species.

Inversion
A 180° reversal of the orientation of a part of a chromosome, relative to some standard chromosome.

Inversion stock
A line of organisms, usually Drosophila, that maintain a balancer chromosome. The presence of a specific balancer chromosome inhibits crossing over, allowing investigators to retain lines of animals that are heterozygous for a specific mutation without screening each generation for the phenotype.

Inverted repeats
Sequences on the same strand that are inverted and complementary.

Ion
Atom with an unbalanced electrical charge caused by the loss or gain of one or more electrons.

Ionic bond
An bond formed by the electro-magnetic attraction between ions of opposite charge.

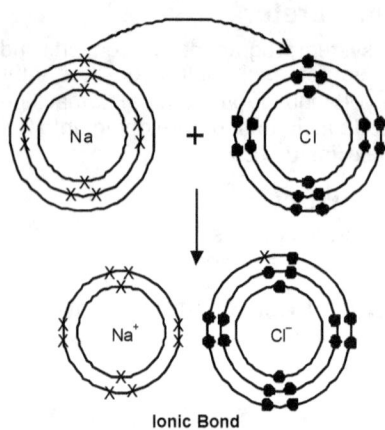

Ionic Bond

Ionic mobility
Defined similarly to the mobility of nonelectrolytic particles, viz., as the speed that the ion obtains in a given solvent when influenced by unit power.

Ionic strength
The weight concentration of ions in solution, computed by multiplying the concentration of each ion in solution (C) by the corresponding square of the charge on the ion (Z) summing this product for all ions in solution and dividing by 2:ionic strength - 1/2 _ Z2 C.

Ip number
Internet Protocol number. A unique number consisting of four parts separated by dots, for example 129.237.247.243. This is the number assigned to a host machine which is retrieved by a DNS when a request for an Internet site is made. These numbers usually correspond to unique domain names, which are easier for people to remember.

Ipts-48
International Practical Temperature Scale of 1948. Fixed points in thermometry as specified by the Ninth

J

J' of peiou
An index used to describe species evenness, the distribution of abundance across species in a community.

Joint venture
A collaboration between two or more companies in a contract.

Joule
The basic unit of thermal energy.

Journal
A journal is that part of a rotor that is in contact with or supported by a bearing in which it revolves.

JPG or JPEG
An efficient method for storing graphic files for transmission across phone lines. Unlike GIF files, JPG files lose a little data when the image is converted, and their files are often much larger than GIFs. However, JPGs are your best choice for photographic images.

Jump dispersal
When individuals of a species travel a relatively long distance to a new environment in which they did not previously occur.

Jun oncogene
A transcription factor that works with fos to initiate transcription of many genes, particularly in response to growth factor signaling. When c-Jun is constitutively expressed, it can cause cellular transformation.

Junction
The point in a thermocouple where the two dissimilar metals are joined.

Junctional diversity
Addition or deletion of nucleotides at the junctions of gene segments brought together in the somatic recombination of genes that encode antibodies and T-cell receptors.

Jupiter
The fifth planet out from the Sun and the first and largest of the gas giants. Jupiter is 5.2 AU away from the Sun, has a mass 318 times that of the Earth and could hold 1400 'Earths' in its volume. It is mainly composed of hydrogen and helium but has a small core of rock and ice.

Jurisprudence
The science of law.

K

K
When referring to memory capacity, two to the tenth power (1024 in decimal notation).

Karyotype
Picture of an individual organism's complete set of metaphase chromosomes.

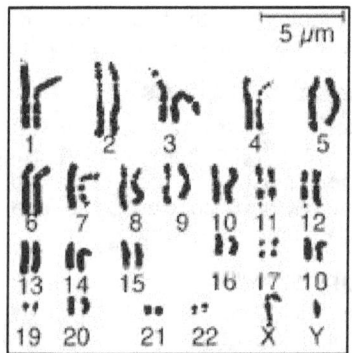

K-band
A band of radio frequencies extending from 10 900 to 36 000 MHz.

Kelvin
The Kelvin (K) is the unit of the absolute temperature scale, in which the temperature of the triple point of water (the temperature at which water can exist simultaneously in solid, liquid and gaseous form) assumes the value of 273.16 K. Kelvin can be converted to degrees Celsius by subtracting 273.15.

Key adaptation
An adaptation that provides the basis for using a new, substantially different habitat or resource.

Keystone species
Species that have effects on communities that far exceed their abundance.

Kilobyte (KB)
A thousand bytes. Due to the binary nature of computers, it's 2^{10} bytes, technically 1024 bytes.

Kilogram
One thousand grams.

Kilowatt (kw)
Equivalent to 1000 watts.

Kilowatthour (KWH)
A power demand of 1,000 watts for one hour. Power company utility rates are typically expressed in rupees per kilowatt-hour.

Kin selection
A form of selection whereby alleles differ in their rate of propagation by influencing the impact of their bearers on the reproductive success of individuals (kin) who carry the same alleles by common descent.

Kin structure
Genetic relationships within a social group.

Kinetic energy
Energy associated with mass in motion, i.e., 1/2 rV2 where r is the density of the moving mass and V is its velocity.

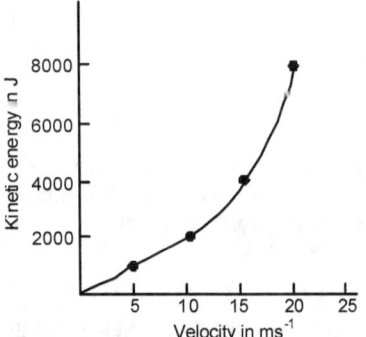

Kinetochore
The set of proteins that assemble on the centromere, providing the point of attachment for spindle microtubules.

Klinefelter syndrome
Human condition in which cells contain one or more Y chromosomes along with multiple X chromosomes (most commonly XXY but may also be XXXY, XXXXY, or XXYY). Persons with Klinefelter syndrome are male in appearance but frequently possess small testes, some breast enlargement, and reduced facial and pubic hair; often taller than normal and sterile, most have normal intelligence.

Knockout
An organism in which the normal gene expression at a given locus (or sometimes multiple loci) has been disrupted. Therefore, this organism has little or no expression of the RNA or protein encoded by this gene.

Knockout mouse
A knockout mouse is a laboratory mouse in which a gene or genes have been turned off or knocked out.

Kourou
Coastal town of French Guiana, just north of the Equator, where France created a launch site in 1964. Since 1977, the site has been exclusively devoted to the Ariane launchers, developed by the European Space Agency and commercially operated by Ariane-Space Agency.

Kruppel transcription factor
A gap protein that has four tandemly repeated zinc finger domains.

K-selection
A form of selection that occurs in an environment at or near carrying capacity, favoring a reproductive strategy in which few offspring are produced.

Kuiper belt
Spherical region of the outer Solar System populated by numerous 'ice dwarfs', otherwise known as Kuiper Belt Objects or trans-Neptunian objects. Several hundred of these have so far been discovered. The planet Pluto appears to be the largest of these objects. The belt seems to occur at 30 - 150 AU from the Sun and is believed to be the source of short-period comets. Named after Dutch-American astronomer Gerard Kuiper who predicted its existence. Also known as the Edgeworth-Kuiper Belt, in recognition of the work of another (Irish) scientist, Kenneth Edgeworth.

L

L1
One of three hybrid crosses used to detect linkage. In the absence of linkage, the progeny distribution in the F3 (F2 x F2) or L1 generation is identical to that in the F2 (F1 x F1) generation.

L2
One of three hybrid crosses used to detect linkage. In the absence of linkage the progeny distribution in the L2 (F2 x P1) generation is identical to that in the B1 (F1 x P1) generation.

L3
One of three hybrid crosses used to detect linkage. In the absence of linkage, the progeny distribution in the L3 (F2 x P2) generation is identical to that in the B2 (F1 x P2) generation.

Lag
1. A time delay between the output of a signal and the response of the instrument to which the signal is sent.
2. A time relationship between two waveforms where a fixed reference point on one wave occurs after the same point of the reference wave.

Lagging strand
DNA strand that is replicated discontinuously.

Lagrangian points
Points where the gravitational forces of three different massive bodies exactly cancel. For the Sun-Earth-Moon system we have five different Lagrange points, known as L1, L2, L3, L4 and L5.

Lahar
A torrential flow of water-saturated volcanic debris down the slope of a volcano in response to gravity. A type of mudflow.

Lamarckism
The theory that evolution is caused by inheritance of character changes acquired during the life of an individual due to its behaviour or to environmental influences.

Laminar flow
Streamlined flow of a fluid where viscous forces are more significant than inertial forces, generally below a Reynolds number of 2000.

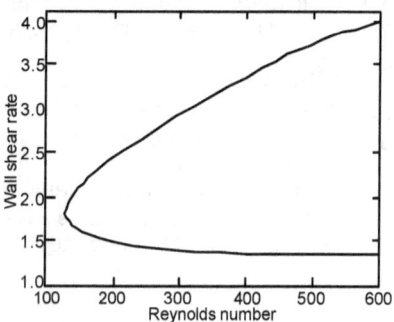

Lan
Local Area Network.

Basic LAN Topology

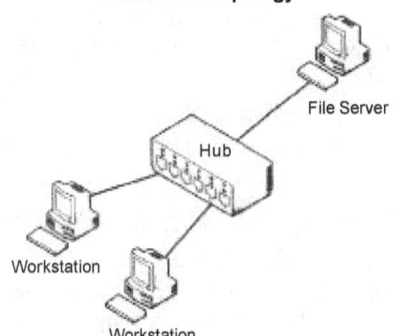

Lander
A small spacecraft designed to land on another solar system body.

Landrace
Domesticated crop plant or livestock that has adaptations specific to the local environment in which it evolved.

Landscape ecolgy
The study of the pattern and interaction between ecosystems within a region of interest, and the way the interactions affect ecological processes, especially the unique effects of spatial heterogeneity on those interactions.

Langley
The unit of solar energy relating to the amount which reaches a specific area of the earth's surface. In general, more "langleys" reach the surface of the earth at the equator than at the poles.

Lapilli
Literally, "little stones;" round to angular rock fragments measuring 1/10 inch to 2-1/2 inches in diameter, which may be ejected in either a solid or molten state.

Large ribosomal subunit
The larger of the two subunits of a functional ribosome.

Large scale integration (lsi)
The combining of about 1,000 to 10,000 circuits on a single chip. Typical examples of LSI circuits are memory chips and microprocessor.

Lariat
1. A structure formed during splicing.
2. Looplike structure created in the splicing of nuclear pre-mRNA in which the 5' end of an intron is attached to a branch point in pre-mRNA.

Latch
Mechanical device that attaches one component, such as a science instrument, to the structure of the telescope and holds it in precisely the right place.

Latent heat
Expressed in BTU per pound. The amount of heat needed (absorbed) to convert a pound of boiling water to a pound of steam.

Latitudinal gradient
For most taxa, as one moves away from the equator, the number of species declines.

Launch window
The time period within which a spacecraft or rocket must be launched in order to achieve the desired orbit or rendezvous.

Launcher
Powered vehicle used to carry one or more satellites into space.

Lava
Magma which has reached the surface through a volcanic eruption.

The term is most commonly applied to streams of liquid rock that flow from a crater or fissure. It also refers to cooled and solidified igneous rock.

Lava flow
An outpouring of lava onto the surface from a vent or fissure. Also, a solidified tongue-like or sheet-like body formed by outpouring lava.

Lava tube
A tunnel formed when the surface of a mafic lava flow cools and solidifies, while the still-molten interior flows through and drains away. These can insulate the flow and allow it to travel great distances.

Laws of Themodynamics
1. The amount of energy in the universe is fixed. It cannot be created or destroyed only changed from one state to another.
2. Heat cannot pass from a cold to a hot body. The opposite condition where heat always flows from a hot to a cold body is valid for the whole universe.

Law of Thermodynamics

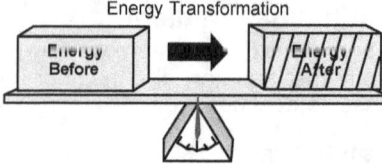

Energy Transformation

Layers of protection analysis
A semi-quantitative risk analysis technique. LOPA results are intended to be conservative (overestimating the risk) and usually adequate to understand the required safety integrity level.

Leaching
the process by which soluble materials in the soil, such as salts, nutrients, pesticide, chemicals or contaminants, are washed into a lower layer of soil or are dissolved and carried away by water.

Leader of mrna
The 5' untranslated region (UTR) of an mRNA molecule.

Leading oil & gas industry competitiveness
An industry funded organisation that works with companies throughout the O&G industry to stimulate collaboration and improve competitiveness.

Leading strand
DNA strand that is replicated continuously.

Leaf
A leaf is an organ of a vascular plant, as defined in botanical terms, and in particular in plant morphology. Foliage is a mass noun that refers to leaves as a feature of plants.

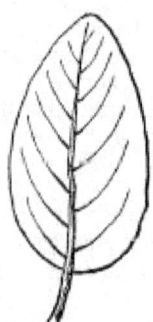

Leakage rate
The maximum rate at which a fluid is permitted or determined to leak through a seal. The type of fluid, the differential Limits of Error: A tolerance band for the thermal electric response of thermocouple wire expressed in degrees or percentage defined by ANSI specification MC-96.1 (1975).

Leaky mutation
When a mutation does not cause a complete loss of function of the wild-type gene.

Least-squares Line
The straight line for which the sum of the squares of the residuals (deviations) is minimized.

Leeward
The side facing away from the wind. When speaking of a mountain range, these areas are generally hotter and drier than on the windward side.

Lek
An aggregation of males for the purpose of performing mating displays.

Lens
Transparent optical element or assembly with either a concave or convex surface, which refracts light to form an image.

Lentic waters
Ponds or lakes (standing water).

Leonids
Meteor shower which occurs around 17 November each year. The meteors appear to radiate from the constellation of Leo. They are caused by dust grains along the orbit of periodic comet Tempel-Tuttle which burn up when they enter the Earth's upper atmosphere. Spectacular displays may occur at approximately 33-year intervals, with the last 'storm' taking place in 1966.

Leptons
Fundamental particles that are relatively non-reactive and capable of an independent existence: electrons, muons, tau particles and neutrinos.

Leptotene
First substage of prophase I in meiosis. In leptotene, chromosomes contract and become visible.

Lethal allele
An allele (usually recessive) that causes virtually complete mortality, usually early in development.

Lethal effect
Effects within a community that occur when predators consume lower trophic levels.

Leucine zipper
A common name for a secondary structural motif in proteins that occurs when two alpha helices interact through leucine amino acids that are located at a specific position in the repeated sequence of amino acids that forms the two helices. The leucine residues interact along the hydrophobic core of the zipper.

Levee
A natural or manmade earthen barrier along the edge of a stream, lake, or river. Land alongside rivers can be protected from flooding by levees.

Lexicography
General lexicography focuses on the design, compilation, use and evaluation of general dictionaries, i.e. dictionaries that provide a description of the language in general use. Such a dictionary is usually called a general dictionary or LGP dictionary (Language for General Purpose). Specialized lexicography focuses on the design, compilation, use and evaluation of specialized dictionaries, i.e. dictionaries that are devoted to a (relatively restricted) set of linguistic and factual elements of one or more specialist subject fields, e.g. legal lexicography. Such a dictionary is

usually called a specialized dictionary or LSP dictionary and following Nielsen 1994, specialized dictionaries are either multi-field, single-field or sub-field dictionaries.

LHV
The heating value is defined as the amount of energy released when a fuel is burned completely in a steady-flow process and the products are returned to the state of the reactants. The heating value is dependent on the phase of water/steam in the combustion products. When H2O is in vapour form the heating value is called LHV (Lower Heating Value).

Lianas
Any of various long-stemmed, woody vines that are rooted in the soil at ground level and use trees, as well as other means of vertical support, to climb up to the canopy in order to get access to well-lit areas of the forest.

Lichens
Composite organisms consisting of a symbiotic association of a fungus with a photosynthetic partner.

Life cycle
The minimum number of pressure cycles the transducer can endure and still remain within a specified tolerance.

Lifestyle
The way of living of a certain individual. Complex concept that includes a person's living environment, eating habits, and exercise.

Lifting operations and lifting equipment regulations
The UK regulations that aim to reduce risks to people's health and safety from lifting equipment provided for use at work.

Light
All electromagnetic radiation can be called light. However, the term 'light' is commonly used for the electromagnetic radiation that the human eye can detect, that is, the 'visible' or 'optical' light.

Light elements
The chemical elements produced during the first minutes of existence of the Universe. They are helium, deuterium (an isotope of hydrogen), lithium, beryllium and boron. They are called 'light elements' because their nuclei are made of just a few nuclear particles, and thus their mass is very low. The other elements - those produced in the core of stars - are 'heavier'; iron, for instance, has 26 protons in its nucleus.

Light use efficiency
The efficiency of using light to fix carbon (i.e., the proportion of light absorbed that is eventually converted to biomass).

Lightning
Sudden high-current discharge caused by a planet atmosphere's electrical breakdown.

Light-year (LY)
The distance travelled by light through space in one year. 1 light-year (ly) equals about 9.5 million million kilometres (= 0.3066 parsecs = 63240 AU = a parallax of 3.259 arcsecs).

Limits of error
A tolerance band for the thermal electric response of thermocouple wire expressed in degrees or percentage defined by ANSI specification MC-96.1.

Limnology
The study of freshwater life.

Line
A pure-breeding group of organisms.

Line (absorption)
Absorption spectra are formed when continuous spectra from a star shine through a gas that absorbs only certain colours of light. The absorption spectra, therefore, look like continuous spectra with dark bands (absorption lines) at discrete wavelengths. These lines characterise the chemical composition of the gas which surrounds the star.

Line of sight
Typically used with reference to telecommunication devices.

Lineage
A series of ancestral and descendant populations through time; usually refers to a single evolving species, but may include several species descended from a common ancestor.

Lineage sorting
The process by which each of several descendant species, carrying several gene lineages inherited from a common ancestral species, acquires a single gene lineage; hence, the derivation of a monophyletic gene tree, in each species, from the paraphyletic gene tree inherited from their common ancestor.

Linear
When a sequence of DNA is in a straight line.

Linear regression
A statistical technique of finding the best fitting straight line through a set of points representing joint values for two variables.

Linearity
The closeness of a calibration curve to a specified straight line. Linearity is expressed as the maximum deviation of any calibration point on a specified straight line during any one calibration cycle.

Linkage
Genetic linkage describes how two genes that are close to one another on the same chromosome are often inherited together.

Linkage disequilibrium
1. A nonrandom relationship between the alleles present at two or more loci, which can cause a genetic correlation.
2. The association of two alleles at two or more loci more frequently (or less frequently) than predicted by their individual frequencies.

Linkage equilibrium
The association of two alleles at two or more loci at the frequency predicted by their individual frequencies.

Linkage group
Genes located together on the same chromosome.

Linkage map
A linkage map is a genetic map of a species or experimental population that shows the position of its known genes or genetic markers relative to each other in terms of recombination frequency, rather than as specific physical distance along each chromosome. Linkage mapping is critical for identifying the location of genes that cause genetic diseases.

Linked genes
Genes located on the same chromosome.

Linked loci
Loci that are on the same chromosome and that show a recombination frequency less than 0.5.

Linker DNA
Stretch of DNA separating two nucleosomes.

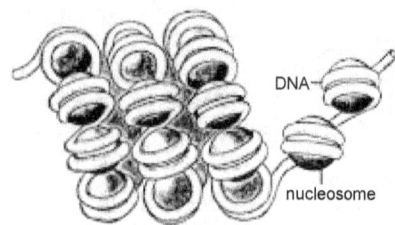

Linux
An operating system that is a UNIX clone. It was created by programmer Linus Torvalds, who gave Linux its name. Linux is under special copyright that allows anyone to improve it, but no one to profit from it.

Liquefied natural gas
The natural gas (mainly methane) refrigerated to reach liquid phase suitable for transportation in specialised vessels or by pipeline.

Liquefied petroleum gas
The butane and propane mixture separated from well fluid stream. LPG can be transported under pressure in refrigerated vessels.

Liquid
A form of matter that can flow easily and takes on the shape of any container into which it is poured. A liquid like milk can be poured from a square milk carton into a roundglass.

Liquid junction potential
The potential difference existing between a liquid-liquid boundary. The sign and size of this potential depends on the composition of the liquids and the type of junction used.

Listserv
A very common programme used to run a mailing list. Because it is so common, mailing lists are often called listservs, even if they are run with different software.

Lithology
The study of the characteristics of rocks.

Litter
The undecomposed plant and animal material found on the forest floor.

Livestock water use
Water used for livestock watering, feed lots, dairy operations, fish farming, and other on-farm needs.

Living thing
Something that is alive and can grow. Living things need food, water, and air.

Load
The electrical demand of a process expressed as power (watts), current (amps) or resistance (ohms).

Load impedance
The impedance presented to the output terminals of a transducer by the associated external circuitry.

Local area network
A local area network (LAN) is a computer network that interconnects computers in a limited area such as a home, school, computer laboratory, or office building. The defining characteristics of LANs, in contrast to wide area networks (WANs), include their usually higher data-transfer rates, smaller geographic area, and lack of a need for leased telecommunication lines.

Local community
A geographically defined community of place, a group of species living and interacting together.

Local extinction
When a species no longer resides in an area of habitat due to suboptimal conditions.

Local variation
Variation in secondary structure within a single molecule.

Locus
1. The position of a gene along a chromosome; often used to refer to the gene itself.
2. A site on a chromosome occupied by a specific gene; more loosely, the gene itself, in all its allelic states.

Locus control region
A cis-acting DNA element that is able to regulate gene expression from a specific region of DNA. The human beta-globin gene cluster is a leading example of genes regulated by a locus control region.

Lod score
The logarithm of the ratio of the probability of obtaining a set of observations, assuming a specified degree of linkage, to the probability of obtaining the same set of observations with independent assortment; used to assess the likelihood of linkage between genes from pedigree data.

Loess
Very fine-grained sediments deposited by wind action. Commonly associated with the margins of continental ice sheets. Large expanses of loess from the recent ice age are in large part responsible for the bountiful corn and wheat fields of the American Midwest.

Logarithmic scale
A method of displaying data (in powers of ten) to yield maximum range while keeping resolution at the low end of the scale.

Logistic equation
An equation describing the idealized growth of a population subject to a density-dependent limiting factor. As density increases, the rate of growth gradually declines until population growth stops.

Logistic population growth
The population growth that levels off as the population size approaches carrying capacity, the ceiling of its growth.

Log-log scale
A scale in which the numbers are proportional to their logarithms.

Log-odds ratio
A log-transformed ratio of likelihoods, used for statistical tests, including testing for the presence of a QTL at a particular location on a genetic map.

Long interspersed element
The long DNA sequence repeated many times and interspersed throughout the genome.

Longevity
The word "longevity" is sometimes used as a synonym for "life expectancy" in demography or known as "long life", especially when it concerns someone or something lasting longer than expected (an ancient tree, for example).

Loop resistance
The total resistance of a thermocouple circuit caused by the resistance of the thermocouple wire. Usually used in reference to analogue pyrometers which have typical loop resistance requirements of 10 ohms.

Loss-of-function mutation
It causes the complete or partial absence of normal function.

Lost time incident
Accident resulting in personnel not being able to work as a result of their injury is called an LTI.

Lotic waters
Flowing waters, as in streams and rivers.

Lotka-volterra models
The simple model that tells us that predator and prey interactions have the potential to cause population cycles, and is useful in understanding and predicting predator-prey population cycles. The model was developed independently by Lotka (1925) and Volterra (1926).

Low copy repeat
A term with variable meaning that is sometimes used synonymously with segmental duplication. It can denote a group of juxtaposed duplicons (duplication block), individual segmental duplication events, or individual duplicons. The term emphasizes the low copy number of repeats (2.50 copies) relative to most transposable elements.

Low pressure
It is often used with reference to a utility or vent line e.g. LP air supply.

Lower explosive limit
Below the LEL a mixture of substance and air lacks sufficient fuel (substance) to burn.

Lsa scale
Low Specific Activity scale found adhering to pipe and equipment internals is mainly due to radium-226 produced from the decay of naturally occurring uranium-238.

Lsd (least-significant digit)
The rightmost active (non-dummy) digit of the display.

LS-TTL compatible
For digital input circuits, a logic 1 is obtained for inputs of 2.0 to 5.5 V which can source 20 µA, and a logic 0 is obtained for inputs of 0 to 0.8 V which can sink 400 µA. For digital output signals, a logic 1 is represented by 2.4 to 5.5 V with a current source capability of at least 400 µA; and a logic 0 is represented by 0 to 0.6 V with a current sink capability of at least 16 MA. "LS" stands for low-power Schottky.

Ls-ttl unit load
A load with LS-TTL voltage levels, which will draw 20 µA for a logic 1 and -400 µA for a logic 0.

Luciferin
The substrate for a basic luminescence assay.

Luciferin/luciferase reporter system
A reporter gene assay system that allows investigators to measure biological activity after transfecting cells with the luciferase gene and conducting an experiment. Activity of the gene after experimental treatment is measured after adding luciferin and measuring luminescence.

Luminescence assay
A method to measure biological activity through a reporter construct that uses the luciferase-luciferin interaction for quantitation.

Luminosity
The amount of radiation emitted by a star or celestial object in a given time.

Lyon hypothesis
It is proposed by Mary Lyon in 1961, this hypothesis proposes that one X chromosome in each female cell becomes inactivated (a Barr body) and suggests that which X becomes

Lysogenic cycle

Life cycle of a bacteriophage in which phage genes first integrate into the bacterial chromosome and are not inactivated is random and varies from cell to cell.

Lytic cycle

Life cycle of a bacteriophage in which phage genes are transcribed and translated, new phage particles are produced, and the host cell is lysed. Phage genes are immediately transcribed and translated.

M

M
Mega; one million. When referring to memory capacity, two to the twentieth power (1,048,576 in decimal notation).

M phase
Period of active cell division; includes mitosis (nuclear division) and cytokinesis (cytoplasmic division).

Mach number
The ratio of the speed of a fluid to the speed of sound in that fluid. If the Mach number is greater than 1, the fluid is moving at a supersonic speed; if the Mach number is greater than 5, the fluid is moving at hypersonic speed.

Machine language
machine language is a system of impartible instructions executed directly by a computer's central processing unit. Each instruction performs a very specific task, typically either an operation on a unit of data (in a register or in memory, e.g. add or move), or a jump operation (deciding which instruction executes next, often conditional on the results of a previous instruction). Every executable programme is made up of a series of these atomic instructions. Machine code may be regarded as a primitive (and cumbersome) programming language or as the lowest-level representation of a compiled and/or assembled computer programme.

Macroalgae
Large algae (such as kelp), often living attached in dense beds in marine intertidal and subtidal zones.

Macroevolution
A vague term, usually meaning the evolution of substantial phenotypic changes, usually great enough to place the changed lineage and its descendants in a distinct genus or higher taxon.

Magma
Molten rock beneath the surface of the earth.

Magma chamber
The subterranean cavity containing magma. When a conduit is opened to the surface, a volcanic eruption is possible.

Magnet
A body which produces a magnetic field. All magnets are di-pole and follow the rule that like poles repel and unlike poles attract.

Magnetic field
Region around a body in which a magnetic force is detected. Fairly weak magnetic fields are generated by dynamo effects inside planets and moons. Magnetic fields more than one billion times stronger may be generated in stars and galaxies. These are capable of controlling the motion of ionised gas and even the shape of objects.

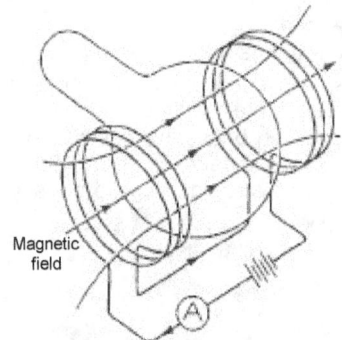

Magnetic force
One of the fundamental forces of Nature. It is a physical phenomenon which arises as a result of moving electric charge and which results in attractive and repulsive forces between objects.

Magnetometer
An instrument for measuring the magnitude and the direction of a magnetic field.

Magnetopause
The outer limit of the magnetosphere, beyond which the magnetic field of a planet is not so relevant in controlling the physical processes taking place.

Magnetoreceptors
Receptors in an organism that allow it to respond to the earth.s magnetic field.

Magnetosphere
Region surrounding a planet which contains charged particles controlled by the planet's magnetic field.

Magnitude
A numerical expression of the amount of energy released by an earthquake, determined by measuring earthquake waves on standardized recording instruments (seismographs). The number scale for magnitude is a modified logarithmic value, rather than arithmetic, and the numbers get real big, real fast; a magnitude 9 earthquake, for example, is 33 times greater than a magnitude 8 earthquake, 1089 times greater than a magnitude 7 earthquake, 35937 times greater than a magnitude 6 earthquake, and so on. The short version? Small quakes don't really do much to relieve stress in the crust.

Magnitude, absolute (M)
How bright a star would appear if it were viewed at a standard distance of 10 parsecs.

Magnitude, apparent (m)
How bright a star appears without any correction made for its distance.

Mailing list
A system that allows people to send e-mail to one address, which is then copied and sent to all of the other subscribers to the mail list. In this way, people who may be using different kinds of e-mail access can participate in discussions together.

Main oil line
Name often given to the oil export line from a platform. Often used as a

prefix to the main export pumps e.g. MOL Pumps.

Main sequence
The main sequence of stars on the Hertzsprung-Russell diagram, containing about 90% of all known stars. A star spends most of its life on the main sequence. The position of the star on the main sequence and the time it spends there depends mainly on the mass of the star.

Major gene
A gene locus responsible for a large proportion of the phenotypic variation in a trait.

Major histocompatibility complex antigen
It belongs to a large and diverse group of antigens found on the surfaces of cells that mark those cells as self; encoded by a large cluster of genes known as the major histocompatibility complex. T cells simultaneously bind to foreign and MHC antigens.

Malignant tumor
It consists of cells that are capable of invading other tissues.

Mammal
An animal that is covered with hair and feeds milk to its babies. Dogs and cats are mammals that make good pets.

Mammography
Radiography of the mammary glands.

Man machine interface
A dated term superseded by SCADA.

Man over board
Some offshore platforms issue personnel with MOB detectors when performing over the side work. These detectors automatically emit a signal when imersed in the sea thereby allowing possible faster rescue.

Mandrel
Metallic structure upon which articles to be turned are placed. Used for example in manufacturing mirrors.

Mandrel (balancing arbor)
An accurately machined shaft on which work is mounted for balancing.

Manifold
A pipe spool in which a number of incoming pipes are combined to feed to a common output line.

Mantle
Layer inside a planet or moon which lies below the crust and above the core. It is intermediate in temperature and density between these two layers. The Earth's mantle is about 2900 km thick and has an average density of $4.5 \, g/cm^3$.

Manual reset (adjustment)
The adjustment on a proportioning controller which shifts the proportioning band in relationship to

the set point to eliminate droop or offset errors.

Manual reset (switch)
The switch in a limit controller that manually resets the controller after the limit has been exceeded.

Manufacturing
Manufacturing is the use of machines, tools and labor to produce goods for use or sale. The term may refer to a range of human activity, from handicraft to high tech, but is most commonly applied to industrial production, in which raw materials are transformed into finished goods on a large scale. Such finished goods may be used for manufacturing other, more complex products, such as aircraft, household appliances or automobiles, or sold to wholesalers, who in turn sell them to retailers, who then sell them to end users – the "consumers".

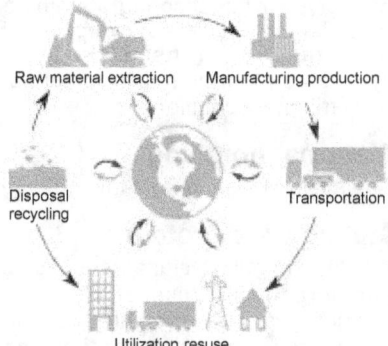

Map density
The number of markers per centimorgan on a genetic map.

Map distance
The distance between two markers on the same chromosome based on recombination frequency, usually measured in centimorgans (cM).

Map-based sequencing
The method of sequencing a genome in which sequenced fragments are ordered into contigs with the use of genetic or physical maps.

Mapping
DNA mapping describes a variety of different methods that can be used to describe the positions of genes.

Mapping population
An experimental population constructed by crossing, designed for the production of a genetic map.

Marigold
A small plant that has bright yellow or orange flowers with a strong smell. Gardeners sometimes plant marigolds because their smell helps to keep insects away from other plants.

Marker
An allele that serves as a probe to follow a specific phenotype.

Marker horizon (or bed)
A distinctive horizon which is used for regional correlation of lithology. A good marker horizon is distinctive, widespread, and represents a relatively short period of geologic time. For example, ash from a volcanic eruption, debris from a meteorite impact, etc. It is GeoMan's opinion that humans will represent one of the earth's finest marker horizons in the geologic record of the future. Our effect on the surface is certainly distinctive and widespread, and, at the rate we are going, it is likely that our species will have a relatively short lifespan (speaking in terms of geologic time, of course).

Markovian MODEL
Alternate name for a Markovian chain in which a sequence of random events

where the current state solely depends on the previous state.

Mark-recapture study
A technique in which animals are captured, marked, and released back into nature. The frequency at which they are recaptured is used to estimate survival or migration rates.

Mars
The fourth planet out from the Sun and the furthest out of the terrestrial planets. Mars is about one-tenth the mass of the Earth and has one third of its gravity. It exhibits geological features suggesting that its early history followed a similar path to that of the Earth.

Mars express mission
ESA's mission to Mars in 2003 is the first of a new type of low cost flexible mission. It will carry seven instruments plus a lander, Beagle 2. The mission will search for water, contribute to the understanding of water and atmospheric loss and the planet's internal structure and geological history, search for signs of past and present life, and map the planet in 3D at very high resolution.

Mass
The total amount of material in a body, a measure of the amount of matter. In his famous equation $E = mc^2$ Albert Einstein stated that mass (m) is equivalent to energy (E) - the two parameters are related via the speed of light (c).

Mass extinction
A highly elevated rate of extinction of species, extending over an interval that is relatively short on a geological time scale (although still very long on a human time scale).

Mass flow rate
Volumetric flowrate times density, i.e. pounds per hour or kilograms per minute.

Mass storage
A device like a disk or magtape that can store large amounts of data readily accessible to the central processing unit.

Material take off
A count of all materials needed to complete a task.

Maternal blood testing
The testing for genetic conditions in a fetus by analyzing the blood of the mother. For example, the level of -fetoprotein in maternal blood provides information about the probability that a fetus has a neural-tube defect.

Maternal effect
A nongenetic effect of a mother on the phenotype of her offspring, stemming from factors such as cytoplasmic inheritance, transmission of symbionts from mother to offspring, or nutritional conditions.

Maternal homolog
The allele of a gene from the mother.

Mating type protein
A protein that designates specific microorganisms (like yeast) as a specific "type" (equivalent to sex in higher organisms), allowing that type to mate with an individual haploid cell of the opposite mating type.

Matrix
The majority of the landscape surrounding the patches (i.e., not the patches).

Matter
A physical substance, having mass and occupying space. At its most

basic level matter consists of fundamental particles such as electrons and quarks. Quarks are the fundamental building blocks of protons and neutrons which are the components of atomic nuclei.

Maximum allowable working pressure
The maximum pressure allowed in a piece of equipment e.g. vessel or pipe at its designated temperature.

Maximum contaminant level (MCL)
The designation given by the U.S. Environmental Protection Agency (EPA) to water-quality standards promulgated under the Safe Drinking Water Act. The MCL is the greatest amount of a contaminant that can be present in drinking water without causing a risk to human health.

Maximum elongation
The strain value where a deviation of more than ±5% occurs with respect to the mean characteristic (diagram of resistance change vs strain).

Maximum excitation
The maximum value of excitation voltage or current that can be applied to the transducer at room conditions without causing damage or performance degradation beyond specified tolerances.

Maximum operating temperature
The maximum temperature at which an instrument or sensor can be safely operated.

Maximum power rating
The maximum power in watts that a device can safely handle.

Mean
The statistic that describes the centre of a distribution of measurements; calculated by dividing the sum of all measurements by the number of measurements; also called the average.

Mean annual biomass
The mean biomass of organisms in a population, group of populations, or trophic level (grams dry mass m to the -2) from samples taken throughout an entire year (e.g., from monthly samples). Other units may be used besides dry mass, such as carbon or the energy unit kilojoules).

Mean fitness
The arithmetic average fitness of all individuals in a population, usually relative to some standard.

Mean square
The sums of squares divided by the degrees of freedom (n . 1).

Mean temperature
The average of the maximum and minimum temperature of a processequilibrium.

Mean time between failures
The time interval between 2 failures of a component. The reciprocal of the failure rate.

Mean time to repair
The average time taken from the failure of a system until it is successfully restarted.

Measurand
A physical quantity, property, or condition which is measured.

Measurements (in-situ)
Measurements made in a place to sample the local environment.

Measurements (remote)
Measurement of physical and chemical parameters of a physical object from a remote location.

Measuring junction
The thermocouple junction referred to as the hot junction that is used to measure an unknown temperature.

Mechanical hysteresis
The difference of the indication with increasing and decreasing strain loading, at identical strain values of the specimen.

Medical genetics
The study of the natural history and etiology of diseases that are at least partially genetic in origin.

Medium effect (f m)
For solvents other than water the medium effect is the activity coefficient related to the standard state in water at zero concentration. It reflects differences in the electrostatic and chemical interactions of the ions with the molecules of various solvents. Solvation is the most significant interaction.

Megaspore
One of the four products of meiosis in plants.

Megasporocyte
In the ovary of a plant, a diploid reproductive cell that undergoes meiosis to produce haploid macrospores.

Meiosis
Meiosis is a special type of cell division necessary for sexual reproduction. The cells produced by meiosis are gametes or spores. The animals' gametes are called sperm and egg cells.

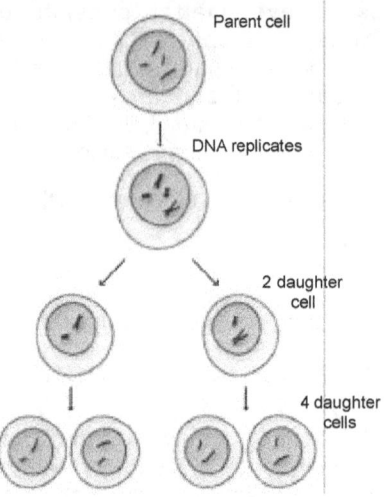

Meiosis I
First phase of meiosis. In meiosis I, chromosome number is reduced by half.

Meiosis II
Second phase of meiosis. Events in meiosis II are essentially the same as those in mitosis.

Meiotic drive
1. A process defined by a deviation from 1:1 Mendelian segregation among the functional gametes produced by a heterozygous genotype.
2. Used broadly to denote a preponderance (> 50 percent) of one allele among the gametes produced by a heterozygote; results in genic selection.

Melting point
The melting point of a solid is the temperature at which it changes state from solid to liquid. At the melting point the solid and liquid phase exist in equilibrium. The melting point of a substance depends (usually slightly)

on pressure and is usually specified at standard pressure. When considered as the temperature of the reverse change from liquid to solid, it is referred to as the freezing point or crystallization point.

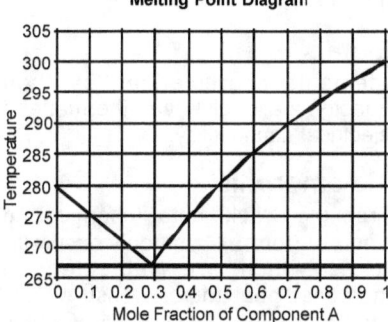

Melting Point Diagram

Because of the ability of some substances to supercool, the freezing point is not considered as a characteristic property of a substance. When the "characteristic freezing point" of a substance is determined, in fact the actual methodology is almost always "the principle of observing the disappearance rather than the formation of ice", that is, the melting point.

Melting temperature
Midpoint of the melting range of DNA.

Membrane
The pH-sensitive glass bulb is the membrane across which the potential difference due to the formation of double layers with ion-exchange properties on the two swollen glass surfaces is developed. The membrane makes contact with and separates the internal element and filling solution from the sample solution.

Memory cell
Long-lived lymphocyte among the clone of cells generated when a foreign antigen is encountered. If the same antigen is encountered again, the memory cells quickly divide and give rise to another clone of cells specific for that particular antigen.

Mendelian population
Group of interbreeding, sexually reproducing individuals.

Mendelian segregation
The production of equal numbers of gametes containing each allele from a heterozygous genotype.

Mendelian trait
Any trait controlled by a genetic locus that can be described by Mendelian principles of inheritance.

Menu bar
A horizontal strip at the top of a window that shows the menus available in a programme.

Mercaptan
Molecules containing sulphur with a low molecular weight and therefore very light.

Mercury
At a distance from the Sun of 0.387 AU, Mercury is the closest planet to our star and the first of the terrestrial planets. Its radius is little more than a third that of the Earth's and it has a very tenuous atmosphere. It is the densest of the planets and gravity at the surface is 3.7 times that of Earth. The average surface temperature is 440 K (170 °C).

Meristic characteristic
Characteristic whose phenotype varies in whole numbers, such as number of vertebrae.

Meroblastic cleavage
Describes a cell division event during development that results in

incomplete cleavage between daughter cells. Meroblastic cleavage is common in zygotes with large concentrations of yolk.

Merozygote
The bacterial cell that has two copies of some genes.one copy on the bacterial chromosome and a second copy on an introduced F plasmid; also called partial diploid.

Messenger RNA
1. RNA molecule that carries genetic information for the amino acid sequence of a protein.
2. The product of transcription and RNA processing that is translated into a polypeptide chain.

Meta-analysis
A statistical technique for jointly analyzing the results of many studies on the same topic.

Metabolic theory of ecology
Theory that aims to find the relationship between body mass and temperature and a variety of ecological phenomena.

Metabolism
The total of physical and chemical processes that occur in an organism to maintain life.

Metacentric chromosome
The chromosome in which the two chromosome arms are approximately the same length.

Metacommunity
It is broadly defined as a collection of communities connected by dispersal.

Metallography
The study of the crystalline structures of metals & alloys.

Metallothionine promoter
A gene promoter that is activated by heavy metals and oxidative stress.

Metallurgy
The process of extracting metals from their ores.

Metals
Elements characterised by their opacity, malleability and thermal and electrical conductivity.

Metamorphic
From the Greek "meta" (change) and "morph" (form). Commonly occurs to rocks which are subjected to increased heat and/or pressure. Also applies to the conversion of snow into glacial ice.

Metamorphosis
The series of changes in shape and function that certain animals go through as they develop from an egg to an adult. The metamorphosis of a tadpole to a frog changes that animal in many ways.

Metaphase
The metaphase is the third phase of mitosis, which is a process that separates the duplicated genetic material carried in the nucleus of a parent cell into two, identical daughter cells.

Metaphase

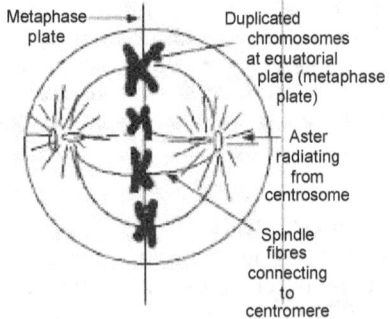

Metaphase I
Stage of meiosis I. In metaphase I, homologous pairs of chromosomes align in the centre of the cell.

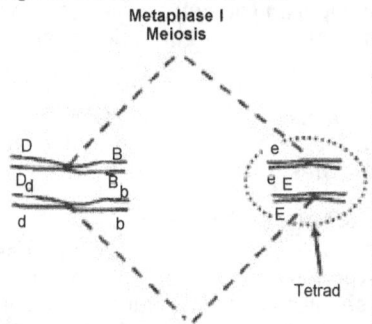

Metaphase II
Stage of meiosis II. In metaphase II, individual chromosomes align on the metaphase plate.

Metaphase plate
Plane in a cell between two spindle poles. In metaphase, chromosomes align on the metaphase plate.

Metapopulation
A set of local populations, among which there may be gene flow and patterns of extinction and recolonization.

Metapopulation theory
The theory that local populations of organisms undergo periodic colonization and extinction, but that these local populations are linked to other populations nearby by migration.

Metastasis
It refers to cells that separate from malignant tumors and travel to other sites, where they establish secondary tumors.

Meteor
Brief streak of light seen in the night sky when a speck of dust burns up as it enters the upper atmosphere. Also known as a shooting star or falling star.

Meteor shower
A group of meteors which appear to radiate from the same part of the sky and which occur over a limited period of a few days or hours. Dozens of annual showers are known though only a few give significant regular displays.

Meteorite
A fragment of rock that survives its fall to Earth from space. Usually named after the place where it fell.

Meteoroid
A piece of rock or dust in space with the potential to enter Earth's atmosphere and become a meteor or meteorite.

Meteorology
The science of the atmosphere and its phenomena.

Methane
A colourless and odorless gas that belongs to the alkane series of the hydrocarbons.

Method of correction
A procedure whereby the mass distribution of a rotor is adjusted to reduce unbalance, or vibration due to unbalance, to an acceptable value. Corrections are usually made by adding material to, or removing it from, the rotor.

Methylation
The addition of a methyl group (-CH3) to a molecule. Extensive methylation of cytosine in DNA is correlated with reduced transcription.

Methylphosphate
A phosphate with one oxygen replaced by a methyl group.

Metric trait
A phenotypic character that is continuously distributed with more than just a few distinct types.

Metrology
The scientific study of weights & measures.

Mica
A transparent mineral used as window material in high-temperature ovens.

Microamp
One millionth of an ampere, 10^{-6} amps, µA.

Microarray
A microarray is a laboratory tool used to detect the expression of thousands of genes at the same time.

Microbe
A plant or animal of microscopic size. Diatoms and protozoa are two types of microbes.

Microbiology
The study of minute living organisms including bacteria, moulds and pathogenic protozoa.

Microclimates
A climate of a relatively small area in which the temperature and moisture of that area can vary significantly from the greater region.

Microcomputer
A microcomputer is a computer with a microprocessor as its central processing unit.

They are physically small compared to mainframe and minicomputers. Many microcomputers (when equipped with a keyboard and screen for input and output) are also personal computers (in the generic sense).

Microevolution
A vague term, usually referring to slight, short-term evolutionary changes within species.

Microgravity
Condition of near-weightlessness experienced by a person or object in free fall as it orbits a star or planet. In a spacecraft orbiting the Earth, gravity is reduced to one ten-thousandth (1/10000) of its value at the planet's surface.

Microhabitat
A small, specialized habitat used by an organism.

Micron
Unit to measure length. It is often used to measure the wavelength of light. 1 micron is a thousandth of a millimetre. 10 000 micron correspond to 1 centimetre.

Microorganism
Any living thing that is too small to be seen with the naked eye. John was only able to see the water microorganisms by using the microscope.

Microrna
The small RNAs, typically 21 or 22 bp in length, that are produced by cleavage of double-stranded RNA arising from small hairpins within RNA that is mostly single stranded. The miRNAs combine with proteins to form a complex that binds (imperfectly) to mRNA molecules and inhibits their translation.

Microsatellites
1. Genetic markers consisting of repeat units 2.9 nucleotides long. Also called simple sequence repeats (SSR), simple sequence repeat polymorphisms (SSRP), or short tandem repeats (STR).
2. A class of repetitive DNA that is made up of repeats that are 2–8 nucleotides in length. They can be highly polymorphic and are frequently used as molecular markers in population genetics studies.

Microscope
A microscope is an instrument used to see objects that are too small for the naked eye. The science of investigating small objects using such an instrument is called microscopy. Microscopic means invisible to the eye unless aided by a microscope.

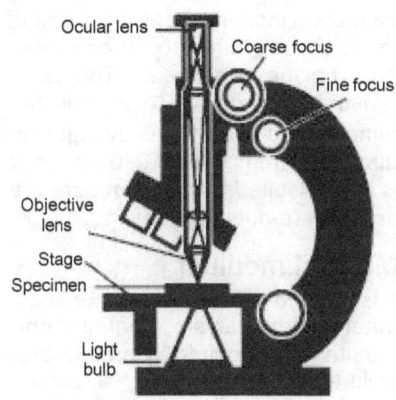

Microspore
Haploid product of meiosis in plants.

Microsporocyte
The diploid reproductive cell in the stamen of a plant; undergoes meiosis to produce four haploid microspores.

Microtubule
The long fiber composed of the protein tubulin; plays an important role in the movement of chromosomes in mitosis and meiosis.

Microvolt
One millionth of a volt, 10^{-6} volts.

Microwave
Light, or electromagnetic radiation, whose wavelength ranges from millimetres to almost one metre. The cosmic microwave background radiation emits strongly in microwaves.

Microwave anisotropy probe (map)
A NASA satellite to study the cosmic microwave background that was launched in 2001.

Mid-domain effect
It predicts a peak of diversity at the midpoint along any domain simply by the fact that the ranges of more species overlap in the middle of a domain (like a mountain or an island) than on the edges.

Mid-ocean gyres
The large areas in the centre of the oceans where nutrients are scarce, resulting in "marine deserts."

Midparent
The average phenotypic value of each pair of parents in an offspring-parent regression.

Migration
It is used in theoretical population genetics as a synonym for gene flow among populations; in other contexts, refers to directed large-scale movements of organisms that do not necessarily result in gene flow.

Mil
One thousandth of an inch (.001").

Milky way
Our Galaxy is seen as a misty band of light which stretches across the night sky. The Milky Way contains about one hundred million stars. It has the shape of a disk with a diameter of about 100 000 light-years. The Sun lies about two-thirds of the way towards the edge of the disk from the centre.

Milliamp
One thousandth of an amp, 10^{-3} amps, symbol mA.

Milligram (mg)
One-thousandth of a gram.

Milligrams per litre (mg/l)
a unit of the concentration of a constituent in water or wastewater. It represents 0.001 gram of a constituent in 1 litre of water. It is approximately equal to one part per million (PPM).

Millimetre
One thousandth of a metre, symbol mm.

Million gallons per day (Mgd)
a rate of flow of water equal to 133,680.56 cubic feet per day, or 1.5472 cubic feet per second, or 3.0689 acre-feet per day. A flow of one million gallons per day for one year equals 1,120 acre-feet (365 million gallons).

Millivolt
Unit of electromotive force. It is the difference in potential required to make a current of 1 millampere flow through a resistance of 1 ohm; one thousandth of a volt, symbol mV.

Mimicry
The similarity of certain characters in two or more species due to convergent evolution when there is an advantage conferred by the resemblance. Common types include Batesian mimicry, in which a palatable mimic experiences lower predation because of its resemblance to an unpalatable model; and MÃ¼an mimicry, in which two or more unpalatable species enjoy reduced predation due to their similarity.

Mineral
A naturally occurring, inorganic, crystalline solid with a definite internal structure and chemical composition.

Mineral-insulated Thermo-couple
A type of thermocouple cable which has an outer metal sheath and mineral (magnesium oxide) insulation inside separating a pair of thermocouple wires from themselves and from the outer sheath. This cable is usually drawn down to compact the mineral insulation and is available in diameters from .375 to .010 inches. It is ideally suited for high-temperature and severe-duty applications.

Minimal medium
It is used to culture bacteria or some other microorganism; contains only the nutrients required by prototrophic (wild-type) cells.typically, a carbon source, essential elements such as nitrogen and phosphorus, certain vitamins, and other required ions and nutrients.

Mining water use
water use during quarrying rocks and extracting minerals from the land.

Minisatellites
A class of repetitive sequences, 7.100 nucleotides each, that span 500.20,000 bp, and are located throughout the genome, towards chromosome ends.

Minor gene
A locus that determines a relatively small proportion of phenotypic variation in a trait.

Minor scale division
On an analogue scale, the smallest indicated division of units on the scale.

Mipeg
An electronic load indicator and monitoring system fitted to cranes - can store data for future analysis and maintenance planning based on the actual crane usage.

Mirror
An optical element that reflects electromagnetic waves (such as visible light, infrared, gamma or X-rays..) towards a camera or detector.

Mismatch repair
The process that corrects mismatched nucleotides in DNA after replication has been completed. Enzymes excise incorrectly paired nucleotides from the newly synthesized strand and use the original nucleotide strand as a template when replacing them.

Missense mutation
It alters a codon in the mRNA, resulting in a different amino acid in the protein.

Mitochondria
Organelles in eukaryotic cells in which the citric acid cycle occurs and ATP is produced.

Mitochondria
Organelles that convert glucose into energy.

Mitochondrial DNA
DNA in mitochondria; has some characteristics in common with eubacterial DNA and typically consists of a circular molecule that lacks histone proteins and encodes some of the rRNAs, tRNAs, and proteins found in mitochondria.

Mitosis
Mitosis is a process of nuclear division in eukaryotic cells that occurs when a parent cell divides to produce two identical daughter cells.

Mitotic spindle
Array of microtubules that radiate from two poles; moves chromosomes in mitosis and meiosis.

Modbus
This Protocol is a messaging structure developed by Modicon in 1979. It is used to establish master-slave/client-server communication between intelligent devices.

Model
A theoretical abstraction of the real world.

Model organism
1. In past decades, the term "model organism" has been narrowly applied to those species.such as mouse or Drosophila.that, because of their small size and short generation times, facilitate experimental laboratory research. However, in the past decade, with the increase in the number of genome-sequencing projects, this definition has broadened. For example, researchers have focused attention on some organisms, such as the tiger pufferfish, because of unique aspects of their genome rather than their feasibility for

experimental studies, and referred to them as "genomic" models.
2. An organism that is widely used in genetic studies because it has characteristics, such as short generation time and large numbers of progeny, that make it well suited to genetic analysis.

Modem
Modulator/Demodulator. A device that transforms digital signals into electrical signals for transmission over telephone lines, and does the reverse for reception.

Moderately repetitive DNA
The DNA consisting of sequences that are from 150 to 300 bp in length and are repeated thousands of times.

Modified base
The Rare base found in some RNA molecules. Such bases are modified forms of the standard bases (adenine, guanine, cytosine, and thymine).

Modifier gene
A gene that alters the phenotypic expression of another gene.

Modularity
The ability of individual parts of an organism, such as segments or organs, to develop or evolve independently from one another; the ability of developmental regulatory genes and pathways to be regulated

independently in different tissues and developmental stages.

Module (satellite)
Part of a satellite that has been designed and built and often tested as an entity.

Molality
A measure of concentration expressed in mols per kilogram of solvent.

Molecular biology
The study of the structure of the molecules which are of importance in biology.

Molecular chaperone
Molecule that assists in the proper folding of another molecule.

Molecular clock
1. Refers to the use of molecular differences to estimate the time of divergence between organisms; assumes a roughly constant rate at which one neutral mutation replaces another.
2. The concept of a steady rate of change in DNA sequences over time, providing a basis for dating the time of divergence of lineages if the rate of change can be estimated.

Molecular cloud
Clouds of interstellar dust and gas in the molecular form. They can be very large - with a diameter of up to a hundred light-years. Most of the gas in these clouds is very cold, only tens of degrees above the absolute zero.

Molecular formula
The number and types of atom in a molecule. For example, the molecular formula of methane is CH_4, one atom of carbon and four atoms of hydrogen.

Molecular genetics
The study of the chemical nature of genetic information and how it is encoded, replicated, and expressed.

Molecular motor
Specialized protein that moves cellular components.

Molecule
A group of atoms bonded together. It is the smallest part of a substance that retains the chemical properties of the whole.

Molt
To shed the hair, feathers, skin, or shell and grow a new covering. The snake molted its old skin and left it behind.

Momentum
The product of mass times velocity. Momentum is conserved in any system of particles.

Monecious/hermaphroditic
Species with no separate sexes.

Monel
A nickel-copper alloy which combines high strength with high ductility these usually being a trade off in metals selection. Also offers excellent general corrosion resistance. Commonly used in seawater applications.

Monitor
Optical instrument used to observe the sky by itself and sometimes as a complement to another instrument.

Monoallelic expression
Expression of a gene from only one of two alleles in a diploid organism.

Monoecious
Refers to the presence of both male and female reproductive structures in the same individual organism.

Monohybrid cross
A cross between two individuals that differ in a single characteristic.more specifically, a cross between individuals that are homozygous for different alleles at the same locus (AA _ aa); also refers to a cross between two individuals that are both heterozygous for two alleles at a single locus (Aa _ Aa).

Monomers
Small molecules that link together to form a polymer.

Monomorphic species
The male and female, of the same species, look and behave in similar ways.

Monophyletic
Refers to a taxon, phylogenetic tree, or gene tree whose members are all derived from a common ancestral taxon. In cladistic taxonomy, the term describes a taxon consisting of all the known species descended from a single ancestral species.

Monosomy
Absence of one of the chromosomes of a homologous pair.

Monovalent ion
An ion with a single positive or negative charge (H+, C1-).

Monozygote
A zygote derived from a single egg.

Monozygotic twins
Identical twins that arise when a single egg fertilized by a single sperm splits into two separate embryos.

Moon
1. The Earth's satellite, which orbits at a distance of 384 500 km. Its mass is one-eighteenth (1/80) and its gravity one-sixth (1/6) of the

Earth's. Surface temperatures range from 80-400 K. It has no atmosphere.
2. General name also given to natural satellites, e.g., the moon of Jupiter and Saturn.

Moraine
A moraine is any glacially formed accumulation of unconsolidated glacial debris (soil and rock) which can occur in currently glaciated and formerly glaciated regions, such as those areas acted upon by a past glacial maximum. This debris may have been plucked off a valley floor as a glacier advanced or it may have fallen off the valley walls as a result of frost wedging or landslide. Moraines may be composed of debris ranging in size from silt-sized glacial flour to large boulders. The debris is typically sub-angular to rounded in shape. Moraines may be on the glacier's surface or deposited as piles or sheets of debris where the glacier has melted. Moraines may also occur when glacier- or iceberg-transported rocks fall into a body of water as the ice melts.

Morphism
The condition of having a form, shape, or observable character.

Morphogen
Molecule whose concentration gradient affects the developmental fate of surrounding cells.

Morphology
Morphology is a branch of bioscience dealing with the study of the form and structure of organisms and their specific structural features. This includes aspects of the outward appearance (shape, structure, colour, pattern) as well as the form and structure of the internal parts like bones and organs. This is in contrast to physiology, which deals primarily with function. Morphology is a branch of life science dealing with the study of gross structure of an organism or Taxon and its component parts.

Mosaic evolution
Evolution of different characters within a lineage or clade at different rates, hence more or less independently of one another.

Mosaicism
Condition in which regions of tissue within a single individual have different chromosome constitutions.

Mother
A mother (or mum/mom) is a woman who has raised a child, given birth to a child, and/or supplied the ovum that grew into a child. Because of the complexity and differences of a mother's social, cultural, and religious definitions and roles, it is challenging to specify a universally acceptable definition for the term. The male equivalent is a father.

Motherboard
In personal computers, a motherboard is the central printed circuit board (PCB) in many modern computers and holds many of the crucial components of the system, providing connectors for other peripherals.

The motherboard is sometimes alternatively known as the mainboard, system board, or, on Apple computers, the logic board. It is also sometimes casually shortened to mobo. In a microcomputer, the motherboard contains the microprocessor and connectors for expansion boards.

Mounting error
The error resultant from installing the transducer, both electrical and mechanical.

Move
To change place or position. It is difficult to move a large box filled with books.

M-phase promoting factor
Protein functioning in the control of the cell cycle; consists of a cyclin combined with cyclin-dependent kinase (CDK). Active MPF stimulates mitosis.

MPI
Magnetic Particle Examination. A form of NDE used to detect surface cracks on castings.

MRNA
mRNA is known as messenger RNA, and is the intermediate form of the genetic code between DNA and protein.

MRNA stability
A measure of the half-life of an mRNA molecule.

MRNA surveillance
Mechanisms for the detection and elimination of mRNAs that contain errors that may create problems in the course of translation.

MSD (most-significant digit)
The leftmost digit of the display.

Mspi endonuclease
A restriction endonuclease that cleaves at the recognition site C/CGG (with the / representing the cleavage site). When the 5'-C is methylated, MspI is inhibited. When the internal C is methylated, MspI can cleave normally.

Mudflow
A flowage of water-saturated earth material possessing a high degree of fluidity during movement. A less-saturated flowing mass is often called a debris flow. A mudflow originating on the flank of a volcano is properly called a lahar.

Mueller bridge
A high-accuracy bridge configuration used to measure three-wire RTD thermometers.

Multifactorial characteristic
Determined by multiple genes and environmental factors.

Multigene family
Set of genes similar in sequence that arose through repeated duplication events; often encode different proteins.

Multimirror
Telescope design employing several mirrors to collect and focus electromagnetic waves, as in ESA's XMM-Newton space observatory.

Multiple 3' cleavage sites
Refers to the presence of more than one 3' cleavage site on a single pre-mRNA, which allows cleavage and polyadenylation to take place at different sites, producing mRNAs of different lengths.

Multiple alleles
Presence in a group of individuals of more than two alleles at a locus.

Although, for the group, the locus has more than two alleles, each member of the group has only two of the possible alleles.

Multiplex
A technique which allows different input (or output) signals to use the same lines at different times, controlled by an external signal. Multiplexing is used to save on wiring and I/O ports.

Multiplexer
A switching device that sequentially connects multiple inputs or outputs in order to process several signal channels with a single A/D or D/A converter.

Multiplication rule
States that the probability of two or more independent events occurring together is calculated by multiplying the probabilities of each of the individual events.

Multi-wavelength (observations)
Observation of a celestial object at different wavelengths, with (possibly) different instruments.

Municipal water system
A water system that has at least five service connections or which regularly serves 25 individuals for 60 days; also called a public water system

Muscles
Body parts that help a person move. Your leg muscles help you run.

Mutagen
Any environmental agent that significantly increases the rate of mutation above the spontaneous rate.

Mutagenesis screen
The method for identifying genes that influence a specific phenotype. Random mutations are induced in a population of organisms, and individual organisms with mutant phenotypes are identified. These individual organisms are crossed to determine the genetic basis of the phenotype and to map the location of mutations that cause the phenotype.

Mutant
A cell or organism harboring a genetic mutation.

Mutant screen
An experiment used in "reverse genetics" to identify the loci responsible for specific phenotypes. Generally, the genetic material of wild-type parental organisms is altered (e.g., by treatment with a chemical mutagen) and organisms are allowed to breed to look for dominant phenotypes (F1) or recessive phenotypes (F2).

Mutation
1. A mutation is a change in a genetic sequence.
2. Any permanent alteration of a DNA molecule.

Mutation frequency
Number of mutations within a group of individual organisms.

Mutation rate
Frequency with which a gene changes from the wild-type to a specific mutant; generally expressed as the number of mutations per biological unit (i.e., mutations per cell division, per gamete, or per round of replication).

Mutational meltdown
A process in which deleterious mutations are fixed due to random

drift in small populations, which further decreases population size and thus increases the rate of fixation of deleterious mutations in a positive feedback loop.

Mutational variance
The increment in the genetic variance of a phenotypic character caused by new mutations in each generation.

Mutation-selection balance
A process in which removal of variation by selection is balanced by the input of new variation into the population by mutation.

Mutualism
A symbiotic relation in which each of two species benefits by their interaction.

Mutualism/mutualisms
The way in which two organisms interact biologically so that each derives a fitness benefit.

Mutualistic associatons
The relationships where one organism shelters another, two organisms exchange resources, or tighter dependencies evolve, such as coevolved relationships between specialized pollinators and flowers. In some cases, species even cultivate others.

Mutualists/mutualistic partners
Species participating in an interaction that involves the exchange of goods or services between the two species where each receives a benefit from the interaction.

Mycology
The study of fungi & fungus diseases.

Mycorrhizae
Fungal mutualists associated with plant roots.

Myoa
A myogenic transcription factor with a helix-loop-helix domain.

Myoblast
An immature muscle cell.

Myod
A transcription factor that can induce differentiation of embryonic muscle fibroblasts to myoblasts in culture. MyoD activates transcription of muscle-specific genes, including MyoA, MyoH, and itself.

Myoh
A myogenic transcription factor with a helix-loop-helix domain.

Myology
The study of muscles.

Myosin
One of the two major proteins of muscle; it makes up the thick filaments.

Myosin heavy chain gene
The gene that encodes the part of the myosin protein that catalyzes ATP and faciliates motor activity.

Myrmecology
The scientific study of ants, a branch of entomology. Some early myrmecologists considered ant society as the ideal form of society and sought to find solutions to human problems by studying them.

N

N/c (no connection)
A connector point for which there is no internal connection.

Nanog
A transcription factor often associated with embryonic stem cells that is thought to be critical for maintaining the pluripotency of these cells.

Naphta
An oil distillate. Naphta is an intermediate product between gasoline and kerosene. It is known as a light product because of the low molecular weight of the hydrocarbons making it up.

Narrow-sense heritability
Proportion of the phenotypic variance that can be attributed to additive genetic variance.

National electrical manufacturers association
The leading US trade association which sets standards relating to electrically powered instrumentation.

Natural gas
Natural gas is a naturally occurring hydrocarbon gas mixture consisting primarily of methane, with up to 20 percent concentration of other hydrocarbons (usually ethane) as well as small amounts of impurities such as carbon dioxide. Natural gas is widely used and is an important energy source in many applications including heating buildings, generating electricity, providing heat and power to industry and vehicles and is also a feedstock in the manufacture of products such as fertilizers.

Natural gas liquification
The name given to the process and the associated plant required to make Liquified Natural Gas.

Natural language processing
Computer understanding, analysis, manipulation and/or generation of natural (human) language.

Natural resource
Materials that come from the earth and can be used by living things, for example: water, oil, and minerals. One reason that trees are an important natural resource is that their wood is used to build houses and to make paper.

Natural selection
The differential survival and/or reproduction of classes of entities that differ in one or more characteristics. To constitute natural selection, the difference in survival and/or reproduction cannot be due to chance, and it must have the potential consequence of altering the proportions of the different entities. Thus, natural selection is also definable as a deterministic difference

in the contribution of different classes of entities to subsequent generations. Usually, the differences are inherited. The entities may be alleles, genotypes or subsets of genotypes, populations, or, in the broadest sense, species.

NDE
Non Destructive Examination e.g. magnetic particle inspection; x-ray etc.

NDT
Non Destructive Testing e.g. magnetic particle inspection; x-ray etc.

Near-Earth asteroid
Rocky object which passes close to the Earth. Most, if not all, seem to have originated in the main asteroid belt. Their Earth-approaching orbits are the result of collisions with other asteroids or the gravitational influence of Jupiter. Many thousands of asteroids inhabit the inner Solar System. The main groups are the Amors, which travel between the Earth and Mars; the Apollos, which cross Earth's orbit; and the Atens, which stay mainly inside Earth's orbit. Occasionally, one of these objects will collide with the Earth, creating a large impact crater and possibly causing mass extinction of life forms.

Nebula
A nebula is an interstellar cloud of dust, hydrogen gas, helium gas and other ionized gases. Originally, *nebula* was a general name for any extended astronomical object including galaxies beyond the Milky Way.

Negative assortative mating
Mating between unlike individuals that is more frequent than would be expected on the basis of chance.

Negative control
Gene regulation in which the binding of a regulatory protein to DNA inhibits transcription (the regulatory protein is a repressor).

Negative selection
The form of natural selection in which rare, deleterious alleles are removed from a population.

Negative temperature coefficient
A decrease in resistance with an increase in temperature.

Negative-strand RNA virus
RNA virus whose genomic RNA molecule carries the complement of the information for viral proteins. A negative-strand RNA virus must first make a complementary copy of its RNA genome, which is then translated into viral proteins.

Nema-12
A standard from the National Electrical Manufacturers Association, which defines enclosures with protection against dirt, dust, splashes by non-corrosive liquids, and salt spray.

Nema-4
A standard from the National Electrical Manufacturers Association, which defines enclosures intended for indoor or outdoor use primarily to provide a degree of protection against windblown dust and rain, splashing water, and hose-directed water.

Nema-7
A standard from the National Electrical Manufacturers Association, which defines explosion-proof enclosures for use in locations classified as Class I, Groups A, B, C or D, as specified in the National Electrical Code.

Nema-size case
An older US case standard for panel metres, which requires a panel cutout of 3.93 x 1.69 inches.

Neoclassical crosses
The F2, F2 B1 and B2 are "classical" hybrid crosses. Neoclassical crosses were named by Collins (1971) and are all addition hybrid crosses. The are often used in estimating the number of segregating genes for quantitative traits.

Neo-darwinism
Neo-Darwinism is the 'modern synthesis' of Darwinian evolution through natural selection with Mendelian genetics, the latter being a set of primary tenets specifying that evolution involves the transmission of characteristics from parent to child through the mechanism of genetic transfer, rather than the 'blending process' of pre-Mendelian evolutionary science. Neo-Darwinism also separates Darwin's ideas of natural selection from his hypothesis of Pangenesis as a Lamarckian source of variation involving blending inheritance.

Neofunctionalization
The divergence of duplicate genes whereby one acquires a new function.

Neopolyploid
A polyploid that has been produced by artificially inducing chromosome doubling.

Neoteny
The heterochronic evolution whereby development of some or all somatic features is retarded relative to sexual maturation, resulting in sexually mature individuals with juvenile features.

Nephelometric turbidity unit (NTU)
Unit of measure for the turbidity of water. Essentially, a measure of the cloudiness of water as measured by a nephelometer. Turbidity is based on the amount of light that is reflected off particles in the water.

Neptune
At more than 30 AU from the Sun, Neptune is the eighth planet away from our star. It is one of the gas giants and has a dense atmosphere consisting mainly of hydrogen. Average surface temperature is 58 K.

Nernst equation
A mathematical description of electrode behaviour: E is the total potential, in millivolts, developed between the sensing and reference electrodes; Ex varies with the choice of electrodes, temperature, and pressure: $2.3RT/nF$ is the Nernst factor (R and F are constants, n is the charge on the ion, including sign, T is the temperature in degrees Kelvin), and ai is the activity of the ion to which the electrode is responding.

Nernst factor (s, slope)
The term $2.3RT/nF$ is the Nernst equation, which is equal (at $T = 25°C$) to 59.16 mV when $n = 1$ and 29.58 mV when $n - 2$, and which includes the sign of the charge on the ion in the term n. The Nerst factor varies with temperature.

Nested paternal half-sibling design
A quantitative genetic design that is well-suited for estimating additive genetic variance, additive genetic correlation, and thus the G matrix. In this design, a few unique females (dams) are mated to each of a number of males (sires), and the traits of interest are measured on a few offspring from each dam. The data are analyzed with nested ANOVA.

Net positive suction head
The minimum suction pressure required by a pump to prevent cavitation.

Net present value
The cost of a product or system calculated in the present-day currency. It is found by subtracting a project's initial investment from the present value of the cash inflows discounted at a rate equal to the firm's cost of capital.

Net primary productivity
The amount of energy primary producers (organisms that produce their own food from an external energy source such as the sun) capture and convert to tissue minus the amount they lose in cellular respiration.

Network
A computer network, often simply referred to as a network, is a collection of hardware components and computers interconnected by communication channels that allow sharing of resources and information. Where at least one process in one device is able to send/receive data to/from at least one process residing in a remote device, then the two devices are said to be in a network. Networks may be classified according to a wide variety of characteristics such as the medium used to transport the data, communications protocol used, scale, topology, and organizational scope.

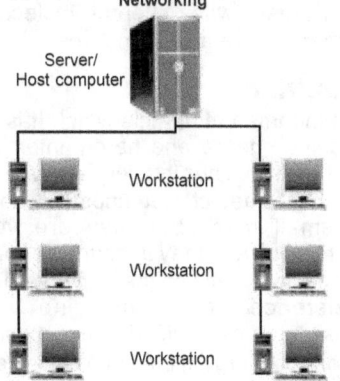

Networking

Neuraminidase
A type II integral membrane glycoprotein that facilitates virus release from cells by removing sialic acid from sialyloligosaccharides on the cell and viral surfaces. It is also a target of the protective immune response.

Neurofibromatosis
An autosomal genetic disorder that results in the growth of tumors along different types of nerves. It can also impact the development of non-nervous system tissues, such as bones and skin.

Neurohormones
Hormones produced and released by neurons.

Neurology
Neurology is a medical specialty dealing with disorders of the nervous system. Specifically, it deals with the diagnosis and treatment of all categories of disease involving the central, peripheral, and autonomic nervous systems, including their coverings, blood vessels, and all effector tissue, such as muscle. The corresponding surgical specialty is neurosurgery. A neurologist is a physician who specializes in neurology, and is trained to investigate, or diagnose and treat neurological disorders. Neurologists may also be involved in clinical research, clinical trials, as well as basic research and translational research.

Neuropathology
Neuropathology is the study of disease of nervous system tissue, usually in the form of either small surgical biopsies or whole autopsy brains. Neuropathology is a subspecialty of anatomic pathology, neurology, and neurosurgery. It should not be

confused with neuro*pathy*, which refers to disorders of the nerves (usually in the peripheral nervous system).

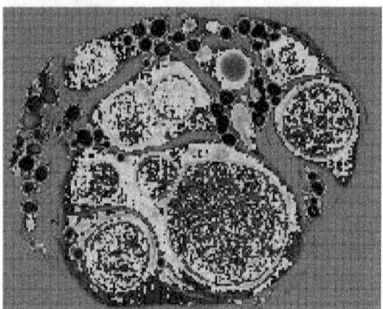

Neutral alleles
Traits or loci that have a negligible effect on fitness. A trait or locus is nearly neutral or effectively neutral if the mean phenotype or allele frequencies are determined more by random genetic drift than by selection.

Neutral equilibrium
An equilibrium in which a perturbed system attains a new state of equilibrium instead of returning to its original equilibrium state.

Neutral models
The differences in relative abundance of any species are caused by historic patterns of abundance and dispersion; these species have equal effects on biodiversity.

Neutral mutation
A neutral mutation is a mutation that has no effect on fitness. In other words, it is neutral with respect to natural selection. some mutations in a DNA triplet or codon do not change which amino acid is introduced: this is known as a synonymous substitution. Unless the mutation also has a regulatory effect, synonymous substitutions are usually neutral. Neutral mutations can accumulate over time due to genetic drift or genetic draft. According to the neutral theory of molecular evolution, while the majority of mutations are deleterious, the majority of mutations that go on to become fixed as differences between species are neutral.

Neutral theory of evolution
The neutral theory claims that the overwhelming majority of evolutionary changes at the molecular level are not caused by selection acting on advantageous mutants, but by random fixation of selectively neutral or very nearly neutral mutants through the cumulative effect of sampling drift (due to finite population number) under continued input of new mutations.

Neutral theory of species diversity
A 2001 theory by Stephen Hubbell proposing that species co-occur for a long time periods because of competitive equivalence.

Neutralization
A reaction in which the characteristics of an acid or base disappear.

Neutral-mutation hypothesis
It proposes that much of the molecular variation seen in natural populations is adaptivoly neutral and unaffected by natural selection. Under this hypothesis, individuals with different molecular variants have equal fitnesses.

Neutrino
A fundamental particle which has no electric charge and hardly interacts with matter. Thus it is very elusive and difficult to detect. Neutrinos only have a small mass but they are very numerous and may account for some of the dark matter in the Universe. The existence of the neutrino was postulated by Enrico Fermi to explain a loss of energy in the radioactive beta

decay. The neutrinos produced in the beta decay carry away the lost energy.

Neutron
Particle in atomic nuclei. A neutron has no charge but a little more mass than the other constituent of atomic nuclei, the proton. Neutrons are made up of three quarks. If neutrons are not bound in an atomic nucleus they decay into a proton, an electron and an antineutrino.

Neutron star
An extremely dense star comprised mainly of neutrons, endpoint of the life of a massive star which has exploded as a supernova. Under huge gravitational forces electrons have been compressed into protons and produced neutrons. A typical neutron star has about 3 times the mass of the Sun but a radius of only 10 kilometres. Fast spinning neutron stars can be observed as pulsars. If the Sun were to become a neutron star it would have a diameter of only 20 km.

Newborn screening
Testing newborn infants for certain genetic disorders; done most commonly for phenylketonuria and other metabolic diseases that can be prevented by early treatment or intervention.

Newsgroup
Usenet newsgroups are Internet discussion groups whose topics are about as diverse as you can imagine. If you have an original idea for a newsgroup, and gather some people who want to subscribe, you can probably begin a newsgroup.

Newtons laws of motion
Classical laws which enable the prediction of the path of any object from a grain of sand to entire galaxies:

1. A body will remain at rest or move with a constant velocity unless acted upon by an outside force.
2. The acceleration of a body is proportional to the applied force. This is expressed by the universal formula:

    Force = mass × acceleration.
3. For every action there is an equal and opposite reaction.

Next generation space telescope (NGST) mission
ESA astronomy mission. The most important goal for NGST is to see light from the very first stars and galaxies forming after the Big Bang - objects which are beyond the reach of today's telescopes.

NGVD
National Geodetic Vertical Datum.
1. As corrected in 1929, a vertical control measure used as a reference for establishing varying elevations.
2. Elevation datum plane previously used by the Federal Emergency Management Agency (FEMA) for the determination of flood elevations. FEMA current uses the North American Vertical Datum Plane.

NGVD of 1929
National Geodetic Vertical Datum of 1929. A geodetic datum derived from a general adjustment of the first order level nets of the United States and Canada. It was formerly called "Sea Level Datum of 1929" or "mean sea level" in the USGS series of reports. Although the datum was derived from the average sea level over a period of many years at 26 tide stations along the Atlantic, Gulf of Mexico, and Pacific Coasts, it does not necessarily represent local mean sea level at any particular place.

Nibble

A nibble (often nybble or even nyble to simulate the spelling of byte) is a four-bit aggregation, or half an octet. As a nibble contains 4 bits, there are sixteen (24) possible values, so a nibble corresponds to a single hexadecimal digit (thus, it is often referred to as a "hex digit" or "hexit"). A full byte (octet) is represented by two hexadecimal digits; therefore, it is common to display a byte of information as two nibbles. The nibble is often called a "semioctet" or a "quartet" in a networking or telecommunication context. Sometimes the set of all 256 byte values is represented as a table 16×16, which gives easily readable hexadecimal codes for each value.

Niche

The particular range of conditions that species. can tolerate, and how their physiological responses impact species. geographic distributions.

Niche space

The multidimensional space encompassing suitable conditions for all factors which represents the conditions under which an individual, population, or species will persist.

Nicrosil/nisil

A nickel chrome/nickel silicone thermal alloy used to measure high temperatures. Inconsistencies in thermoelectric voltages exist in these alloys with respect to the wire gage.

Nitrification

The process by which ammonia is converted to nitrite (NO2-) and then nitrate (NO3-) by microorganisms.

Nitrogen

A chemical element, symbol N, with atomic number 14, under normal conditions it is a diatomic gas (N_2). One of the main constituents of proteins and a major constituent of Earth's atmosphere.

Nitrogen cycle

The nitrogen cycle is the process by which nitrogen is converted between its various chemical forms. This transformation can be carried out by both biological and non-biological processes. Important processes in the nitrogen cycle include fixation, mineralization, nitrification, and denitrification. The majority of Earth's atmosphere (approximately 78%) is nitrogen, making it the largest pool of nitrogen. However, atmospheric nitrogen has limited availability for biological use, leading to a scarcity of usable nitrogen in many types of ecosystems. The nitrogen cycle is of particular interest toecologists because nitrogen availability can affect the rate of key ecosystem processes, including primary production and decomposition. Human activities such as fossil fuel combustion, use of artificial nitrogen fertilizers, and release of nitrogen in wastewater have dramatically altered the global nitrogen cycle.

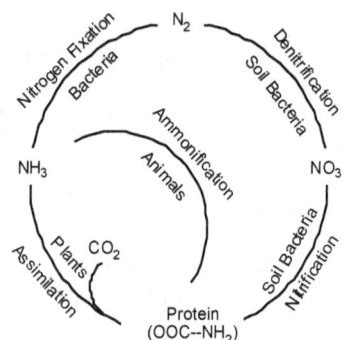

Nitrogen deposition
The input of reactive nitrogen forms from the atmosphere to the land.

Nitrogen oxides
The term used to describe the sum of nitric oxide (NO); nitric dioxide (NO_2) and other oxides of nitrogen which play a major role in the formation of ozone.

Nitrogenous base
A nitrogenous (nitrogen-containing) base is a nitrogen-containing molecule having the chemical properties of a base. It is an organic compound that owes its property as a base to the lone pair of electrons of a nitrogen atom. In biological sciences, nitrogenous bases are typically classified as the derivatives of two parent compounds, pyrimidine and purine. They are non-polar and due to their aromaticity, planar. Both pyrimidines and purines resemble pyridine and are thus weak bases and relatively unreactive towards electrophilic aromatic substitution.

NMR (normal-mode rejection)
The ability of a panel metre to filter out noise superimposed on the signal and applied across the SIG HI to SIG LO input terminals. Normally expressed in dB at 50/60 Hz.

NMR specroscopy
A powerful method for determining the structure of organic compounds.

Noble gases
The noble gases are a group of chemical elements with very similar properties: under standard conditions, they are all odourless, colourless, monatomic gases, with very low chemical reactivity. The six noble gases that occur naturally are helium (He), neon (Ne), argon (Ar), krypton (Kr), xenon (Xe), and the radioactive radon (Rn).

Node
Point in a phylogenetic tree that represents an organism. Terminal nodes are those that are at the outmost branches of the tree and represent organisms for which data have been obtained. Internal nodes represent ancestors common to organisms on different branches of the tree.

Noise
The word noise means any unwanted sound. In both analogue and digital electronics, noise is random unwanted perturbation to a wanted signal; it is called noise as a generalisation of the acoustic noise ("static") heard when listening to a weak radio transmission with significant electrical noise. Signal noise is heard as acoustic noise if the signal is converted into sound (e.g., played through a loudspeaker); it manifests as "snow" on a television or video image. High noise levels can block, distort, change or interfere with the meaning of a message in human, animal and electronic communication.

Nomology
The study of law making or scientific laws.

Nonadditive genetic variance
The sum of the dominance and epistatic variance.

Nonallelic homologous recombination
Homologous recombination between paralogous sequences (for example, segmental duplication and repetitive sequence); a major mechanism of recurrent rearrangements, also known as unequal crossing-over.

Nonautonomous element
Transposable element that cannot transpose on its own but can transpose in the presence of an autonomous element of the same family.

Non-baryonic matter
Matter that is not made of baryons (i.e. of neutrons and protons), and is thus different from the matter which makes up the planets, human beings and everything you can see around you. It has been proposed that part of the dark matter in the Universe is non-baryonic matter. It is classified as 'cold' non-baryonic matter or 'hot' non-baryonic matter. Cold non-baryonic matter would be made of particles moving much slower than light (there are several non-detected candidates); hot non-baryonic matter is made of particles moving very fast, such as neutrinos. Non-baryonic matter (hot or cold) is supposed to interact weakly with radiation. Therefore, the 'imprints' left by the non-baryonic matter in the cosmic background radiation would be different than those left by the baryonic matter. This attribute could be used to measure the contribution of non-baryonic matter to the total amount of mass in the Universe.

Noncoding RNA
RNA in a cell that does not encode a protein.

Non-coding rnas
An RNA molecule that is not translated into a protein.

Nondisjunction
Failure of homologous chromosomes or sister chromatids to separate in meiosis or mitosis.

Non-equilibrium view
Whether a system really tend toward steady state at all and emphasizes that disturbance in time and space constantly interact to influence the ecology and evolutionary trajectories in the ecosystems. This more current framework focuses attention on the importance of variation and transient dynamics rather than expecting steady states.

Non-functional dna
The segments of DNA with no known biological function or importance.

Nonhistone chromosomal protein
One of a heterogeneous assortment of nonhistone proteins in chromatin.

Non-lethal effect/non-consumptive effect
It effect within a community that occur when prey react to predators by altering their behavior, morphology, and/or habitat selection.

Nonlinear allometries
When the scaling relationship between organ and body is not linear on a log-log scale.

Nonoverlapping genetic code
It refers to the fact that generally each nucleotide is a part of only one codon and codes for only one amino acid in a protein.

Nonparametric analysis
Analysis widely used for studying populations that take on a ranked order (such as movie reviews receiving one to four stars). The use of this analysis may be necessary when data have a ranking but no clear numerical interpretation, such as when assessing preferences.

Non-point source (NPS) pollution
Pollution discharged over a wide land area, not from one specific location.

These are forms of diffuse pollution caused by sediment, nutrients, organic and toxic substances originating from land-use activities, which are carried to lakes and streams by surface runoff. Non-point source pollution is contamination that occurs when rainwater, snowmelt, or irrigation washes off plowed fields, city streets, or suburban backyards. As this runoff moves across the land surface, it picks up soil particles and pollutants, such as nutrients and pesticides.

Nonreciprocal translocation
The movement of a chromosome segment to a nonhomologous chromosome or region without any (or with unequal) reciprocal exchange of segments.

Nonrecombinant gamete
Contains only original combinations of genes present in the parents.

Nonrecombinant progeny
Possesses the original combinations of traits possessed by the parents.

Nonreplicative transposition
Type of transposition in which a transposable element excises from an old site and moves to a new site, resulting in no net increase in the number of copies of the transposable element.

Nonsegregating generations
Generation in which there is one genotype (excluding sex chromosomes). These are the P1, P2, F1, and F1R generations.

Nonsense codon
Codon in mRNA that signals the end of translation; also called stop codon or termination codon. There are three common nonsense codons: UAA, UAG, and UGA.

Nonsense mutation
A nonsense mutation is a genetic mutation in a DNA sequence that results in a shorter, unfinished protein product.

Nonsense-mediated mrna decay
Process that brings about the rapid elimination of mRNA that has a premature stop codon.

Nonstop RNA decay
Mechanism in eukaryotic cells for dealing with ribosomes stalled at the 3' end of an mRNA that lacks a termination codon. A protein binds to the A site of the stalled ribosome and recruits other proteins that degrade the mRNA from the 3' end.

Nonsynonymous substitution
A base pair substitution in DNA that results in an amino acid substitution in the protein product; also called replacement substitution.

Nontemplate strand
The DNA strand that is complementary to the template strand; not ordinarily used as a template during transcription.

Nontransmissible disease
A disorder that cannot be passed between organisms.

Norite
Norite is a mafic intrusive igneous rock composed largely of the calcium-rich plagioclase labradorite and hypersthene with olivine. Norite is essentially indistinguishable from gabbro without thin section study under the petrographic microscope.

Norm of reaction
Range of phenotypes produced by a particular genotype in different environmental conditions.

Normal (axial) stress
The force per unit area on a given plane within a body a = F/A

Normal distribution
A bell-shaped frequency distribution of a variable; the expected distribution if many factors with independent, small effects determine the value of a variable; the basis for many statistical formulations.

Normal hydrogen electrode
A reversible hydrogen electrode (Pt) in contact with hydrogen gas at 1 atmosphere partial pressure and immersed in a solution containing hydrogen ions at unit activity.

Normal Temperature and Pressure
NTP is used in many thermodynamic calculations and tabulations and is defined as 20 degrees Celsius and 1 atmosphere of pressure.

Normal-mode rejection ratio
The ability of an instrument to reject interference usually of line frequency (50-60 Hz) across its input terminals.

Normoxic
The state of the environment in which oxygen concentration is at normal levels.

Northern blot
A Northern blot is a laboratory method used to detect specific RNA molecules from a mixture of RNA molecules.

Northern blotting
Process by which RNA is transferred from a gel to a solid support such as a nitrocellulose or nylon filter.

Nosology
Nosology is a branch of medicine that deals with classification of diseases.

Notified body
The independent Testing Laboratory recognised to perform tests; audit quality systems and issue reports and certificates of conformity.

Nova
A star which suddenly increases in brightness by a factor of more than hundred. Novae are close binary stars of which one component is a white dwarf star. Material from the companion star is transferred onto the white dwarf and triggers explosive nuclear reactions, resulting in the increased brightness.

Nuclear envelope
Membrane that surrounds the genetic material in eukaryotic cells to form a nucleus; segregates the DNA from other cellular contents.

Nuclear factor-kappa B
A family of dimeric transcription factors that regulate a variety of cellular signaling events. NF-kappaB monomers are held inactive via binding to an inhibitory protein called I-kappaB. When I-kappaB is phosphorylated, the interaction with NF-kappaB is released and allowed to dimerize, thus promoting its interaction with DNA.

Nuclear fusion
Nuclear fusion is the process by which two or more atomic nuclei join together, or "fuse", to form a single heavier nucleus. This is usually accompanied by the release or absorption of large quantities of energy. Fusion is the process that powers active stars, the hydrogen bomb and experimental devices examining fusion power forelectrical generation. The fusion of two nuclei with lower masses than iron (which, along with nickel, has the largest

binding energy per nucleon) generally releases energy, while the fusion of nuclei heavier than iron *absorbs* energy. The opposite is true for the reverse process, nuclear fission. This means that fusion generally occurs for lighter elements only, and likewise, that fission normally occurs only for heavier elements. There are extreme astrophysical events that can lead to short periods of fusion with heavier nuclei. This is the process that gives rise to nucleosynthesis, the creation of the heavy elements during events like supernovas.

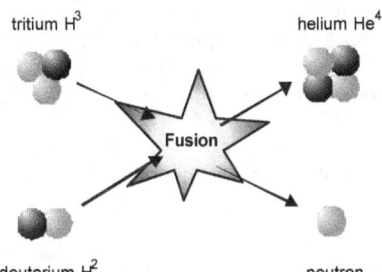

Nuclear lamina

The nuclear lamina is a dense (~30 to 100 nm thick) fibrillar network inside the nucleus of a eukaryotic cell. It is composed of intermediate filaments and membrane associated proteins. Besides providing mechanical support, the nuclear lamina regulates important cellular events such as DNA replication and cell division. Additionally, it participates in chromatin organization and it anchors the nuclear pore complexes embedded in the nuclear envelope. The nuclear lamina is associated with the inner face of the bilayer nuclear envelope whereas the outer face stays continuous with the endoplasmic reticulum.

Nuclear magnetic resonance

Nuclear magnetic resonance (NMR) is a physical phenomenon in which magnetic nuclei in a magnetic field absorb and re-emit electromagnetic radiation. This energy is at a specific resonance frequency which depends on the strength of the magnetic field and the magnetic properties of the isotope of the atoms. NMR allows the observation of specific quantum mechanical magnetic properties of the atomic nucleus. Many scientific techniques exploit NMR phenomena to study molecular physics, crystals, and non-crystalline materials through NMR spectroscopy. NMR is also routinely used in advanced medical imaging techniques, such as in magnetic resonance imaging (MRI).

Nuclear matrix

The nuclear matrix is the network of fibres found throughout the inside of a cell nucleus and is somewhat analogous to the cell cytoskeleton. However, in contrast to the cytoskeleton, the nuclear matrix has been proposed to be a highly dynamic structure, perhaps more like a dynamic sponge with open compartments for free diffusion of molecules in the nucleus. The exact function of this matrix is still disputed, and its very existence has recently been called into question. There is evidence that the nuclear matrix is involved in regulation of gene expression in *Arabidopsis thaliana*.

Nuclear pore

The nuclear pore is a protein-lined channel in the nuclear envelope that regulates the transportation of molecules between the nucleus and the cytoplasm.

Nuclear power

Nuclear power is the use of sustained nuclear fission to generate heat and electricity. Nuclear power plants provide about 6% of the world's energy and 13–14% of the world's electricity, with the U.S., France, and Japan together accounting for about 50% of nuclear generated electricity. In 2007, the IAEA reported there were 439 nuclear power reactors in operation in the world, operating in 31 countries. Also, more than 150 naval vessels using nuclear propulsion have been built.

Nuclear power plant

A nuclear power plant (NPP) is a thermal power station in which the heat source is one or more nuclear reactors. As in a conventional thermal power station the heat is used to generate steam which drives a steam turbine connected to a generator which produces electricity. Nuclear power plants are usually considered to be base load stations, which are best suited to constant power output.

Nuclear pre-mrna introns

Class of introns in protein-encoding genes that reside in the nuclei of eukaryotic cells; removed by spliceosomal-mediated splicing.

Nuclear run-off assay

A method for measuring gene transcription at a specific time that involves incorporating radioactive nucleotides into growing mRNA chains combined with Northern blotting.

Nucleic acid

Nucleic acids are biological molecules essential for life, and include DNA (deoxyribonucleic acid) and RNA (ribonucleic acid). Together with proteins, nucleic acids make up the most important macromolecules; each is found in abundance in all living things, where they function in encoding, transmitting and expressing genetic information. Nucleic acids were first discovered by Friedrich Miescher in 1871.

Experimental studies of nucleic acids constitute a major part of modern biological and medical research, and form a foundation for genome and forensic science, as well as the biotechnology and pharmaceutical industries.

Nucleoid

The nucleoid (meaning *nucleus-like*) is an irregularly-shaped region within the cell of a prokaryote that contains all or most of the genetic material. In contrast to the nucleus of a eukaryotic cell, it is not surrounded by a nuclear membrane. The genome of prokaryotic organisms generally is a circular, double-stranded piece of DNA, of which multiple copies may exist at any time. The length of a genome widely varies, but generally is at least a few million base pairs.

Nucleolytic

Enzymatic activity that describes the ability to cleave nucleic acid.

Nucleoside

Nucleosides are glycosylamines consisting of a nucleobase (often referred to as simply *base*) bound to a ribose or deoxyribose sugar via abeta-glycosidic linkage. Examples of nucleosides include cytidine, uridine, adenosine, guanosine, thymidine and inosine.

Nucleosome

Nucleosomes are the basic unit of DNA packaging in eukaryotes, consisting of a segment of DNA wound around a histone protein core. This structure is often compared to thread wrapped around a spool. Nucleosomes form the fundamental repeating units of eukaryotic chromatin, which is used to pack the large eukaryotic genomes into the nucleus while still ensuring appropriate access to it (in mammalian cells approximately 2 m of linear DNA have to be packed into a nucleus of roughly 10 μm diameter). Nucleosomes are folded through a series of successively higher order structures to eventually form a chromosome; this both compacts DNA and creates an added layer of regulatory control, which ensures correct gene expression.

Nucleosynthesis

The chemical reaction by which atomic nuclei (of any chemical element) are created. Nucleosynthesis took place when the Universe was very young. Today it takes place, for instance, in the stars' cores: the hydrogen, the most abundant component of a star, is converted into helium (this is referred to as helium nucleosynthesis) a process by which a huge amount of energy is released. This is the energy that allows the star to keep shining. When the hydrogen is used up then the star begins to transform the helium into other elements, and so on. The elements are hence used as fuel for the star, and the kind of element used in each stage of the star's life is an indication of how long it has been shining. Therefore, the chemical components of a star can provide a lot of information about its history.

Nucleotide

1. One of the building blocks of DNA or RNA; each contains a nitrogenous base attached to a five-carbon sugar.
2. Repeating unit of DNA, made up of a sugar, a phosphate, and a base.

Nucleotide substitution

The complete replacement of one nucleotide base pair by another within a lineage over evolutionary time.

Nucleotide-excision repair

DNA repair that removes bulky DNA lesions and other types of DNA damage.

Nucleus

The nucleus is a membrane-enclosed organelle found in eukaryotic cells. It contains most of the cell's genetic material, organized as multiple long linear DNA molecules in complex with a large variety of proteins, such ashistones, to form chromosomes. The genes within these chromosomes are the cell's nuclear genome. The function of the nucleus is to maintain the integrity of these genes and to control the activities of the cell by regulating gene expression — the nucleus is, therefore, the control centre of the cell.

Nuée ardente

A French term applied to a highly heated mass of gas-charge ash which is expelled with explosive force down the mountainside. Common to intermediate volcanoes. Can be quite deadly. Also known as a "glowing avalanche."

Null

A condition, such as balance, which results in a minimum absolute value of output.

Null allele

A null allele is a mutant copy of a gene that completely lacks that gene's normal function. This can be the result of the complete absence of the gene product (protein, RNA) at the molecular level, or the expression of a non-functional gene product. At the phenotypic level, a null allele is indistinguishable from a deletion of the entire locus.

Null hypothesis
The statistical hypothesis that states that there will be no differences between observed and expected data.

Null model
A hypothesis used for statistical testing that states random processes create observed patterns and compared to alternative hypotheses.

Nullisomy
Absence of both chromosomes of a homologous pair (2n - 1).

Numerology
The study of numbers, study of the date and year of one's birth to determine their influence on one's future life.

Numismatics
Numismatics is the study or collection of currency, including coins, tokens, paper money, and related objects.

Nutrient cycling
While numismatists are often characterized as students or collectors ofcoins, the discipline also includes the broader study of money and other payment media used to resolve debts and the exchange of goods.

Nusa factor
Protein subunit of bacterial RNA polymerase that facilitates the termination of transcription.

Nutrient cycling
The cycling of nutrients between organisms and the physical environment.

O

Objective lens
The lower lens in a microscope that is closest to what is being looked at. She rotated the objective lens into position, just above the slide.

Obligate slave-maker
A type of social parasitism in ants whereby the colonies require slave ants in order to survive.

Observational variance components
In a sibling analysis, the portions of the phenotypic variance that are due to the different factors (i.e., sires, dams) in the mating design.

Observed
The number of organisms with specific characteristics after an experiment is performed.

Obsessive-compulsive disorder
An anxiety disorder characterized by repeated, upsetting thoughts called obsessions and by repetitive behaviors aimed at reducing the obsessions.

Obsidian
Obsidian is a naturally occurring volcanic glass formed as an extrusive igneous rock. It is produced when felsic lava extruded from a volcano cools rapidly with minimum crystal growth. Obsidian is commonly found within the margins of rhyolitic lava flows known as obsidian flows, where the chemical composition (high silica content) induces a high viscosity and polymerization degree of the lava. The inhibition of atomic diffusion through this highly viscous and polymerized lava explains the lack of crystal growth.

Occultation
An occultation is an event that occurs when one object is hidden by another object that passes between it and the observer. The word is used in astronomy (see below). It can also refer to any situation wherein an object in the foreground blocks from view (occults) an object in the background. In this general sense, occultation applies to the visual scene observed from low-flying aircraft (or computer-generated imagery) wherein foreground objects obscure distant

dynamically, as the scene changes over time.

Occupation
The primary employment of a person.

Occupational Safety and Health Administration
The department of the US government with the responsibility to ensure safety and healthful work environments.

Oceanic crust
Oceanic crust is the part of Earth's lithosphere that surfaces in the ocean basins. Oceanic crust is primarily composed of mafic rocks, or sima, which is rich in iron and magnesium. It is thinner than continental crust, or sial, generally less than 10 kilometres thick, however it is denser, having a mean density of about 3.3 grams per cubic centimetre.

Oceanic islands
Islands that have emerged from the sea floor in the ocean.

Oct4 transcription factor
A POU family homeodomain containing transcription factor.

Octal
The octal numeral system, or oct for short, is the base-8 number system, and uses the digits 0 to 7. Numerals can be made from binary numerals by grouping consecutive binary digits into groups of three (starting from the right). For example, the binary representation for decimal 74 is 1001010, which can be grouped into (00)1 001 010 — so the octal representation is 112.

Octane number
A measurement of a fuel's resistance to spontaneous ignition. The higher the octane number greater the fuel's resistance to spontaneous ignition.

Ocular lens
An ocular lens, is a type of lens that is attached to a variety of optical devices such as telescopes and microscopes. It is so named because it is usually the lens that is closest to the eye when someone looks through the device. The objective lens or mirror collects light and brings it to focus creating an image. The eyepiece is placed near the focal point of the objective to magnify this image. The amount of magnification depends on the focal length of the eyepiece.

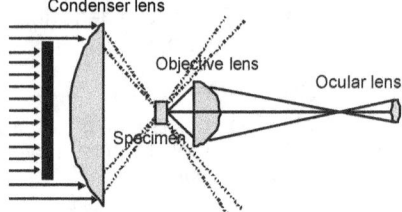

Odontography
A description of the teeth.

Odontology
The scientific study of the teeth.

Oenology
Oenology is the science and study of all aspects of wine and winemaking except vine-growing and grape-harvesting, which is a subfield called viticulture. "Viticulture & oenology" is a common designation for training programmes and research centres that include both the "outdoors" and "indoors" aspects of wine production.

Offset
The difference in temperature between the set point and the actual process temperature. Also, referred to as droop.

Offspring
The children resulting from a cross between two parents.

Offspring parent regression
A quantitative genetic design that is well suited for estimating additive genetic variance, additive genetic correlation, and thus the G matrix. In this design, the traits of interest are measured on a number of mothers, fathers, and their offspring. The slope of the regression line is an estimate of heritability.

OFHC
Oxygen-free high-conductivity copper. The industrial designation of the pure copper used in a Type T thermocouple.

OGP
The International Association of Oil & Gas producers. It is formed in 1974 to develop effective communications between the upstream industry and the complex network of international regulators.

Ohmeter
An ohmmeter is an electrical instrument that measures electrical resistance, the opposition to an electric current. Micro-ohmmeters (microhmmeter or microohmmeter) make low resistance measurements. Megohmmeters (aka megaohmmeter or in the case of a trademarked device Megger) measure large values of resistance. The unit of measurement for resistance is ohms ( ).

Okazaki fragment
Short stretch of newly synthesized DNA; produced by discontinuous replication on the lagging strand, these fragments are eventually joined together.

Old field
Lands that are cultivated or grazed and them abandoned.

Oligo
A short polymer of nucleotides, usually ranging between 2 and 50 nucleotides in length.

Oligogenic trait
A trait affected by a few loci.

Oligonucleotide-directed mutagenesis
Method of site-directed mutagenesis that utilizes an oligonucleotide to introduce a mutant sequence into a DNA molecule.

Omnivore
An animal that feeds on animals, but also on either live plants or dead ones (detritus).

On/off controller
A controller whose action is fully on or fully off.

Oncogene
Dominant-acting gene that stimulates cell division, leading to the formation of tumors and contributing to cancer; arises from mutated copies of a normal cellular gene (protooncogene).

Oncology
The study of tumour.

One gene, one enzyme hypothesis
Idea proposed by Beadle and Tatum that each gene encodes a separate enzyme.

One gene, one polypeptide hypothesis
Modification of the one gene, one enzyme hypothesis; proposes that each gene encodes a separate polypeptide chain.

Oneirology
Oneirology is the scientific study of dreams. Current research seeks correlations between dreaming and current knowledge about the functions of the brain, as well as understanding of how the brain works during dreaming as pertains to memory formation and mental disorders. The study of oneirology can be distinguished from dream analysis in that the aim is to quantitatively study the process of dreams instead of analyzing the meaning behind them.

Ontogenetic
Allometry the relationship of x and y that are traits measured in the same individual through developmental time.

Ontogeny
The development of an individual organism, from fertilized zygote until death.

Ontology
A hierarchical organization of concepts, typically used to denote 'more-general-than' and/or 'part-of' relationships.

Oogenesis
Oogenesis is the creation of an ovum (egg cell). It is the female form of gametogenesis. The male equivalent isspermatogenesis. It involves the development of the various stages of the immature ovum.

Oogonium
Diploid cell in the ovary; capable of undergoing meiosis to produce an egg cell.

Oology
The study of eggs.

Oort cloud
Swarm of billions of comets thought to surround the Solar System between 2000 and 20 000 AU from the Sun. First proposed by E. Öpik in 1932 and later developed by J. Oort in the 1950s. Its existence is based on studies of long-period comet orbits, which seem to have their aphelia in this zone.

Opec
Organisation of the Petroleum Exporting Countries a permanent inter-governmental organization currently made up of 11 oil producing and exporting countries. Its aim is to co-ordinate and unify the petroleum policies of the Member Countries and to determine the best means for safeguarding their individual and collective interests.

Open circuit
The lack of electrical contact in any part of the measuring circuit. An open circuit is usually characterized by rapid large jumps in displayed potential, followed by an off-scale reading.

Open reading frame
Continuous sequence of DNA nucleotides that contains a start codon and a stop codon in the same reading frame; is assumed to be a gene that encodes a protein but, in many cases, the protein has not yet been identified.

Operating system
An operating system (OS) is a set of programmes that manage computer hardware resources and provide common services for application software. The operating system is the most important type of system software in a computer system. A user cannot run an application programme

on the computer without an operating system, unless the application programme is self booting. Time-sharing operating systems schedule tasks for efficient use of the system and may also include accounting for cost allocation of processor time, mass storage, printing, and other resources.

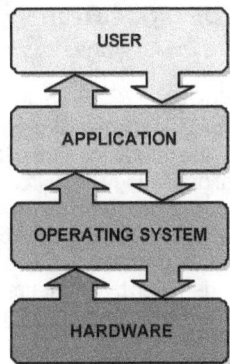

Operational ph
The determination of sample pH by relating to pH measurements in a primary standard solution. This relationship assumes that electrode errors such as sensitivity and changes in asymmetry potential can be disregarded or compensated for, provided the liquid junction potential remains constant between standard and sample.

Operator
DNA sequence in the operon of a bacterial cell. A regulator protein binds to the operator and affects the rate of transcription of structural genes.

Operator
The term used to describe a company appointed by venture stake holders to take primary responsibility for day-to-day operations for a specific plant or activity.

Operon
Set of structural genes in a bacterial cell along with a common promoter and other sequences (such as an operator) that control the transcription of the structural genes.

Opposition
The point at which a planet that is further away from the Sun than the Earth, lines up with the Sun and Earth. Opposition is a good time for observation because the planet is near its closest point to Earth.

Optical isolation
Two networks which are connected only through an LED transmitter and photoelectric receiver with no electrical continuity between the two networks.

Optical light (visible light)
The light that can be detected by the human eye. It has a wavelength between 4000 and 7000 angstroms (or between 0.00004 and 0.00007 cm).

Optics
Optics is the branch of physics which involves the behavior and properties of light, including its interactions with matter and the construction of instruments that use ordetect it. Optics usually describes the behavior of visible, ultraviolet, and infrared light. Because light is an electromagnetic wave, other forms of electromagnetic radiationsuch as X-rays, microwaves, and radio waves exhibit similar properties.

Optimal foraging theory
Relates the costs of moving among different habitat patches to habitat quality and the distances separating patches.

Orbit
An orbit is the gravitationally curved path of an object around a point in space, for example the orbit of a planet around the centre of a star system, such as theSolar System. Orbits of planets are typically elliptical. Current understanding of the mechanics of orbital motion is based on Albert Einstein's general theory of relativity, which accounts for gravity as due to curvature of space-time, with orbits following geodesics. For ease of calculation, relativity is commonly approximated by the force-based theory of universal gravitation based on Kepler's laws of planetary motion.

Orbit acquisition
Reception of the telemetry containing the information about the orbital parameters of the spacecraft.

Orbiter
A spacecraft orbiting around a planet or other celestial body to act as a telecommunications relay or from which remote sensing observations can be made.

Organelles
Specialized organs within cells.

Organic compounds
Substances that contain Carbon.

Organic matter
Plant and animal residues, or substances made by living organisms. All are based upon carbon compounds.

Organics
Carbon-based material.

Organism
Usually used to refer to an individual member of a species.

Orientation
Position in space relative to a reference point.

Origin
In electrophoresis, the location in a gel where the sample is placed.

Origin of replication
Site where DNA synthesis is initiated.

Ornithology
Ornithology is a branch of zoology that concerns the study of birds. Several aspects of ornithology differ from related disciplines, due partly to the high visibility and the aesthetic appeal of birds. Most marked among these is the extent of studies undertaken by amateurs working within the parameters of strict scientific methodology.

Orthoepy
The study of correct pronunciation.

Orthologous genes
1. Loci in two species that are derived from a common ancestral locus by a speciation event. This is different from paralogous members of a gene family that are derived from duplication events.
2. Homologous genes found in different species, because the two species have a common ancestor that also possessed the gene.

Orthopedics
The science of prevention, diagnosis and treatment of diseases and abnormalities of musculoskeletal systems.

Osmosis
The movement of water molecules through a thin membrane. The osmosis process occurs in our bodies and is also one method of desalinating saline water.

Ospar
The Convention for the Protection of the Marine Environment of the North-East Atlantic - the OSPAR Convention. It replaces the Oslo and Paris Conventions but decisions; recommendations and all other agreements adopted under those Conventions continue to be applicable.

Osteology
Osteology is the scientific study of bones, practiced by osteologists. A subdiscipline of anatomy, anthropology, and archeology, osteology is a detailed study of the structure of bones, skeletal elements, teeth, morphology, function, disease, pathology, the process of ossification (from cartilaginous molds), the resistance and hardness of bones (biophysics), etc. often used by scientists with identification of human remains with regard to age, death, sex, growth, and development in a biocultural context.

Osteopathology
Any disease of bones.

Osteopathy
A therapeutic system based upon detecting and correcting faulty structure.

Outboard rotor
A two-journal rotor which has its centre of gravity between the journals.

Outbreeding depression
A decline in fitness resulting from mating between distantly related individuals, especially those from different locally adapted populations.

Outcrossing
Mating between unrelated individuals that is more frequent than would be expected on the basis of chance.

Outfall
The place where a sewer, drain, or stream discharges; the outlet or structure through which reclaimed water or treated effluent is finally discharged to a receiving water body.

Outgroup
A taxon that diverged from a group of other taxa before they diverged from one another.

Output
The electrical signal which is produced by an applied input to the transducer.

Output impedance
The resistance as measured on the output terminals of a pressure transducer.

Output noise
The RMS, peak-to-peak (as specified) ac component of a transducer's dc output in the absence of a measurand variation.

Ovalbumin
The main protein in egg whites.

Overdominance
The phenomenon in which the heterozygous genotype has a higher phenotypic value (especially for fitness) than either homozygous genotype.

Overshoot
The number of degrees that a process exceeds the set point temperature when coming up to the set point temperature.

Overstory
The larger, taller trees that of a forest that overtop and shade younger and smaller trees and shrubs.

Oviduct
In mammals, the tube serving to transport eggs to the uterus or to outside of the body.

Oviparous
Describes an animal that lays eggs.

Ovum
An ovum (plural ova, from the Latin word ovum meaning egg or egg cell) is a haploid female reproductive cell or gamete. Both animals and embryophytes have ova.

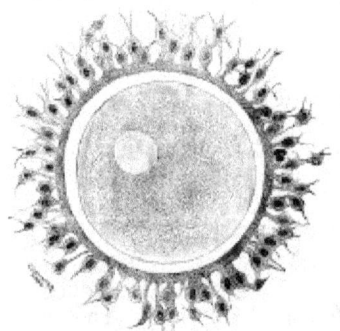

The term ovule is used for the young ovum of an animal, as well as the plant structure that carries the female gametophyte and egg cell and develops into a seed after fertilization. In lower plants and algae, the ovum is also often called oosphere.

Oxygen demand
The need for molecular oxygen to meet the needs of biological and chemical processes in water. Even though very little oxygen will dissolve in water, it is extremely important in biological and chemical processes.

Ozone
An isotope of oxygen that blocks ultraviolet radiation. Normally found in the stratosphere.

Ozone layer
A layer in the Earth's atmosphere at 15-30 km altitude in which ozone is at higher concentration than at lower or higher altitudes. The ozone is created by a series of processes beginning with the splitting up of the oxygen molecule to single oxygen atoms. The ozone layer protects the Earth from UV radiation harmful to life.

P

P generation
First set of parents in a genetic cross.

Pachytene
Third substage of prophase I in meiosis. The synaptonemal complex forms during pachytene.

Paedomorphosis
Possession in the adult stage of features typical of the juvenile stage of the organism's ancestor.

Pahoehoe
Hawaiian term for a fluid volcanic eruption resulting in broad basaltic shield volcanoes. The highly fluid magma flows readily, and hardens into ropey forms as it cools. It can be very impressive to view an active flow!

Pain
A subjective characterization of sensation associated with physical damage to the body. The perception of pain is protective; it provides feedback that allows the avoidance of further injury or of dangerous situations.

Pair-rule genes
Set of segmentation genes in fruit flies that define regional sections of the embryo and affect alternate segments. Mutations in these genes often cause the deletion of every other segment.

Paleobotany
The study of fossil plants.

Paleoecology
Using data from fossils to reconstruct ecosystems of the past.

Paleontology
Paleontology is the study of prehistoric life. It includes the study of fossils to determine organisms' evolution and interactions with each other and their environments (their paleoecology). As a "historical science" it attempts to explain causes rather than conduct experiments to observe effects. Paleontological observations have been documented as far back as the 5th century BC. The science became established in the 18th century as a result ofGeorges Cuvier's work on comparative anatomy, and developed rapidly in the 19th century.

Palindrome
Sequence of nucleotides that reads the same on complementary strands; inverted repeats.

Palynology
Palynology is the science that studies contemporary and fossil palynomorphs, including pollen, spores, orbicules, dinoflagellate cysts, acritarchs, chitinozoansand scolecodonts, together with particulate organic matter (POM) and

kerogen found in sedimentary rocks and sediments. Palynology does not include diatoms, foraminiferans or other organisms with siliceous or calcareous exoskeletons. Palynology is an interdisciplinary science and is a branch of earth science (geology or geological science) and biological science (biology), particularly plant science (botany). Stratigraphical palynology is a branch of micropalaeontology and paleobotany which studies fossil palynomorphs from the Precambrian to the Holocene.

Pancreas
A gland located near the stomach of vertebrates that secretes digestive enzymes into the small intestine and releases insulin into the bloodstream.

Pandemic flu
An influenza virus of a new subtype to which the general population has little or no immunity that causes disease in humans and spreads efficiently from person to person, causing community-wide outbreaks and resulting in a global outbreak of influenza.

Pangenesis
Early concept of heredity proposing that particles carry genetic information from different parts of the body to the reproductive organs.

Panmictic
A population in which any member of the species can potentially mate with any other member of the opposite sex; often used as a synonym for random mating.

Panmixia
Random mating among members of a population.

Parabolic (mirror)
A mirror whose surface is figured to the shape of a paraboloid, a particular form of open curve.

Paracentric inversion
Chromosome inversion that does not include the centromere in the inverted region.

Parallax
An optical illusion which occurs in analogue metres and causes reading errors. It occurs when the viewing eye is not in the same plane, perpendicular to the metre face, as the indicating needle.

Parallel evolution
The evolution of similar or identical features independently in related lineages, thought usually to be based on similar modifications of the same developmental pathways.

Parallel transmission
Sending all data bits simultaneously. Commonly used for communications between computers and printer devices.

Paralogous
1. Two (or more) genes located at different locations in the genome of an organism that are related, based on sequence similarity, suggesting they derived from a common ancestor gene earlier in their evolution via mutation or genetic drift.
2. Refers to the homologous relationship between two different members of a gene family, within a species or in a comparison of different species.

Parapatric
Parapatry is a term from biogeography, referring to organisms whose ranges

do not significantly overlap but are immediately adjacent to each other; they only occur together in the narrow contact zone, if at all. This geographical distribution is opposed to sympatry (same area) & allopatry or peripatry (2 cases of distinct areas). This distribution may along time cause speciation into sister species, a process called parapatric speciation.

Paraphyletic
It refers to a taxon, phylogenetic tree, or gene tree whose members are all derived from a single ancestor, but which does not include all the descendants of that ancestor.

Parasitism
The situation in which an individual organism, the parasite, consumes nutrients from another organism, its host, resulting in a decrease in fitness to the host as a result of the interaction.

Parasitoid
A parasitoid is an organism that spends a significant portion of its life history attached to or within a single host organism in a relationship that is in essence parasitic; unlike a true parasite, however, it ultimately sterilises or kills, and sometimes consumes, the host. Thus parasitoids are similar to typical parasites except in the more dire prognosis for the host.

Parental effect
Nongenetic effect of parents on traits present in their offspring.

Parental investment
Parental activities or processes that enhance the survival of existing offspring but whose costs reduce the parent's subsequent reproductive success.

Parental line
The line used for the first generation of a genetic cross; usually a pure-breeding stain.

Parity
A technique for testing transmitting data. Typically, a binary digit is added to the data to make the sum of all the digits of the binary data either always even (even parity) or always odd (odd parity).

P-arm
The short arm of a chromosome.

Parsec (pc)
A distance equal to 3.26 light-years, often used as a unit for measuring distances to stars and galaxies. One million parsecs are more conveniently expressed as 1 Megaparsec (Mpc).

Parsimony
Economy in the use of means to an end; the principle of accounting for observations by that hypothesis requiring the fewest or simplest assumptions that lack evidence; in systematics, the principle of invoking the minimal number of evolutionary changes to infer phylogenetic relationships.

Parthenogenesis
Parthenogenesis is a form of asexual reproduction where growth and development of embryos occur without fertilization. In plants, parthenogenesis means development of an embryo from an unfertilized egg cell, and is a component process of apomixis. The term is sometimes used inaccurately to describe reproduction modes in hermaphroditic species that can reproduce by themselves because they contain reproductive organs of both sexes in a single individual's body.

Partial diploid
The bacterial cell that possesses two copies of genes, including one copy on the bacterial chromosome and the other on an extra piece of DNA (usually a plasmid); also called merozygote.

Partial dominance
When one trait is not fully dominant over another; here, one can see a "mixing" of the characteristics. Incomplete dominance and codominance are two types of partial dominance.

Particle size
The diameter, in millimetres, of suspended sediment or bed material. Particle-size classifications are:
[1] Clay—0.00024-0.004 millimetres (mm);
[2] Silt—0.004-0.062 mm;
[3] Sand—0.062-2.0 mm; and
[4] Gravel—2.0-64.0 mm.

Particle(s)
A fundamental constituent of matter. About 200 different elementary particles are thought to exist.

Particulate inheritance
The model described by Mendel which suggested that transmission of inherited traits occurs through distinct units (particles) in contrast to a blending of characters from each parent.

Parts per billion
The number of "parts" by weight of a substance per billion parts of water. Used to measure extremely small concentrations.

Parts per million
The number of "parts" by weight of a substance per million parts of water. This unit is commonly used to represent pollutant concentrations.

Passive restoration
Allowing natural succession to occur in an ecosystem after removing a source of disturbance. The recovery of the deciduous forests in the eastern United States after the abandonment of agriculture is a classic.

Patau syndrome
Characterized by severe mental retardation, a small head, sloping forehead, small eyes, cleft lip and palate, extra fingers and toes, and other disabilities; results from the presence of three copies of chromosome 13 (trisomy 13).

Patch
An area of an ecosystem differing from its surroundings, often the smallest ecologically distinct feature in a landscape mapping and classification system.

Patch-corridor-matrix concept
Landscapes are conceptualized and analyzed as mosaics of discrete patches recognizing the three major elements that can be recognized in the landscape.

Patent
A property right granted by the government of the United States of America to an inventor .to exclude others from making, using, offering for sale, or selling the invention throughout the United States or importing the invention into the United States. for a limited time in exchange for public disclosure of the invention when the patent is granted.

Paternal homolog
An allele of a locus that was inherited from the genetic contribution of the father.

Paternity
Fatherhood; the state of being a father. Establishing who is the father of an offspring.

Path integration
The ability to remember the distances and directions traveled, to sum them, and then to calculate their return path.

Pathogen
A disease-producing agent; usually applied to a living organism. Generally, any viruses, bacteria, or fungi that cause disease.

Pathology
Pathology is the precise study and diagnosis of disease. Pathologization, to pathologize, refers to the process of defining a condition or behaviour as pathological, e.g. pathological gambling. Pathologies is synonymous with diseases. The suffix "path" is used to indicate a disease, e.g. psychopath.

Payload
Cargo of a spacecraft. Scientific instruments are part of a satellite's payload. For ESA scientific missions, they are usually designed and built by scientists at their home institutes.

Payload module
Some satellites are built in a modular way. They consist of a payload module with the scientific instruments and a service module with the housekeeping equipment.

Peak flow
The maximum instantaneous discharge of a stream or river at a given location. It usually occurs at or near the time of maximum stage.

Peak shift
Change in allele frequencies within a population from one to another local maximum of mean fitness by passage through states of lower mean fitness.

Pedagogy
Pedagogy is also occasionally referred to as the correct use of instructive strategies. For example, Paulo Freire referred to his method of teaching adult humans as "critical pedagogy". In correlation with those instructive strategies the instructor's own philosophical beliefs of instruction are harboured and governed by the pupil's background knowledge and experience, situation, and environment, as well as learning goals set by the student and teacher. One example would be the Socratic schools of thought.

Pedigree
Pictorial representation of a family history outlining the inheritance of one or more traits or diseases.

Pedology
Pedology is the study of soils in their natural environment. It is one of two main branches of soil science, the other being edaphology. Pedology deals with pedogenesis, soil morphology, and soil classification, while edaphology studies the way soils influence plants, fungi, and other living things.

P-element
A transposable DNA element in Drosophila that is frequently used to facilitate insertional mutagenesis for genetic screens.

Peltier effect
When a current flows through a thermocouple junction, heat will either be absorbed or evolved depending on the direction of current flow. This effect is independent of joule I^2R heating.

Penetrance
Penetrance is a measure of the proportion of individuals in a population who carry a specific gene and express the related trait.

Penology
The study of prisons & treatment of criminals.

Peptide
Peptides are short polymers of amino acid monomers linked by peptide bonds. They are distinguished from proteins on the basis of size, typically containing less than 50 monomer units. The shortest peptides are dipeptides, consisting of two amino acids joined by a single peptide bond. There are also tripeptides, tetrapeptides, etc. Amino acids which have been incorporated into a peptide are termed "residues"; every peptide has a N-terminus and C-terminus residue on the ends of the peptide (except for cyclic peptides). A polypeptide is a long, continuous, and unbranched peptide. Proteins consist of one or more polypeptides arranged in a biologically functional way and are often bound to cofactors, or other proteins.

Peptide bond
A peptide bond (amide bond) is a covalent chemical bond formed between two molecules when the carboxyl group of one molecule reacts with the amino group of the other molecule, causing the release of a molecule of water (H_2O), hence the process is a dehydration synthesis reaction (also known as a condensation reaction), and usually occurs between amino acids. The resulting C(O)NH bond is called a peptide bond, and the resulting molecule is an amide. The four-atom functional group -C(=O)NH- is called a peptide link. Polypeptides and proteins are chains of amino acids held together by peptide bonds, as is the backbone of PNA.

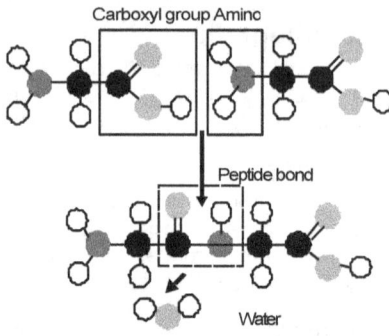

Peptidyl site
One of three sites in a ribosome occupied by a tRNA in translation. In the elongation stage of protein synthesis, tRNAs move from the aminoacyl (A) site into the P site.

Peptidyl transferase
Activity in the ribosome that creates a peptide bond between two amino acids. Evidence suggests that this activity is carried out by one of the RNA components of the ribosome.

Per capita use
The average amount of water used per person during a standard time period, generally per day.

Percolation
1. The movement of water through the openings in rock or soil.
2. The entrance of a portion of the streamflow into the channel materials to contribute to ground water replenishment.

Perennating organ
Tissues that give rise to new growth the following season, and are therefore sensitive to climatic conditions.

Perfectly balanced rotor
A rotor is perfectly balanced when its mass distribution is such that it transmits no vibratory force or motion to its bearings as a result of centrifugal forces.

Periapsis
The point of an orbit nearest to the centre of attraction of an orbiting body.

Pericentre
The point on a spacecraft's orbit at which it is nearest to the centre of mass of the system.

Pericentric inversion
Chromosome inversion that includes the centromere in the inverted region.

Perigee
Perigee is the point at which an object makes its closest approach to the Earth. Often the term is used in a broader sense to define the point in an orbit where the orbiting body is closest to the body it orbits. The opposite is the apogee, the farthest or highest point.

Perihelic opposition
When the Earth passes between a planet and the Sun when the planet is at its closest from the Sun.

Perihelion
The point in a planet's orbit when it is nearest to the Sun.

Period
Time interval between two consecutive and similar phases of a regularly occurring event. For example, the period of rotation of the Earth is the time taken to complete one revolution; the period of a variable star is the time between two successive maxima or minima on its light-curve.

Peripatric
Of a population, peripheral to most of the other populations of a species.

Peripatric speciation
The speciation by evolution of reproductive isolation in peripatric populations as a consequence of a combination of genetic drift and natural selection.

Peripheral
A peripheral is a device attached to a host computer, but not part of it, and is more or less dependent on the host. It expands the host's capabilities, but does not form part of the core computer architecture. Examples are computer printers, image scanners, tape drives, microphones, loudspeakers, web-cams, and digital cameras.

Peripheral populations
The population of a species that resides towards the margin of its habitat.

Permanent inquilines
An animal that completely lives in the nest, burrow, or colony of another species.

Permeability
The ability of a material to allow the passage of a liquid, such as water through rocks. Permeable materials, such as gravel and sand, allow water to move quickly through them, whereas unpermeable material, such as clay, don't allow water to flow freely.

Personal computer (PC)
A microcomputer with its own processor and hard drive. Although technically this refers to all such computers, including Macs, the term PC is nearly synonymous with only the IBM-compatible microcomputers.

Personal protective equipment
The collective term used for coveralls; gloves; hard hat; protective foot wear; accessories etc designed to create a barrier against workplace hazards.

Personel locator beacon
Device issued to each traveler when traveling offshore on a helicopter. It automatically emits a signal when submersed in the sea thereby giving potential for speedier rescue in event of helicopter ditching.

Persons on Board
It is used in reference to the number of people allowed on offshore installations.

Pesticide rotation
Systematic change in the pesticide used to control a pest.

Pfa
A fluorocarbon polymer used for insulation of electrical wires.

Ph
A measure of the relative acidity or alkalinity of water. Water with a pH of 7 is neutral; lower pH levels indicate increasing acidity, while pH levels higher than 7 indicate increasingly alkalinity.

Ph junctions
The Junction of a reference electrode or combination electrode is a permeable membrane through which the fill solution escapes (called the liquid junction).

Ph scale
The strength of acids and bases. Pure water has a pH value of 7, acids have a lower value and bases higher.

Ph(S) (Standard ph Scale)
The conventional standard pH scale established on the basis that an individual ionic activity coefficient can be calculated from the Debye-Huckel law for primary buffers.

Phage
Virus that infects bacterial cells. Phages are widely distributed in locations populated by bacterial hosts, such as soil or the intestines of animals. One of the densest natural sources for phages and other viruses is sea water, where up to 9×10^8 virions per millilitre have been found in microbial mats at the surface, and up to 70% of marine bacteria may be infected by phages. They have been used for over 90 years as an alternative to antibiotics in the former Soviet Union and Eastern Europe as well as in France. They are seen as a possible therapy against multi-drug-resistant strains of many bacteria.

Phanerophytes
Plants with their perennating organs greater than 0.5 metres above the ground (normally woody perennials).

Pharmacogenomics
The use of genetic information to guide drug prescribing.

Pharyngology
The science of the pharynx & its diseases.

Phase
A time based relationship between a periodic function and a reference. In electricity, it is expressed in angular degrees to describe the voltage or current relationship of two alternating waveforms.

Phase changes
Freezing or boiling.

Phase difference
The time expressed in degrees between the same reference point on two periodic waveforms.

Phase proportioning
A form of temperature control where the power supplied to the process is controlled by limiting the phase angle of the line voltage.

Phenetics
Phenetics, also known as taximetrics, is an attempt to classify organisms based on overall similarity, usually in morphology or other observable traits, regardless of their phylogeny or evolutionary relation. It is closely related to numerical taxonomy which is concerned with the use of numerical methods for taxonomic classification. Many people contributed to the development of phenetics, but the most influential were Peter Sneath and Robert R. Sokal. Their books are still primary references for this sub-discipline, although now somewhat dated and out of print

Phenocopy
Phenotype that is produced by environmental effects and is the same as the phenotype produced by a genotype.

Phenology
The timeframe for any seasonal biological phenomena. The study of the relationship between climate and the timing of ecological events such as the date and emergence of leaves and flowers, the first flight of butterflies and the first appearance of migratory birds.

Phenotype
1. The outward appearance of an organism for a given characteristic.
2. The morphological, physiological, biochemical, behavioural, and other properties of an organism manifested throughout its life; or any subset of such properties, especially those affected by a particular allele or other portion of the genotype.

Phenotypic adaptive landscape
A three-dimensional representation of the relationship between two phenotypic traits and population mean fitness.

Phenotypic correlation
A standardized measure of the degree to which two traits covary among individuals in the population.

Phenotypic plasticity
1. The condition in which the same genotype produces different phenotypes in different environments.
2. The capacity of an organism to develop any of several phenotypic states, depending on the environment; usually this capacity is assumed to be adaptive.

Phenotypic value
The measurement of a given quantitative trait for a given individual.

Phenotypic variance
Measures the degree of phenotypic differences among a group of individuals; composed of genetic, environmental, and genetic-environmental interaction variances.

Phenylketonuria
The Genetic disease characterized by mental retardation, light skin, and eczema; caused by mutations in the gene that encodes phenylalanine hydroxylase (PAH), a liver enzyme that normally metabolizes the amino acid phenylalanine. When the enzyme is

defective, phenylalanine is not metabolized and builds up to high levels in the body, eventually causing mental retardation and other characteristics of the disease. The disease is inherited as an autosomal recessive disorder and can be effectively treated by limiting phenylalanine in the diet.

Philately
Philately is the study of stamps and postal history and other related items. Philately involves more than just stamp collecting, which does not necessarily involve the study of stamps. It is possible to be a philatelist without owning any stamps. For instance, the stamps being studied may be very rare, or exist only in museums.

Philology
Philology is the study of language in written historical sources; it is a combination of literary studies, history and linguistics.

Phonetics
Phonetics is a branch of linguistics that comprises the study of the sounds of human speech, or—in the case of sign languages—the equivalent aspects of sign. It is concerned with the physical properties of speech sounds or signs (phones): their physiological production, acoustic properties, auditory perception, and neurophysiological status. Phonology, on the other hand, is concerned with the abstract, grammatical characterization of systems of sounds or signs.

Phosphate backbone
The sugar-phosphate backbone forms the structural framework of nucleic acids, like DNA and RNA, and is composed of alternating sugar and phosphate groups.

Phosphate group
A phosphorus atom attached to four oxygen atoms; one of the three components of a nucleotide.

Phosphodiester
Molecule containing R.O.P.O.R, in which R is a carbon-containing group, O is oxygen, and P is phosphorus.

Phosphodiester bond
A phosphodiester bond is a group of strong covalent bonds between a phosphate group and two 5-carbon ring carbohydrates (pentoses) over two ester bonds. Phosphodiester bonds are central to all known life, as they make up the backbone of each helical strand of DNA. In DNA and RNA, the phosphodiester bond is the linkage between the 3' carbon atom of one sugar molecule and the 5' carbon atom of another; the sugar molecules being deoxyribose in DNA and ribose in RNA. Phosphodiester bonds are also found in O-phosphonolipids (phospholipids)

Phosphodiester linkage
Phosphodiester bond connecting two nucleotides in a polynucleotide strand.

Phosphorothioate
A phosphate with one oxygen replaced with a sulphur; this can also refer to an oligo with phosphorothioate linkages.

Phosphorylation
The enzymatic addition of a phosphate group to a protein.

Photoautotrophs
Organisms that are able to synthesize their own food from collected light energy through photosynthesis.

Photobiology
Photobiology is the scientific study of the interactions of light (technically,

non-ionizing radiation) and living organisms. The field includes the study of photosynthesis, photomorphogenesis, visual processing, circadian rhythms, bioluminescence, and ultraviolet radiation effects. The division between ionizing radiation and nonionizing radiation is typically considered to be 10 eV, the energy required to ionize an oxygen atom.

Photochemistry
Photochemistry, a sub-discipline of chemistry, is the study of chemical reactions that proceed with the absorption of light by atoms or molecules. Everyday examples include photosynthesis, the degradation of plastics and the formation of vitamin D with sunlight.

Photometer
In astronomy, an instrument to measure the amount of light that reaches the telescope.

Photons
A photon is an elementary particle, the quantum of light and all other forms of electromagnetic radiation, and the force carrier for the electromagnetic force. The effects of this force are easily observable at both the microscopic and macroscopic level, because the photon has no rest mass; this allows for interactions at long distances. Like all elementary particles, photons are currently best explained by quantum mechanics and will exhibit wave–particle duality, exhibiting properties of both waves and particles.

Photosynthesis
The process by which organisms capture energy from the sun, convert it to chemical energy, and either store the energy in chemical bonds or use the energy to build biomass.

Photosynthetic capability
How much energy an organism is able to capture from the sun to, through a series of chemical steps, synthesize sugars; how much energy an organism is able to convert from light energy to chemical energy.

Photosynthetic pigment
A photosynthetic pigment (accessory pigment; chloroplast pigment; antenna pigment) is a pigment that is present in chloroplasts or photosynthetic bacteria and captures the light energy necessary for photosynthesis.

Photosynthetic reaction centre
A photosynthetic reaction centre (or photosynthetic reaction centre) is a complex of several proteins, pigments and other co-factors assembled together to execute the primary energy conversion reactions of photosynthesis. Molecular excitations, either originating directly from sunlight or transferred as excitation energy via light-harvesting antenna systems, give rise to electron transfer reactions along a series of protein-bound co-factors. These co-factors are light-absorbing molecules (also named chromophores or pigments) such as chlorophyll and phaeophytin, as well as quinones. The energy of the photon is used to promote an electron to a higher molecular energy level of a pigment. The free energy created is then used to reduce a chain of nearby electron acceptors, which have subsequently lowered redox-potentials. These electron transfer steps are the initial phase of a series of energy conversion reactions, ultimately resulting in the production of chemical energy during photosynthesis.

Phreatic eruption (explosion)
An explosive volcanic eruption caused when water and heated volcanic rocks interact to produce a violent expulsion of steam and pulverized rocks. Magma is not involved.

Phrenology
The study of the faculties & qualities of mind from the shape of the skull.

Phthisiology
Phthisiology is the care, treatment, and study of tuberculosis of the lung. It is therefore considered a specialisation within the area of pulmonology.

Phycology
Phycology is the scientific study of algae. Phycology is a branch of life science and often is regarded as a subdiscipline of botany. Algae are important plants as primary producers in aquatic ecosystems. Most algae are eukaryotic, photosynthetic organisms that live in a wet environment. They are distinguished from the higher plants by a lack of true roots, stems or leaves. Many species are single-celled and microscopic (including phytoplankton and other microalgae); many others are multicellular to one degree or another, some of these growing to large size (for example, seaweeds such as kelp and Sargassum).

Phylogenetic distance
A measure of the degree of separation between two organisms or their genomes on an evolutionary scale, usually expressed as the number of accumulated sequence changes, number of years, or number of generations.

Phylogenetic profile
The presence-and-absence pattern of genes in different species, which may be used to infer gene function. A presence-and-absence pattern that is the same in different organisms suggests that the genes may be functionally related.

Phylogenetic species concept
Any of several related concepts of species as sets of populations that are diagnosably different from other populations.

Phylogenetic trees
The branching diagram or .tree. showing the deduced evolutionary relationships among organisms.

Phylogeny
The history of descent of a group of taxa such as species from their common ancestors, including the order of branching and sometimes the absolute times of divergence; also applied to the genealogy of genes derived from a common ancestral gene.

Physical distance
The actual distance between two loci in terms of the number of nucleotides in the DNA, usually measured in units of thousands of base pairs (kilobases, kb) or millions of base pairs (megabases, Mb).

Physical linkage
Phenomenon in which two genes are located on the same chromosome.

Physical map
Map of physical distances between loci, genetic markers, or other chromosome segments; measured in base pairs.

Physical science
The study of natural laws and process other than those peculiar to living matters, as in Physics,

Chemistry and Astronomy.

Physics

Physics is a natural science that involves the study of matter and its motion through spacetime, along with related concepts such as energy and force. More broadly, it is the general analysis of nature, conducted in order to understand how the universe behaves. Physics is one of the oldest academic disciplines, perhaps the oldest through its inclusion of astronomy. Over the last two millennia, physics was a part of natural philosophy along with chemistry, certain branches of mathematics, and biology, but during the Scientific Revolution in the 16th century, the natural sciences emerged as unique research programmes in their own right.

Physiography

Physical geography (also known as geosystems or physiography) is one of the two major subfields of geography. Physical geography is that branch of natural science which deals with the study of processes and patterns in the natural environment like the atmosphere, biosphere and geosphere, as opposed to the cultural or built environment, the domain of human geography.

Physiology

Physiology is the science of the function of living systems. This includes how organisms, organ systems, organs, cells, and biomolecules carry out the chemical or physical functions that exist in a living system. The highest honor awarded in physiology is the Nobel Prize in Physiology or Medicine, awarded since 1901 by the Royal Swedish Academy of Sciences. Many U.S. universities offer physiology as a major.

Phytogeny

Origin and growth of plants.

Picture

Visual representation of something, such as the image of a star obtained by a telescope.

Pid

Proportional, integral, derivative. A three mode control action where the controller has time proportioning, integral (auto reset) and derivative rate action.

Piezoelectric accelerometer

A transducer that produces an electrical charge in direct proportion to the vibratory acceleration.

Piezoresistance

Resistance that changes with stress.

Pig

A device used for cleaning a pipeline or separating two liquids being moved down the pipeline. Intelligent pigs are fitted with sensors allowing measurement of corrosion and identification of pipeline defects.

Pillow lava

Interconnected, sack-like bodies of lava that form underwater.

Pilus

Extension of the surface of some bacteria that allows conjugation to take place. When a pilus on one cell makes contact with a receptor on another cell, the pilus contracts and pulls the two cells together.

Ping

Packet Internet Gopher. A TCP/IP application that sends a message to another computer, waits for a reply, and displays the time the transmission took. This serves to identify what computers are available on the Internet and how long wait-times are.

Pioneer community
A community composed of the initial inhabitants (early seral stage).

Pioneer species
Species that colonize early in a vegetational succession; pioneer species possess characteristics like rapid growth, the production of copious, small, easily dispersed seed, and the ability to germinate and establish themselves on open sites.

Pipe-line (processing)
Analysis and processing of scientific data in a sequential manner.

Pixel
Picture element. Definable locations on a display screen that are used to form images on the screen. For graphic displays, screens with more pixels provide higher resolution.

Plain text
This is text without extraneous codes that designate font size, font style, et cetera.

Planck constant
The Planck constant, h, is a fundamental physical constant. Electromagnetic radiation has a dual nature. It can be considered to be composed of waves or of particles (photons). The wavelike and particle-like properties are related by Planck's Law in which the constant of proportionality is h. (h = 6.62 x 10^{-34} Joule seconds).

Planck mission
ESA astronomy mission, which will observe the cosmic microwave background with an unprecedented precision allowing different theoretical models explaining how the Universe formed after the Big Bang occurred to be evaluated.

Planck's law
Planck's law describes the amount of energy emitted by a black body in radiation of a certain wavelength (i.e. the spectral radiance of a black body). The law is named after Max Planck, who originally proposed it in 1900. The law was the first to accurately describe black body radiation, and resolved the ultraviolet catastrophe. It is a pioneer result of modern physics and quantum theory.

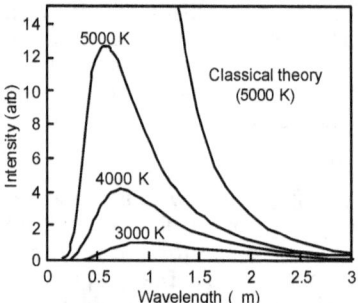

Plane (focal)
A surface upon which the image of all points in the field of view of an optical instrument is created

Plane separation
Of a balancing machine, is the operation of reducing the correction plane interference ratio for a particular rotor.

Planet
Large, spherical, rocky or icy body which orbits the Sun or another star.

Planetary nebula
A bright cloud of dust and gas surrounding an old star, namely a red giant. Towards the end of its life the star ejects the dust and gas violently, losing most of its mass and becoming a white dwarf. The nebula disappears

after approximately 100,000 years. They are called 'planetary' because originally astronomers thought they looked like planetary discs.

Planktonic
Living in open water.

Plant
A living thing is green, and needs water, light, and air to grow. Many rain forest plants have large leaves and tall stems.

Plaque
Clear patch of lysed cells on a continuous layer of bacteria on the agar surface of a petri plate. Each plaque represents a single original phage that multiplied and lysed many cells.

Plasma
Matter containing more or less equal amounts of positively charged ions and negatively charged electrons. It is usually extremely hot and found in or near stars.

Plasmid
A plasmid is a small, circular, double-stranded DNA molecule, which is distinct from chromosomal DNA.

Plastic deformation (or flow)
Permanent bending or folding of rock (or ice) as a result of directed pressure. In rock, usually occurs below the Brittle-Ductile Transition Zone, and is commonly associated with metamorphism.

Plate
1. A thin, flat piece of bone. One dinosaur had a row of pointed plates running down its back.
2. A very large slab of rock that makes up the crust and mantle of the Earth. The Himalayan Mountains were created when one plate collided with another plate.

Plate tectonics
The theory that the earth's crust is broken into about fragments (plates,) which move in relation to one another, shifting continents, forming new ocean crust, and causing volcanic eruptions.

Platform
Main supporting structure of a spacecraft accommodating its main subsystems such as propellant, flight electronics and communications.

Platinum
Platinum is a chemical element with the chemical symbol Pt and an atomic number of 78. Its name is derived from the Spanish term platina del Pinto, which is literally translated into "little silver of the Pinto River." It is a dense, malleable, ductile, precious, gray-white transition metal. Even though it has six naturally occurring isotopes, platinum is one of the rarest elements in the Earth's crust and has an average abundance of approximately 0.005 mg/kg. It is the least reactive metal.

Platinum 10% rhodium
The platinum-rhodium alloy used as the positive wire in conjunction with pure platinum to form a Type S thermocouple.

Platinum 13% rhodium
The platinum-rhodium alloy used as the positive wire in conjunction with pure platinum to form a Type R thermocouple.

Platinum 30% rhodium
The platinum-rhodium alloy used as the positive wire in conjunction with platinum 6% rhodium to form a Type B thermocouple.

Platinum 6% rhodium
The platinum-rhodium alloy used as the negative wire in conjunction with

platinum-30% rhodium to form a Type B thermocouple.

Platinum 67
To develop thermal emf tables for thermocouples, the National Bureau of Standards paired each thermocouple alloy against a pure platinum wire (designated Platinum 2 prior to 1973, and currently Platinum 67). The thermal emf's of any alloy combination can be determined by summing the "vs. Pt-67" emf's of the alloys, i.e., the emf table for a Type K thermocouple is derived from the Chromel vs. Pt-67 and the Alumel vs. Pt-67 values.

Pleiades
The Pleiades star cluster, also known as the seven sisters or M45, is a young star cluster in the constellation Taurus. It is no more than 80 million years old and lies at a distance of about 400 light-years from the Sun. The cluster contains thousands of stars, of which 6 are visible with the naked-eye: Alcyone, Maia, Atlas, Electra, Merope and Taygeta.

Pleiotropy
The phenomenon in which one locus affects more than one phenotypic trait, causing a genetic correlation.

Ploidy
The number of chromosome complements in an organism.

Plug
Solidified lava that fills the conduit of a volcano. Plugs (also called volcanic necks) are usually more resistant to erosion than the material making up the surrounding cone, and may remain standing as a solitary pinnacle when the rest of the original structure has eroded away.

Plug dome
The steep-sided, rounded mound formed when viscous lava wells up into a crater and is too stiff to flow away. It piles up as a dome-shaped mass, often completely filling the vent from which it emerged.

Plug-in
A small piece of software that adds features to already existing, usually large, programmes.

Plumes
Feather-like formation of hot, rising gas in the atmosphere of a star or planet caused by convection.

Pluto
Originally considered the ninth planet in our Solar System as now classified a dwarf planet. Pluto is much smaller than the Moon. Its highly eccentric orbit, with an average radius of 39.4 AU, sometimes takes it within the orbit of Neptune. Pluto has a very thin atmosphere consisting mainly of methane and nitrogen. The average surface temperature is 50 K.

Pluton
A large igneous intrusion formed at great depth in the crust.

Poineer species
Species that colonize early in a vegetational succession; species possessing characteristics like rapid growth, the production of copious, small, easily dispersed seed, and the ability to germinate and establish themselves on open sites.

Point mutation
A change in a single nucleotide in a DNA sequence. See also transition, transversion.

Pointed teeth
Sharp teeth that are good for tearing food. Most meat-eating dinosaurs had pointed teeth.

Point-source pollution
Water pollution coming from a single point, such as a sewage-outflow pipe.

Poisson ratio
The ratio between the strain of expansion in the direction of force and the strain of contraction perpendicular to that force v = -Et/E1.

Polarisation
Polarization (also polarisation) is a property of certain types of waves that describes the orientation of their oscillations. Electromagnetic waves, such as light, and gravitational waves exhibit polarization; acoustic waves (sound waves) in a gas or liquid do not have polarization because the direction of vibration and direction of propagation are the same. By convention, the polarization of light is described by specifying the orientation of the wave's electric field at a point in space over one period of the oscillation. When light travels in free space, in most cases it propagates as a transverse wave—the polarization is perpendicular to the wave's direction of travel.

Polarity
In electricity, the quality of having two oppositely charged poles, one positive one negative.

Polarization
The inability of an electrode to reproduce a reading after a small electrical current has been passed through the membrane. Glass pH electrodes are especially prone to polarization errors caused by small currents flowing from the pH metre input circuit and from static electrical charges built up as the electrodes are removed from the sample solution, or when the electrodes are wiped.

Pole
Usually the coldest regions on a planet, being the areas around an axis through the planet perpendicular to the plane of rotation about the Sun.

Pollen
In seed plants, the microscopic grains containing the male gametophyte and gamete.

Polluted
Containing waste materials or other unwanted substances. The river that runs through town is polluted.

Poly(A) addition sequence
An AAUAAA sequence in the 3' end of a growing mRNA that binds to several proteins that signal the end of the templated molecule, cleavage of the mRNA molecule, and subsequent polyadenylation.

Poly(A) tail
String of adenine nucleotides added to the 3' end of a eukaryotic mRNA after transcription.

Poly(A)-binding protein
Binds to the poly(A) tail of eukaryotic mRNA and makes the mRNA more stable. There are several types of PABPs, one of which is PABII.

Poly-A tail
The poly-A tail is a long chain of adenines nucleotides that is added to a messenger RNA (mRNA) molecule during RNA processing to increase the stability of the mRNA molecule.

Polychlorinated biphenyls (pcbs)
A group of synthetic, toxic industrial chemical compounds once used in making paint and electrical transformers, which are chemically

inert and not biodegradable. PCBs were frequently found in industrial wastes, and subsequently found their way into surface and ground waters. As a result of their persistence, they tend to accumulate in the environment. In terms of streams and rivers, PCBs are drawn to sediment, to which they attach and can remain virtually indefinitely.

Polycystic kidney disease
A kidney disorder passed down through families in which multiple cysts form on the kidneys, causing them to become enlarged.

Polygenic character
A character whose variation is based wholly or in part on allelic variation at more than a few loci.

Polymerase chain reaction
The polymerase chain reaction (PCR) is a scientific technique in molecular biology to amplify a single or a few copies of a piece of DNA across several orders of magnitude, generating thousands to millions of copies of a particular DNA sequence.

Polymerisation
The repetitive bonding of small molecules (monomers) to produce large molecules (polymers).

Polymers
A polymer is a large molecule (macromolecule) composed of repeating structural units. These subunits are typically connected by covalent chemical bonds. Although the term polymer is sometimes taken to refer to plastics, it actually encompasses a large class of compounds comprising both natural and synthetic materials with a wide variety of properties.

Polymorphic
A population that has more than one relatively common allele present at a given locus.

Polymorphism
The existence within a population of two or more genotypes, the rarest of which exceeds some arbitrarily low frequency (say, 1 percent); more rarely, the existence of phenotypic variation within a population, whether or not genetically based.

Polynucleotide strand
Series of nucleotides linked together by phosphodiester bonds.

Polypeptide
Chain of amino acids linked by peptide bonds; also called a protein.

Polyphenism
The capacity of a species or genotype to develop two or more forms, with the specific form depending on specific environmental conditions or cues, such as temperature or day length. A polyphenism is distinct from a polymorphism in that the former is the property of a single genotype, whereas the latter refers to multiple forms encoded by two or more different genotypes.

Polyphyletic
Refers to a taxon, phylogenetic tree, or gene tree composed of members derived by evolution from ancestors in more than one ancestral taxon; hence, composed of members that do not share a unique common ancestor.

Polyploid
Of a cell or organism, possessing more than two chromosome complements.

Polyribosome
Messenger RNA molecule with several ribosomes attached to it.

Polysomy
Polysomy is a condition in which an organism has at least one more chromosome than normal, i.e. the number of a particular chromosome is not diploid - there may be three or more copies of the chromosome rather than the expected two copies. Polysomy is usually caused by non-disjunction (the failure of a pair of homologous chromosomes to separate) during meiosis, but may also be due to a translocation mutation. Down's syndrome is an example of polysomy where affected individuals possess three copies (trisomy) of chromosome 21.

Polytene chromosome
Giant chromosome in the salivary glands of Drosophila melanogaster; each polytene chromosome consists of a number of DNA molecules lying side by side.

Pomology
Pomology (from Latin pomum (fruit) + -logy) is a branch of botany that studies and cultivates pome fruit, particularly from the genera Malus, Prunus and Pyrus belonging to the Rosaceae. The term is sometimes applied more broadly, to the cultivation of any type of fruit. In the latter case, the denomination fruticulture—introduced from romance languages (from Latin fructus and cultura) —is also used. Pomological research is mainly focused on the development, cultivation and physiological studies of stone fruit trees. The goals of fruit tree improvement include enhancement of fruit quality, regulation of production periods, and reduction of production cost.

Pond
A small body of water. Fish and frogs often live in a pond.

Pool habitat
A stream location with constant stream bottom height.

Population
A group of conspecific organisms that occupy a more or less well-defined geographic region and exhibit reproductive continuity from generation to generation; ecological and reproductive interactions are more frequent among these individuals than with members of other populations of the same species.

Population bottleneck
A population bottleneck is an event that drastically reduces the size of a population.

Population differentiation
Differences between populations in allele frequencies at one or more loci, or in mean phenotype, in a common environment.

Population ecology
The study of individual populations (of a single species), including their birth, death, and growth rates in numbers and their growth rates of individual mass and population biomass; also includes their spatial distributions and rates of movement (immigration, emigration).

Population genetics
Study of the genetic composition of populations (groups of individuals of the same species) and how a population's collective group of genes changes through time.

Porosity
A measure of the water-bearing capacity of subsurface rock. With respect to water movement, it is not just the total magnitude of porosity that is important, but the size of the

voids and the extent to which they are interconnected, as the pores in a formation may be open, or interconnected, or closed and isolated.

Port
A communications connection on an electronic or computer based device.

Portfolio effect
If the abundance of different species fluctuates independently, or at least out of phase with one another, then these fluctuations will average each other out, leading to less variation over time in a diverse assemblage.

Position effect
Dependence of the expression of a gene on the gene's location in the genome.

Positional cloning
Positional cloning is a method of gene identification in which a gene for a specific phenotype is identified, with only its approximate chromosomal location (but not the function) known, also known as the candidate region. Initially, the candidate region can be defined using techniques such as linkage analysis, and positional cloning is then used to narrow the candidate region until the gene and its mutations are found. Positional cloning typically involves the isolation of partially overlapping DNA segments from genomic libraries to progress along the chromosome toward a specific gene. During the course of positional cloning, one needs to determine whether the DNA segment currently under consideration is part of the gene.

Positive allometry
For ontogenetic allometry, when the organ has a higher growth rate than the body as whole, a > 1; for static/ evolutionary allometry, when an organ is proportionally larger in larger individuals/species.

Positive assortative mating
Mating between like individuals that is more frequent than would be expected on the basis of chance.

Positive control
Gene regulation in which the binding of a regulatory protein to DNA stimulates transcription (the regulatory protein is an activator).

Positive selection
The selection for an allele that increases fitness.

Positive temperature coefficient
An increase in resistance due to an increase in temperature.

Positive-strand RNA virus
RNA virus whose genomic RNA molecule codes directly for viral proteins.

Positron
The antiparticle of the electron. A positron has the same characteristics as an electron but it has a positive charge instead of a negative one.

Post-copulatory selection
Occurs during and after mating and it refers to selection on traits that influence the likelihood of fertilization and subsequent investment in offspring.

Postnatal
Postnatal (Latin for after birth, from post, meaning after, and natalis, meaning of birth) is the period beginning immediately after the birth of a child and extending for about six weeks. Another term would be postpartum period, as it refers to the

mother (whereas postnatal refers to the infant). Less frequently used is puerperium. It is the time after birth, a time in which the mother's body, including hormone levels and uterus size, returns to a non-pregnant state. Lochia is post-partum vaginal discharge, containing blood, mucus, and placental tissue.

Post-transcriptional regulation

Multiple processes that regulate the efficiency of translation after mRNA is transcribed, including mRNA stability.

Posttranslational modification

Alteration of a protein after translation; may include cleavage from a larger precursor protein, the removal of amino acids, and the attachment of other molecules to the protein.

Postzygotic

Occurring after union of the nuclei of uniting gametes; usually refers to inviability or sterility that confers reproductive isolation.

Potable water

Drinking water or potable water is water pure enough to be consumed or used with low risk of immediate or long term harm. In most developed countries, the water supplied to households, commerce and industry is all of drinking water standard, even though only a very small proportion is actually consumed or used in food preparation. Typical uses include washing or landscape irrigation. Drinking or using such water in food preparation leads to widespread acute and chronic illnesses and is a major cause of death and misery in many countries. Reduction of waterborne diseases is a major public health goal in developing countries.

Potential difference

The voltage difference between two points. Electricity flows from a high to low level of potential.

Potential energy

Energy related to the position or height above a place to which fluid could possibly flow.

Potential energy (gravitational)

The stored energy of a substance. Water has a lot of this if there is an elevation difference. Potential energy can be converted to kinetic energy if the water (or other substance) is allowed to move.

Potentiometer

1. A variable resistor often used to control a circuit.
2. A balancing bridge used to measure voltage.

Power

Amount of work done per second.

Power supply

A power supply is a device that supplies electrical energy to one or more electric loads. The term is most commonly applied to devices that convert one form of electrical energy to another, though it may also refer to devices that convert another form of energy (e.g., mechanical, chemical, solar) to electrical energy. A regulated power supply is one that controls the output voltage or current to a specific value; the controlled value is held nearly constant despite variations in either load current or the voltage supplied by the power supply's energy source.

PPM

Abbreviation for "parts per million," sometimes used to express temperature coefficients. For instance, 100 ppm is identical to 0.01%.

Prader-Willi syndrome
Prader-Willi syndrome (PWS) is a metabolic disorder caused by genetic defects; among its features are short stature, mental retardation, poor muscle tone, and hyperphagia, which leads to childhood obesity.

Praire restoration
An attempt to recreate a prairie climax community within 10 years, when this process naturally takes several hundred years through manipulation of mechanisms of succession to rapidly achieve climax conditions by greatly increasing seed availability, reducing competition by early-successional species, and amending soil to better match late-succession conditions.

Preadaptation
Possession of the necessary properties to permit a shift to a new niche, habitat, or function. A structure is preadapted for a new function if it can assume that function without evolutionary modification.

Prebiotic
Related to the period before life appears on a planet.

Precipitation
The falling of water in the form of rain, sleet, hail, or snow. During the last big winter storm, the precipitation took the form of snow and sleet.

Preconception
The time before a pregnancy has occurred.

Pre-copulatory sexual selection
Refers to selection on traits that influence likelihood of mating.

Predation
Biological interaction where an one organism, the predator, kills and eats another, the prey.

Predator
Predation describes a biological interaction where a predator (an organism that is hunting) feeds on its prey (the organism that is attacked). Predators may or may not kill their prey prior to feeding on them, but the act of predation always results in the death of its prey and the eventual absorption of the prey's tissue through consumption. Other categories of consumption are herbivory (eating parts of plants) and detritivory, the consumption of dead organic material (detritus). All these consumption categories fall under the rubric of consumer-resource systems. It can often be difficult to separate various types of feeding behaviours

Preformationism
Early concept of inheritance proposing that a miniature adult (homunculus) resides in either the egg or the sperm and increases in size during development, with all traits being inherited from the parent that contributes the homunculus.

Preimplantation genetic diagnosis
Used to select an embryo produced by in vitro fertilization before implantation of the embryo in the uterus.

Preliminary design review
A major review of the design for a spacecraft before construction can begin. The preliminary design review marks the boundary between the design phase and the construction phase.

Pre-messenger RNA
Eukaryotic RNA molecule that is modified after transcription to become mRNA.

Prenatal
The period between conception and birth.

Presymptomatic diagnosis
The identification of a disease before a patient exhibits physical manifestations of the disease.

Presymptomatic genetic testing
Testing people to determine whether they have inherited a disease-causing gene before the symptoms of the disease have appeared.

Prevention
Action taken to avoid getting a disease.

Prey
The organism consumed.

Prezygotic
Occurring before union of the nuclei of uniting gametes; usually refers to events in the reproductive process that cause reproductive isolation.

Primaeval soup
Mixture of water and chemical ingredients that constituted the oceans on Earth about three or four billion years ago. Among the chemicals were simple organic molecules. The primeval soup is thought to have been the place where life originated.

Primary device
Part of a flowmeter which is mounted internally or externally to the fluid conduit and produces a signal corresponding to the flowrate and from which the flow may be determined.

Primary down syndrome
Caused by the presence of three copies of chromosome 21.

Primary immune response
Initial clone of cells specific for a particular antigen and generated when the antigen is first encountered by the immune system.

Primary mirror
Large mirror in a reflecting telescope the size of which determines the light-gathering power of the prism.

Primary oocyte
Oogonium that has entered prophase I.

Primary producers
Organisms that convert energy from light or heat into organic tissue. Plants are an example of a primary producer.

Primary production
The amount of light energy from the sun converted to chemical energy (organic compounds) by autotrophs (e.g. plants, algae, many bacteria) in an ecosystem within a period of time.

Primary standards
Aqueous pH buffer solutions established by the National Bureau of Standards within the 2.5 to 11.5 pH range of ionic strength less than 0.1 and which provide stable liquid junction potential and uniformity of electrode sensitivity.

Primary structure of a protein
The amino acid sequence of a protein.

Primary succession
The loss of the entire soil complex due to large, extreme disturbances

such as volcanic eruptions or glaciers that Â result in very slow succession due to complete mortality of all living individuals in the system.

Primary wastewater treatment
The first stage of the wastewater-treatment process where mechanical methods, such as filters and scrapers, are used to remove pollutants. Solid material in sewage also settles out in this process.

Primase
Primase is an enzyme that synthesizes short RNA sequences called primers, which serve as starting points for DNA synthesis.

Primer
1. A primer is a short nucleic acid sequence that provides a starting point for DNA synthesis.
2. Short stretch of RNA on a DNA template; provides a 3'-OH group for the attachment of a DNA nucleotide at the initiation of replication.

Primordial nucleosynthesis
The first time that nuclear atomic particles, neutrons and protons, could combine to make atomic nuclei. This happened during the first thousand seconds of existence of the Universe. The first atomic nuclei made were those of the light elements.

Primordium
A group of embryonic or larval cells destined to give rise to a particular adult structure.

Principal axes
The axes of maximum and minimum normal stress.

Principle of independent assortment
The principle of independent assortment describes how different genes independently separate from one another during the formation of reproductive cells.

Principle of segregation
The principle of segregation describes how pairs of gene variants are separated into reproductive cells.

Principle of uniformity
States that the F1 progeny of two parents that differ in a trait should all have the same appearance.

Principles of inheritance
The term that describes the three principles described by Gregor Mendel that summarized his extensive experiments studying the patterns of heredity for acquired characteristics.

Prion
Infectious agent that lacks nucleic acid; believed to replicate by altering the shape of proteins produced by cellular genes.

Prior appropriation doctrine
The system for allocating water to private individuals used in most Western states. The doctrine of Prior Appropriation was in common use throughout the arid West as early settlers and miners began to develop the land. The prior appropriation doctrine is based on the concept of "First in Time, First in Right." The first person to take a quantity of water and put it to beneficial use has a higher priority of right than a subsequent user. The rights can be lost through nonuse; they can also be sold or transferred apart from the land.

Priority effects
Species arrival in a community prevents the invasion of other species.

Prism
Device that breaks light into its composite wavelength spectrum.

Probability
Likelihood of a particular event occurring; more formally, the number of times a particular event occurs divided by the number of all possible outcomes. Probability values range from 0 to 1.

Proband
A person with a trait or disease for whom a pedigree is constructed.

Probe
The known sequence of DNA or RNA that is complementary to a sequence of interest and will pair with it; used to find specific DNA sequences.

Problem
A situation which is generally uncomfortable, or otherwise undesirable. I always seem to have several - how about you?

Process metre
A panel metre with sizeable zero and span adjustment capabilities, which can be scaled for readout in engineering units for signals such as 4-20 mA, 10-50 mA and 1-5 V.

Processed pseudogene
A pseudogene that has arisen via the retrotransposition of mRNA into cDNA.

Processing of mrna
The process of adding different features to a nascent mRNA strand in eukaryotes, including the addition of a 5' cap, splicing, editing, and polyadenylation.

Producers
Organisms that can produce their own food either by photosynthesis or chemosynthesis.

Productivity
Productivity or production refers to the rate of generation of biomass in an ecosystem. It is usually expressed in units of mass per unit surface (or volume) per unit time, for instance grams per square metre per day. The mass unit may relate to dry matter or to the mass of carbon generated. Productivity of autotrophs such as plants is called primary productivity, while that of heterotrophs such as animals is called secondary productivity.

Products
The substances produced in a chemical reaction.

Progenesis
A decrease during evolution of the duration of ontogenetic development, resulting in retention of juvenile features in the sexually mature adult.

Programme
A list of instructions that a computer follows to perform a task.

Programmable logic controller
The computer based monitoring and control package where control actions are primarily based on equipment and alarm status.

Prokaryote
The prokaryotes are a group of organisms that lack a cell nucleus (= karyon), or any other membrane-bound organelles.

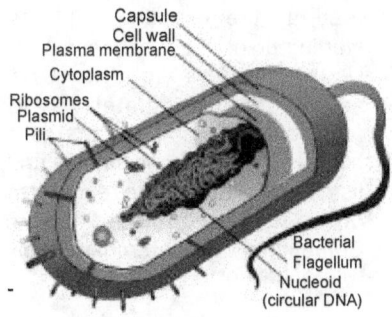

are called eukaryotes. Most prokaryotes are unicellular, but a few such as myxobacteria have multicellular stages in their life cycles.

Prom
Programmable read-only memory. A semiconductor memory whose contents cannot be changed by the computer after it has been programmed.

Prometaphase
Prometaphase is the second phase of mitosis, which is a process that separates the duplicated genetic material carried in the nucleus of a parent cell into two, identical daughter cells.

Prominence (solar)
Large cloud of plasma extending above the Sun's chromosphere. They are divided into two main classes. Quiescent types show little motion, may last for several solar rotations and disappear slowly. Eruptive or active types form and disappear very quickly, and may grow to tremendous size.

Promoter
1. DNA sequence to which the transcription apparatus binds so as to initiate transcription; indicates the direction of transcription, which of the two DNA strands is to be read as the template, and the starting point of transcription.
2. Usually refers to the DNA sequences immediately 5' to (upstream of) a gene that are bound by the RNA polymerase and its cofactors and/or are required in order to transcribe the gene. Sometimes used interchangeably with enhancer.

Pronucleus
The nucleus in a sperm cell or oocyte prior to fertilization.

Proof pressure
The specified pressure which may be applied to the sensing element of a transducer without causing a permanent change in the output characteristics.

Proofreading
The ability of DNA polymerases to remove and replace incorrectly paired nucleotides in the course of replication.

Prophage
The phage genome that is integrated into a bacterial chromosome.

Prophase
The prophase is the first phase of mitosis, which is a process that separates the duplicated genetic material carried in the nucleus of a parent cell into two, identical daughter cells

Prophase I
The stage of meiosis I. In prophase I, chromosomes condense and pair, crossing over takes place, the nuclear membrane breaks down, and the spindle forms.

Prophase II
The stage of meiosis after interkinesis. In prophase II, chromosomes condense, the nuclear membrane breaks down, and the spindle forms. Some cells skip this stage.

Proportion of polymorphic loci
Percentage of loci in which more than one allele is present in a population.
Proportional counter

Instrument used for detecting gamma rays and X-rays in which radiation triggers an electrical discharge resulting in a pulse of electric current whose strength is proportional to the energy of the radiation.

Proportioning band
A temperature band expressed in degrees within which a temperature controller's time proportioning function is active.

Proportioning control mode
A time proportioning controller where the amount of time that the relay is energized is dependent upon the system's temperature.

Proportioning control plus derivative function
A time proportioning controller with derivative function. The derivative function senses the rate at which a system's temperature is either increasing or decreasing and adjusts the cycle time of the controller to minimize overshoot or undershoot.

Proportioning control plus integral
A two-mode controller with time proportioning and integral (auto reset) action. The integral function automatically adjusts the temperature at which a system has stabilized back to the setpoint temperature, thereby eliminating droop in the system.

Proportioning control with integral and derivative functions
Three mode PID controller. A time proportioning controller with integral and derivative functions. The integral function automatically adjusts the system temperature to the set point temperature to eliminate droop due to

the time proportioning function. The derivative function senses the rate of rise or fall of the system temperature and automatically adjusts the cycle time of the controller to minimize overshoot or undershoot.

Propulsion
Process by which something can be moved by producing a reaction with a force of thrust.

Proteasomal regulation
Protein stability mediated by the proteasome, a cellular organelle that degrades misfolded proteins that are often tagged with ubiquitin.

Proteasome
A multiprotein structure shaped like a barrel through which misfolded proteins pass and are dismantled.

Protection head
An enclosure usually made out of metal at the end of a heater or probe where connections are made.

Protection tube
A metal or ceramic tube, closed at one end into which a temperature sensor is inserted. The tube protects the sensor from the medium into which it is inserted.

Protein
1. One of the most fundamental building substances of living organisms. A long-chain polymer of amino acids with twenty different common side chains. Occurs with its polymer chain extended in fibrous proteins, or coiled into a compact macromolecule in enzymes and other globular proteins.
2. A type of macromolecule that is the direct product of genetic information; a chain of amino acids.

Protein domain
The region of a protein that has a specific shape or function.

Protein kinase
An enzyme that adds phosphate groups to other cellular proteins.

Protein kinase A
A signaling protein that phosphorylates other proteins in response to cAMP signals.

Protein kinase B
A family of protein kinases (Akt1, Akt2 and Akt3) that mediate an array of intracellular signaling cascades. For example, Akt1 is generally thought to mediate cellular survival, and Akt2 is a primary component of insulin signaling.

Protein kinase C
A family of protein kinases that can be divided ubti three subgroups can be identified depending on their mechanism of action.conventional, novel, or atypical.

Protein-coding region
The part of mRNA consisting of the nucleotides that specify the amino acid sequence of a protein.

Protein-protein association
When two proteins bind and have an affinity for each other.

Proteome
A proteome is the complete set of proteins expressed by an organism

Protocol
A formal definition that describes how data is to be exchanged.

Proton
Positively charged constituent of all atomic nuclei. A proton is made up of three quarks. The number of protons in a nucleus is called the atomic number and determines the chemical element.

Proton rocket
Russia's largest operational launch vehicle. The four-stage booster has a length of more than 57 m, its total lift-off mass is almost 700 tonnes. Over the past 30 years it has been used in more than 230 launches.

Proto-oncogene
The normal cellular gene that controls cell division. When mutated, it may become an oncogene and contribute to cancer progression.

Protoplanetary disc
The disc of dust surrounding a star out of which planets might form.

Protostellar object
The earliest stages of star formation, when the nuclear reactions in the star's core have not begun yet. Stars form in opaque clouds of very cold dust and gas, which can be seen only with infrared telescopes.

Provinciality
The degree to which the taxonomic composition of a biota is differentiated among major geographic regions.

Provirus
A provirus is a virus genome that is integrated into the DNA of a host cell. This state can be a stage of virus replication, or a state that persists over longer periods of time as either inactive viral infections or an endogenous retrovirus. In inactive viral infections the virus will not replicate itself but through replication of its host cell. This state can last over many host cell generations. A provirus does not directly make new DNA copies of itself while integrated into a host genome in this way. Instead, it is

passively replicated along with the host genome and passed on to the original cell's offspring; all descendants of the infected cell will also bear proviruses in their genomes.

Pseudoautosomal region
The small region of the X and Y chromosomes that contains homologous gene sequences.

Pseudodominance
The expression of a normally recessive allele owing to a deletion on the homologous chromosome.

Pseudogene
A nonfunctional member of a gene family that has been derived from a functional gene.

Psia
Pounds per square inch absolute. Pressure referenced to a vacuum.

Psi-blast
A variation of BLAST that uses profiles that are based on sequence multiple-alignments to improve the sensitivity of protein database searches.

Psid
Pounds per square inch differential. Pressure difference between two points.

Psig
Pound per square inch gage. Pressure referenced to ambient air pressure.

Psis
Pounds per square inch standard. Pressure referenced to a standard atmosphere.

Psychology
The study of human and animal behaviour.

Public supply
Water withdrawn by public governments and agencies, such as a county water department, and by private companies that is then delivered to users. Public suppliers provide water for domestic, commercial, thermoelectric power, industrial, and public water users. Most people's household water is delivered by a public water supplier. The systems have at least 15 service connections (such as households, businesses, or schools) or regularly serve at least 25 individuals daily for at least 60 days out of the year.

Public water use
Water supplied from a public-water supply and used for such purposes as firefighting, street washing, and municipal parks and swimming pools.

Pulldown menu
A list of options that "pulls down" when you select a menu at the top of a window. For example, the File menu in most programmes is a pulldown menu that reveals commands such as open, new, and save.

Pulsar
A stellar source, such as a rotating single star or pair of stars, emitting electromagnetic radiation which is characterised by rapid frequency and regularity.

Pulse labeling
The addition of a labeled biochemical to cells in order to follow that specific chemical in cells of an organism or in culture.

Pulse width modulation
An output in the form of duty cycle which varies as a function of the applied measurand.

Pulse-chase assay
An experiment that requires the treatment of cells for a short time with a radioactive biochemical. The radioactive chemical is removed from the cells and the material that was incorporated into the cell is followed over time.

Pumice
Light-coloured, frothy volcanic rock, usually of dacite or rhyolite composition, formed by the expansion of gas in erupting lava. Commonly seen as lumps or fragments of pea-size and larger, but can also occur abundantly as ash-sized particles.

Punctuated equilibria
A pattern of rapid evolutionary change in the phenotype of a lineage separated by long periods of little change; also, a hypothesis intended to explain such a pattern, whereby phenotypic change transpires rapidly in small populations, in concert with the evolution of reproductive isolation.

Pyroclastic
Pertaining to fragmented (clastic) rock material formed by a volcanic explosion or ejection from a volcanic vent.

Pyroclastic flow
Lateral flowage of a turbulent mixture of hot gases (H"400°C) and unsorted pyroclastic material (volcanic fragments, crystals, ash, pumice, and glass shards) that can move at high speed (100 miles an hour or more). Also known as a "glowing avalanche" or "nueé ardente."

Pyrolyser
An instrument that breaks complex molecules into constituents by using heat.

Qbe
Query By Example. A search method for databases in which the user fills out the form by following the examples given.

Qualification model
Satellite prototype used to confirm the design and performance of the final flight model.

Quantam electrodynamics
Quantum electrodynamics (QED) is the relativistic quantum field theory of electrodynamics. In essence, it describes how light and matter interact and is the first theory where full agreement between quantum mechanics and special relativity is achieved. QED mathematically describes all phenomena involving electrically charged particles interacting by means of exchange of photons and represents the quantum counterpart of classical electrodynamics giving a complete account of matter and light interaction.

Quantum field theory
Quantum field theory (QFT) provides a theoretical framework for constructing quantum mechanical models of systems classically parametrized (represented) by an infinite number of dynamical degrees of freedom, that is, fields and (in a condensed matter context) many-body systems.

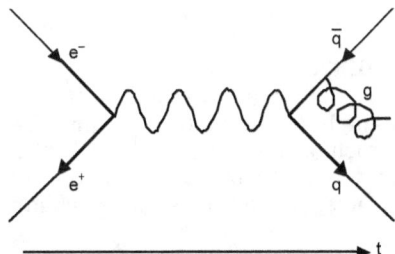

It is the natural and quantitative language of particle physics and condensed matter physics. Most theories in modern particle physics, including the Standard Model of elementary particles and their interactions, are formulated as relativistic quantum field theories. Quantum field theories are used in many contexts, and are especially vital in elementary particle physics, where the particle count/number may change over the course of a reaction.

Quantum mechanics
Theory of physics that explains the behaviour of nature and its forces on a very small, subatomic scale. It states that physical quantities can only have discrete values (this is quantization). According to quantum mechanics photons or electrons may be considered as particles but they can also be diffracted like waves (this is referred to as wave-particle duality). This quantum theory was proposed by Max Planck in 1900. Quantum

mechanics is the more formal mathematical description of his theory which was developed in the 1920's. It also incorporates the uncertainty principle, which states that you cannot measure a particle's position and velocity at the same time.

Quantum theory
The theory that energy can only be absorbed or radiated in discrete values or quanta. All particles are subject to quantum theory.

Quark
An elementary particle which is believed to be the fundamental structural unit from which all other particles are made. There are six quarks: up, down, strange, charm, top and bottom. A proton is made up of one down quark and two up quarks.

Quasar
A quasi-stellar radio source ("quasar") is a very energetic and distant active galactic nucleus. Quasars are extremely luminous and were first identified as being high redshift sources of electromagnetic energy, including radio waves and visible light, that were point-like, similar to stars, rather than extended sources similar to galaxies.

Quick-look analysis
Initial examination of scientific data before further processing and investigation.

Radiation

Radiation is a process in which energetic particles or energetic waves travel through a medium or space. Two types of radiation are commonly differentiated in the way they interact with normal chemical matter: ionizing and non-ionizing radiation. The word radiation is often colloquially used in reference to ionizing radiation (i.e., radiation having sufficient energy to ionize an atom), but the term radiation may correctly also refer to non-ionizing radiation (e.g., radio waves, heat or visible light). The particles or waves radiate (i.e., travel outward in all directions) from a source. This aspect leads to a system of measurements and physical units that are applicable to all types of radiation.

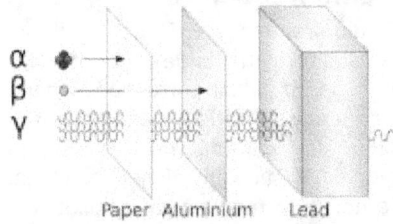

Radiation belt (Van Allen)

The Van Allen radiation belt is a torus of energetic charged particles (plasma) around Earth, which is held in place by Earth's magnetic field. It is believed that most of the particles that form the belts come from solar wind, and other particles by cosmic rays. It is named after its discoverer, James Van Allen, and is located in the inner region of the Earth's magnetosphere. It is split into two distinct belts, with energetic electrons forming the outer belt and a combination of protons and electrons forming the inner belts. In addition, the radiation belts contain lesser amounts of other nuclei, such as alpha particles. The belts pose a hazard to satellites, which must protect their sensitive components with adequate shielding if their orbit spends significant time in the radiation belts.

Radiation pattern

In the field of antenna design the term radiation pattern most commonly refers to the directional (angular) dependence of the strength of the radio waves from the antenna or other source (synonyms: antenna pattern, far-field pattern).

Radiation pressure

Radiation pressure is the pressure exerted upon any surface exposed to electromagnetic radiation. If absorbed, the pressure is the power flux density divided by the speed of light. If the radiation is totally reflected, the radiation pressure is doubled. For example, the radiation of the Sun at the Earth has a power flux density of 1,370 W/m^2, so the radiation pressure is 4.6 µPa (absorbed).

Radiation therapy
Radiation therapy sometimes abbreviated to XRT or DXT, is the medical use of ionizing radiation, generally as part of cancer treatment to control or kill malignant cells. Radiation therapy may be curative in a number of types of cancer if they are localized to one area of the body. It may also be used as part of curative therapy, to prevent tumor recurrence after surgery to remove a primary malignant tumor (for example, early stages of breast cancer). Radiation therapy is synergistic with chemotheraphy, and has been used before, during, and after chemotherapy in susceptible cancers.

Radio
Radio is the transmission of signals through free space by modulation of electromagnetic waves with frequencies below those of visible light. Electromagnetic radiation travels by means of oscillating electromagnetic fields that pass through the air and the vacuum of space. Information is carried by systematically changing (modulating) some property of the radiated waves, such as amplitude, frequency, phase, or pulse width. When radio waves pass through an electrical conductor, the oscillating fields induce an alternating current in the conductor. This can be detected and transformed into sound or other signals that carry information.

Radio astronomy
Radio astronomy is a subfield of astronomy that studies celestial objects at radio frequencies. The initial detection of radio waves from an astronomical object was made in the 1930s, when Karl Jansky observed radiation coming from the Milky Way. Subsequent observations have identified a number of different sources of radio emission. These include stars and galaxies, as well as entirely new classes of objects, such as radio galaxies, quasars, pulsars, and masers. The discovery of the cosmic microwave background radiation, which provided compelling evidence for the Big Bang, was made through radio astronomy.

Radio broadcasting
Radio broadcasting is a one-way wireless transmission over radio waves intended to reach a wide audience. Stations can be linked in radio networks to broadcast a common radio format, either in broadcast syndication or simulcast or both. Audio broadcasting also can be done via cable radio, local wire television networks, satellite radio, and internet radio via streaming media on the Internet. The signal types can be either analog audio or digital audio.

Radio frequency
Radio frequency (RF) is a rate of oscillation in the range of about 3 KHz to 300 GHz, which corresponds to the frequency of radio waves, and the alternating currents which carry radio signals. RF usually refers to electrical rather than mechanical oscillations, although mechanical RF systems do exist.

Radio frequency interference
The noise induced upon signal wires by ambient radio-frequency electromagnetic radiation with the effect of obscuring an instrument signal.

Radio waves

Radio waves are a type of electromagnetic radiation with wavelengths in the electromagnetic spectrum longer than infrared light. Radio waves have frequencies from 300 GHz to as low as 3 KHz, and corresponding wavelengths from 1 millimeter to 100 kilometers. Like all other electromagnetic waves, they travel at the speed of light. Naturally occurring radio waves are made by lightning, or by astronomical objects. Artificially generated radio waves are used for fixed and mobile radio communication, broadcasting, radar and other navigation systems, satellite communication, computer networks and innumerable other applications. Different frequencies of radio waves have different propagation characteristics in the Earth's atmosphere; long waves may cover a part of the Earth very consistently, shorter waves can reflect off the ionosphere and travel around the world, and much shorter wavelengths bend or reflect very little and travel on a line of sight.

Radioactive suicide

The death of cells due to incorporation of a radioactive substrate with high specific activity. Radioactive suicide can be used as a technique to select for mutants that are unable to incorporate a particular substrate.

Radioactivity

Spontaneous decay of atomic nuclei. An unstable nucleus may decay to one or more lighter nuclei. During the process radiation is emitted. There are three types of radioactive emissions: alpha particles (nuclei of helium), beta-rays (fast electrons) and gamma rays (high-energy photons). In the Universe radioactive atoms are formed in supernova explosions.

Radiobiology

Radiobiology (also known as radiation biology), as a field of clinical and basic medical sciences, originated from Leopold Freund's 1896 demonstration of the therapeutic treatment of a hairy mole using a new type of electromagnetic radiation called x-rays, which was discovered 1 year previously by the German physicist, Wilhelm Rontgen. At the same time, Pierre and Marie Curie discovered the radioactive polonium and radium later used to treat cancer. In simplest terms, radiobiology is the study of the action of ionizing radiation on living things.

Radiology

Radiology is a medical specialty that employs the use of imaging to both diagnose and treat disease visualized within the human body. Radiologists use an array of imaging technologies (such as x-ray radiography, ultrasound, computed tomography (CT), nuclear medicine, positron emission tomography (PET) and magnetic resonance imaging (MRI)) to diagnose or treat diseases. Interventional radiology is the performance of (usually minimally invasive) medical procedures with the guidance of imaging technologies. The acquisition of medical imaging is usually carried out by the radiographer or radiologic technologist.

Radiology information system

A radiology information system (RIS) is a computerized database used by radiology departments to store, manipulate and distribute patient radiological data and imagery. The system generally consists of patient tracking and scheduling, result reporting and image tracking capabilities. RIS complements HIS (Hospital Information Systems) and is critical to efficient workflow to radiology practices.

Raised face
Description of the mating face of a flange.

RAM
Random access memory (RAM) is a form of computer data storage. Today, it takes the form of integrated circuits that allow stored data to be accessed in any order with a worst case performance of constant time. Strictly speaking, modern types of DRAM are therefore not random access, as data is read in bursts, although the nameDRAM / RAM has stuck. However, many types of SRAM, ROM, OTP, and NOR flash are still random access even in a strict sense. RAM is often associated with volatiletypes of memory (such as DRAM memory modules), where its stored information is lost if the power is removed. Many other types of non-volatile memory are RAM as well, including most types of ROM and a type of flash memory called NOR-Flash. The first RAM modules to come into the market were created in 1951 and were sold until the late 1960s and early 1970s.

Random primed synthesis
If you have a DNA clone and you want to produce radioactive copies of it, one way is to denature it (separate the strands), then hybridize to that template a mixture of all possible 6-mer oligonucleotides. Those oligos will act as primers for the synthesis of labeled strands by DNA polymerase (in the presence of radiolabeled precursors).

Random primers
A set of short oligonucleotides with variable sequences. Within a population of random oligonucleotides, some will anneal to complementary sequences in a DNA or RNA template. Use of random primers to initiate DNA synthesis in the presence of a radiolabeled (or chemiluminescent) dexoynucleotide (dNTP) will yield probes representing the sequences found in the template DNA. The labeled probes can then be used to identify other sequences homologous to this DNA (e.g. by Southern blotting).

Range
Those values over which a transducer is intended to measure, specified by its upper and lower limits.

Rangeability
The ratio of the maximum flowrate to the minimum flowrate of a meter.

Rankine cycle
The Rankine cycle is a cycle that converts heat into work. The heat is supplied externally to a closed loop, which usually uses water. This cycle generates about 90% of all electric power used throughout the world, including virtually all solar thermal, biomass, coal and nuclear power plants. It is named after William John Macquorn Rankine, a Scottish polymath and Glasgow University professor. The Rankine cycle is the fundamental thermodynamic underpinning of the steam engine.

Rankine method
Rankine's method is a technique for laying out circular curves by a combination of chaining and angles at circumference, fully exploiting the theodolite and making a substantial improvement in accuracy and productivity over existing methods.

Rankine scale (°r)
Rankine is a thermodynamic (absolute) temperature scale named after the Glasgow University engineer

and physicist William John Macquorn Rankine, who proposed it in 1859. (The Kelvin scale was first proposed in 1848.) The symbol for degrees Rankine is R (or Ra if necessary to distinguish it from the Rømer and Réaumur scales). Zero on both the Kelvin and Rankine scales is absolute zero, but the Rankine degree is defined as equal to one degree Fahrenheit, rather than the one degree Celsius used by the Kelvin scale. A temperature of "459.67 °F is exactly equal to 0 R.

Rate action
The derivative function of a temperature controller.

Rate time
the time interval over which the system temperature is sampled for the derivative function.

Rating curve
A Rating curve is a graph of discharge versus stage for a given point on a stream, usually at gauging stations, where the stream discharge is measured across the stream channel with a flow meter. Numerous measurements of stream discharge are made over a range of stream stages. The rating curve is usually plotted as stage on x-axis versus discharge on y-axis.

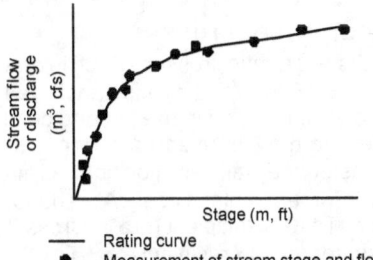

— Rating curve
● Measurement of stream stage and flow

Ratiometric measurement
A measurement technique where an external signal is used to provide the voltage reference for the dual-slope A/D converter. The external signal can be derived from the voltage excitation applied to a bridge circuit or pick-off supply, thereby eliminating errors due to power supply fluctuations.

Reactants
The substances that take part in a chemical reaction.

Read only memory (ROM)
Read-only memory (ROM) is a class of storage medium used in computers and other electronic devices. Data stored in ROM cannot be modified, or can be modified only slowly or with difficulty, so it is mainly used to distribute firmware (software that is very closely tied to specific hardware, and unlikely to need frequent updates).

Reading frame
The sequence of nucleotides which is read as consecutive triplets during translation of mRNA into protein. A sequence of codons that continues without encountering a stop codon is called an open reading frame (ORF). A sequence of DNA will often have one ORF, but in some cases a sequence of DNA will include overlapping ORFs that encode distinct polypeptides.

Read-through
Failure to stop transcription at a normal termination signal.

Reagent
A reagent is a "substance or compound that is added to a system in order to bring about a chemical reaction, or added to see if a reaction occurs."[1] Although the terms reactant and reagent are often used interchangeably, a reactant is less specifically a "substance that is consumed in the course of a chemical

reaction". Solvents and catalysts, although they are involved in the reaction, are usually not referred to as reactants.

Real-time
The time interval over which the system temperature is sampled for the derivative function.

Real-time computing
In computer science, real-time computing (RTC), or reactive computing, is the study of hardware and software systems that are subject to a "real-time constraint"— e.g. operational deadlines from event to system response. Real-time programmes must guarantee response within strict time constraints. Often real-time response times are understood to be in the order of milliseconds and sometimes microseconds. In contrast, a non-real-time system is one that cannot guarantee a response time in any situation, even if a fast response is the usual result.

Real-time strategy
Real-time strategy (RTS) is a sub-genre of strategy video game which does not progress incrementally in turns. Brett Sperry is credited with coining the term to market Dune II.

Reboost
Reboost is the process of boosting the altitude of an artificial satellite, to increase the time until its orbit will decay and it re-enters the atmosphere. For example, the International Space Station has been given a reboost by the Space Shuttle, the Progress resupply vehicle, and the Automated Transfer Vehicle every time they docked in, because it is in a low Earth orbit which experiences significant atmospheric drag.

Reboot
In computing, rebooting is the process by which a running computer system is restarted, either intentionally or unintentionally. Reboots can be either hard (alternatively known as cold) whereby the power to the system is physically turned off, or soft (alternatively known as warm) where the system restarts without the need to interrupt the power or trigger a reset line.

Reca protein
The protein encoded by the *recA* gene which is essential for homologous recombination. The RecA protein is also involved in the induction of the SOS response and the induction of lambda prophage in response to DNA damaging agents.

Recessive
A genetic trait that is not expressed in a heterozygous or partially heterozygous cell.

Recessive gene
A gene which must be present on both chromosomes in a pair to show outward signs of a certain characteristic.

Recharge
Water added to an aquifer. For instance, rainfall that seeps into the ground.

Reciprocal crosses
Pairs of genetic crosses which in one case DNA from strain #1 is transferred into strain #2 and in the second case the strain #2 is used as a donor to transfer the same region into strain #1. For example: Cross A = donor (pro::Tn10) x recipient (pro$^+$) Cross B = donor (pro$^+$) x recipient (pro::Tn10)

Reciprocal recombination
A precise exchange of genetic information like that expected for a simple cut, exchange, and rejoin

mechanism. That is, a region of DNA simply moves from the donor molecule to the recipient molecule in exchange for the identical region from the recipient molecule.

Reclaimed wastewater
Reclaimed water or recycled water, is former wastewater (sewage) that is treated to remove solids and certain impurities, and used in sustainable landscaping irrigation or to recharge groundwater aquifers. The purpose of these processes is sustainability and water conservation, rather than discharging the treated water to surface waters such as rivers and oceans.

Recombinant DNA
A molecule of DNA in which a DNA fragment from a different source has been inserted.

Recombinant DNA molecules
A combination of DNA molecules of different origin that are joined using recombinant DNA technologies.

Recombinant DNA technologies
Procedures used to join together DNA segments in a cell- free system (an environment outside a cell or organism). Under appropriate conditions, a recombinant DNA molecule can enter a cell and replicate there, either autonomously or after it has become integrated into a cellular chromosome.

Recombinase
An enzyme that catalyzes genetic recombination.

Recombination
The process by which progeny derive a combination of genes different from that of either parent. In higher organisms, this can occur by crossing over.

Recombination era
The time when matter and radiation first separated. The Universe became 'transparent'; the cosmic microwave background was emitted. The 'decoupling' between matter and radiation happened because the Universe was cool enough already to allow protons to capture one electron and form a neutral atom of hydrogen: the electrons, charged particles that interact strongly with light, were not free anymore, and light could propagate. This happened some 3 lakh years after the Big Bang.

Recombination frequency
The number of recombinants divided by the total number of progeny. The recombination frequency is proportional to the physical distance between two genetic markers, and thus recombination frequencies can be used to draw genetic maps showing the relative distance between genetic markers.

Recombineering ("Recombination-mediated genetic engineering")
A term coined by Don Court to describe a method for vector construction based on homologous recombination in E. coli using lambda phage recombination proteins exo, bet, and gam. This process allows homologous recombination between much shorter DNA sequences than the E. coli homologous recombination system.

Record
A row—also called a record or tuple—represents a single, implicitly structured data item in a table. In simple terms, a database table can be thought of as consisting of *rows* and columns or fields. Each row in a table represents a set of related data, and

every row in the table has the same structure.

Recovery time
The length of time which it takes a transducer to return to normal after applying a proof pressure.

Recycle
Recycling is processing used materials (waste) into new products to prevent waste of potentially useful materials, reduce the consumption of fresh raw materials, reduce energy usage, reduce air pollution (from incineration) and water pollution (from landfilling) by reducing the need for "conventional" waste disposal, and lower greenhouse gas emissions as compared to virgin production. Recycling is a key component of modern waste reduction and is the third component of the "Reduce,Reuse, Recycle" waste hierarchy.

Recycled water
Water that is used more than one time before it passes back into the natural hydrologic system.

Red giant
An old star that has used up all the hydrogen in its nucleus (see Nucleosynthesis) and uses instead other elements as fuel to keep shining. The Sun will become a red giant in the future. These stars can be 25 times as big as the Sun, and hundreds of times brighter.

Redox potential
Reduction potential (also known as redox potential, oxidation / reduction potential, ORP or E_h) is a measure of the tendency of a chemical species to acquire electrons and thereby be reduced. Reduction potential is measured in volts (V), or millivolts (mV). Each species has its own intrinsic reduction potential; the more positive the potential, the greater the species' affinity for electrons and tendency to be reduced.

Redshift
When a distant object moves away from the observer the lines in its spectrum are shifted to longer (redder) wavelengths. This is because of the apparent stretching of the wave of light due to the recession of the object: as a result of this stretching the wave 'lengthens' and thus shifts towards the red side of the electromagnetic spectrum. The redshift of an astronomical object is an indication of the speed at which this object is receding. This data, combined with the Hubble Constant, will lead to an estimate of the distance of the object. The redshift of an object is symbolised by 'z'.

Reduction
A chemical reaction in which electrons are gained, or the chemical addition of hydrogen takes place.

Redundancy
Redundancy is the duplication of critical components or functions of a system with the intention of increasing reliability of the system, usually in the case of a backup or fail-safe. In many safety-critical systems, such as fly-by-wire and hydraulic systems in aircraft, some parts of the control system may be triplicated, which is formally termed triple modular

redundancy (TMR). An error in one component may then be out-voted by the other two. In a triply redundant system, the system has three sub components, all three of which must fail before the system fails. Since each one rarely fails, and the sub components are expected to fail independently, the probability of all three failing is calculated to be extremely small; often outweighed by other risk factors, e.g., human error. Redundancy may also be known by the terms "majority voting systems" or "voting logic".

Redundant genes
Multiple copies of a gene or different genes with the same function.

Reference junction
The cold junction in a thermocouple circuit which is held at a stable known temperature. The standard reference temperature is 0°C (32°F). However, other temperatures can also be used.

Reference mark
Any diagnostic point or mark which can be used to relate a position during rotation of a part to its location when stopped.

Reference plane
Any plane perpendicular to the shaft axis to which an amount of unbalance is referred.

Reflecting telescope
A reflecting telescope (also called a reflector) is an optical telescope which uses a single or combination of curved mirrors that reflect light and form an image. The reflecting telescope was invented in the 17th century as an alternative to the refracting telescope which, at that time, was a design that suffered from severe chromatic aberration. Although reflecting telescopes produce other types of optical aberrations, it is a design that allows for very large diameter objectives. Almost all of the major telescopes used in astronomy research are reflectors. Reflecting telescopes come in many design variations and may employ extra optical elements to improve image quality or place the image in a mechanically advantageous position. Since reflecting telescopes use mirrors, the design is sometimes referred to as a "catoptric" telescope.

Reflector
A telescope that uses a mirror - instead of a lens - to collect and focus the light coming from astronomical objects. The term 'reflector' is also used for the mirror itself.

Reflexology
Reflexology, or zone therapy, is an alternative medicine involving the physical act of applying pressure to the feet, hands, or ears with specific thumb, finger, and hand techniques without the use of oil or lotion. It is based on what reflexologists claim to be a system of zones and reflex areas that they say reflect an image of the body on the feet and hands, with the premise that such work effects a physical change to the body.

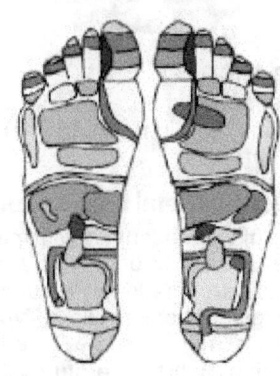

A 2009 systematic review of randomised controlled trials concludes that "The best evidence available to date does not demonstrate convincingly that reflexology is an effective treatment for any medical condition."

Refracting telescope

A refracting or refractor telescope is a type of optical telescope that uses a lens as its objective to form an image (also referred to a dioptric telescope). The refracting telescope design was originally used in spy glasses and astronomical telescopes but is also used for long focus camera lenses. Although large refracting telescopes were very popular in the second half of the 19th century, for most research purposes the refracting telescope has been superseded by the reflecting telescope.

Refraction

The deflection of a wave as it passes from one medium to another, eg through a lens.

Refractory metal thermocouple

A class of thermocouples with melting points above 3600°F. The most common are made from tungsten and tungsten/rhenium alloys Types G and C. They can be used for measuring high temperatures up to 4000°F (2200°C) in non-oxidizing, inert, or vacuum environments.

Reggae

Reggae is a music genre first developed in Jamaica in the late 1960s. While sometimes used in a broader sense to refer to most types of Jamaican music, the term reggae more properly denotes a particular music style that originated following the development of ska and rocksteady. Reggae is most easily recognized by the rhythmic accents on the off-beat, usually played by guitar and/or piano, known as the *skank*. This pattern accents the second and fourth beat in each bar (or the "and"s of each beat depending on how the music is counted) and combines with the drums emphasis on beat three to create a unique feel and sense of phrasing in contrast to most other popular genres focus on beat one, the "downbeat".

Register

A storage device with a specific capacity, such as a bit, byte or word.

Regulatory regions or sequences

A DNA base sequence that controls gene expression.

Regulon

A group of genes or operons located at different positions on the chromosome but respond to a common regulatory protein.

Reimbursable

A type of contract where contractor is re-imbursed for all time taken to carry out and complete the assignment.

Relative atomic mass (RAM)

The mass of an atom relative to one atom of carbon. Carbon has a RAM of 12.

Relativity
The relative values of time, motion, mass and energy of a body in motion.

Relay (mechanical)
An electromechanical device that completes or interrupts a circuit by physically moving electrical contacts into contact with each other.

Relay (solid state)
A solid state switching device which completes or interrupts a circuit electrically with no moving parts.

Release factors (RF)
Proteins that facilitate the termination of translation. Translation termination occurs when a ribosome encounters one of the three stop codons (UAA, UAG, or UGA). These codons are not recognized by a tRNA but by protein release factors. RF-1 recognizes UAA and UAG, RF-2 recognizes UAA and UGA. RF-3 stimulates the activity of RF-1 and RF-2. Interaction of the RF with a stop codon causes the peptidyl transferase activity of the ribosome to catalyze the hydrolysis of the ester bond between the tRNA and the polypeptide chain, releasing the polypeptide chain and resulting in dissociation of the ribosome.

Remote
Not hard-wired; communicating via switched lines, such as telephone lines. Usually refers to peripheral devices that are located a site away from the CPU.

Remote control
A remote control is a component of an electronics device, most commonly a television set, DVD player and home theater systems originally used for operating the television device wirelessly from a short line-of-sight distance. Remote control has continually evolved and advanced over recent years to include Bluetooth connectivity, motion sensor enabled capabilities and voice control.

Remote sensing
Remote sensing is the acquisition of information about an object or phenomenon, without making physical contact with the object. In modern usage, the term generally refers to the use of aerial sensor technologies to detect and classify objects on Earth (both on the surface, and in the atmosphere and oceans) by means of propagated signals (e.g. electromagnetic radiation emitted from aircraft or satellites).

Repeat sequences
The length of a nucleotide sequence that is repeated in a tandem cluster.

Repeatability
The ability of a transducer to reproduce output readings when the same measurand value is applied to it consecutively, under the same conditions, and in the same direction. Repeatability is expressed as the maximum difference between output readings.

Repetitive DNA
A surprising portion of any genome consists not of genes or structural elements, but of frequently repeated simple sequences. These may be short repeats just a few nt long, like CACACA etc. They can also range up to a few hundred nt long. Examples of the latter include Alu repeats, LINEs, SINEs. The function of these elements is often unknown. In shorter repeats like di- and tri-nucleotide repeats, the number of repeating units can occasionally change during evolution and descent. They are thus useful

markers for familial relationships and have been used in paternity testing, forensic science and in the identification of human remains.

Repetitive strain injury
Injury occurring from repeated physical movements which causes damage to tendons; nerves; muscles and other soft body tissues. It is repeated movements can be simple and not necessarily strenuous e.g. keyboard use etc.

Replica plating
A technique for transferring an identical pattern of bacterial colonies from one petrie plate (the master plate) to a series of other plates containing different media. A plate containing bacterial colonies is pressed against a cylindrical block covered with velveteen, resulting in the transfer of many of the bacteria from each colony onto the corresponding position on the velveteen. Then a series of sterile plates are sequentially pressed against the velveteen to transfer cells from the velveteen to the corresponding position on each petrie plate. After incubation, if the cells can grow on the particular medium in a plate colonies will appear at identical positions on each plate. Typically about 10 replica plates can be made from each master plate with about 200 isolated colonies on the master plate.

Replication
Replication is the process of sharing information so as to ensure consistency between redundant resources, such as software or hardware components, to improve reliability, fault-tolerance, or accessibility. It could be data replication if the same data is stored on multiple storage devices, or computation replication if the same computing task is executed many times. A computational task is typically replicated in space, i.e. executed on separate devices, or it could be replicated in time, if it is executed repeatedly on a single device.

Replication fork
The region on a replicating double stranded DNA molecule where synthesis of new DNA is taking place. The replicating fork produces a Y shaped region in the DNA molecule where the two strands have separated and replication is taking place.

Replication origin
The origin of replication (also called the replication origin) is a particular sequence in a genome at which replication is initiated. This can either be DNA replication in living organisms such as prokaryotes and eukaryotes, or RNA replication in RNA viruses, such as double-stranded RNA viruses. DNA replication may proceed from this point bidirectionally or unidirectionally. The specific structure of the origin of replication varies somewhat from species to species, but all share some common characteristics such as high AT content. The origin of replication binds the pre-replication complex, a protein complex that recognizes, unwinds, and begins to copy DNA.

Replication restart
An event that occurs when replication forks that collapse or disintegrate spontaneously do not progress to the completion of the chromosome; the replication fork is reasembled at the site of its collapse.

Replicative transposition
The insertion of a transposable element at a new location without loss from the original location.

Replicon
A DNA molecule that is able to initiate its own replication. A replicon must

have an origin of replication and usually also has the necessary regulatory information required for the proper initiation of DNA replication.

Replicon fusion
The integration of one replicon into another to form a single replicon. May occur by recombination between homologous regions of two replicons or by formation of a cointegrate during transposition of a transposable element located on one of the replicons.

Reporter gene
A gene which can be placed downstream of a promoter and expression of the gene followed by a relatively easy assay (often a colorimetric assay).

Repression
Switching off the expression of a gene or a group of genes in response to a chemical or other stimulus.

Repressor
A gene product that negatively regulates gene expression. Usually refers to a DNA-binding protein that inhibits transcription under certain conditions. Transcriptional repressors typically decrease the transcription of certain other genes by specifically binding to operator sites one or more short DNA sequences located upstream of the structural gene. Regulation of repression is usually modulated by a ligand which binds to the repressor protein and alters its DNA-binding properties. DNA-binding may be increased by association with a co-repressor or DNA-binding may be decreased by association with an inducer.

Reproducibility
The closeness of agreement among repeated measurements of an output for the same value of input made under the same operating conditions over a period of time.

Reproduction
Reproduction is the process by which a new organism is produced. The first stage in the production of any organism is the fertilisation of an ova by spermatozoa (or spores on the case of plants). Fertilisation produces a single cell called a zygote which contains all the information required to build the adult organism. The progression (growth) from zygote to adult is achieved through cell division.

Reptile
Reptiles (Reptilia) are members of a group of air-breathing, ectothermic (cold-blooded) vertebrates which are characterized by laying shelled eggs (except for some vipers and constrictor snakes that give live birth), and having skin covered in scales and/or scutes. They are tetrapods, either having four limbs or being descended from four-limbed ancestors. Modern reptiles inhabit every continent with the exception of Antarctica. Reptiles originated around 320-310 million years ago during the Carboniferous period, having evolved from advanced reptile-like amphibians that became increasingly adapted to life on dry land.

Reserved word
A word that has a defined function in the language, and cannot be used as a variable name.

Reservoir
A reservoir, artificial lake or dam is used to store water. Reservoirs may be created in river valleys by the construction of a dam or may be built by excavation in the ground or by conventional construction techniques such as brickwork or cast concrete.

The term reservoir may also be used to describe underground reservoirs such as an oil or water well.

Residual (final) unbalance
Residual unbalance is that unbalance of any kind that remains after balancing.

Resistance
The resistance to the flow of electric current measured in ohms (1/2) for a conductor. Resistance is function of diameter, resistivity (an intrinsic property of the material) and length.

Resistance ratio characteristic
For thermistors, the ratio of the resistance of the thermistor at 25°C to the resistance at 125°C.

Resistance temperature characteristic
A relationship between a thermistor's resistance and the temperature.

Resistance temperature detector
Resistance Temperature Detectors (RTD's) provide temperature measurement through changes in electrical resistance.

Resistance transfer factor (RTF)
The component of an R-plasmid that encodes the ability to conjugate and to transfer DNA.

Resolution
The smallest detectable increment of measurement. Resolution is usually limited by the number of bits used to quantize the input signal. For example, a 12-bit A/D can resolve to one part in 4096 (2 to the 12 power equals 4096).

Resolution
Degree of molecular detail on a physical map of DNA, ranging from low to high.

Resolution (angular, spectral)
Ability to discriminate fine detail in an image, a spectrum or data. The angular resolution of a telescope is the smallest angle between two point objects that produces distinct images. In a spectrum, the resolution determines how well closely spaced features in the wavelength spectrum can be detected.

Resolvase
An enzyme which resolves a co-integrate molecule into its two component replicons.

Resonance
Resonance is the tendency of a system to oscillate at a greater amplitude at some frequencies than at others. These are known as the system's resonant frequencies (or resonance frequencies). At these frequencies, even small periodic driving forces can produce large amplitude oscillations, because the system stores vibrational energy.

Resonant frequency
The measurand frequency at which a transducer responds with maximum amplitude.

Respiration
The production of energy by the oxidisation of glucose.

Response element
By definition, a "response element" is a portion of a gene which must be present in order for that gene to respond to some hormone or other stimulus. Response elements are binding sites for transcription factors.

Certain transcription factors are activated by stimuli such as hormones or heat shock. A gene may respond to the presence of that hormone because the gene has in its promoter region a binding site for hormone-activated transcription factor.

Response regulator

A regulatory protein that responds to sensor protein of a "two-component" regulatory system. Interaction with the transmitter domain of the sensor protein, leads to the phosphorylation or dephosphorylation of an aspartate residue on the response regulator. The modified protein regulates gene expression in response to the changes in the environment.

Response time

The length of time required for the output of a transducer to rise to a specified percentage of its final value as a result of a step change of input.

Response time (time constant)

The time required by a sensor to reach 63.2% of a step change in temperature under a specified set of conditions. Five time constants are required for the sensor to stabilize at 600 of the step change value.

Rest

To lie down or sit quietly; to give the muscles a break from working. After you exercise, you should rest.

Restriction

To "restrict" DNA means to cut it with a restriction enzyme. The recognition site is thus said to be palindromic, which is typical of restriction sites. Every copy of a plasmid is identical in sequence, so if BamHI cuts a particular circular plasmid at three sites producing three "restriction fragments", then a million copies of that plasmid will produce those same restriction fragments a million times over. There are more than six hundred known restriction enzymes.

Restriction analysis

Determination of the number and sizes of the DNA fragments produced when a particular DNA molecule is cut with a particular restriction endonuclease.

Restriction endonuclease

An endonuclease cuts double stranded DNA by binding to specific sites, in many cases arranged in palindromes. Several different classes of restriction endonucleases can be differentiated based upon their binding and cleavage sites and their required cofactors. Although restriction endonucleases have specific recognition sites, cleavage may occur at specific or random sites depending on the class of the endonuclease. Also called restriction enzymes.

Restriction enzyme cutting site

A specific nucleotide sequence of DNA at which a particular restriction enzyme cuts the DNA. Some sites occur frequently in DNA (e.g., every several hundred base pairs), others much less frequently (rare- cutter; e.g., every 10,000 base pairs).

Restriction enzyme cutting site

A specific sequence of DNA at which a particular restriction enzyme cuts the DNA.

Restriction enzyme, endonuclease

A protein that recognizes specific, short nucleotide sequences and cuts

DNA at those sites. Bacteria contain over 400 such enzymes that recognize and cut over 100 different DNA sequences.

Restriction enzyme, endonuclease
A protein that recognizes specific, short sequences of DNA and cuts at those sites.

Restriction fragment
The piece of DNA released after restriction digestion of plasmids or genomic DNA. One can digest a plasmid and isolate one particular restriction fragment (actually a set of identical fragments). The term also describes the fragments detected on a genomic blot which carry the gene of interest. The map usually indicates the approximate length of the entire piece (scale on the bottom), as well as the position within the piece at which designated enzymes will cut. This map happens to be of a plasmid, and the two ends are joined together with about 25 nt between the EcoRI and HindIII sites.

Restriction fragment length polymorphism (RFLP)
Variation between individuals in DNA fragment sizes cut by specific restriction enzymes; polymorphic sequences that result in RFLPs are used as markers on both physical maps and genetic linkage maps. RFLPs are usually caused by mutation at a cutting site.

Restriction map
A map showing the positions of different restriction sites in a DNA molecule.

Restriction site
A DNA sequence recognized and cleaved by a restriction endonuclease. Restriction sites are often 4 to 6 bp, but some sites are 8 bp or longer. The presence or absence of specific nucleotide modifications (e.g. methylation) determines whether the restriction endonuclease cleaves at its cognate restriction site.

Restriction-modification
The modification of host DNA to prevent cutting by a restriction endonuclease. The modification is often via methylation of a specific restriction site sequence.

Restrictive conditions
The particular environmental conditions which do not allow growth of a conditional lethal mutant but result in the expression of the mutant phenotype.

Retinitis pigmentosa
Group of hereditary ocular disorders with progressive retinal degeneration. Autosomal dominant, autosomal recessive, and x-linked forms.

Retinoblastoma
Retinoblastoma (Rb) is a rapidly developing cancer that develops in the cells of retina, the light-detecting tissue of the eye. In the developed world, Rb has one of the best cure rates of all childhood cancers (95-98%), with more than nine out of every ten sufferers surviving into adulthood.

Retrograde
The motion of a planet or other Solar System body in a clockwise direction. Most Solar System bodies orbit or rotate about their axes in an anti-clockwise direction when looked at from the north pole of the body or the Sun.

Retroregulation
The effect of a downstream RNA sequence upon the expression of an

upstream sequence. First used to describe the regulation of the phage lambda xis gene.

Retrotransposon
A genetic element that transposes to a new location in DNA by first making an RNA copy of itself, then making a DNA copy of this RNA with a reverse transcriptase, and then inserting the DNA copy into the target DNA.

Return flow
(1) That part of a diverted flow that is not consumptively used and returned to its original source or another body of water.
(2) Drainage water from irrigated farmlands that re-enters the water system to be used further downstream.

Return flow (irrigation)
Irrigation water that is applied to an area and which is not consumed in evaporation or transpiration and returns to a surface stream or aquifer.

Return on capital employed
The ratio of operating profits generated to the amount of operating capital invested. In effect it is a measure of how productively a company manages its assets.

Reverse genetics
An approach where a cloned gene with an unknown function is used to disrupt the corresponding chromosomal gene to examine the resulting phenotype.

Reverse osmosis
(1) (Desalination) The process of removing salts from water using a membrane. With reverse osmosis, the product water passes through a fine membrane that the salts are unable to pass through, while the salt waste (brine) is removed and disposed. This process differs from electrodialysis, where the salts are extracted from the feedwater by using a membrane with an electrical current to separate the ions. The positive ions go through one membrane, while the negative ions flow through a different membrane, leaving the end product of freshwater.
(2) (Water Quality) An advanced method of water or wastewater treatment that relies on a semi-permeable membrane to separate waters from pollutants. An external force is used to reverse the normal osmotic process resulting in the solvent moving from a solution of higher concentration to one of lower concentration.

Reverse transcriptase
An enzyme produced by retroviruses that can synthesize a strand of DNA complimentary to an RNA template. (Reverse transcriptase can also synthesize DNA from a DNA template.) Used to make cDNA clones from mRNA.

Reverse transcriptase
An enzyme which will make a DNA copy of an RNA template - a DNA-dependant RNA polymerase. RT is used to make cDNA; one begins by isolating polyadenylated mRNA, providing oligo-dT as a primer, and adding nucleotide triphosphates and RT to copy the RNA into cDNA.

Reversion
Any mutation that restores the wild-type phenotype of a mutant.

Revolution
A rotation through a full circle, or 360 degrees.

Rewheel
To change out the internals (bundle) of a compressor to alter its throughput capabilities.

Reynolds number
The ratio of inertial and viscous forces in a fluid defined by the formula Re = rVD/μ, where:
r = Density of fluid,
μ = Viscosity in centipoise (CP),
V = Velocity, and
D = Inside diameter of pipe.

R-factor
A transmissible plasmid that carries genes coding for resistance to several different antibiotics. Also called R-plasmid.

RFI
Radio frequency interference.

RFLP
Restriction fragment length polymorphism; the acronym is pronounced "riflip". Although two individuals of the same species have almost identical genomes, they will always differ at a few nucleotides. Some of these differences will produce new restriction sites (or remove them), and thus the banding pattern seen on a genomic Southern will thus be affected.

Rheology
The study of the deformation, flow of matter.

Rheostat
A variable resistor.

Rho factor
A protein which catalyzes transcription termination at certain sites or when an extended stretch on nontranslated, unstructured RNA is present.

Rhyolite
Volcanic rock (or lava) that characteristically is light in color, contains 69 percent silica or more, and is rich in potassium and sodium. It is fine grained, which although different in texture, has the same composition as granite

Ribonucleic acid (RNA)
A chemical found in the nucleus and cytoplasm of cells; it plays an important role in protein synthesis and other chemical activities of the cell. The structure of RNA is similar to that of DNA. There are several classes of RNA molecules, including messenger RNA, transfer RNA, ribosomal RNA, and other small RNAs, each serving a different purpose.

Riboprobe
A strand of RNA synthesized *in-vitro* (usually radiolabeled) and used as a probe for hybridization reactions. An RNA probe can be synthesized at very high specific activity, is single stranded (and therefore will not self anneal), and can be used for very sensitive detection of DNA or RNA.

Ribosomal (rrna)
An RNA molecule that forms part of the structure of a ribosome.

Ribosomal protein
one of the ribonucleoprotein particles that are the sites of translation.

Ribosomal RNA (rrna)
Ribosomal ribonucleic acid (rRNA) is the RNA component of the ribosome, the enzyme that is the site of protein synthesis in all living cells. Ribosomal RNA provides a mechanism for decoding mRNA into amino acids and interacts with tRNAs during translation by providing peptidyl transferase activity. The tRNAs bring

the necessary amino acids corresponding to the appropriate mRNA codon.

Ribosome
A ribosome is a component of cells that synthesizes protein chains. It assembles the twenty specific amino acid molecules to form the particular protein molecule determined by the nucleotide sequence of an RNA molecule.

Ribosome binding site
A short nucleotide sequence upstream of a gene which forms the site on the mRNA molecule where the ribosome binds.

Rich medium
A growth medium in which not all the components have been identified. Most "rich" media have a variety of complex, undefined components.

Ridge, oceanic
A major submarine mountain range. Commonly the sites of crustal rifting and plate separation, and the eruption of mafic basaltic lavas.

Rift system
The oceanic ridges formed where tectonic plates are separating and a new crust is being created; also, their on-land counterparts like the East African Rift.

Rigid rotor
A rotor is considered rigid when it can be corrected in any two (arbitrarily selected) planes and after that correction, its unbalance does not significantly exceed the balancing tolerances (relative to the shaft axis) at any speed up to maximum operating speed and when running under conditions which approximate closely to those of the final supporting system.

RII locus
A region from phage T4 that determines whether this phage can grow on *E. coli* K or B strains. Fine structure genetic mapping of the rII locus by Sydney Benzer first unveiled a variety of important facets of gene structure and function.

Ring of Fire
The regions of mountain-building earthquakes and volcanoes which surround the Pacific Ocean.

Ring type joint
The description of the mating face of a flange where the mating face has a machined groove into which the gasket is inserted.

Rings (saturn's)
A series of rings surrounding Saturn, composed of dust and solid fragments and distributed in the equatorial plane of the planet at several distances. The rings are just a few hundred meters high and can not collapse into a satellite, because they are located inside the Roche limit.

Riparian water rights
The rights of an owner whose land abuts water. They differ from state to state and often depend on whether the water is a river, lake, or ocean. The doctrine of riparian rights is an old one, having its origins in English common law. Specifically, persons who own land adjacent to a stream have the right to make reasonable use of the stream. Riparian users of a stream share the streamflow among themselves, and the concept of priority of use is not applicable.

Rise time
The time required for a sensor or system to respond to an instantaneous

step function, measured from the 10% to 90% points on the response waveforms.

Riser
Steel or flexible pipe which transfer well fluids from the seabed to the surface.

Ritchey-chretien
A modern optical design for two-mirror reflecting telescopes. It is a derivative of the Cassegrain concept in which the primary mirror has a hyperbolic cross-section.

River
A natural stream of water of considerable volume, larger than a brook or creek.

RNA phage
A phage that carries RNA as its genetic material. Some examples include phage MS2 and Qß.

RNA polymerase (RNAP)
An enzyme complex that polymerizes RNA from ribonucleotides (NTPs), using one strand of DNA as template (hence called "DNA-dependent RNA polymerase). The core RNAP from E. coli is composed of five subunits: 2 alpha subunits, beta, beta', and omega. Upon binding another subunit called sigma, RNAP is called a holoenzyme. The sigma subunit (or sigma factor) reduces the nonspecific affinity of RNAP for DNA and increases the specific binding to certain promoter sequences. A variety of different sigma subunits exist, each promoting RNAP binding to different promoters under specific physiological conditions.

RNAi
'RNA interference' (a.k.a. 'RNA silencing') is the mechanism by which small double-stranded RNAs can interfere with expression of any mRNA having a similar sequence. Those small RNAs are known as 'siRNA', for short interfering RNAs. The mode of action for siRNA appears to be via dissociation of its strands, hybridization to the target RNA, extension of those fragments by an RNA-dependent RNA polymerase, then fragmentation of the target. Importantly, the remnants of the target molecule appears to then act as an siRNA itself; thus the effect of a small amount of starting siRNA is effectively amplified and can have long-lasting effects on the recipient cell.

Rnase
Ribonuclease; an enzyme which degrades RNA. It is ubiquitous in living organisms and is exceptionally stable. The prevention of RNase activity is the primary problem in handling RNA.

Rnase protection assay
This is a sensitive method to determine (1) the amount of a specific mRNA present in a complex mixture of mRNA and/or (2) the sizes of exons which comprise the mRNA of interest. A radioactive DNA or RNA probe (in excess) is allowed to hybridize with a sample of mRNA (for example, total mRNA isolated from tissue), after which the mixture is digested with single-strand specific nuclease. Only the probe which is hybridized to the specific mRNA will escape the nuclease treatment, and can be detected on a gel.

Robot
A robot is a mechanical or virtual intelligent agent that can perform tasks automatically or with guidance, typically by remote control. In practice a robot is usually an electro-mechanical machine that is guided by computer and electronic

programming. Robots can be autonomous, semi-autonomous or remotely controlled. Robots range from humanoids such as ASIMO and TOPIO to Nano robots, Swarm robots, Industrial robots, military robots, mobile and servicing robots. By mimicking a lifelike appearance or automating movements, a robot may convey a sense that it has intent or agency of its own. The branch of technology that deals with robots is robotics.

Roche limit
The Roche limit, sometimes referred to as the Roche radius, is the distance within which a celestial body, held together only by its own gravity, will disintegrate due to a second celestial body's tidal forces exceeding the first body's gravitational self-attraction. Inside the Roche limit, orbiting material will tend to disperse and form rings, while outside the limit, material will tend to coalesce. The term is named after Édouard Roche, the French astronomer who first calculated this theoretical limit in 1848.

Rock flour
Finely ground rock material, usually associated with glaciers (or faults). Can be mixed with water and formed into loaves which, when baked for 45 minutes at 350°, are totally unedible.

Rocket
A rocket is a missile, spacecraft, aircraft or other vehicle which obtains thrust from a rocket engine. In all rockets, the exhaust is formed entirely from propellants carried within the rocket before use. Rocket engines work by action and reaction. Rocket engines push rockets forwards simply by throwing their exhaust backwards extremely fast.

Roll
To move by turning over and over. A round object like an orange will roll down a ramp.

Rolling circle (sigma) replication
A type of DNA replication where a replication fork moves around a circular DNA molecule, producing a single-stranded concatamer (much like the way toilet paper peels off the roll). The resulting single-stranded DNA may become double-stranded by the synthesis of a complementary strand.

ROM
Read Only Memory. Readable memory that cannot be corrupted by accidental erasure. ROM retains its data when the computer is turned off.

Room conditions
Ambient environmental conditions under which transducers must commonly operate.

Root mean square (RMS)
Square root of the mean of the square of the signal taken during one full cycle.

Rosetta mission
ESA cornerstone mission to explore Comet Wirtanen. Scheduled for launch in January 2003. On its way to the comet, it will fly past the Earth and Mars, and investigate two main belt asteroids, Siwa and Otawara.

Rotation
A rotation is a circular movement of an object around a center (or point) of rotation. A three-dimensional object rotates always around an imaginary line called a rotation axis. If the axis is within the body, and passes through its center of mass the body is

said to rotate upon itself, or spin. A rotation about an external point, e.g. the Earth about the Sun, is called a revolution or orbital revolution, typically when it is produced by gravity.

Rotor
A rotor is a rotating body whose journals are supported by bearings.

Round and round
A push-and-pull motion. Wheels, tops, balls, and many other objects move in a round and round motion.

Rover
A small remote-controlled vehicle for exploring the terrain close to a lander situated on a planetary surface.

RPM
Revolutions per minute. Often used to describe the velocity of a centrifuge.

RRNA
"Ribosomal RNA"; any of several RNAs which become part of the ribosome, and thus are involved in translating mRNA and synthesizing proteins. They are the most abundant RNA in the cell (on a mass basis).

Rubinstein-Taybi syndrome
Condition with multiple congenital anomalies including: mental deficiency, broad thumbs, small head, broad nasal bridge and beaked nose.

Runoff
(1) That part of the precipitation, snow melt, or irrigation water that appears in uncontrolled surface streams, rivers, drains or sewers. Runoff may be classified according to speed of appearance after rainfall or melting snow as direct runoff or base runoff, and according to source as surface runoff, storm interflow, or ground-water runoff.

(2) The total discharge described in (1), above, during a specified period of time. (3) Also defined as the depth to which a drainage area would be covered if all of the runoff for a given period of time were uniformly distributed over it.

S

S1 end mapping
A technique to determine where the end of an RNA transcript lies with respect to its template DNA (the gene).

S1 nuclease
An enzyme which digests only single-stranded nucleic acids.

Safety integrity level
A discrete level (1 to 4) for specifying the safety integrity requirements of the safety functions to be allocated to a loop.

Safety training and observation programme
DuPont initiated scheme designed to create a culture of spotting potential hazards before they cause an accident.

Sagittarius (astrology)
Sagittarius is the ninth astrological sign in the Zodiac, which spans the zodiac between the 240th and 269th degree of celestial longitude. According to the tropical zodiac of western astrology, the Sun transits this area of the zodiac between November 22 and December 21 each year (sometimes the dates vary slightly).

Saline water
Saline water is a general term for water that contains a significant concentration of dissolved salts (NaCl). The concentration is usually expressed in parts per million (ppm) of salt. Water that is saline contains significant amounts (referred to as "concentrations") of dissolved salts. In this case, the concentration is the amount (by weight) of salt in water, as expressed in "parts per million" (ppm). If water has a concentration of 10,000 ppm of dissolved salts, then one percent (10,000 divided by 1,000,000) of the weight of the water comes from dissolved salts. The salinity concentration level used by United States Geological Survey classifies saline water in three categories. Slightly saline water contains around 1,000 to 3,000 ppm. Moderately saline water contains roughly 3,000 to 10,000 ppm. Highly saline water has around 10,000 to 35,000 ppm of salt. Seawater has a salinity of roughly 35,000 ppm, equivalent to 35 g/L.

Salt bridge
The salt bridge of a reference electrode is that part of the electrode which contains the filling solution to establish the electrolytic connection between reference internal cell and the test solution. Auxiliary Salt Bridge: A glass tube open at one end to receive intermediate electrolyte filling solution, and the reference electrode tip and a junction at the other end to make contact with the sample.

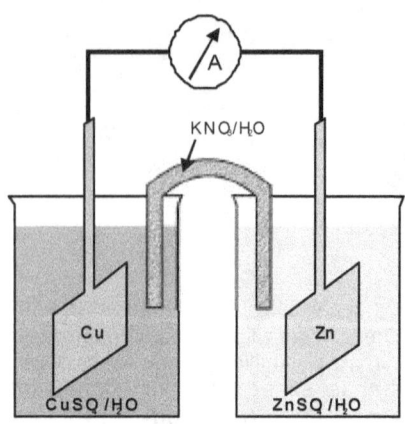

Salt Effect (fx)
The effect on the activity coefficient due to salts in the solution.

Sama
Scientific Apparatus Makers Association. An association that has issued standards covering platinum, nickel, and copper resistance elements (RTDs).

Same-sense mutation
A mutation which changes the nucleotide sequence of a codon but does not change the amino acid encoded due to the degeneracy of the genetic code. For example, both CCC and CCA encode proline.

Sanger sequence
"Plus and minus" or "primed synthesis" method; DNA is synthesized so it is radioactively labeled and the reaction terminates specifically at the position corresponding to a given base.

Sanger sequencing
DNA sequencing includes several methods and technologies that are used for determining the order of the nucleotide bases—adenine, guanine, cytosine, and thymine—in a molecule of DNA. Knowledge of DNA sequences has become indispensable for basic biological research, other research branches utilizing DNA sequencing, and in numerous applied fields such as diagnostic, biotechnology, forensic biology and biological systematics. The advent of DNA sequencing has significantly accelerated biological research and discovery. The rapid speed of sequencing attained with modern DNA sequencing technology has been instrumental in the sequencing of the human genome, in the Human Genome Project. Related projects, often by scientific collaboration across continents, have generated the complete DNA sequences of many animal, plant, and microbial genomes.

Satellite
(1) A small, natural celestial body (such as our Moon) revolving around a larger one.
(2) A man-made object (such as a spacecraft) placed in orbit around the Earth, another planet or the Sun.

Saturn
The sixth planet out from the Sun, famous for its ring system. Saturn, a gas giant, is 9.5 AU from the Sun and has a volume 845 times greater than that of the Earth. The atmosphere of hydrogen and helium surrounds a zone of metallic hydrogen, which covers an ice-silicate core.

S-band
The S band is defined by an IEEE standard for radio waves with frequencies that range from 2 to 4 GHz, crossing the conventional boundary between UHF and SHF at 3.0 GHz. It is part of the microwave band of the electromagnetic spectrum.

The S band is used by weather radar, surface ship radar, and some communications satellites, especially those used by NASA to communicate with the Space Shuttle and the International Space Station. The 10-cm radar short-band ranges roughly from 1.55 to 5.2 GHz.

Scaffolding proteins

Proteins which facilitate the assembly of a cell structure but are not included in the final structure. For example, phage encoded proteins that are required for procapsid assembly but are removed after the procapsid is constructed.

Scalar

A scalar is a simple physical quantity that is not changed by coordinate system rotations or translations (in Newtonian mechanics), or by Lorentz transformations or space-time translations (in relativity). This is in contrast to a vector. A related concept is a pseudoscalar, which is invariant under proper rotations but (like a pseudovector) flips sign under improper rotations.

Scatology

The study of excrement; obscene language.

Score

To determine the presence or absence of a phenotype by testing for growth under different conditions (e.g., plus and minus an auxotrophic supplement or permissive and nonpermissive conditions). Usually done by replica plating or patching colonies onto each type of plate.

Screen

To determine the presence or absence of a phenotype by testing for growth under different conditions (e.g., plus and minus an auxotrophic supplement or permissive and nonpermissive conditions). Usually done by replica plating or patching colonies onto each type of plate.

Screening

To screen a library is to select and isolate individual clones out of the mixture of clones. For example, if you needed a cDNA clone of the pituitary glycoprotein hormone alpha subunit, you would need to make (or buy) a pituitary cDNA library, then screen that library in order to detect and isolate those few bacteria carrying alpha subunit cDNA. There are two methods of screening which are particularly worth describing screening by hybridization, and screening by antibody.

Scroll

To move all or part of the screen material up to down, left or right, to allow new information to appear.

Sea level

The top of the ocean, where the water meets the atmosphere. It's not necessarily level!

Seafloor spreading

The mechanism by which new seafloor crust is created at oceanic ridges and slowly spreads away as tectonic plates separate.

Search engine

A web search engine is designed to search for information on the World Wide Web and FTP servers. The search results are generally presented in a list of results often referred to as SERPS, or "search engine results pages". The information may consist of web pages, images, information and other types of files. Some search engines also mine data available in databases or open directories. Unlike web directories, which are maintained only by human editors, search engines also maintain real-time information by running an algorithm on a web crawler. Some popular search engines are Metacrawler, Alta Vista, and Excite.

Secondary device

A part of the flowmeter which receives a signal proportional to the flowrate, from the primary device, and displays, records and/or transmits the signal.

Secondary mirror

In a two-mirror reflecting telescope, the secondary mirror sits in front of the larger primary mirror and reflects light to the point at which it will be detected and recorded by an instrument. In simple telescopes, the secondary mirror is flat and bounces the light out the side of the tube to an eyepiece. In more complex and larger telescopes, it is convex and reflects light through a hole in the primary mirror.

Secondary standard

pH buffer solutions which do not meet the requirements of primary standard solutions but provide coverage of the pH range not covered by primary standards. Used when the pH value of the primary standard is not close to the sample pH value.

Secondary wastewater treatment

Treatment (following primary wastewater treatment) involving the biological process of reducing suspended, colloidal, and dissolved organic matter in effluent from primary treatment systems and which generally removes 80 to 95 percent of the Biochemical Oxygen Demand (BOD) and suspended matter. Secondary wastewater treatment may be accomplished by biological or chemical-physical methods. Activated sludge and trickling filters are two of the most common means of secondary treatment. It is accomplished by bringing together waste, bacteria, and oxygen in trickling filters or in the activated sludge process. This treatment removes floating and settleable solids and about 90 percent of the oxygen-demanding substances and suspended solids.

Secreted protein

A protein that is exported through the cytoplasmic membrane. Most secreted proteins have specific signal sequences that promote interaction with the export apparatus in the membrane.

Sediment

Sediment is naturally occurring material that is broken down by processes of weathering and erosion, and is subsequently transported by the action of fluids such as wind, water, or ice, and/or by the force of gravity acting on the particle itself. Sediments are most often transported by water (fluvial processes), wind (aeolian processes) and glaciers. Beach sands and river channel deposits are examples of fluvial transport and deposition, though sediment also often settles out of slow-moving or standing water in lakes and oceans. Desert sand dunes and loess are examples of aeolian transport and deposition. Glacial moraine deposits and till are ice-transported sediments.

Sedimentary basin

The term sedimentary basin is used to refer to any geographical feature exhibiting subsidence and consequent infilling by sedimentation. As the sediments are buried, they are subjected to increasing pressure and begin the process of lithification. A number of basins formed in extensional settings can undergo inversion which has accounted for a number of the economically viable oil reserves on earth which were formerly basins.

Sedimentary depositional environment

Sedimentary depositional environment describes the combination of physical, chemical and biological processes associated with the deposition of a particular type of sediment and, therefore, the rock types that will be formed after lithification, if the sediment is preserved in the rock record. In most cases the environments associated with particular rock types or associations of rock types can be matched to existing analogues. However, the further back in geological time sediments were deposited, the more likely that direct modern analogues are not available (e.g. banded iron formations).

Sedimentary rock

Rock formed of sediment, and specifically:
(1) sandstone and shale, formed of fragments of other rock transported from their sources and deposited in water; and
(2) rocks formed by or from secretions of organisms, such as most limestone. Many sedimentary rocks show distinct layering, which is the result of different types of sediment being deposited in succession.

Sedimentary structure

Sedimentary structures are those structures formed during sediment deposition. Sedimentary structures such as cross bedding, graded bedding and ripple marks are utilized in stratigraphic studies to indicate original position of strata in geologically complex terrains and understand the depositional environment of the sediment.

Sedimentation

Sedimentation is the tendency for particles in suspension to settle out of the fluid in which they are entrained, and come to rest against a barrier. This is due to their motion through the fluid in response to the forces acting on them: these forces can be due to gravity, centrifugal acceleration or electromagnetism. In geology sedimentation is often used as the polar opposite of erosion, i.e., the terminal end of sediment transport. In that sense it includes the termination of transport by saltation or true bedload transport. Settling is the falling of suspended particles through the liquid, whereas sedimentation is the termination of the settling process.

Sedimentation tanks

wastewater tanks in which floating wastes are skimmed off and settled solids are removed for disposal.

Seebeck coefficient

The derivative (rate of change) of thermal EMF with respect to temperature normally expressed as millivolts per degree.

Seebeck effect

When a circuit is formed by a junction of two dissimilar metals and the junctions are held at different temperatures, a current will flow in the circuit caused by the difference in temperature between the two junctions.

Seebeck EMF
The open circuit voltage caused by the difference in temperature between the hot and cold junctions of a circuit made from two dissimilar metals.

Seed
A seed is a small embryonic plant enclosed in a covering called the seed coat, usually with some stored food. It is the product of the ripened ovule of gymnosperm and angiosperm plants which occurs after fertilization and some growth within the mother plant. The formation of the seed completes the process of reproduction in seed plants (started with the development of flowers and pollination), with the embryo developed from the zygote and the seed coat from the integuments of the ovule.

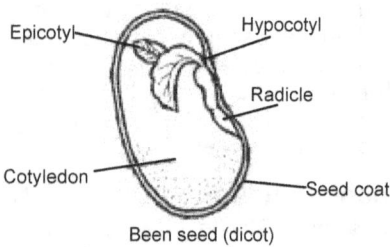

Been seed (dicot)

Seepage
(1) The slow movement of water through small cracks, pores, Interstices, etc., of a material into or out of a body of surface or subsurface water.
(2) The loss of water by infiltration into the soil from a canal, ditches, laterals, watercourse, reservoir, storage facilities, or other body of water, or from a field.

Segregration
The loss of one allele during cell division. For example, one allele maybe lost from because it fails to replicate or partition into one of the daughter cells.

Seismograph
An instrument that measures and records the Earth's vibrations. The seismograph indicated that an earthquake was coming.

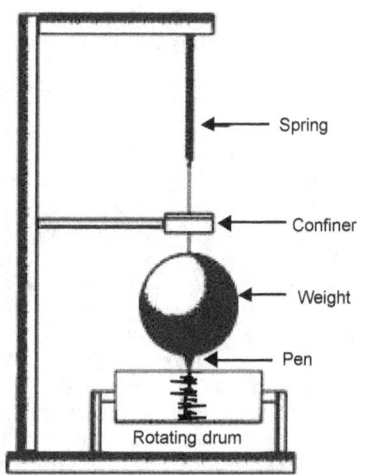

Seismology
The study of earthquakes and the phenomena associated with it.

Seismometer
Seismometers are instruments that measure motions of the ground, including those of seismic waves generated by earthquakes, volcanic eruptions, and other seismic sources. Records of seismic waves allow seismologists to map the interior of the Earth, and locate and measure the size of these different sources.

Selectable marker
A mutation that confers a phenotype on a cell such that when grown on a certain medium only those cells with the mutation will grow. For example, the mutation rpsL1 makes cells resistant to the antibiotic streptomycin

— when grown on medium with streptomycin rpsL1 mutants will grow but rpsL⁺ cells will die.

Selected marker
An allele that allows growth under a particular selective condition.

Selection
The process of determining the relative share allotted individuals of different genotypes in the propagation of a population; the selective effect of a gene can be defined by the probability that carriers of the gene will reproduce.

Selective media
Growth media that only allow growth of mutant or recombinant cells with a particular phenotype grow. For example, media containing tetracycline would select for tetracycline resistant bacteria, preventing growth of parental tetracycline sensitive bacteria.

Selenology
The geology of the Moon (sometimes called selenology, although the latter term can refer more generally to "lunar science") is quite different from that of the Earth. The Moon lacks a significant atmosphere and any bodies of water, which eliminates erosion due to weather; it does not possess any form of plate tectonics, it has a lower gravity, and because of its small size, it cools more rapidly. The complex geomorphology of the lunar surface has been formed by a combination of processes, chief among which are impact cratering and volcanism. The Moon is a differentiated body, possessing a crust, mantle and core.

Selex
A method for isolation of high-affinity RNA- or DNA-protein interactions through successive rounds of selection for increased nucleic acid binding.

Self heating
Internal heating of a transducer as a result of power dissipation.

Selfish DNA
A DNA sequence that does not contribute to the fitness of an organism but is maintained in the genome because it promotes its own replication.

Self-supplied water
Water withdrawn from a surface- or ground-water source by a user rather than being obtained from a public supply. An example would be homeowners getting their water from their own well.

Sense strand
The strand of DNA that has the same nucleotide sequence as the mRNA (except the DNA has T where the RNA has U residues).

Sensing element
That part of the transducer which reacts directly in response to the input.

Sensitivity
The minimum change in input signal to which an instrument can respond.

Sensitivity shift
A change in slope of the calibration curve due to a change in sensitivity.

Sensor
A sensor (also called detectors) is a device that measures a physical quantity and converts it into a signal which can be read by n observer or by an instrument. For example, a mercury-in-glass thermometer converts the measured temperature into expansion and contraction of a

liquid which can be read on a calibrated glass tube. A thermocouple converts temperature to an output voltage which can be read by a voltmeter. For accuracy, most sensors are calibrated against known standards.

Separation (satellite)
The instant at which a satellite is released from its launcher.

Septic tank
A septic tank is a key component of the septic system, a small-scale sewage treatment system common in areas with no connection to main sewage pipes provided by local governments or private corporations. (Other components, typically mandated and/or restricted by local governments, optionally include pumps, alarms, sand filters, and clarified liquid effluent disposal means such as a septic drain field, ponds, natural stone fiber filter plants or peat moss beds.) Septic systems are a type of On-Site Sewage Facility (OSSF). In North America, approximately 25% of the population relies on septic tanks; this can include suburbs and small towns as well as rural areas (Indianapolis is an example of a large city where many of the city's neighborhoods are still on separate septic systems). In Europe, they are in general limited to rural areas only.

Septum
The growth of the cell membrane and wall between opposite ends of a growing cell, ultimately separating the cell into two daughter cells.

Sequence
As a noun, the sequence of a DNA is a buzz word for the structure of a DNA molecule, in terms of the sequence of bases it contains. As a verb, "to sequence" is to determine the structure of a piece of DNA; i.e. the sequence of nucleotides it contains.

Sequence tagged site (STS)
Short (200 to 500 base pairs) DNA sequence that has a single occurrence in the human genome and whose location and base sequence are known. Detectable by polymerase chain reaction, STSs are useful for localizing and orienting the mapping and sequence data reported from many different laboratories and serve as landmarks on the developing physical map of the human genome. Expressed sequence tags (ESTs) are STSs derived from cDNAs.

Sequencer
An apparatus used for deciphering the order of bases in a strand of DNA.

Sequencing
Determination of the order of nucleotides (base sequences) in a DNA or RNA molecule or the order of amino acids in a protein.

Sequential access
In computer science, sequential access means that a group of elements (e.g. data in a memory array or a disk file or on magnetic tape data storage) is accessed in a predetermined, ordered sequence. Sequential access is sometimes the only way of accessing the data, for example if it is on a tape. It may also be the access method of choice, for example if we simply want to process a sequence of data elements in order.

Serendipity
Serendipity means a "happy accident" or "pleasant surprise"; specifically, the accident of finding something good or useful without looking for it. The word has been voted one of the ten English words hardest to translate in June 2004 by a British translation

company. However, due to its sociological use, the word has been exported into many other languages.

Serial transmission
Sending one bit at a time on a single transmission line. Compare with parallel transmission.

Sericulture
Sericulture, or silk farming, is the rearing of silkworms for the production of raw silk. Although there are several commercial species of silkworms, Bombyx mori is the most widely used and intensively studied.

Serovars
Different strains of the same species of bacterium that can be distinguished by different reactions to certain antibodies (anti-sera). The name derives from the terms SEROlogical VARiety.

Server
A computer or software package that provides a specific service to client software running on other computers. The term can refer to a particular piece of software, such as a WWW server, or to the machine on which the software is running, hence the popular phrase: "The server's down."

Service module
Part of a satellite which contains the housekeeping equipment, i.e. power generation, conditioning and control, stabilisation and ground-satellite link.

Servicing mission
Auxiliary mission to have astronauts perform repairs and upgrades to satellite equipment in space.

Set point
The temperature at which a controller is set to control a system.

Settlement rule
The UK tax rule that aims to stop you passing income to someone else in the family or giving income or assets to someone else on the basis that you will have it back later in an effort to reduce your overall income tax bill.

Settling pond (water quality)
An open lagoon into which wastewater contaminated with solid pollutants is placed and allowed to stand. The solid pollutants suspended in the water sink to the bottom of the lagoon and the liquid is allowed to overflow out of the enclosure.

Settling time
The time taken for the display to settle within one digit final value when a step is applied to the meter input.

Sewage treatment plant
A facility designed to receive the wastewater from domestic sources and to remove materials that damage water quality and threaten public health and safety when discharged into receiving streams or bodies of water. The substances removed are classified into four basic areas:
(1) greases and fats;
(2) solids from human waste and other sources;
(3) dissolved pollutants from human waste and decomposition products; and
(4) dangerous microorganisms.
Most facilities employ a combination of mechanical removal steps and bacterial decomposition to achieve the desired results. Chlorine is often added to discharges from the plants to reduce the danger of spreading disease by the release of pathogenic bacteria.

Sewer
A system of underground pipes that collect and deliver wastewater to treatment facilities or streams.

Sex chromosomes
The X and Y chromosomes in human beings that determine the sex of an individual. Females have two X chromosomes in diploid cells; males have an X and a Y chromosome. The sex chromosomes comprise the 23rd chromosome pair in a karyotype.

Sex determination
The mechanism in a given species by which sex is determined; in many species sex is determined at fertilization by the nature of the sperm that fertilizes the egg.

Sexual PCR
PCR amplification in which similar, but not identical, DNA sequences are reassembled to obtain novel combinations of related, but variable sequences. When different combinations of a gene sequence are constructed, some of the resulting genes may possess improved characteristics. By repeating many rounds of PCR amplification and selection, an enormous amount of sequence variation can be obtained.

Seyfert (galaxy)
Type of galaxy with a point-like nucleus and very faint spiral arms, first described in 1943 by American astrophysicist Carl Seyfert. Such galaxies have since been shown to belong to a wider class of objects known as active galactic nuclei.

Shear modulus
The ratio of the shear stress and the angular shear distortion.

Shear stress
A shear stress, denoted (Greek: tau), is defined as the component of stress coplanar with a material cross section. Shear stress arises from the force vector component parallel to the cross section. Normal stress, on the other hand, arises from the force vector component perpendicular or antiparallel to the material cross section on which it acts.

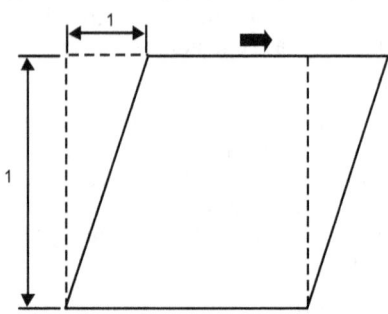

Shearing
Shearing in continuum mechanics refers to the occurrence of a shear strain, which is a deformation of a material substance in which parallel internal surfaces slide past one another. It is induced by a shear stress in the material. Shear strain is distinguished from volumetric strain, the change in a material's volume in response to stress.

Shearing strain
A measure of angular distortion also directly measurable, but not as easily as axial strain.

Sheath thermocouple
A thermocouple made out of mineral-insulated thermocouple cable which has an outer metal sheath.

Shell
A surface made of thin material.

Shelter
A place where an animal can rest and be safe. An animal stores food and raises its young in a shelter.

Shield volcano
A gently sloping volcano in the shape of a flattened dome, built almost exclusively of mafic lava flows. The Hawaiian Islands are a good example.

Shine-Delgarno sequence
A sequence in the mRNA which can pair with the ribosome facilitating the initiation of protein synthesis.

Shoemaker-Levy 9 (comet)
The only comet ever seen to collide with a planet. Discovered by Carolyn and Eugene Shoemaker and David Levy on 25 March 1993 while it was in orbit around Jupiter. After approaching too close to Jupiter, it broke into about 20 separate fragments. These struck the planet 16 - 22 July 1994, creating fireballs which produced dark clouds in Jupiter's atmosphere.

Shotgun cloning
The practice of randomly clipping a larger DNA fragment into various smaller pieces, cloning everything, and then studying the resulting individual clones to figure out what happened. For example, if one was studying a 50 kb gene, it "may" be a bit difficult to figure out the restriction map.

Shotgun method
Cloning of DNA fragments randomly generated from a genome.

Shotgun sequencing
A way of determining the sequence of a large DNA fragment which requires little brainpower but lots of late nights. The large fragment is shotgun cloned (see above), and then each of the resulting smaller clones ("subclones") is sequenced. By finding out where the subclones overlap, the sequence of the larger piece becomes apparent. Note that some of the regions will get sequenced several times just by chance.

Shuttle vector
A vector that can replicate in the cells of more than one organism (e.g. in both E. coli and in yeast).

SI
System Internationale. The name given to the standard metric system of units.

Siblings
Two cells that arose by the division of a parent cell.

Sibs
An abbreviation for siblings.

Sickle cell anemia
An hereditary, chronic form of hemolytic anemia characterized by breakdown of the red blood cells; red blood cells undergo a reversible alteration in shape when the oxygen tension of the plasma falls slightly and a sickle-like shape forms.

Sigma factor
A protein that functions as a subunit of bacterial RNA polymerases and is responsible for specificity of recognition of promoters. Different sigma factors allow recognition of different promoter sequences.

Signal
An electrical transmittance (either input or output) that conveys information.

Signal conditioner
A circuit module which offsets, attenuates, amplifies, linearizes and/or filters the signal for input to the A/D converter. The typical output signal conditioner is +2 V dc.

Signal conditioning
To process the form or mode of a signal so as to make it intelligible to, or compatible with, a given device, including such manipulation as pulse shaping, pulse clipping, compensating, digitizing, and linearizing.

Signal transduction
Conditions that alter the conformation of a protein which regulates expression of other genes. Initially signal transduction was used to refer to extracellular conditions that alter the conformation of a membrane protein and cause it to relay the regulatory signal inside the cell, but more recently the term has been broadly applied to a variety of regulatory cascades.

Silent mutation
A mutation which changes the nucleotide sequence but does not cause a detectable change in the phenotype.

Silica
The chemical compound silicon dioxide, also known as silica (from the Latin silex), is an oxide of silicon with the chemical formula SiO_2. It has been known for its hardness since antiquity. Silica is most commonly found in nature as sand or quartz, as well as in the cell walls of diatoms. Silica is manufactured in several forms including fused quartz, crystal, fumed silica (or pyrogenic silica, trademarked Aerosil or Cab-O-Sil), colloidal silica, silica gel, and aerogel.

Silicate
A silicate is a compound containing a silicon bearing anion. The great majority of silicates are oxides, including hexafluorosilicate $(SiF_6)^{2-}$. This definition focuses mainly on the Si-O anions.

Silicates comprise the majority of the earth's crust, as well as the other terrestrial planets, rocky moons, and asteroids. Sand, Portland cement, and thousands of minerals are examples of silicates.

Silicon
Silicon is the eighth most common element in the universe by mass, but very rarely occurs as the pure free element in nature. It is most widely distributed in dusts, sands, planetoids, and planets as various forms of silicon dioxide (silica) or silicates. Over 90% of the Earth's crust is composed of silicate minerals, making silicon the second most abundant element in the earth's crust (about 28% by mass) after oxygen.

Silicon graphics
Silicon Graphics, Inc. (commonly initialised to SGI, historically sometimes referred to as Silicon Graphics Computer Systems or SGCS) was a manufacturer of high-performance computing solutions, including computer hardware and software, founded in 1981 by Jim Clark. Its initial market was 3D graphics display terminals, but its products, strategies and market positions evolved significantly over time.

Similarity
Sequence identity between two nucleotide sequences. For example, 85% similarity means that 85 nucleotide positions out of 100 are identical in the two nucleotide sequences. Sequence similarity does not necessarily indicate that two sequences have common ancestry.

Simple harmonic motion
Simple harmonic motion is a type of periodic motion where the restoring

force is directly proportional to the displacement. It can serve as a mathematical model of a variety of motions, such as the oscillation of a spring. In addition, other phenomena can be approximated by simple harmonic motion, including the motion of a simple pendulum as well as molecular vibration. Simple harmonic motion is typified by the motion of a mass on a spring when it is subject to the linear elastic restoring force given by Hooke's Law. The motion is sinusoidal in time and demonstrates a single resonant frequency.

Simultaneous drilling & production

A technique of drilling a new well on a platform while it continues to produce oil or gas.

Single line diagram

A one-line diagram or single-line diagram is a simplified notation for representing a three-phase power system. The one-line diagram has its largest application in power flow studies. Electrical elements such as circuit breakers, transformers, capacitors, bus bars, and conductors are shown by standardized schematic symbols. Instead of representing each of three phases with a separate line or terminal, only one conductor is represented. It is a form of block diagram graphically depicting the paths for power flow between entities of the system. Elements on the diagram do not represent the physical size or location of the electrical equipment, but it is a common convention to organize the diagram with the same left-to-right, top-to-bottom sequence as the switchgear or other apparatus represented.

Single precision

The degree of numeric accuracy that requires the use of one computer word. In single precision, seven digits are stored, and up to seven digits are printed. Contrast with double precision.

Single strand

One half of a DNA double helix.

Single-ended Input

A signal-input circuit where SIG LO (or sometimes SIG HI) is tied to METER GND. Ground loops are normally not a problem in AC-powered meters, since METER GND is transformer-isolated from AC GND.

Single-gene disorder

A single gene disorder is the result of a single mutated gene. There are estimated to be over 4000 human diseases caused by single gene defects. Single gene disorders can be passed on to subsequent generations in several ways. Genomic imprinting and uniparental disomy, however, may affect inheritance patterns. The divisions between recessive and dominant types are not "hard and fast" although the divisions between autosomal and X-linked types are (since the latter types are distinguished purely based on the chromosomal location of the gene).

Single-plane (static) balancing machine

A single plane balancing machine is a gravitational or centrifugal balancing machine that provides information for accomplishing single plane balancing.

Single-strand DNA binding protein (ssb)

The small basic protein that has a high affinity for single-stranded DNA. Ssb protein protects single-stranded DNA from nuclease attack and inhibits it from reannealing into double-stranded DNA.

Sinkhole
A depression in the Earth's surface caused by dissolving of underlying limestone, salt, or gypsum. Drainage is provided through underground channels that may be enlarged by the collapse of a cavern roof.

Site acceptance test
A test of equipment carried out at site following installation of equipment but prior to commissioning.

Site-directed mutagenesis
A method for introducing specific mutations at a defined site in a nucleotide sequence.

Site-specific recombination
Genetic exchange that occurs between particular, short DNA sequences. Site-specific recombination systems do not require RecA. Instead, each site-specific recombination system requires unique enzymes that catalyze the genetic exchange. Unlike RecA mediated recombination, site-specific recombination requires little sequence homology between the two DNA molecules. The best understood example is the integration of lambda into the E. coli chromosome by recombination between attP and attD catalyzed by the lambda integrase protein.

Slot blot
Similar to a dot blot, but the analyte is put onto the membrane using a slot-shaped template. The template produces a consistently shaped spot, thus decreasing errors and improving the accuracy of the analysis.

Smallest bending radius
The smallest radius that a strain gage can withstand in one direction, without special treatment, without suffering visible damage.

SMART-1 mission
The first of the European Space Agency's 'Small Missions for Advanced Research in Technology'. Due to be launched in 2002 towards the Moon, the spacecraft will demonstrate new technologies such as solar electric propulsion to be used on future deep-space missions.

Sniceball
A snowball which has been stored in the freezer for several months (or more). Useful for surprising unwelcome visitors during the spring and summer months.

Snirtball
A combination of snow and dirt. Snirtballs are produced by accident when the total snowfall on bare ground is less than 0.537 inches.

Snockball
A combination of snow and rock: generally an innocent-looking snowball with a dense, rocky core. Snockballs are always premeditated, and are not known to occur naturally on earth. Giant snockballs from space (also called comets) may be responsible to the initial introduction of water onto our planet.

Snowball
A snowball is a spherical object made from snow, usually created by scooping snow with the hands, and compacting it into a roughly fist-sized ball. The snowball is often used to engage in games, such as snowball fights. Snowball fights are usually light-hearted and involve throwing snowballs at one's friends or family. The pressure exerted by the hands on the snow is a determinant for the final result. Reduced pressure leads to a light and soft snowball. Compacting humid or "packy" snow,

by applying a high pressure produces a harder snowball or iceball, which eventually can be considered harmful during a snowball fight.

Snowball earth

The Snowball Earth hypothesis posits that the Earth's surface became entirely or nearly entirely frozen at least once, some time earlier than 650 Ma (million years ago). Proponents of the hypothesis argue that it best explains sedimentary deposits generally regarded as of glacial origin at tropical paleolatitudes, and other otherwise enigmatic features in the geological record. Opponents of the hypothesis contest the implications of the geological evidence for global glaciation, the geophysical feasibility of an ice- or slush-covered ocean, and the difficulty of escaping an all-frozen condition.

Snowline

The lower limit of any year's permanent snowfall. Separates the Zone of Accumulation from the Zone of Ablation.

SNP

Single Nucleotide Polymorphism (SNP) - a position in a genomic DNA sequence that varies from one individual to another. It is thought that the primary source of genetic difference between any two humans is due to the presence of single nucleotide polymorphisms in their DNA. Furthermore, these SNPs can be extremely useful in genetic mapping (see 'Genetic Mapping') to follow inheritance of specific segments of DNA in a lineage. SNP-typing is the process of determining the exact nucleotide at positions known to be polymorphic.

Snrna

Small nuclear RNA; forms complexes with proteins to form snRNPs; involved in RNA splicing, polyadenylation reactions, other unknown functions (probably).

Snrnp

Small Nuclear RiboNucleoProtein particles, which are complexes between small nuclear RNAs and proteins, and which are involved in RNA splicing and polyadenylation reactions.

Sociology

Sociology is the scientific study of society. It is a social science which uses various methods of empirical investigation and critical analysis to develop a body of knowledge about human social activity. For many sociologists the goal is to conduct research which may be applied directly to social policy and welfare, while others focus primarily on refining the theoretical understanding of social processes. Subject matter ranges from the micro level of individual agency and interaction to the macro level of systems and the social structure.

Software

Computer software, or just software, is a collection of computer programmes and related data that provides the instructions for telling a computer what to do and how to do it. In other words, software is a conceptual entity which is a set of computer programmes, procedures, and associated documentation concerned with the operation of a data processing system. We can also say software refers to one or more computer programmes and data held in the storage of the computer for some purposes. In other words software is a set of programmes, procedures, algorithms and its documentation. Programme software performs the function of the programme it implements, either by directly providing instructions to the computer hardware or by serving as input to another piece of software.

Soil

Soil is a natural body consisting of layers (soil horizons) of primarily mineral constituents of variable thicknesses, which differ from the parent materials in their morphological, physical, chemical, and mineralogical characteristics. In engineering, soil is referred to as regolith, or loose rock material. Strictly speaking, soil is the depth of regolith that influences and has been influenced by plant roots. Soil is composed of particles of broken rock that have been altered by chemical and mechanical processes that include weathering and erosion. Soil differs from its parent rock due to interactions between the lithosphere, hydrosphere, atmosphere, and the biosphere. It is a mixture of mineral and organic constituents that are in solid, gaseous and aqueous states. Soil is commonly referred to as earth or dirt; technically, the term dirt should be restricted to displaced soil.

Solar and heliospheric observatory (SOHO) mission

ESA-NASA spacecraft launched in 1995 to investigate the interior of the Sun, its atmosphere and the solar wind. Led to a number of major discoveries about the Sun.

Solar array

Panel on a spacecraft used to generate electrical power. It comprises a large number of solar cells which generate electricity when exposed to sunlight.

Solar flare

Sudden violent explosion on the Sun which occurs above complex active regions in the photosphere. They usually last only a few minutes, but their temperatures may reach hundreds of millions of degrees. Most of their radiation is emitted as X-rays, but they can also be observed in visible light and radio waves. Charged particles ejected by flares can cause aurorae when they reach the Earth a few days later.

Solar storm

Violent outburst of explosive activity on the Sun.

Solar system

The Solar System consists of the Sun and the astronomical objects gravitationally bound in orbit around it, all of which formed from the collapse of a giant molecular cloud approximately 4.6 billion years ago. The vast majority of the system's mass (well over 99%) is in the Sun. Of the many objects that orbit the Sun, most of the mass is contained within eight relatively solitary planets whose orbits are almost circular and lie within a nearly flat disc called the ecliptic plane. The four smaller inner planets, Mercury, Venus, Earth and Mars, also called the terrestrial planets, are primarily composed of rock and metal. The four outer planets, the gas giants, are substantially more massive than the terrestrials. The two largest, Jupiter and Saturn, are composed mainly of hydrogen and helium; the two outermost planets, Uranus and Neptune, are composed largely of ices, such as water, ammonia and methane, and are often referred to separately as "ice giants".

Solar wind

The solar wind is a stream of charged particles ejected from the upper atmosphere of the Sun. It mostly consists of electrons and protons with energies usually between 1.5 and 10 keV. The stream of particles varies in temperature and speed over time. These particles can escape the Sun's gravity because of their high kinetic energy and the high temperature of the corona. The solar wind creates the heliosphere, a vast bubble in the interstellar medium that surrounds the Solar System. Other phenomena include geomagnetic storms that can knock out power grids on Earth, theaurorae (northern and southern lights), and the plasma tails of comets that always point away from the Sun.

Solas
Safety of Life at Sea (SOLAS) requirements stipulate minimum equipment to be provided in liferafts. The liferafts are provided on offshore installations, helicopters etc.

Solid
Solid is one of the three classical states of matter (the others being gas and liquid). It is characterized by structural rigidity and resistance to changes of shape or volume. Unlike a liquid, a solid object does not flow to take on the shape of its container, nor does it expand to fill the entire volume available to it like a gas does. The atoms in a solid are tightly bound to each other, either in a regular geometric lattice (crystalline solids, which include metals and ordinary water ice) or irregularly (an amorphous solid such as common window glass).

Solid state
In metamorphism, indicates the change of mineral identity without melting. All ion migration occurs while the rock (or pre-glacial ice) is still solid.

Solute
A substance that is dissolved in another substance, thus forming a solution.

Solution
A mixture of a solvent and a solute. In some solutions, such as sugar water, the substances mix so thoroughly that the solute cannot be seen. But in other solutions, such as water mixed with dye, the solution is visibly changed.

Solution hybridization
A method closely related to RNase protection. Solution hybridization is designed to measure the levels of a specific mRNA species in a complex population of RNA. An excess of radioactive probe is allowed to hybridize to the RNA, then single-strand specific nuclease is used to destroy the remaining unhybridized probe and RNA. The "protected" probe is separated from the degraded fragments, and the amount of radioactivity in it is proportional to the amount of mRNA in the sample which was capable of hybridization. This can be a very sensitive detection method.

Solutions integrator
A type of consulting business that helps other businesses integrate new technology into their existing structure. The technology being integrated includes: supply-chain management systems, sales-force automation systems, e-commerce, Internet development telecommunications, computer telephony, etc.

Solvation
Solvation, also sometimes called dissolution, is the process of attraction

and association of molecules of a solvent with molecules or ions of a solute. As ions dissolve in a solvent they spread out and become surrounded by solvent molecules.

Solvation shell
A Solvation shell is a shell of any chemical species acting as a solvent, surrounding a solute species. When the solvent is water it is often referred to as a hydration shell or hydration sphere. A classic example is water molecules solvating a metal ion. The electronegative oxygen atom contained in the water molecule attracts electrostatically to the positive charge on the metal ion. The result is a 'solvation shell' of water molecules surrounding the ion. This shell can be several molecules thick, dependent on the charge of the ion.

Solvent
A solvent is a liquid, solid, or gas that dissolves another solid, liquid, or gaseous solute, resulting in a solution that is soluble in a certain volume of solvent at a specified temperature. Common uses for organic solvents are in dry cleaning (e.g., tetrachloroethylene), as a paint thinner (e.g., toluene, turpentine), as nail polish removers and glue solvents (acetone, methyl acetate, ethyl acetate), in spot removers (e.g., hexane, petrol ether), in detergents (citrus terpenes), in perfumes (ethanol), nail polish and in chemical synthesis. The use of inorganic solvents (other than water) is typically limited to research chemistry and some technological processes.

Somatic cell hybrid
Hybrid cell line derived from two different species; contains a complete chromosomal complement of one species and a partial chromosomal complement of the other; human/hamster hybrids grow and divide, losing human chromosomes with each generation until they finally stabilize, the hybrid cell line established is then utilized to detect the presence of genes on the remaining human chromosome.

Somatic cells
A somatic cell (diploid) is any biological cell forming the body of an organism; that is, in a multicellular organism, any cell other than a gamete, germ cell, gametocyte or undifferentiated stem cell. By contrast, gametes are cells that fuse during sexual reproduction, for organisms that reproduce sexually; Germ cells are cells that give rise to gametes; Stem cells are cells that can divide through mitosis and differentiate into diverse specialized cell types. For example, in mammals, somatic cells make up all the internal organs, skin, bones, blood, and connective tissue. By contrast, mammalian germ cells give rise to spermatozoa and ova which fuse during fertilization to produce a cell called a zygote, which develops into an embryo.

Somatic mutation
A mutation occurring in any cell that is not destined to become a germ cell; if the mutant cell continues to divide, the individual will come to contain a patch of tissue of genotype different from the cells of the rest of the body.

SOS box
The operator sequence recognised by the LexA repressor protein.

SOS response
The coordinate induction of many genes in response to certain types of DNA damage. Many of the induced gene products facilitate repair of the damaged DNA, but the repair

processes result in a high frequency of mistakes in the repaired DNA, a process often called error-prone repair. The SOS response in enteric bacteria is initiated by RecA protein, which becomes activated by DNA damage, and stimulates the autoproteolysis of several other proteins, including the LexA protein and the lambda cl repressor protein. The LexA protein is a global repressor that normally turns off expression of many other genes in the SOS regulon.

Sound engineering practice
The PED classification whereby equipment is required to be designed and manufactured according to 'sound engineering practice'.

Sour
A sour fluid is a fluid that contains hydrogen sulphide (H_2S) at 10 ppm or more.

Source
Celestial object which emits electromagnetic radiation.

Source code
A non-executable programme written in a high-level language. A compiler or assembler must translate the source code into object code (machine language) that the computer can understand and process.

Southern blot
A method for detecting specific DNA fragments seperated on an agarose gel. DNA fragments are first seperated by electrophoresis through an agarose gel. After electrophoresis, the DNA in the gel is denatured by soaking the gel in an alkaline solution. Then a nitrocellulose or nylon membrane is layed on top of the agarose gel and absorbant paper is layered on top of the membrane. The aqueous solution passes from the agarose gel through the membrane into the absorbant paper by capillary action. The DNA moves with the aqueous solution but becomes trapped on the membrane. The DNA is then detected by annealing a labelled single stranded DNA probe to the fragments of denatured DNA on the membrane, hybridization detected by autoradiography.

Southern blotting
A technique for transferring electrophoretically resolved DNA segments from an agarose gel to a nitrocellulose filter paper sheet via capillary action; the DNA segment of interest is probed with a radioactive, complementary nucleic acid, and its position is determined by autoradiography.

Soyuz (-Fregat) rocket
Russian rocket which has been launched 1500 times since 1963. It is 43.5 m high and can bring a payload of up to 6 tonnes to 400 km. A manned version used to carry crews to space stations such as Mir now defunct, while an unmanned version is used to launch satellites and Progress cargo craft. A fourth stage called Fregat may also be added to the standard three-stage booster.

Space infrared telescope facility (sirtf)
A NASA infrared space telescope due for launch in 2002. Its main mirror will have a diameter of 0.85 m. It will have a 3-year lifetime.

Space weather
The changing conditions in interplanetary space caused by fluctuations in the solar wind.

Spacecraft
A spacecraft or spaceship is a craft, vehicle, vessel or machine designed

for spaceflight. Spacecraft are used for a variety of purposes, including communications, earth observation, meteorology, navigation, planetary exploration and transportation of humans and cargo.

Span

The difference between the upper and lower limits of a range expressed in the same units as the range.

Span adjustment

The ability to adjust the gain of a process or strain meter so that a specified display span in engineering units corresponds to a specified signal span. For instance, a display span of 200°F may correspond to the 16 mA span of a 4-20 mA transmitter signal.

Spare

A connector point reserved for options, specials, or other configurations. The point is identified by an (E) for location on the electrical schematic.

Special relativity

The observable effects on a body in motion. As velocity increases, time slows down, mass increases and lengths contract.

Specialized transduction

A method of gene transfer between bacteria in which a specific region of the bacterial donor DNA is carried by a phage. The host DNA carried by a specialized transducing phage arises by abbarent excision of a prophage. Thus, only regions of DNA adjacent to an integrated phage can be transferred by this method.

Speciation

A group of organisms that are able to interbreed all belong to the same species. It follows then that organisms that are unable to interbreed belong to separate species.

Specific conductance

A measure of the ability of water to conduct an electrical current as measured using a 1-cm cell and expressed in units of electrical conductance, i.e., Siemens per centimeter at 25 degrees Celsius. Specific conductance can be used for approximating the total dissolved solids content of water by testing its capacity to carry an electrical current. In water quality, specific conductance is used in ground water monitoring as an indication of the presence of ions of chemical substances that may have been released by a leaking landfill or other waste storage or disposal facility. A higher specific conductance in water drawn from downgradient wells when compared to upgradient wells indicates possible contamination from the facility.

Specific gravity

Specific gravity is the ratio of the density (mass of a unit volume) of a substance to the density (mass of the same unit volume) of a reference substance. Apparent specific gravity is the ratio of the weight of a volume of the substance to the weight of an equal volume of the reference substance. The reference substance is nearly always water for liquids or air for gases. Temperature and pressure must be specified for both the sample and the reference. Pressure is nearly always 1 atm equal to 101.325 kPa. Temperatures for both sample and reference vary from industry to industry. In British brewing practice the specific gravity as specified above is multiplied by 1000. Specific gravity is commonly used in industry as a simple means of obtaining information about the concentration of solutions of various materials such as brines, hydrocarbons, sugar solutions (syrups, juices, honeys, brewers wort, must etc.) and acids.

Specific heat

The ratio of thermal energy required to raise the temperature of a body 1° to the thermal energy required to raise an equal mass of water 1°.

Spectral class (of a star)

The spectral class of a star is characterised by the absorption and emission lines that are found in its atmosphere. Each spectral class corresponds to a temperature and is denoted by a letter, from O the hottest and more massive stars to M for the coldest and smallest stars. A mnemonic to remember the series of spectral types is: 'Oh Be A Fine Girl (or Guy) Kiss Me' = OBAFGKM. A new class of stars, designated L, has recently been detected. A spectral class is subdivided into subclasses, designated by a number (0-9).

Spectral filter

A filter which allows only a specific band width of the electromagnetic spectrum to pass, i.e., 4 to 8 micron infrared radiation.

Spectral lines

The lines that appear in the spectrum of an astronomical object. They are an indicator of the chemical elements present in the object, as well as of its physical conditions.

Spectrograph

An instrument used to disperse or separate the light into all its wavelengths which allows quantitative measurements of intensity to be made. As an instrument on a telescope, the spectrograph obtains the spectrum of the light from the astronomical objects. Each spectrum contains a wealth of information. For instance, each chemical element has a distinctive spectrum, which varies with temperature. By analyzing the spectrum of a star astronomers can learn about its chemical composition, its temperature.

Spectrometer

A spectrometer (spectrophotometer, spectrograph or spectroscope) is an instrument used to measure properties of light over a specific portion of the electromagnetic spectrum, typically used in spectroscopic analysis to identify materials. The variable measured is most often the light's intensity but could also, for instance, be the polarization state. The independent variable is usually the wavelength of the light or a unit directly proportional to the photon energy, such as wave number or electron volts, which has a reciprocal relationship to wavelength. A spectrometer is used in spectroscopy for producing spectral lines and measuring their wavelengths and intensities. Spectrometer is a term that is applied to instruments that operate over a very wide range of wavelengths, from gamma rays and X-rays into the far infrared. If the instrument is designed to measure the spectrum in absolute units rather than relative units, then it is typically called a spectrophotometer. The majority of spectrophotomers are used in spectral regions near the visible spectrum.

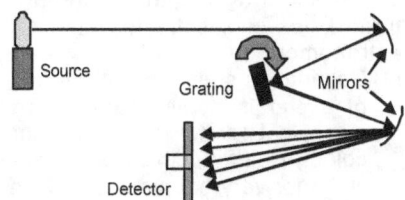

Spectrometer (mass)
An instrument for producing ions in a gas and determining their mass and hence composition.

Spectrometer (mossbauer)
An instrument that provides information on the bonding of an atom in a mineral by bombarding it with gamma rays and measuring small shifts in the velocity or energy of the gamma rays emitted. It is most commonly used to identify the nature of iron in a mineral.

Spectrophotometer
An instrument which determines the energy distribution in a spectrum.

Spectroscopy
Spectroscopy is the study of the interaction between matter and radiated energy. Historically, spectroscopy originated through the study of visible light dispersed according to its wavelength, e.g., by a prism. Later the concept was expanded greatly to comprise any interaction with radiative energy as a function of its wavelength or frequency. Spectroscopic data is often represented by a spectrum, a plot of the response of interest as a function of wavelength or frequency.

Spectrum
Electromagnetic radiation whose beam is dispersed like a natural rainbow so that components with different wavelengths are separated in space in order of increasing or decreasing wavelength. There are three kinds of spectra that interest astronomers.
(1) Continuous spectra: The surface of a star is heated to such an extent that it glows with a particular colour. Red for cool stars, bluish-white for very hot stars. Because the light emitted at the surface has been absorbed and transmitted by many atoms by the time it reaches the surface, the discrete colours of the emission spectra of the atoms have been evened out to form a continuous spectra.
(2) Emission Spectra: These usually arise from gas that is in the outer regions of stars, where the light is not absorbed and emitted many times before being transmitted to space. An emission spectrum consists of sharp peaks in the spectrum corresponding to the wavelengths of the emitted light.

Spectrum analysis
Utilizing frequency components of a vibration signal to determine the source and cause of vibration.

Speed
The rate at which something moves. A bicyclist's speed usually drops when riding up a steep hill.

Spelology
The study of caves.

Spherical aberration
Image defect caused by a mismatch in the shapes of the reflecting surfaces of the primary and secondary mirrors. Light from different annular regions on the primary mirror comes to a focus at different distances from the secondary mirror, and there is no one position where all of the light is in focus.

Spheroplast
Partial removal of the cell wall resulting in osmotically sensitive cells.

Spina bifida
A congenital condition that results from altered fetal development of the spinal cord, part of the neural plate

fails to join together and bone and muscle are unable to grow over this open section.

Spines
Horn-like projections formed upon a lava dome.

Spontaneous mutation
A mutation that occurs without known exposure to a mutagen.

Spore
A highly resistant, resting state of an organism. Under the proper condiditons s spore will germinate to form a viable, reproducing organism. Bacterial spores are often very resistant to heat and dessication.

Spot size
The diameter of the circle formed by the cross section of the field of view of an optical instrument at a given distance.

Spray irrigation
An common irrigation method where water is shot from high-pressure sprayers onto crops. Because water is shot high into the air onto crops, some water is lost to evaporation.

Spring
A water body formed when the side of a hill, a valley bottom or other excavation intersects a flowing body of groundwater at or below the local water table, below which the subsurface material is saturated with water.

Spud
To spud a well to start the actual drilling of a well.

Spurious error
Random or erratic malfunction.

SSR
Simple Sequence Repeat.

Stability
The quality of an instrument or sensor to maintain a consistent output when a constant input is applied.

Stability (satellite)
Artificial satellite's ability to maintain a constant orientation in space.

Stable transfection
A form of transfection experiment designed to produce permanent lines of cultured cells with a new gene inserted into their genome. Usually this is done by linking the desired gene with a "selectable" gene, i.e. a gene which confers resistance to a toxin (like G418, aka Geneticin). Upon putting the toxin into the culture medium, only those cells which incorporate the resistance gene will survive, and essentially all of those will also have incorporated the experimenter's gene.

Stagnation pressure
Stagnation pressure is the static pressure at a stagnation point in a fluid flow. At a stagnation point the fluid velocity is zero and all kinetic energy has been converted into pressure energy (isentropically). Stagnation pressure is equal to the sum of the free-stream dynamic pressure and free-stream static pressure. Stagnation pressure is sometimes referred to as pitot pressure because it is measured using a pitot tube.

Standard electrode potential (e0)
The standard potential $E0$ of an electrode is the reversible emf between the normal hydrogen electrode and the electrode with all components at unit activity.

Standard model
The organization and relationships between fundamental particles.

Standard temperature and pressure
STP is used in many thermodynamic calculations and tabulations and is defined as 0 degrees Celsius and 1 atmosphere of pressure.

Standardization
A process of equalizing electrode potentials in one standardizing solution (buffer) so that potentials developed in unknown solutions can be converted to pH values.

Standby vessel
The rescue vessel that is always within 5 miles of the rig or platform. Close standby i.e. closer than 5 miles is provided if activities on the asset increase the risk of man overboard.

Star
Giant ball of gas in space which produces vast amounts of energy through nuclear reactions in its core. There are many different types of stars, which are classified according to their temperatures, colours, ages and compositions.

Starburst galaxy
A starburst galaxy is a galaxy in the process of an exceptionally high rate of star formation, compared to the usual star formation rate seen in most galaxies. Galaxies are often observed to have a burst of star formation after a collision or close encounter between two galaxies. The rate of star formation is so great for a galaxy undergoing a starburst that, if the rate was sustained, the gas reservoirs from which stars are formed would be used up on timescales much shorter than the age of the galaxy. For this reason, it is presumed that starbursts are temporary. Well-known starburst galaxies include M82, NGC 4038/NGC 4039 (the Antennae Galaxies), and IC 10.

Start (initiation) codon
The codon on mRNA where polypeptide synthesis is initiated. The most common start codon is AUG but sometimes GUG or rarely UUG can be used as a start codon.

Static calibration
A calibration recording pressure versus output at fixed points at room temperature.

Static error band
The error band applicable at room temperature.

Static pressure
Pressure of a fluid whether in motion or at rest. It can be sensed in a small hole drilled perpendicular to and flush with the flow boundaries so as not to disturb the fluid in any way.

Static unbalance
Static unbalance is that condition of unbalance for which the central principal axis is displayed only parallel to the shaft axis

Steady flow
When all the time derivatives of a flow field vanish, the flow is considered to be a steady flow. Steady-state flow refers to the condition where the fluid properties at a point in the system do not change over time. Otherwise, flow is called unsteady. Whether a particular flow is steady or unsteady, can depend on the chosen frame of reference. For instance, laminar flow over a sphere is steady in the frame of reference that is stationary with

respect to the sphere. In a frame of reference that is stationary with respect to a background flow, the flow is unsteady.

Steady state vibration
That condition of vibration induced by an unchanging continuing periodic force.

Stellite
Stellite alloy is a range of cobalt-chromium alloys designed for wear resistance. It may also contain tungsten or molybdenum and a small but important amount of carbon. It is a trademarked name of the Deloro Stellite Company and was invented by Elwood Haynes in the early 1900s as a substitute for flatware that stained (or that had to be constantly cleaned).

Sticky (cohesive) ends
The two complementary single-stranded ends of a DNA duplex. For example, resulting from digestion with a Class II restriction endonuclease.

Stiffness
The ratio of the force required to create a certain deflection or movement of a part expressed as (Force/deflection) lbs/in or grams/cm.

Stochastic
A random process; a process determined by a random distribution of probabilities.

Stonewall
The maximum stable flow and maximum head condition for a centrifugal compressor.

Stop (nonsense) codon
A UAG, UAA. or UGA codons which is not representing any cognate aminoacyl tRNA in most organisms. When the ribosome encounters a stop codon in the mRNA, a termination factor interacts with the ribosome causing polypeptide synthesis to stop and the ribosome to dissociate from the mRNA.

Stop bit
A signal following a character or block that prepares the receiving device to receive the next character or block.

Storm sewer
A sewer that carries only surface runoff, street wash, and snow melt from the land. In a separate sewer system, storm sewers are completely separate from those that carry domestic and commercial wastewater (sanitary sewers).

Strain
An organism that is different from other organisms of the same species due to genetic differences. Strain is commonly used in two ways:
(i) organisms of the same species that when initially isolated are found to have certain different properties (due to unknown mutations) are called different strains;
(ii) derivatives of an organism that have distinct genotypes due to known mutations are called different strains.

Strain gage
A measuring element for converting force, pressure, tension, etc., into an electrical signal.

Strand slippage
The denaturation and aberrant mispairing of a template strand during DNA replication. Results in frameshift mutations.

Stratovolcano
A volcano composed of both lava flows and pyroclastic material. Also

called "Composite" volcanoes. Common at convergent boundaries. Excellent examples in the U.S. include Mt. St. Helens, Mt. Shasta, and the other peaks of the Cascade Range of California, Oregon, and Washington.

Stream
A general term for a body of flowing water; natural water course containing water at least part of the year. In hydrology, it is generally applied to the water flowing in a natural channel as distinct from a canal.

Streamflow
The water discharge that occurs in a natural channel. A more general term than runoff, streamflow may be applied to discharge whether or not it is affected by diversion or regulation.

Streptomycin
An antibiotic that inhibits protein synthesis in bacteria by binding to the S12 protein of the 30s ribosomal subunit and inhibiting translation. A high level of Str^R can result from chromosomal mutations in the gene for the S12 protein (rpsL) which prevent streptomycin from binding to the ribosome. Only mutant ribosomes are Str^R, so resistance to streptomycin is recessive to streptomycin sensitivity. Because streptomycin rapidly inhibits protein synthesis, when cells acquire the rpsL gene phenotypic expression is required before the cells become streptomycin resistant.

Stress
Stress is a measure of the internal forces acting within a deformable body. Quantitatively, it is a measure of the average force per unit area of a surface within the body on which internal forces act. These internal forces are a reaction to external forces applied on the body. Because the loaded deformable body is assumed to behave as a continuum, these internal forces are distributed continuously within the volume of the material body, and result in deformation of the body's shape. Beyond certain limits of material strength, this can lead to a permanent shape change or structural failure.

Stretch
To make longer by pulling. Before exercising, she will stretch and bend.

Striations (glacial)
Grooves eroded into bedrock by rock debris frozen into the base of a glacier.

Strike-slip fault
A nearly vertical fault with side-slipping displacement.

String
The entire length of casing; tubing or drill pipe used in a drilling operation.

Stringency
Conditions affecting the hybridization of nucleotide sequences. Higher stringency conditions require more base pairing between the two sequences. Higher stringency conditions can be obtained by higher temperatures, lighter salt concentrations, or addition of formamide.

Stringency
A term used to describe the conditions of hybridization. By varying the conditions (especially salt concentration and temperature) a given probe sequence may be allowed to hybridize only with its exact complement (high stringency), or with any somewhat related sequences (relaxed or low stringency). Increasing the temperature or decreasing the salt concentration will tend to increase the selectivity of a hybridization

reaction, and thus will raise the stringency.

Stringent response
The ability of a bacterium to limit the synthesis of tRNA and rRNA during amino acid starvation. The alarmones ppGpp and pppGpp are at least partially responsible for the stringent response. The concentrations of these alarmones are controlled by the relA and spot gene products in E. coli.

Strong promoter
An efficient promoter that can direct synthesis of RNA transcripts at a relatively fast rate.

Strouhal number
A nondimensional parameter important in vortex meter design defined as:
$s = Fh/V$
where
f = frequency,
V = velocity, and
h = a reference length

Structural and thermal model
Satellite prototype used to test the space performance of the final flight model.

Structural gene
The portion of a gene encoding a functional polypeptide or RNA molecule.

Structural protein
A protein which fulfill a purely structural role (i.e. not enzymatic). This includes phage capsid proteins, some ribosomal proteins, "histone-like" proteins, etc.

Stuffer fragment
The part of a lambda replacement vector that is removed during insertion of new DNA.

Sub-cloning
If you have a cloned piece of DNA (say, inserted into a plasmid) and you need unlimited copies of only a part of it, you might "sub-clone" it. This involves starting with several million copies of the original plasmid, cutting with restriction enzymes, and purifying the desired fragment out of the mixture. That fragment can then be inserted into a new plasmid for replication.

Subduction zone
The zone of convergence of two tectonic plates, one of which usually overrides the other.

Sublimation
Sublimation is the process of transition of a substance from the solid phase to the gas phase without passing through an intermediate liquid phase. Sublimation is anendothermic phase transition that occurs at temperatures and pressures below a substance's triple point in its phase diagram

Submillimetre (sub-mm)
Electromagnetic radiation with a wavelength shorter than 1 mm.

Subsidence
A dropping of the land surface as a result of ground water being pumped. Cracks and fissures can appear in the land. Subsidence is virtually an irreversible process.

Substrate
A chemical recognized by an enzyme.

Substution mutation
A mutation that replaces one nucleotide in a DNA sequence with another nucleotide.

Subtraction library
A cDNA library that only contains those cDNAs that are expressed in a

particular type of cell or tissue or under particular growth conditions. The cDNA common to all conditions is removed by hybridization with excess RNA from other cells (i.e. subtraction), leaving only the unique RNA behind.

Suicide plasmid

A plasmid that cannot replicate in a given host, used to force the; integration into host replicons of genetic determinants carried by the plasmid or phage. It is usually necessary to have a direct selection for the desired recombinants.

Sulphur oxides

Sulphur oxide gases (principally Sulphur dioxide - SO_2) are formed when fuel e.g. coal and oil; containing sulphur is burned.

Sun

Our nearest star and the central object in the Solar System. Compared with other stars it is fairly average in terms of size and temperature. It seems to have formed from a cloud of dust and gas about 5 billion years ago. A giant ball of gas, mainly hydrogen and helium, it contains 745 times as much mass as all of the planets put together. Energy is generated through nuclear fusion in its core. The temperature of the core is about 15 million degrees Celsius, while the temperature of its visible surface (the photosphere) is 5700 °C. Above the photosphere are the chromosphere and the corona, where the temperature exceeds one million degrees. The energy generated in the core takes 30 000 years to reach the surface, when it is mostly emitted as light and infrared (heat) radiation.

Sunflower

Sunflower (Helianthus annuus) is an annual plant native to the Americas. It possesses a large inflorescence (flowering head). The sunflower got its name from its huge, fiery blooms, whose shape and image is often used to depict the sun. The sunflower has a rough, hairy stem, broad, coarsely toothed, rough leaves and circular heads of flowers. The heads consist of 1,000-2,000 individual flowers joined together by a receptacle base.

Sunspot

A relatively cool, dark region on the Sun's surface (photosphere) which is created by the Sun's magnetic field. May occur individually or in groups. Number of sunspots increases every 11 years. The most recent sunspot occurred in 2000.

Sunspot cycle

Periodic variation in the number of sunspots which is related to changes in overall solar activity. The period of the cycle is 10 - 11 years. At the beginning of the cycle there are few, if any, sunspots, but numbers increase as time goes by, then decrease once maximum has passed. This cycle seems to be caused by the interaction between the 'dynamo' which generates the Sun's magnetic field and the Sun's rotation.

Super cooling

Supercooling, also known as undercooling, is the process of lowering the temperature of a liquid or a gas below its freezing point without it becoming a solid. A liquid below its standard freezing point will crystallize in the presence of a seed crystal or nucleus around which a crystal structure can form. However, lacking any such nucleus, the liquid phase can be maintained all the way down to the temperature at which crystal homogeneous nucleation occurs. The homogeneous nucleation can occur above the glass transition where the system is an amorphous (non-crystalline) solid.

Super heating
1. The heating of a liquid above its boiling temperature without the formation of the gaseous phase.
2. The heating of the gaseous phase considerably above the boiling-point temperature to improve the thermodynamic efficiency of a system.

Supercoiled DNA
Double-stranded circular DNA in which either overwinding or underwinding of the duplex makes the circle twist. The conformation of a covalently closed-circular DNA molecule, which is coiled by torsional strain into the shape taken by a wound up elastic band.

Superinfection
Superinfection is the process by which a cell, that has previously been infected by one virus, gets coinfected with a different strain of the virus, or another virus at a later point in time.[1] Viral superinfections of serious conditions can lead to resistant strains of the virus, which may prompt a change of treatment. For example, an individual superinfected with two separate strains of HIV may contract a strain that is resistant to antiretroviral treatment. The combined infection has also been shown to reduce the overall effectiveness of the immune response

Superinfection exclusion
A process whereby the presence of one phage in a cell prevents the secondary infection by other. There are many different mechanisms of superinfection exclusion, including changes in cell surface receptors or the expression of a restriction system.

Supernova
Explosion of a massive star at the end of its life. Supernova explosions are so luminous that they can outshine a galaxy. There are two types of supernovae. A supernova type I is most likely a white dwarf star in a binary system which accretes material that builds up until a nuclear explosion disrupts the star. A supernova type II is a massive star which has used up all its nuclear fuel. The star then collapses and the impact of all the material produces a shock wave which blasts the outer layers of the star out.

Supervisory control and data acquisition (SCADA)
A term commonly used to describe a PC based software package that allows operator control of a process from a PC and has the PC collecting and storing process information.

Suppression
The restoration (or partial restoration) of a wild-type phenotype by a second mutation. There are many different mechanisms of suppression.

Suppressor gene
A mutated gene which produces a product which reverses the effect of a previous specific mutation without actually correcting the original mutation in the DNA can be either intergenic or intragenic.

Suppressor mutation
A mutation that restores, partially or completely, the loss of function caused by another mutation. Many suppressor mutations are in genes encoding a transfer RNA species; the altered tRNA can recognise the original mutant codon and, during translation, insert an acceptable substitute amino acid into the polypeptide.

Suppressor trna
A mutant tRNA that recognizes a stop codon instead of the codon for the cognate amino acid. This property is sometimes, but not always, due to a base substitution in the anticodon.

Surface tension
The attraction of molecules to each other on a liquid's surface. Thus, a barrier is created between the air and the liquid.

Surface water
Surface water is water collecting on the ground or in a stream, river, lake, wetland, or ocean; it is related to water collecting as groundwater or atmospheric water. Surface water is naturally replenished by precipitation and naturally lost through discharge to evaporation and sub-surface seepage into the ground. Although there are other sources of groundwater, such as connate water and magmatic water, precipitation is the major one and groundwater originated in this way is called meteoric water.

Surge
An unstable operating condition when the flow through a compressor is decreased to the point that momentary flow reversals occur.

Surge current
A current of short duration that occurs when power is first applied to capacitive loads or temperature dependent resistive loads such as tungsten or molybdenum heaters- usually lasting no more than several cycles.

Suspended sediment
Very fine soil particles that remain in suspension in water for a considerable period of time without contact with the bottom. Such material remains in suspension due to the upward components of turbulence and currents and/or by suspension.

Suspended solids
solids that are not in true solution and that can be removed by filtration. Such suspended solids usually contribute directly to turbidity. Defined in waste management, these are small particles of solid pollutants that resist separation by conventional methods. Suspended-sediment concentration the ratio of the mass of dry sediment in a water-sediment mixture to the mass of the water-sediment mixture. Typically expressed in milligrams of dry sediment per liter of water-sediment mixture.

Suspended-sediment discharge
The quantity of suspended sediment passing a point in a stream over a specified period of time. When expressed in tons per day, it is computed by multiplying water discharge (in cubic feet per second) by the suspended-sediment concentration (in milligrams per liter) and by the factor 0.0027.

Suspension effect
The source of error due to varied reference liquid junction potential depending upon whether the electrodes are immersed in the supernatant fluid or deeper in the sediment. Normally encountered with solutions containing resins or charged colloids.

Swing-by
A particular manoeuvre that exploits the gravitational force of a moon or a planet to modify the trajectory of a spacecraft and to boost it into space.

SWOT
Strengths; Weaknesses; Opportunities and Threats. A technique employed for analysing a competitive situation or proposal.

Synapsis
The pairing of homologous chromosomes or of homologous chromosomal regions.

Synchrotron radiation
Electromagnetic radiation emitted by a very high-energy electron, moving in a magnetic field.

Syndrome
A syndrome is the association of several clinically recognizable features, signs (observed by someone other than the patient), symptoms (reported by the patient), phenomena or characteristics that often occur together, so that the presence of one or more features alerts the healthcare provider to the possible presence of the others. In recent decades, the term has been used outside medicine to refer to a combination of phenomena seen in association.

Syntax
The rules governing the structure of a language.

Synteny
Genes which occur in the same order on the chromosome of different species.

Sysop
Systems operator. A person responsible for the operations of a computer system or network. Part of such operations are security checks and routine maintenance.

Systems engineering review
A review which verifies that the systems engineering (design and construction) of a spacecraft corresponds to the requirements as contained in the design drawings.

Sythetic lethal mutations
Two mutations are synthetically lethal if cells with either of the single mutations are viable but cells with both mutations are inviable. As with suppressor analysis, synthetic lethal mutations often indicate that the two mutations affect a single function or pathway.

Sythetic phenotype
A distinct phenotype that requires the presence of two mutations, and either of the mutations alone does not exhibit the same phenotype. Also note the defination of Synthetic lethal mutations.

T

T-1
One of the fastest leased-line connections used for the Internet. It is capable of transmitting data at roughly 1.5 million bits per second, still not fast enough for full-screen, full-motion video.

Tandem bicycle
The tandem bicycle or twin is a form of bicycle (occasionally, a tricycle) designed to be ridden by more than one person. The term tandem refers to the seating arrangement (fore to aft, not side-by-side), not the number of riders. A bike with two riders side-by-side is called a sociable.

Tandem duplication
A DNA sequence that is repeated in direct orientation.

Tandem repeat sequences
Multiple copies of the same base sequence on a chromosome; used as a marker in physical mapping.

Tandem repeats
Tandem repeats occur in DNA when a pattern of two or more nucleotides is repeated and the repetitions are directly adjacent to each other.

Tandem repeat locus
Variable number of tandem repeat locus (VNTR locus) is any DNA sequence that exist in multiple copies strung together in a variety of tandem lengths.

Tandem rotors
Tandem rotor helicopters have two large horizontal rotor assemblies mounted one in front of the other. Currently this configuration is mainly used for large cargo helicopters.

Tape
A recording media for data or computer programmes. Tape can be in permanent form, such as perforated paper tape, or erasable, such as magnetic tape. Generally, tape is used as a mass storage medium, in magnetic form, and has a much higher storage capacity than disk storage, but it takes much longer to write or recover data from tape than from a disk.

Tape drive
A tape drive is a data storage device that reads and performs digital recording, writes data on a magnetic tape. Magnetic tape data storage is typically used for offline, archival data storage. Tape media generally has a favorable unit cost and long archival stability.

Taq polymerase
A DNA polymerase isolated from the bacterium Thermophilis aquaticus and which is very stable to high temperatures. It is used in PCR procedures and high temperature sequencing.

TATA box
A sequence found in the promoter (part of the 5' flanking region) of many genes. Deletion of this site (the binding site of transcription factor TFIID) causes a marked reduction in transcription, and gives rise to heterogeneous transcription initiation sites.

Tautomeric shift
A reversible change in the position of a hydrogen atom in a molecule which results in the conversion of the molecule between different isomers. A shift between the keto group and a enoyl group in nucleotides can result in altered base-pairing.

Taxonomy
Taxonomy is the science of identifying and naming species, and arranging them into a classification. The field of taxonomy, sometimes referred to as "biological taxonomy", revolves around the description and use of taxonomic units, known as taxa (singular taxon). A resulting taxonomy is a particular classification ("the taxonomy of..."), arranged in a hierarchical structure or classification scheme. An example of a modern classification is the one published in 2009 by the Angiosperm Phylogeny Group for all living flowering plant families (the APG III system).

Tay-Sachs disease
A fatal degenerative disease of the nervous system due to a deficiency of hexosamidase A, causing mental deficiency, paralysis, mental deterioration, and blindness; found primarily but not exclusively among Ashkenazi Jews. Autosomal recessive.

TCP/IP
Transmission Control Protocol/Internet Protocol. The programing protocols invented by individuals in the U.S. Department of Defence to carry messages around the Internet.

T-DNA
The portion of the Ti plasmid transferred from Agrobacterium to the plant DNA.

Technology
The application of scientific discoveries to the development and improvement of goods and services that ideally improve the life of humans and their environment. Such goods and services include materials, machinery, and processes that improve production or solve problems. In schools, technology ranges from pencils, books, and furniture to lighting, transportation, computers, and more. Most common references in schools imply computing or computer-related programmes.

Technology transfer
The process of converting scientific findings from research laboratories into useful products by the commercial sector.

Telecommunication
Synonym for data communication. The transmission of information from one point to another.

Telemetry
Data and commands sent from the spacecraft to ground stations.

Teleology
The study of the evidences of design or purpose in nature.

Telepathy
Communication between minds by some means other than sensory perception.

Telescope
A telescope is an instrument that aids in the observation of remote objects

by collecting electromagnetic radiation (such as visible light). The first known practical telescopes were invented in the Netherlands at the beginning of the 1600s (the 17th century), using glass lenses. They found use in terrestrial applications and astronomy.

Telescope (wolter)
German physicist Hans Wolter (1911-1978) conceived a series of designs for grazing-incidence telescopes, requiring photons to undergo two successive reflections from combinations of paraboloid-hyperboloid (particularly suited for extended field of view imaging) or paraboloid-ellipsoid surfaces.

Telomere
The terminal part of a linear chromosome. Replication of the ends of linear DNA molecules requires specialized enzymes or structures. Often the telomers have a DNA sequence with a single-stranded end that can fold into a hairpin structure.

Tempco
Abbreviation for "temperature coefficient": the error introduced by a change in temperature. Normally expressed in %/°C or ppm/°C.

Temperate phage
A phage that is capable of becoming a prophage in the bacterial host (i.e. maintain itself in a relatively quiescent state). Improperly but frequently called a lysogenic phage.

Temperature
Temperature is a physical property of matter that quantitatively expresses the common notions of hot and cold. Objects of low temperature are cold, while various degrees of higher temperatures are referred to as warm or hot. Heat spontaneously flows from bodies of a higher temperature to bodies of lower temperature. No net heat will be exchanged between bodies of the same temperature; such bodies The temperature of a substance varies with the microscopic speed of the fundamental particles that it contains, raised to the second power; that is, it is proportional to the mean kinetic energy of its particles. are said to be in "thermal equilibrium".

Temperature error
The maximum change in output, at any measurand value within the specified range, when the transducer temperature is changed from room temperature to specified temperature extremes.

Temperature range, compensated
The range of ambient temperatures within which all tolerances specified for Thermal Zero Shift and Thermal Sensitivity Shift are applicable (temperature error).

Temperature range, operable
The range of ambient temperatures, given by their extremes, within which

the transducer may be operated. Exceeding compensated range may require recalibration.

Temperature-sensitive mutation
A mutation that results in a gene product that is functional within a certain temperature range (e.g. at less than 30°C), but nonfunctional at different temperatures (e.g. at 42°C).

Template
A single-stranded polynucleotide (or region of a polynuceotide) that can be copied to produce a complementary polynucleotide.

Temporary refuge
The area on a platform; usually within accommodation block; designed to give temporary refuge to personel during emergency situations e.g. fire; gas leak etc.

Tephra
Tephra is fragmental material produced by a volcanic eruption regardless of composition, fragment size or emplacement mechanism. Volcanologists also refer to airborne fragments as pyroclasts. Once clasts have fallen to the ground they remain as tephra unless hot enough to fuse together into pyroclastic rock or tuff.

Teratogens
Any agent that raises the incidence of congenital malformations.

Tetralogy
Teratology is the study of abnormalities of physiological development. It is often thought of as the study of human birth defects, but it is much broader than that, taking in other non-birth developmental stages, including puberty; and other non-human life forms, including plants. A newer term developmental toxicity includes all manifestations of abnormal development, not only frank terata. These may include growth retardation or delayed mental development without any structural malformations.

Terminal
An input/output device used to enter data into a computer and record the output.

Terminal redundancy
The presence of identical DNA sequences repeated at the two ends of DNA molecule (e.g. phage particles).

Terminator
In genetics, a terminator, or transcription terminator is a section of genetic sequence that marks the end of gene or operon on genomic DNA for transcription. In prokaryotes, two classes of transcription terminators are known:
1. Intrinsic transcription terminators where a hairpin structure forms within the nascent transcript that disrupts the mRNA-DNA-RNA polymerase ternary complex.
2. Rho-dependent transcription terminators that require Rho factor, an RNA helicase protein complex, to disrupt the nascent mRNA-DNA-RNA polymerase ternary complex.

Terminus
The region of DNA sequences where DNA replication terminates.

Terrestrial planets
The four innermost planets in the Solar System, which have solid rocky surfaces.

Tertiary wastewater treatment
Selected biological, physical, and chemical separation processes to

remove organic and inorganic substances that resist conventional treatment practices; the additional treatment of effluent beyond that of primary and secondary treatment methods to obtain a very high quality of effluent. The complete wastewater treatment process typically involves a three-phase process:
(1) First, in the primary wastewater treatment process, which incorporates physical aspects, untreated water is passed through a series of screens to remove solid wastes;
(2) Second, in the secondary wastewater treatment process, typically involving biological and chemical processes, screened wastewater is then passed a series of holding and aeration tanks and ponds; and
(3) Third, the tertiary wastewater treatment process consists of flocculation basins, clarifiers, filters, and chlorine basins or ozone or ultraviolet radiation processes.

Testing (spacecraft)
All the procedures, including the simulation of space environment, to ascertain that a spacecraft is ready for launch. The name given to the process of injecting drilling debris back in to the well.

Tetracycline (tet)
An antibiotic that inhibits protein synthesis by preventing aminoacyl tRNA from binding to ribosomes. There are several possible mechanisms of Tetracycline resistance. Tet^R encoded by Tn10 and pBR plasmids is due to a membrane protein that actively transports tetracycline out of the cell.

Tetrad
The four products of a single meiosis.

Tetrad analysis
A method for establishing linkage relationships in fungi by analysing the four products from individual meiotic divisions.

Theory of plate tectonics
The theory explaining that the Earth's plates, or large slabs of rock, are constantly moving, causing continents and oceans to form, be destroyed, and reform over very long periods of time. The theory of plate tectonics explains what causes earthquakes.

Therapeutics
The science and art of healing.

Thermal coefficient of resistance
The change in resistance of a semiconductor per unit change in temperature over a specific range of temperature.

Thermal conductivity
The property of a material to conduct heat in the form of thermal energy.

Thermal expansion
An increase in size due to an increase in temperature expressed in units of an increase in length or increase in size per degree, i.e. inches/inch/degree C.

Thermal gradient
A temperature gradient is a physical quantity that describes in which direction and at what rate the temperature changes the most rapidly around a particular location. The temperature gradient is a dimensional quantity expressed in units of degrees (on a particular temperature scale) per unit length. The SI unit is kelvin per meter (K/m). Temperature gradients in the atmosphere are important in the

atmospheric sciences (meteorology, climatology and related fields).

Thermal pollution

Thermal pollution is the degradation of water quality by any process that changes ambient water temperature. A common cause of thermal pollution is the use of water as a coolant by power plants and industrial manufacturers. When water used as a coolant is returned to the natural environment at a higher temperature, the change in temperature decreases oxygen supply, and affects ecosystem composition. Urban runoff—stormwater discharged to surface waters from roads and parking lots—can also be a source of elevated water temperatures.

Thermal sensitivity shift

The sensitivity shift due to changes of the ambient temperature from room temperature to the specified limits of the compensated temperature range.

Thermal zero shift

An error due to changes in ambient temperature in which the zero pressure output shifts. Thus, the entire calibration curve moves in a parallel displacement.

Thermistor

A thermistor is a type of resistor whose resistance varies significantly with temperature, more so than in standard resistors. The word is a portmanteau of thermal and resistor. Thermistors are widely used as inrush current limiters, temperature sensors, self-resetting overcurrent protectors, and self-regulating heating elements. Thermistors differ from resistance temperature detectors (RTD) in that the material used in a thermistor is generally a ceramic or polymer, while RTDs use pure metals. The temperature response is also different; RTDs are useful over larger temperature ranges, while thermistors typically achieve a higher precision within a limited temperature range, typically -90 °C to 130 °C.

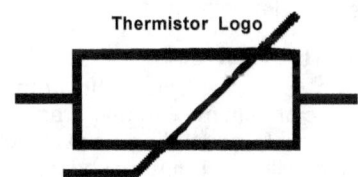
Thermistor Logo

Thermocouple

The junction of two dissimilar metals which has a voltage output proportional to the difference in temperature between the hot junction and the lead wires (cold junction).

Thermoelectric power water use

Water used in the process of the generation of thermoelectric power. Power plants that burn coal and oil are examples of thermoelectric-power facilities.

Thermopile

An arrangement of thermocouples in series such that alternate junctions are at the measuring temperature and the reference temperature. This arrangement amplifies the thermoelectric voltage. Thermopiles are usually used as infrared detectors in radiation pyrometry.

Thermowell

A closed-end tube designed to protect temperature sensors from harsh environments, high pressure, and flows. They can be installed into a system by pipe thread or welded flange and are usually made of corrosion-resistant metal or ceramic material depending upon the application.

Theta-replication
Replication of a circular molecule of double-stranded DNA by initiation at a unique origin and proceeding in one or both directions around the molecule. The resulting intermediate looks like the greek letter theta.

Thomson effect
When current flows through a conductor within a thermal gradient, a reversible absorption or evolution of heat will occur in the conductor at the gradient boundaries.

Three-factor cross
A method for determining the genetic map position of three linked loci based upon relative frequency of coinheritance of each locus during a cross between two strains with different allelic forms in each gene.

Throughput
The total amount of raw materials processed by a refinery or other plant in a given period.

Thrusters
Small reaction engines on a spacecraft that can provide thrust used to control its orbit, orientation and attitude.

Thunderstorm
A storm that produces lightning and thunder and often heavy rain and strong wind. When the weather is hazy, hot, and humid, thunderstorms are likely to develop.

Thymine (T)
Thymine (T, Thy) is one of the four nucleobases in the nucleic acid of DNA that are represented by the letters G–C–A–T. The others are adenine, guanine, and cytosine. Thymine is also known as 5-methyluracil, a pyrimidine nucleobase. As the name suggests, thymine may be derived by methylation of uracil at the 5th carbon. In RNA, thymine is replaced with uracil in most cases. In DNA, thymine (T) binds to adenine (A) via two hydrogen bonds, thus stabilizing the nucleic acid structures. Thymine combined with deoxyribose creates the nucleoside deoxythymidine, which is synonymous with the term thymidine. Thymidine can be phosphorylated with one, two, or three phosphoric acid groups, creating, respectively, TMP, TDP, or TTP (thymidine mono-, di-, or triphosphate).

Ti plasmid
The large plasmid found in those Agrobacterium tumefaciens cells able to direct crown gall formation on certain species of plants.

Till (glacial)
Till or glacial till is unsorted glacial sediment. Glacial drift is a general term for the coarsely graded and extremely heterogeneous sediments of glacial origin. Glacial till is that part of glacial drift which was deposited directly by the glacier. Its content may vary from clays to mixtures of clay, sand, gravel and boulders. This material is mostly derived from the subglacial erosion and entrainment by the moving ice of the glaciers of previously available unconsolidated sediments. Bedrock can also be eroded through the action of glacial plucking and abrasion and the resulting clasts of various sizes will be incorporated to the glacier's bed. Eventually, the sedimentary

assemblage forming this bed will be abandoned some distance down-ice from its various sources.

Tissue-specific expression
Gene function which is restricted to a particular tissue or cell type. For example, the glycoprotein hormone alpha subunit is produced only in certain cell types of the anterior pituitary and placenta, not in lungs or skin; thus expression of the glycoprotein hormone alpha-chain gene is said to be tissue-specific. Tissue specific expression is usually the result of an enhancer which is activated only in the proper cell type.

Titan
The largest and most intriguing moon of Saturn. Titan is the second largest moon in the Solar System after Ganymede (one of Jupiter's moons), and is larger than the planet Mercury. Titan was discovered by the Dutch astronomer Christian Huygens on March 25 1655.

Tm
The melting point for a double-stranded nucleic acid. Technically, this is defined as the temperature at which 50% of the strands are in double-stranded form and 50% are single-stranded, i.e. midway in the melting curve. A primer has a specific Tm because it is assumed that it will find an opposite strand of appropriate character.

Toolpusher
The Foreman in charge of drilling rig operations and crew members.

Topographic map
A topographic map is a type of map characterized by large-scale detail and quantitative representation of relief, usually using contour lines in modern mapping, but historically using a variety of methods. Traditional definitions require a topographic map to show both natural and man-made features. A topographic map is typically published as a map series, made up of two or more map sheets that combine to form the whole map. A contour line is a combination of two line segments that connect but do not intersect; these represent elevation on a topographic map.

Topography
Topography is the study of Earth's surface shape and features or those of planets, moons, and asteroids. It is also the description of such surface shapes and features (especially their depiction in maps). The topography of an area can also mean the surface shape and features themselves.

Topoisomerase
An enzyme which introduces or removes overwinding or underwinding of the DNA circular duplex by causing a nick, rotating the strands, and then ligating them.

Torque
Torque, moment or moment of force is the tendency of a force to rotate an object about an axis, fulcrum, or pivot. Just as a force is a push or a pull, a torque can be thought of as a twist.

Toxicology
Toxicology (from the Greek words - toxicos "poisonous" and logos) is a branch of biology, chemistry, and medicine concerned with the study of the adverse effects of chemicals on living organisms. It is the study of symptoms, mechanisms, treatments and detection of poisoning, especially the poisoning of people.

Toxicology testing
Toxicology testing, also known as safety testing, or toxicity testing, is conducted by pharmaceutical companies testing drugs, or by contract animal testing facilities such as Huntingdon Life Sciences and Inveresk Research International on behalf of a wide variety of customers, including the manufacturer of medicines and household products.

Tracking
Ground facilities employed to follow the progress and to communicate with a satellite.

Trait
A trait is a distinct variant of a phenotypic character of an organism that may be inherited, environmentally determined or be a combination of the two. For example, eye color is a character or abstraction of an attribute, while blue, brown and hazel are traits.

Trans
Genes located on different DNA molecules present in the same cell (the opposite of cis). For example, one copy of a particular gene may reside on the chromosome and the cooond copy may reside on a plasmid.

Trans acting factor
A molecule that can diffuse through the cell to act at a distance from where it is made. Often used to distinguish gene products (protein or RNA) that regulate gene expression in trans vs the DNA site where the gene products binds.

Transcript
A strand of RNA copied from a DNA template.

Transcription
Transcription is the process of creating a complementary RNA copy of a sequence of DNA. Both RNA and DNA are nucleic acids, which use base pairs of nucleotides as a complementary language that can be converted back and forth from DNA to RNA by the action of the correct enzymes. During transcription, a DNA sequence is read by RNA polymerase, which produces a complementary, antiparallel RNA strand. As opposed to DNA replication, transcription results in an RNA complement that includes uracil (U) in all instances where thymine (T) would have occurred in a DNA complement. Transcription can be explained easily in 4 or 5 steps, each moving like a wave along the DNA.
1. RNA Polymerase moves the transcription bubble, a stretch of unpaired nucleotides, by breaking the hydrogen bonds between complementary nucleotides.
2. RNA Polymerase adds matching RNA nucleotides that are paired with complementary DNA bases.
3. RNA sugar-phosphate backbone forms with assistance from RNA polymerase.
4. Hydrogen bonds of the untwisted RNA+DNA helix break, freeing the newly synthesized RNA strand.
5. If the cell has a nucleus, the RNA is further processed (addition of a 3' poly-A tail and a 5' cap) and exits through to the cytoplasm through the nuclear pore complex.

Transcription bubble
A region where the double-stranded DNA is separated while RNA polymerase is actively transcribing RNA. A short region of RNA-DNA duplex is formed between the newly synthesized RNA and the template DNA in this region.

Transcription factor
A protein which is involved in the transcription of genes. These usually

bind to DNA as part of their function (but not necessarily). A transcription factor may be general (i.e. acting on many or all genes in all tissues), or tissue-specific (i.e. present only in a particular cell type, and activating the genes restricted to that cell type). Its activity may be constitutive, or may depend on the presence of some stimulus; for example, the glucocorticoid receptor is a transcription factor which is active only when glucocorticoids are present.

Transcription terminator
A nucleotide sequence that acts as a signal for termination of transcription. There are two common types of transcription terminators: Rho-independant terminators (usually a stem-loop structure in the transcribed RNA followed by a run of U residues) are typically located at the end of operons, and Rho-dependant terminators (typically an unstructured region of RNA that, when untranslated, is recognized by Rho factor) are typically responsible for translational polarity.

Transcription unit
A region of DNA (a gene or an operon) transcribed as a single RNA.

Transcriptome
The complete set of RNA transcripts made by a cell under a particular condition. Typically determined by microarray analysis.

Trans-dimer synthesis
A process which permits nucleotides to be inserted opposite a pyrimidine dimer. Because this process is not based upon complementary base pairing, the wrong base pairs may be inserted, resulting in a mutation.

Transducer
A transducer is a device that converts one form of energy to another. Energy types include (but are not limited to) electrical, mechanical, electromagnetic (including light), chemical, acoustic or thermal energy. While the term transducer commonly implies the use of a sensor/detector, any device which converts energy can be considered a transducer. Transducers are widely used in measuring instruments.

Transducer vibration
Generally, any device which converts movement, either shock or steady state vibration, into an electrical signal proportional to the movement; a sensor.

Transductant
A genetic recombinant formed by transduction.

Transduction
A method of gene transfer between bacteria in which the bacterial donor DNA is carried by a phage. There are two types of transduction: generalized transduction and specialized transduction. Generalized transduction can transfer of any region of the chromosome from the bacterial host into a recipient cell. Specialized transduction can only transfer regions of DNA adjacent to an integrated phage (prophage).

Transfection
A method by which experimental DNA may be put into a cultured mammalian cell. Such experiments are usually performed using cloned DNA containing coding sequences and control regions (promoters, etc) in order to test whether the DNA will be expressed. Since the cloned DNA may have been extensively modified (for example, protein binding sites on the promoter may have been altered or removed), this procedure is often used to test whether a particular modification affects the function of a gene.

Transfer RNA (trna)

Adaptor molecules which translate the triplet code from the mRNA sequence into the corresponding chain of amino acids. tRNAs are short (about 74-95 bases), single-stranded RNA molecules that contain a high proportion of modified nucleosides. When drawn in two-dimensions, tRNAs can be folded into a characteristic cloverleaf structure with three stem-loop structures. The anticodon at the base of the second loop region. A specific amino acid is are added to the 3' end of each tRNA by a specific aminoacyl tRNA synthetase.

Transferase

A transferase is an enzyme that catalyzes the transfer of a functional group (e.g., a methyl or phosphate group) from one molecule (called the donor) to another (called the acceptor). For example, an enzyme that catalyzed this reaction would be a transferase:

$$A - X + B \rightarrow A + B - X$$

In this example, A would be the donor, and B would be the acceptor. The donor is often a coenzyme.

Transformation

Transformation is the genetic alteration of a cell resulting from the direct uptake, incorporation and expression of exogenous genetic material (exogenous DNA) from its surroundings and taken up through the cell membrane(s). Transformation occurs naturally in some species of bacteria, but it can also be effected by artificial means in other cells. Bacteria that are capable of being transformed, whether naturally or artificially, are called competent. Transformation is one of three processes by which exogenous genetic material may be introduced into a bacterial cell, the other two being conjugation (transfer of genetic material between two bacterial cells in direct contact), and transduction (injection of foreign DNA by a bacteriophage virus into the host bacterium). Transformation may also be used to describe the insertion of new genetic material into nonbacterial cells including animal and plant cells; however, because "transformation" has a special meaning in relation to animal cells, indicating progression to a cancerous state, the term should be avoided for animal cells when describing introduction of exogenous genetic material. Introduction of foreign DNA into eukaryotic cells is usually called "transfection".

Transformation (with respect to bacteria)

The process by which a bacteria acquires a plasmid and becomes antibiotic resistant. This term most commonly refers to a bench procedure performed by the investigator which introduces experimental plasmids into bacteria.

Transformation (with respect to cultured cells)

A change in cell morphology and behavior which is generally related to carcinogenesis. Transformed cells tend to exhibit characteristics known collectively as the "transformed phenotype" (rounded cell bodies, reduced attachment dependence, increased growth rate, loss of contact inhibition, etc). There are different "degrees" of transformation, and cells may exhibit only a subset of these characteristics.

Transformation frequency

The relative proportion of cells in a population that are transformed in a single experiment.

Transgenic mouse
A mouse which carries experimentally introduced DNA. The procedure by which one makes a transgenic mouse involves the injection of DNA into a fertilized embryo at the pro-nuclear stage. The DNA is generally cloned, and may be experimentally altered. It will become incorporated into the genome of the embryo. That embryo is implanted into a foster mother, who gives birth to an animal carrying the new gene.

Transgenic organism
one into which a cloned genetic material has been experimentally transferred, a subset of these foreign gene express themselves in their offspring.Turner syndrome a chromosomal condition in females (usually 45,XO) due to monosomy of the X- chromosome; characterized by short stature, failure to develop secondary sex characteristics and infertility.

Transient transfection
When DNA is transfected into cultured cells, it is able to stay in those cells for about 2-3 days, but then will be lost (unless steps are taken to ensure that it is retained). During those 2-3 days, the DNA is functional, and any functional genes it contains will be expressed. Investigators take advantage of this transient expression period to test gene function.

Transient vibration
A temporary vibration or movement of a mechanical system.

Transition mutation
A base substitution mutation where a purine is replaced by a different purine, or a pyrimidine is replaced by a different pyrimidine.

Transitional flow
Flow between laminar and turbulent flow, usually between a pipe Reynolds number of 2000 and 4000.

Translation
The process of decoding a strand of mRNA, thereby producing a protein based on the code. This process requires ribosomes (which are composed of rRNA along with various proteins) to perform the synthesis, and tRNA to bring in the amino acids. Sometimes, however, people speak of "translating" the DNA or RNA when they are merely reading the nucleotide sequence andpredicting from it the sequence of the encoded protein. This might be more accurately termed "conceptual translation".

Translesion synthesis
A mechanism that resumes stalled replication due to a damage on the template strand. The stalled replicative polymerase is replaced by translesion polymerase(s) that synthesises a short stretch of DNA across the lesion. Once this occurs, the replicative polymerase resumes DNA synthesis.

Translocation
A chromosome aberration which results in a change in position of a chromosomal segment within the genome, but does not change the total number of genes present.

Transmissibility (ground water)
The capacity of a rock to transmit water under pressure. The coefficient of transmissibility is the rate of flow of water, at the prevailing water temperature, in gallons per day, through a vertical strip of the aquifer one foot wide, extending the full saturated height of the aquifer under

a hydraulic gradient of 100-percent. A hydraulic gradient of 100-percent means a one foot drop in head in one foot of flow distance.

Transmitter (two-wire)
1. A device which is used to transmit data from a sensor via a two-wire current loop. The loop has an external power supply and the transmitter acts as a variable resistor with respect to its input signal.
2. A device which translates the low level output of a sensor or transducer to a higher level signal suitable for transmission to a site where it can be further processed.

Transpiration
Transpiration is a process similar to evaporation. It is a part of the water cycle, and it is the loss of water vapor from parts of plants (similar to sweating), especially in leaves but also in stems, flowers and roots. Leaf surfaces are dotted with openings which are collectively called stomata, and in most plants they are more numerous on the undersides of the foliage. The stomata are bordered by guard cells that open and close the pore. Leaf transpiration occurs through stomata, and can be thought of as a necessary "cost" associated with the opening of the stomata to allow the diffusion of carbon dioxide gas from the air for photosynthesis. Transpiration also cools plants and enables mass flow of mineral nutrients and water from roots to shoots.

Transpiration pull
The differential pressure (suction) of transpirational pull could only be measured indirectly, by applying external pressure with a pressure bomb to counteract it. When the technology to perform direct measurements with a pressure probe was developed, there was initially some controversy about whether the classic theory was correct, because some workers were unable to demonstrate negative pressures. More recent measurements do tend to validate the classic theory, for the most part. Xylem transport is driven by a combination of transpirational pull from above and root pressure from below, which makes the interpretation of measurements more complicated.

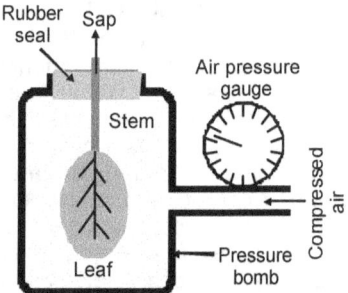

Transposable element
A transposon or insertion sequence. An element that can insert in a variety of DNA sequences.

Transposase
An enzyme (or enzyme complex) required for the transposition of a particular transposable element. A transposase must recognize specific sites on the ends of a transposon, cut the transposon out of the original site, and insert the transposon into a new site.

Transposition
The movement of a discrete segment of DNA from one location in the genome to another.

Transposon
A genetic element which, in addition to encoding the proteins required for its own transposition, confers one or

more new observable phenotypes (often resistance to one or more specific drugs) on the host cell.

Transposon tag
Use of a transposon insertion in a gene to follow the inheritance of the gene. Because transposons often express phenotypes that are simple to select and screen for (e.g. antibiotic resistance), it is often much easier to follow inheritance of the transposon insertion than the unmarked gene.

Transversion
A base substitution mutation where a pyrimidine replaces a purine, or a purine replaces a pyrimidine.

Triac
A solid state switching device used to switch alternating current wave forms.

Triboelectric noise
The generation of electrical charges caused by layers of cable insulation. This is especially troublesome in high impedance accelerometers.

Tributary
A smaller river or stream that flows into a larger river or stream. Usually, a number of smaller tributaries merge to form a river.

Triethylene glycol
A colourless odourless non volatile hygroscopic liquid whose major application is as a drying agent for natural gas. Synonyms for TEG are triglycol; 2.2-(Ethylene-dioxy) diethanol and ethylene glycol dihydroxydiethyl ether.

Trim
Name given to the internals i.e. plug and seat of a valve. Rather than replace a complete valve the trim is often replaced utilising the existing body and actuator.

Triple point
The temperature and pressure at which solid, liquid, and gas phases of a given substance are all present simultaneously in varying amounts.

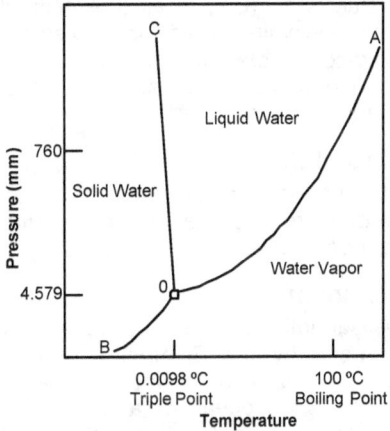

Triple point (water)
The thermodynamic state where all three phases, solid, liquid, and gas may all be present in equilibrium. The triple point of water is .01°C.

Triplet
A sequence of three nucleotides. Typically refers to the codons and the corresponding genetic code.

Triplet code
a code in which a given amino acid is specified by a set of three nucleotides.

Trna
"Transfer RNA"; one of a class of rather small RNAs used by the cell to carry amino acids to the enzyme complex (the ribosome) which builds proteins, using an mRNA as a guide.

Tropical rain forest
A type of rain forest where conditions are very warm and humid. Many types of parrots live in tropical rain forests around the world.

True RMS
The true root-mean-square value of an AC or AC-plus-DC signal, often used to determine power of a signal. For a perfect sine wave, the RMS value is 1.11072 times the rectified average value, which is utilized for low-cost metering. For significantly non-sinusoidal signals, a true RMS converter is required.

Truncation
To shorten. For example, a truncated protein results if a premature stop codon interrupts the gene.

Tsunami
A tsunami is a series of water waves caused by the displacement of a large volume of a body of water, typically an ocean or a large lake. Earthquakes, volcanic eruptions and other underwater explosions (including detonations of underwater nuclear devices), landslides, glacier calvings, meteorite impacts and other disturbances above or below water all have the potential to generate a tsunami

TTL
Transistor-to-transistor logic. A form of solid state logic which uses only transistors to form the logic gates.

TTL unit load
A load with TTL voltage levels, which will draw 40 µA for a logic 1 and -1.6 mA for a logic 0.

TTL-compatible
For digital input circuits, a logic 1 is obtained for inputs of 2.0 to 5.5 V which can source 40 µA, and a logic 0 is obtained for inputs of 0 to 0.8 V which can sink 1.6 mA. For digital output signals, a logic 1 is represented by 2.4 to 5.5 V with a current source capability of at least 400 µA; and a logic 0 is represented by 0 to 0.6 V with a current sink capability of at least 16 mA.

Tube
Cylindrical or conical structure in a telescope between its optics and its focal plane.

Tuff
Tuff (from the Italian tufo) is a type of rock consisting of consolidated volcanic ash ejected from vents during a volcanic eruption. Tuff is sometimes called tufa, particularly when used as construction material, although tufa also refers to a quite different rock. Rock that contains greater than 50% tuff is considered tuffaceous.

Tumor suppressor
A gene that inhibits progression towards neoplastic transformation. The best-known examples of tumor suppressors are the proteins p53 and Rb.

Tumor suppressor gene
Genes that normally function to restrain the growth of tumors; the best understood case is for hereditary retinoblastoma.

Tupe
Transfer of Undertakings (Protection of Employment) Regulations. The UK regulations designed to safeguard employees' rights when the business in which they work changes hands between employers.

Turbidity
The amount of solid particles that are suspended in water and that cause light rays shining through the water to scatter. Thus, turbidity makes the water cloudy or even opaque in extreme cases. Turbidity is measured in nephelometric turbidity units (NTU).

Turbulent flow
When forces due to inertia are more significant than forces due to viscosity. This typically occurs with a Reynolds number in excess of 4000.

Turnkey
A type of contract where contractor carries out and completes his assignment for a fixed fee; opposite of a reimbursable contract.

Two μm circle
A plasmid found in the yeast Saccharomyces cerevisiae and used as the basis for a series of cloning vectors.

Two-componant system
A regulatory mechanism that includes at least two functional activities defined as a sensor and a response regulator. Phosphorylation of the sensor domain is modulated in response to specific physiological stimulus. Phosphotransfer between a histidine residue on the sensor domain and an aspartate residue inÊthe response regulator domain determines the phosphorylation state of the response regulator. The phosphorylation state of the response regulator determines its physiological role (DNA binding, repression, activation, protein-protein interactions, or enzymatic activity). In many cases the two components are present on separate proteins, but in some cases both components are present in a single protein, and in other cases there are more than two proteins involved in the phosphotransfer reactions.

Typical
Error is within plus or minus one standard deviation (±1%) of the nominal specified value, as computed from the total population.

U

Uhuru satellite
Uhuru was the first satellite launched specifically for the purpose of X-ray astronomy. It was also known as the X-ray Explorer Satellite, SAS-A (for "Small Astronomy Satellite" A, being first of the three-spacecraft SAS series), SAS 1, or Explorer 42. The observatory was launched on 12 December 1970 into an initial orbit of about 560 km apogee, 520 km perigee, 3 degrees inclination, with a period of 96 minutes. The mission ended in March 1973. Uhuru was a scanning mission, with a spin period of ~12 minutes. It performed the first comprehensive survey of the entire sky for X-ray sources, with a sensitivity of about 0.001 times the intensity of the Crab nebula.

Uida
The gene encoding Beta-glucuronidase (abbreviated GUS). Commonly used for constructing operon or gene fusions in organisms with high endogenous Beta-galactosidase activity. A variety of analogs exist that make it easy to detect GUS expression on solid medium and to assay the activity of the enzyme in cells.

Ul
Underwriters Laboratories, Inc. An independent laboratory that establishes standards for commercial and industrial products.

Ultra luminous infrared galaxies (ulirg)
A type of galaxy which is very bright when observed at infrared wavelengths. They were discovered by the IRAS satellite. Astronomers are now investigating the cause of their enormous infrared luminosity.

Ultraviolet
Ultraviolet (UV) light is electromagnetic radiation with a wavelength shorter than that of visible light, but longer than X-rays, in the range 10 nm to 400 nm, and energies from 3 eV to 124 eV. It is named because the spectrum consists of electromagnetic waves with frequencies higher than those that humans identify as the colour violet. These frequencies are invisible to humans, but visible to a number of insects. They are also indirectly detectable, through their induction of secondary fluorescense at visible wavelengths.

Ultraviolet (UV) radiation
The part of the invisible electromagnetic spectrum (just below violet) with wavelengths between about 100-400nm.

Ultraviolet light
Region of the electromagnetic spectrum spanning wavelengths from 91.2 nm to 350 nm, wavelengths largely blocked by the Earth's atmosphere.

Ulysses mission
A joint ESA/NASA mission launched in 1990, to explore the region of space above the poles of the Sun.

Umber
Umber is a natural brown clay pigment which contains iron and manganese oxides. The color becomes more intense when calcined (heated), and the resulting pigment is called burnt umber. Its name derives from the Latin word umbra (shadow) and was originally extracted in Umbria, a mountainous region of central Italy,[1] but it is found in many parts of the world. Some of the finest umber comes from Cyprus. It has been used as a pigment since prehistoric times.

Unbalance
That condition which exists in a rotor when vibratory force or motion is imparted to its bearings as a result of centrifugal forces.

Unbalance tolerance
The unbalance tolerance with respect to a radial plane (measuring plane or correction plane) is that amount of unbalance which is specified as the maximum below which the state of unbalance is considered acceptable.

Uncertainty
It is impossible to know exactly where something is and where it is going. This is a fundamental law of nature has a major effect on quantum theory.

Undefined medium
A growth medium in which not all the components have been identified. Most "rich" media have a variety of complex, undefined componants.

Undershoot
The difference in temperature between the temperature a process goes to, below the set point, after the cooling cycle is turned off and the set point temperature.

Understory
The level of the rain forest just below the canopy. Insects flew through the understory.

Unequal cross-over
A recombination event that occurs between DNA molecules that are not fully aligned. For example, a crossover may occur between repeated DNA sequences resulting in the deletion or duplication the intervening DNA sequence.

UNESCO
The United Nations Educational, Scientific and Cultural Organization (French L'Organisation des Nations unies pour l'éducation, la science et la culture) is a specialized agency of the United Nations. Its stated purpose is to contribute to peace and security by promoting international collaboration through education, science, and culture in order to further universal respect for justice, the rule of law, and human rights along with fundamental freedoms proclaimed in the UN Charter. It is the heir of the League of Nations' International Commission on Intellectual Cooperation.

Ungrounded junction
A form of construction of a thermocouple probe where the hot or measuring junction is fully enclosed by and insulated from the sheath material.

Unidirectional replication
DNA replication that proceeds in only one direction along the DNA template.

Union
A form of pipe fitting where two extension pipes are joined at a separable coupling.

Universe
The universe is commonly defined as the totality of everything that exists, including all matter and energy, the planets, stars, galaxies, and the contents of intergalactic space. Definitions and usage vary and similar terms include the cosmos, the world and nature. Scientific observation of earlier stages in the development of the universe, which can be seen at great distances, suggests that the universe has been governed by the same physical laws and constants throughout most of its extent and history. There are various multiverse theories, in which physicists have suggested that our universe is one among many universes that likewise exist.

Unix
A multi-user operating system that was used to create most of the programmes and protocols that built the Internet.

Unsaturated zone
the zone immediately below the land surface where the pores contain both water and air, but are not totally saturated with water. These zones differ from an aquifer, where the pores are saturated with water.

Unselected marker
A genetic marker that may be co-inherited with an adjacent, selected marker but inheritance of the unselected marker is not demanded. For example, in a genetic cross you may select for one gene and screen for inheritance of an adjacent, unselected gene.

Up
Toward the sky. The ball flew high up in the sky before falling back to earth.

Up promoter mutation
A mutation that increasses expression from a promoter.

Upstream
A sequence located in front of a particular site relative to the direction of transcription and translation (i.e. located in the 5' direction relative to a particular site). For example, the lac promoter is located upstream of the lacZ structural gene.

Upstream activator sequence
A binding site for transcription factors, generally part of a promoter region. A UAS may be found upstream of the TATA sequence (if there is one), and its function is (like an enhancer) to increase transcription. Unlike an enhancer, it can not be positioned just anywhere or in any orientation.

Upstream activator sequence (UAS)
A DNA sequence some distance in front of a gene that increases transcription of the gene. Such sequences often stimulate binding of RNA polymerase to the promoter.

Upstream/downstream
In an RNA, anything towards the 5' end of a reference point is "upstream" of that point. This orientation reflects the direction of both the synthesis of mRNA, and its translation from the 5' end to the 3' end. In DNA, the situation is a bit more complicated. In the vicinity of a gene (or in a cDNA), the DNA has two strands, but one strand is virtually a duplicate of the RNA, so it's 5' and 3' ends determine upstream and downstream, respectively.

Uracil (U)
Uracil is one of the four nucleobases in the nucleic acid of RNA that are represented by the letters A, G, C and

U. The others are adenine, cytosine, and guanine. In RNA, uracil (U) binds to adenine (A) via two hydrogen bonds. In DNA, the uracil nucleobase is replaced by thymine. Uracil is a common and naturally occurring pyrimidine derivative. Originally discovered in 1900, it was isolated by hydrolysis of yeast nuclein that was found in bovine thymus and spleen, herring sperm, and wheat germ. It is a planar, unsaturated compound that has the ability to absorb light.

Uracil-N-glycosylase
A repair enzyme that removes uracil from DNA by cleaving the bond between the base and the sugar backbone. This enzyme ensures that DNA contains T instead of U residues.

Uranus
Uranus is the seventh planet from the Sun. It has the third-largest planetary radius and fourth-largest planetary mass in the Solar System. It is named after the ancient Greek deity of the sky Uranus, the father of Cronus (Saturn) and grandfather of Zeus (Jupiter). Though it is visible to the naked eye like the five classical planets, it was never recognized as a planet by ancient observers because of its dimness and slow orbit. Sir William Herschel announced its discovery on March 13, 1781, expanding the known boundaries of the Solar System for the first time in modern history. Uranus was also the first planet discovered with a telescope.

URL
A uniform resource locator or universal resource locator (URL) is a specific character string that constitutes a reference to an Internet resource. A URL is technically a type of uniform resource identifier (URI) but in many technical documents and verbal discussions URL is often used as a synonym for URI.

UV absorbance spectroscopy
A method for measuring the concentration of a compound by determining the amount of ultraviolet radiation absorbed by a sample.

UV reactivation
A phenomenon in which survival of an ultraviolet-irradiated phage is greater upon infecting a host that has also been irradiated with UV than upon infecting a host that has not been irradiated with UV. The increased survival in the UV irradiated host is due to the induction of the SOS-repair system in the host.

Uvrabc
An enzyme complex that functions as an endonuclease, cutting the DNA on both sides of DNA lesions that distort the double-helix (for example, T-T dimers). The DNA fragment is subsequently excised allowing resynthesis and repairing the DNA damage.

V

Vacuum
Vacuum is space that is empty of matter. The word stems from the Latin adjective vacuus for "empty". An approximation to such vacuum is a region with a gaseous pressure much less than atmospheric pressure. Physicists often discuss ideal test results that would occur in a perfect vacuum, which they sometimes simply call "vacuum" or free space, and use the term partial vacuum to refer to an actual imperfect vacuum as one might have in a laboratory or in space. The Latin term in vacuo is used to describe an object as being in what would otherwise be a vacuum.

Valence
Valence, also known as valency or valence number, is a measure of the number of bonds formed by an atom of a given element. "Valence" can be defined as the number of valence bonds[1] a given atom has formed, or can form, with one or more other atoms. For most elements the number of bonds can vary. The IUPAC definition limits valence to the maximum number of univalent atoms that may combine with the atom, that is the maximum number of valence bonds that is possible for the given element.

Valance shell
The valence shell is the outermost shell of an atom. It is usually (and misleadingly) said that the electrons in this shell make up its valence electrons, that is, the electrons that determine how the atom behaves in chemical reactions. Just as atoms with complete valence shells (noble gases) are the most chemically non-reactive, those with only one electron in their valence shells (alkalis) or just missing one electron from having a complete shell (halogens) are the most reactive

Valve flow coefficient
A measurement of valve capacity. The number of gallons per minute of room temperature water that will flow through the valve with a pressure drop of 1 psi across the valve.

Vapour (water)
A vapor or vapour is a substance in the gas phase at a temperature lower than its critical point. This means that the vapor can be condensed to a liquid or to a solid by increasing its pressure without reducing the temperature.

Variable speed drive
An electrical system that allows a motor to be controlled to run at different speeds.

Vector
The DNA "vehicle" used to carry experimental DNA and to clone it. The vector provides all sequences

essential for replicating the test DNA. Typical vectors include plasmids, cosmids, phages and YACs.

Velocity

Velocity is speed in a given direction. Speed describes only how fast an object is moving, whereas velocity gives both the speed and direction of the object's motion. To have a constant velocity, an object must have a constant speed and motion in a constant direction. Constant direction typically constrains the object to motion in a straight path. A car moving at a constant 20 kilometers per hour in a circular path does not have a constant velocity. The rate of change in velocity is acceleration. Velocity is a vector physical quantity; both magnitude and direction are required to define it. The scalar absolute value (magnitude) of velocity is speed, a quantity that is measured in metres per second (m/s or ms-1) when using the SI (metric) system.

Vent

The opening at the earth's surface through which volcanic materials reach the surface.

Venus

Venus is the second planet from the Sun, orbiting it every 224.7 Earth days. The planet is named after Venus, the Roman goddess of love and beauty. After the Moon, it is the brightest natural object in the night sky, reaching an apparent magnitude of -4.6, bright enough to cast shadows. Because Venus is an inferior planet from Earth, it never appears to venture far from the Sun: its elongation reaches a maximum of 47.8°. Venus reaches its maximum brightness shortly before sunrise or shortly after sunset, for which reason it has been known as the Morning Star or Evening Star. Venus is classified as a terrestrial planet and it is sometimes called Earth's "sister planet" due to the similar size, gravity, and bulk composition.

Vesicular basalt

Holes and other openings in basaltic flow which are the result of trapped gas bubbles. Vesicles are often filled at a later date with a wide variety of materials, including, quartz, agate, zeolites, and many other minerals.

Vesicular texture

Vesicular texture is a volcanic rock texture characterised by a rock being pitted with many cavities (known as vesicles) at its surface and inside.[1] The texture is often found in extrusive aphanitic, or glassy, igneous rock. These vesicles form during the extrusion of magma to the surface; as the pressure decreases dissolved, magmatic gases are able to come out of solution, forming gas bubbles (the cavities) in the magma. When the magma is extruded as lava and cools the lava solidifies around the gas bubbles, preserving them as vesicles.

VGA

Video Graphics Array (VGA) refers specifically to the display hardware first introduced with the IBM PS/2 line of computers in 1987, but through its widespread adoption has also come to mean either an analog computer display standard, the 15-pin D-subminiature VGA connector or the 640×480 resolution itself.

While this resolution was superseded in the personal computer market in the 1990s, it is becoming a popular resolution on mobile devices.

Viability
Viable or viability is the ability of a thing (a living organism, an artificial system, an idea, etc.) to maintain itself or recover its potentialities.

Viability (fetal)
Fetal viability is the ability of a fetus to survive outside the uterus.

Viable system model
The viable systems model, or VSM is a model of the organisational structure of any viable or autonomous system. A viable system is any system organised in such a way as to meet the demands of surviving in the changing environment. One of the prime features of systems that survive is that they are adaptable. The VSM expresses a model for a viable system, which is an abstracted cybernetic (regulation theory) description that is applicable to any organisation that is a viable system and capable of autonomy.

Vibration error
The maximum change in output of a transducer when a specific amplitude and range of frequencies are applied to a specific axis at room temperature.

Vibration error band
The error recorded in output of a transducer when subjected to a given set of amplitudes and frequencies.

Virion
Virus particles (known as virions) consist of two or three parts: the genetic material made from either DNA or RNA, long molecules that carry genetic information; a protein coat that protects these genes; and in some cases an envelope of lipids that surrounds the protein coat when they are outside a cell. The shapes of viruses range from simple helical and icosahedral forms to more complex structures. The average virus is about one one-hundredth the size of the average bacterium. Most viruses are too small to be seen directly with a light microscope.

Virology
Virology is the study of viruses and virus-like agents: their structure, classification and evolution, their ways to infect and exploit host cells for virus reproduction, their interaction with host organism physiology and immunity, the diseases they cause, the techniques to isolate and culture them, and their use in research and therapy. Virology is considered to be a subfield of microbiology or of medicine.

Virtual
With regard to memory, virtual refers to temporarily storing information on the hard drive. Virtual memory is controlled automatically by the operating system.

Virtual private network
The use of encryption to provide a secure connection through an otherwise insecure network e.g. typically the Internet. The encryption may be performed by firewall software or possibly by routers.

Virulence
The relative ability of an organism to cause disease.

Virulence factor
Any gene product which enhances the ability of an organism to cause disease.

Virulence gene
Slang for a gene encoding a virulence factor.

Virulent phage
A bacteriophage which always grows lytically.

Virus
A small, infectious, obligate intracellular parasite. The virus genome is composed of either DNA or RNA. Within an appropriate host cell, the viral genome is replicated and uses cellular systems to direct the synthesis of other viral components. Progeny viruses are formed by de novo assembly from the newly synthesized components within the host cell. Transmission of the progeny viruses occurs by release from the host cell, and infection of new host cells.

Visbreaker
A thermal cracking process unit in a refinery used to break up large molecules into smaller ones. It is applied to the residue of vacuum distillation as part of the overall conversion process.

Viscosity
Viscosity is a measure of the resistance of a fluid which is being deformed by either shear or tensile stress. In everyday terms (and for fluids only), viscosity is "thickness" or "internal friction". Thus, water is "thin", having a lower viscosity, while honey is "thick", having a higher viscosity. Put simply, the less viscous the fluid is, the greater its ease of movement (fluidity).

Visibility
Periods at which a celestial object, either natural or artificial, is visible from a point on Earth.

Vitamin
A vitamin is an organic compound required as a vital nutrient in tiny amounts by an organism. In other words, an organic chemical compound (or related set of compounds) is called a vitamin when it cannot be synthesized in sufficient quantities by an organism, and must be obtained from the diet. Thus, the term is conditional both on the circumstances and on the particular organism. For example, ascorbic acid (vitamin C) is a vitamin for humans, but not for most other animals, and biotin and vitamin D are required in the human diet only in certain circumstances. By convention, the term vitamin does not include other essential nutrients such as dietary minerals, essential fatty acids, or essential amino acids (which are needed in larger amounts than vitamins), nor does it encompass the large number of other nutrients that promote health but are otherwise required less often. Thirteen vitamins are universally recognized at present.

Vitamin A
Vitamin A (or Vitamin A Retinol, retinal, and four carotenoids including beta carotene) is a vitamin that is needed by the retina of the eye in the form of a specific metabolite, the light-absorbing molecule retinal, that is necessary for both low-light (scotopic vision) and color vision. Vitamin A also functions in a very different role as an irreversibly oxidized form of retinol known as retinoic acid, which is an important hormone-like growth factor for epithelial and other cells.

Vitamin B
B vitamins are a group of water-soluble vitamins that play important roles in cell metabolism. The B vitamins were once thought to be a single vitamin,

referred to as vitamin B (much as people refer to vitamin C or vitamin D).

Vitamin C

Vitamin C or L-ascorbic acid or L-ascorbate is an essential nutrient for humans and certain other animal species. In living organisms ascorbate acts as an antioxidant by protecting the body against oxidative stress.

Vitamin D

Vitamin D is a group of fat-soluble secosteroids. In humans, vitamin D is unique both because it functions as a prohormone and because the body can synthesize it (as vitamin D3) when sun exposure is adequate (hence its nickname, the "sunshine vitamin").

VLSI

Very large- scale integration allowing over 100,000 transistors on a chip.

Vntr

Variable number tandem repeats; any gene whose alleles contain different numbers of tandemly repeated oligonucleotide sequences.

Volcanic neck

Solidified lava that fills the conduit of a volcano. Volcanic necks (also called plugs) are usually more resistant to erosion than the material making up the surrounding cone, and may remain standing as a solitary pinnacle when the rest of the original structure has eroded away.

Volt

The (electrical) potential difference between two points in a circuit. The fundamental unit is derived as work per unit charge-($V = W/Q$). One volt is the potential difference required to move one coulomb of charge between two points in a circuit while using one joule of energy.

Voltage

Voltage, otherwise known as electrical potential difference or electric tension (denoted V and measured in volts, or joules per coulomb) is the potential difference between two points — or the difference in electric potential energy per unit charge between two points. Voltage is equal to the work which would have to be done, per unit charge, against a static electric field to move the charge between two points. A voltage may represent either a source of energy (electromotive force), or it may represent lost or stored energy (potential drop). A voltmeter can be used to measure the voltage (or potential difference) between two points in a system; usually a common reference potential such as the ground of the system is used as one of the points. Voltage can be caused by static electric fields, by electric current through a magnetic field, by time-varying magnetic fields, or a combination of all three

Voltmeter

An instrument used to measure voltage.

Volume flow rate

Calculated using the area of the full closed conduit and the average fluid velocity in the form, $Q = V \times A$, to arrive at the total volume quantity of flow. Q = volumetric flowrate, V = average fluid velocity, and A = cross sectional area of the pipe.

Von Hippel-Lindau syndrome
An autosomal dominant condition characterized by the anomalous growth and proliferation of blood vessels on the retina of the eye and the cerebellum of the brain; cysts and cancers in the kidneys, pancreas, and adrenal glands.

Voyager satellite
The name of two NASA spacecraft designed to study the outer planets (Jupiter, Saturn, Uranus and Neptune) of our Solar System.

VSP repair
"Very short patch" DNA repair. A DNA repair mechanism that corrects G-T mismatches arising from deamination of 5-methyl cytosine in enteric bacteria. A short DNA fragment including the mismatch is excised and resynthesized.

Vulcan
Vulcan is the god of beneficial and hindering fire, including the fire of volcanoes in ancient Roman religion and Roman Neopaganism. Vulcan is usually depicted with a thunderbolt.

Wais
Wide Area Information Server. A software system intended to search large database servers on the Web, and then rank the findings or hits.

Wan
Wide Area Network. This network connects several computer so they can share files and sometimes equipment, as well as exchange e-mail. A wide area network connects computers across a large geographic area, such as a city, state, or country. The World Wide Web is a WAN.

Warm up
Movements done to get the body ready to exercise. The runner stretched to warm up before the race.

Wastewater
Water that has been used in homes, industries, and businesses that is not for reuse unless it is treated.

Wastewater-treatment return flow
Water returned to the environment by wastewater-treatment facilities.

Water cycle
The circuit of water movement from the oceans to the atmosphere and to the Earth and return to the atmosphere through various stages or processes such as precipitation, interception, runoff, infiltration, percolation, storage, evaporation, and transportation.

Water quality
A term used to describe the chemical, physical, and biological characteristics of water, usually in respect to its suitability for a particular purpose.

Water table
The water table is the surface where the water pressure head is equal to the atmospheric pressure (where gauge pressure = 0). It may be conveniently visualized as the 'surface' of the subsurface materials that are saturated with groundwater in a given vicinity. However, saturated conditions may extend above the water table as surface tension holds water in some pores below atmospheric pressure. Individual points on the water table are typically measured as the elevation that the water rises to in a well screened in the shallow groundwater.

Water use
Water that is used for a specific purpose, such as for domestic use, irrigation, or industrial processing. Water use pertains to human's interaction with and influence on the hydrologic cycle, and includes elements, such as water withdrawal from surface- and ground-water sources, water delivery to homes and businesses, consumptive use of water,

water released from wastewater-treatment plants, water returned to the environment, and instream uses, such as using water to produce hydroelectric power.

Watershed
The land area that drains water to a particular stream, river, or lake. It is a land feature that can be identified by tracing a line along the highest elevations between two areas on a map, often a ridge. Large watersheds, like the Mississippi River basin contain thousands of smaller watersheds.

Watson-Crick rules
The normal base pairing rules for DNA and RNA: A pairs with T or U, and G pairs with C.

Watt (W)
Unit of power in the SI unit system. 1 Watt = 1 Joule per second.

Watt density
The watts emanating from each square inch of heated surface area of a heater. Expressed in units of watts per square inch.

Watthour (Wh)
An electrical energy unit of measure equal to one watt of power supplied to, or taken from, an electrical circuit steadily for one hour.

Wavelength
the wavelength of a sinusoidal wave is the spatial period of the wave—the distance over which the wave's shape repeats. It is usually determined by considering the distance between consecutive corresponding points of the same phase, such as crests, troughs, or zero crossings, and is a characteristic of both traveling waves and standing waves, as well as other spatial wave patterns. Wavelength is commonly designated by the Greek letter lambda ( ). The concept can also be applied to periodic waves of non-sinusoidal shape. The term wavelength is also sometimes applied to modulated waves, and to the sinusoidal envelopes of modulated waves or waves formed by interference of several sinusoids. The SI unit of wavelength is the meter.

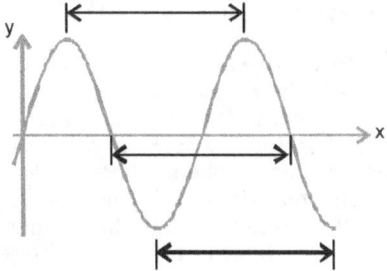

Weathering (surface)
"Making little ones out of big ones." Waethering includes the processes which mechanically and chemically break down the mountains into little pieces, so they can be eroded and transported to the beach.

Weight
In science and engineering, the weight of an object is the force on the object due to gravity. Its magnitude (a scalar quantity), often denoted by an italic letter W, is the product of the mass m of the object and the magnitude of the local gravitational acceleration g; thus: $W = mg$. When considered a vector, weight is often denoted by a bold letter W. The unit of measurement for weight is that of force, which in the International System of Units (SI) is the newton. For example, an object with a mass of one kilogram has a weight of about 9.8 newtons on the surface of the Earth, about one-sixth as much on the Moon, and very nearly zero when in deep space far away from all bodies imparting gravitational influence.

Weigle reactivation
The increased survival of phage after UV irradiation if they infect cells that have previously been exposed to a lose dose of UV. Due to induction of UV repair systems in the infected cells.

Well
A hole dug into the ground in the attempt to intersect water or other subsurface fluids.

Well (water)
an artificial excavation put down by any method for the purposes of withdrawing water from the underground aquifers. A bored, drilled, or driven shaft, or a dug hole whose depth is greater than the largest surface dimension and whose purpose is to reach underground water supplies or oil, or to store or bury fluids below ground.

West texas intermediate
A specific grade of crude oil that is a benchmark commodity of the U.S. oil industry.

Western blot
The western blot (sometimes called the protein immunoblot) is a widely used analytical technique used to detect specific proteins in the given sample of tissue homogenate or extract. It uses gel electrophoresis to separate native proteins by 3-D structure or denatured proteins by the length of the polypeptide. The proteins are then transferred to a membrane (typically nitrocellulose or PVDF), where they are probed (detected) using antibodies specific to the target protein.

Western blotting analysis
A technique used to identify a specific protein; the probe is a radioactively labeled antibody raised against the protein in question.

Wheatstone bridge
A network of four resistances, an emf source, and a galvanometer connected such that when the four resistances are matched, the galvanometer will show a zero deflection or "null" reading.

Wheel
A wheel is a device that allows heavy objects to be moved easily through rotating on an axle through its center, facilitating movement or transportation while supporting a load, or performing labor in machines. Common examples are found in transport applications. A wheel, together with an axle, overcomes friction by facilitating motion by rolling. In order for wheels to rotate, a moment needs to be applied to the wheel about its axis, either by way of gravity, or by application of another external force. More generally the term is also used for other circular objects that rotate or turn, such as a ship's wheel, steering wheel and flywheel.

White dwarf
A very dense star with a mass below 1.4 solar masses that is no longer burning nuclear fuel. The Sun will one day evolve into a white dwarf with a diameter of 10 000 km.

Wide area network
A wide area network (WAN) is a telecommunication network that covers a broad area (i.e., any network that links across metropolitan, regional, or national boundaries). Business and government entities utilize WANs to relay data among employees, clients, buyers, and suppliers from various geographical locations. In essence this mode of telecommunication allows a business to effectively carry out its daily function regardless of location.

Wildcat
A well drilled in unproven territory.

Wild-type
A strain used as a standard reference to compare any mutant derivatives. A wild-type strain may have certain nutritional requirements depending upon the species. Often a wild-type strain is simply one of the most convient strains of a particular species obtained from nature.

Window (Microsoft)
In computer graphics, Microsoft Windows is a series of operating systems produced by Microsoft. Microsoft introduced an operating environment named Windows on November 20, 1985 as an add-on to MS-DOS in response to the growing interest in graphical user interfaces (GUIs). Microsoft Windows came to dominate the world's personal computer market, overtaking Mac OS, which had been introduced in 1984. The most recent client version of Windows is Windows 7; the most recent server version is Windows Server 2008 R2; the most recent mobile version is Windows Phone 7.

Windward
The side facing into the wind. When speaking of a mountain range, these areas are generally cooler and wetter than on the leeward side.

Wirtanen (comet)
Periodic comet which orbits the Sun once every 5.45 years. Discovered in 1948 at the Lick Observatory, California, by Carl A. Wirtanen. It is a so-called 'Jupiter-type' comet, whose orbit is strongly influenced by that planet. Perihelion is at 159 million km (1.06 AU) from the Sun, i.e. just outside the orbit of the Earth. Aphelion is at a distance of about 768 million km (5.13 AU), near the orbit of Jupiter. Target of ESA's Rosetta mission, which will go into orbit around the nucleus and deploy a lander on its surface.

Withdrawal
Water removed from a ground- or surface-water source for use.

Wobbe index
A comparative measure of thermal energy flow through a given size of orifice. A measure of the interchangeability of gases used for combustion. The gases which have the same Wobbe index can replace each other without a change in the relative air-fuel ratio at the same fuel metering settings.

Wobble
A hypothesis proposed by Francis Crick to explain how one tRNA may recognize two different codons that differ in the third position. The three bases in the anticodon of each tRNA are antiparallel to the three bases of the codon in the mRNA. Normal Watson-Crick base pairing occurs between the first two bases of the codon with the complementary bases of the anticodon. However, the first (5') base of the anticodon can pair with the third (3') base of the codon in different ways: in this position of the anticodon G can pair with either C or U in the mRNA, U can pair with either A or G in the mRNA, and I can pair with A, C, or U in the mRNA.

Word
Number of bits treated as a single unit by the CPU. In an 8-bit machine, the word length is 8 bits; in a sixteen bit machine, it is 16 bits.

Word processor
The software used to produce documents, such as letters, posters,

reports, and syllabi. Common word processors used in schools are MS Works, MS Word, or ClarisWorks.

Work
The amount of energy transferred to a system.

Working standard
A standard of unit measurement calibrated from either a primary or secondary standard which is used to calibrate other devices or make comparison measurements.

Workover
To carry out remedial operations on a producing well with the intention of restoring or increasing production.

Write
To record data in a storage device or on a data medium.

Wysiwyg
What You See Is What You Get. Monitor output that closely resembles the printed output. Most software now offers WYSIWYG options, like "print preview."

X-band

The X band is a segment of the microwave radio region of the electromagnetic spectrum. In some cases, such as in communication engineering, the frequency range of X band is rather indefinitely set at approximately 7.0 to 11.2 gigahertz (GHz). In radar engineering, the frequency range is specified by the IEEE at 8.0 to 12.0 GHz. The term "X-band" is also used informally and inaccurately to refer to the extended AM broadcast band, where the "X" stands for "extended".

X-band radar

X band is used in radar applications including continuous-wave, pulsed, single-polarization, dual-polarization, synthetic aperture radar, and phased arrays. X band radar frequency sub-bands are used in civil, military, and government institutions for weather monitoring, air traffic control, maritime vessel traffic control, defense tracking, and vehicle speed detection for law enforcement.

Xbar

Crossbar. A kind of multiplexor for which one of a number of channels are hardware-selected. Crossbars are used extensively in the CATV system, and have applications in the Switchyard as well.

Xbar and R chart

In statistical quality control, the $\bar{x}$ and R chart is a type of control chart used to monitor a variable's data when samples are collected at regular intervals from a business or industrial process.

Xbase++

Xbase++ is an object oriented programming language which has multiple inheritance and polymorphism. It is based on the XBase language dialect and conventions. It is 100% Clipper compatible language supporting multiple inheritance, polymorphism, object oriented programming. It supports the xBase data types, including Codeblocks. With Xbase++ it is possible to generate applications for Windows NT, 95, 98, Me, 2000,XP, VISTA and Windows 7.

XBASIC

XBasic is a variant of the BASIC programming language that was developed in the late 1980s for the Motorola 88000 CPU and Unix by Max Reason. In the early 1990s it was ported to Windows and Linux, and since 1999 it has been available as open source software with its runtime library under the LGPL license. Max Reason discontinued his support, and development since has been overseen by Eddie Penninkhof. Together with a few other enthusiastic programmers, XBasic is slowly being further developed and improved.

Xeriscaping

Xeriscaping and xerogardening refers to landscaping and gardening in ways that reduce or eliminate the need for supplemental water from irrigation. It is promoted in regions that do not have easily accessible, plentiful, or reliable supplies of fresh water, and is gaining acceptance in other areas as climate patterns shift.

Xerography

Xerography (or electrophotography) is a dry photocopying technique invented by Chester Carlson in 1938, for which he was awarded U.S. Patent 2,297,691 on October 6, 1942. Carlson originally called his invention electrophotography. It was later renamed xerography—from the Greek roots xeros "dry" and graphia "writing"—to emphasize that, unlike reproduction techniques then in use such as cyanotype, this process used no liquid chemicals.

Xerox

Xerox Corporation (NYSE: XRX) is an American multinational document management corporation that produced and sells a range of color and black-and-white printers, multifunction systems, photo copiers, digital production printing presses, and related consulting services and supplies.

Xerox 530

An obsolete computer, no longer supported by Xerox, which was formerly used to control the accelerator. The most recent, and final accelerator to be converted from the XEROX system to ACNET was the Booster. The MAC-16 computers used by MR.barf are the remnants of the old system.

XEUS

XEUS, X-ray Evolving Universe Spectroscopy, was space observatory plan developed by the European Space Agency as a successor to the successful XMM-Newton X-ray satellite telescope. It was merged to the International X-ray Observatory around 2008, but as that project ran into issues in 2010, the ESA component was forked off into Advanced Telescope for High Energy Astrophysics (ATHENA). XEUS consisted of a mirror spacecraft that carried a large X-ray telescope, with a mirror area of about 5 m^2 and an imaging resolution better than 5" for X-ray radiation with an energy of 1 keV. A detector spacecraft would have flown in formation with the telescope at a distance of approximately 35 m, in the focus of the telescope.

XEUS mission

Future global X-ray astronomy mission.

X-gal

A common abbreviation for 5-bromo-4-chloro-3-indolyl-ß-D-galactoside. A sensitive, color indicator for ß-galactosidase. X-gal is a colorless compound but upon hydrolysis by beta-galactosidase releases an indolyl moiety. This product is not colored, but dimerizes after oxidation to form an insoluble and highly colored indigo dye. The oxidation is promoted by atmospheric oxygen, hence the color does not form anaerobically.

X-glu

A common abbreviation for 5-bromo-4-chloro-3-indolyl-glucuronide. A color indicator for beta-Glucuronidase (GUS). X-glu (AKA X-gluc) is a colorless compound but upon hydrolysis by GUS the indolyl moiety is oxidized to form a blue colored product. GUS is often used as a reporter gene in organisms that have high background levels of beta-galactosidase, often due to multiple genes encoding lacZ homologues.

X-inactivation

The repression of one of the two X-chromosomes in the somatic cells of females as a method of dosage compensation; at an early embryonic stage in the normal female, one of the two X-chromosomes undergoes inactivation, apparently at random, from this point on all descendent cells will have the same X-chromosome inactivated as the cell from which they arose, thus a female is a mosaic composed of two types of cells, one which expresses only the paternal X-chromosome, and another which expresses only the maternal X-chromosome.

XMM-Newton (X-ray Multi-Mirror) mission

ESA's X-ray space observatory mission, with its X-ray Multi-Module design using three telescopes each with 58 nested X-ray mirrors. Named also in honour of Sir Isaac Newton.

XMIT button

A button at the keypad of each ACNET console which allows the user to leave an operating programme and return to the index page without having to move the cursor. It is used when control of the cursor has been lost. Also known as the application abort button.

Xmodem

XMODEM is a simple file transfer protocol developed as a quick hack by Ward Christensen for use in his 1977 MODEM.ASM terminal programme. XMODEM became extremely popular in the early bulletin board system (BBS) market, largely because it was so simple to implement. It was also fairly inefficient, and as modem speeds increased this problem led to the development of a number of modified versions of XMODEM to improve performance or address other problems with the protocol. Chuck Forsberg collected a number of these into his YMODEM protocol, but poor implementation led to a further fracturing before they were re-unified by his later ZMODEM protocol.

X-over

An abbreviation for cross-over.

X-p

A common abbreviation for 5-bromo-4-chloro-3-indolyl phosphate. A sensitive, color indicator for alkaline phosphatase activity. X-P is a colorless compound but upon hydrolysis by a phosphatase the indolyl moiety is released, and upon oxidization it forms a blue colored product.

X-ray

The part of the electromagnetic spectrum whose radiation has somewhat greater frequencies and smaller wavelengths than those of ultraviolet radiation. Because x-rays are absorbed by the Earth's atmosphere, x-ray astronomy is performed in space.

X-ray (hard)

Higher-energy part of the X-ray spectrum ranging from approximately 5 keV to 100 keV.

X-ray (soft)

Band of low energy X-rays, between 0.1 keV and approximately 5 keV.

Xylem

Xylem is one of the two types of transport tissue in vascular plants (phloem is the other). The word xylem is derived from the (xylon), meaning "wood"; the best-known xylem tissue is wood, though it is found throughout the plant. Its basic function is to transport water, but it also transports some nutrients through the plant.

Xylology

The study of the structure of wood.

XYY syndrome

Genetic condition in males with extra Y chromosome (in 1 in 1000 male births). Symptoms: tall stature (over 6'), may including sterility, developmental delay, learning problems.

Y

Yac

A yeast artificial chromosome (YAC) is a vector used to clone DNA fragments larger than 100 kb and up to 3000 kb. YACs are useful for the physical mapping of complex genomes and for the cloning of large genes. First described in 1983 by Murray and Szostak, a YAC is an artificially constructed chromosome and contains the telomeric, centromeric, and replication originsequences named autonomous replicating sequence needed for replication and preservation in yeast cells. A YAC is built using an initial circular plasmid, which is typically broken into two linear molecules using restriction enzymes; DNA ligase is then used to ligate a sequence or gene of interest between the two linear molecules, forming a single large linear piece of DNA.

Yeast

Yeasts are eukaryotic microorganisms classified in the kingdom Fungi, with 1,500 species currently described estimated to be only 1% of all fungal species. Most reproduce asexually by mitosis, and many do so by an asymmetric division process called budding. Yeasts are unicellular, although some species with yeast forms may become multicellular through the formation of a string of connected budding cells known as pseudohyphae, or false hyphae, as seen in most molds. Yeast size can vary greatly depending on the species, typically measuring 3–4 µm in diameter, although some yeasts can reach over 40 µm.

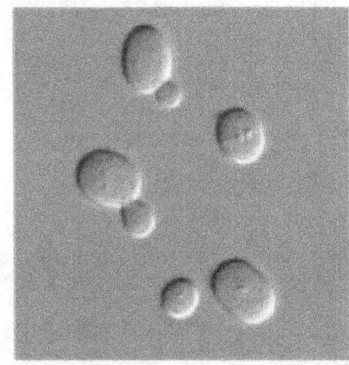

Yeast episomal plasmid (yep)

A yeast vector carrying the 2 µm circle origin of replication.

Yeast extract

Yeast extract is the common name for various forms of processed yeast products made by extracting the cell contents (removing the cell walls); they are used as food additives or flavourings, or as nutrients for bacterial culture media. They are often used to create savory flavors and umami taste sensations. Monosodium glutamate (MSG) is used for umami. Yeast extract, like MSG, often contains free glutamic acid. Yeast extracts in liquid form can be dried to a light paste or a dry powder. Glutamic acid in yeast extracts are produced from an acid-base fermentation cycle, only found in some yeasts, typically ones bred for use in baking.

Yeast hydrolyzed
Hydrolyzed yeast or hydrolyzed yeast extract is another version used as a food additive for flavouring purposes. Exogenous enzymes or acids are used to hydrolyze the proteins.

Yeast infection
Candidiasis or thrush is a fungal infection (mycosis) of any of the Candida species (all yeasts), of which Candida albicans is the most common. Also commonly referred to as a yeast infection, candidiasis is also technically known as candidosis, moniliasis, and oidiomycosis.

Yeast integrative plasmid (yip)
A yeast vector that relies on integration into the host chromosome for replication.

Yeast replicative plasmid (yrp)
A yeast vector that carries a chromosomal origin of replication.

Yeast two-hybrid system
An approach developed by Stan Fields and colleagues in 1989 to identify protein-protein interactions in vivo. Proteins (aka "prey") that interact with other, known proteins (aka "bait") are identified by using a reporter system that relies upon interaction between the two proteins. A variety of versions of this system are available, but the basic format involves the construction of two distinct hybrid proteins fused to different reporter genes: in the first the "bait" protein is fused to a transcription factor, and in the second the "prey" protein is fused to a related transcription factor. If the bait and prey proteins interact the two reporter genes fused to the proteins are brought into proximity with each other, producing a specific signal.

Yield (chemistry)
Yield, also referred to as chemical yield and reaction yield, is the amount of product obtained in a chemical reaction. The absolute yield can be given as the weight in grams or in moles (molar yield). The fractional yield, relative yield, or percentage yield, which serve to measure the effectiveness of a synthetic procedure, is calculated by dividing the amount of the obtained product by the theoretical yield.

Yield (engineering)
The yield strength or yield point of a material is defined in engineering and materials science as the stress at which a material begins to deform plastically. Prior to the yield point the material will deform elastically and will return to its original shape when the applied stress is removed. Once the yield point is passed, some fraction of the deformation will be permanent and non-reversible. In the three-dimensional space of the principal stresses ($_{1,\ 2,\ 3}$), an infinite number of yield points form together a yield surface.

Yield
Mass per unit time per unit area.

Yield of paper pulp
The ratio of pulp solid mass to the solid mass of the original wood that it was derived from. High-yield pulps are produced by mechanical refining or grinding.

Ymmv
E-mail and chat abbreviation for "your mileage may vary," indicating that your results may vary.

Ytterbium

Symbol: "Yb" Atomic Number: "70" Atomic Mass: 173.04amu. Ytterbium is one of the elements in the lanthanide series of inner transition elements. It may also be classified as a rare earth element. This silvery metal can be found in several minerals. It is never found as a pure element in nature, always in compounds.

Yttrium

Symbol:"Y" Atomic Number:"39" Atomic Mass: 88.91amu. This is one of the transition elements found in period five of the periodic table. One of the rare Earth metals, yttrium is used in TV tubes, alloys, and has even been found on the Moon.

Young's modulus

Young's modulus, also known as the tensile modulus, is a measure of the stiffness of an elastic material and is a quantity used to characterize materials. It is defined as the ratio of the uniaxial stress over the uniaxial strain in the range of stress in which Hooke's Law holds. In solid mechanics, the slope of the stress-strain curve at any point is called the tangent modulus. The tangent modulus of the initial, linear portion of a stress-strain curve is called Young's modulus. It can be experimentally determined from the slope of a stress-strain curve created during tensile tests conducted on a sample of the material. In anisotropic materials, Young's modulus may have different values depending on the direction of the applied force with respect to the material's structure. It is also commonly called the elastic modulus or modulus of elasticity, because Young's modulus is the most common elastic modulus used, but there are other elastic moduli measured, too, such as the bulk modulus and the shear modulus.

Z

Z boson
The W and Z bosons (together known as the weak bosons) are the elementary particles that mediate the weak interaction; their symbols are W^+, W^- and Z. The W bosons have a positive and negative electric charge of 1 elementary charge respectively and are each other's antiparticle. The Z boson is electrically neutral and its own antiparticle. All three of these particles are very short-lived with a half-life of about 3×10^{-25} s. Their discovery was a major success for what is now called the Standard Model of particle physics.

Z dna
Z-DNA is one of the many possible double helical structures of DNA. It is a left-handed double helical structure in which the double helix winds to the left in a zig-zag pattern (instead of to the right, like the more common B-DNA form). Z-DNA is thought to be one of three biologically active double helical structures along with A- and B-DNA.

Zeeman effect
The Zeeman effect is the splitting of a spectral line into several components in the presence of a static magnetic field. It is analogous to the Stark effect, the splitting of a spectral line into several components in the presence of an electric field. The Zeeman effect is very important in applications such as nuclear magnetic resonance spectroscopy, electron spin resonance spectroscopy, magnetic resonance imaging (MRI) and Mössbauer spectroscopy. It may also be utilized to improve accuracy in Atomic absorption spectroscopy.

Zero adjustment
The ability to adjust the display of a process or strain meter so that zero on the display corresponds to a non-zero signal, such as 4 mA, 10 mA, or 1 V dc. The adjustment range is normally expressed in counts.

Zero offset
1. The difference expressed in degrees between true zero and an indication given by a measuring instrument.
2. See Zero Suppression

Zero point
The electrical zero point where zero millivolts would be displayed. Used in conjunction with the slope control to provide a narrower range calibration.

Zero power resistance
The resistance of a thermistor or RTD element with no power being dissipated.

Zero suppression
The span of an indicator or chart recorder may be offset from zero

(zero suppressed) such that neither limit of the span will be zero. For example, a temperature recorder which records a 100° span from 400° to 500° is said to have 400° zero suppression.

Zero voltage switching
The making or breaking of circuit timed such that the transition occurs when the voltage wave form crosses zero voltage; typically only found in solid state switching devices.

Zeroth law of thermodynamics
If body A is in thermal equilibrium with body B, and B is also in thermal equilibrium with C, then A is necessarily in thermal equilibrium with C.

Zinc finger
A protein structural motif common in DNA binding proteins. Four Cys residues are found for each "finger" and one finger can bind a molecule of zinc. A typical configuration is CysXxxXxxCys—(intervening 12 or so aa's)—CysXxxXxxCys.

Zip (file format)
Zip is a file format used for data compression and archiving. A zip file contains one or more files that have been compressed, to reduce file size, or stored as is. The zip file format permits a number of compression algorithms. The zip format is now supported by many software utilities other than PKZIP. Microsoft has included built-in zip support (under the name "compressed folders") in versions of Microsoft Windows since 1998. Apple has included built-in zip support in Mac OS X 10.3 (via BOMArchiveHelper, now Archive Utility) and later, along with other compression formats. Zip files generally use the file extensions ".zip" or ".ZIP" and the MIME media type application/zip. Zip is used as a base file format by many programmes, usually under a different name.

Zipped files
Zipped files are files that are compressed and must be "unzipped" to be read. Zipped files download faster because they are smaller than an uncompressed equivalent.

Zonal wind
Atmospheric wind component which flows along the latitude.

Zone of ablation (or wastage)
The area below the snowline where snow melt exceeds snowfall, and material is lost from a glacier.

Zone of accumulation
The area above the snowline where snowfall exceeds snow melt, and material is added to a glacier.

Zoo blot
A zoo blot or garden blot is a type of Southern blot that demonstrates the similarity between specific, usually protein-coding, DNA sequences of different species. A zoo blot compares animal species while a garden blot compares plant species.

Zov
Zinc-Oxide Varistor. Used for detecting Voltage To Ground spurts in Main Ring and Tevatron power supplies.

Zoogeography
The study of the distribution of animals on the surface of the globe.

Zoology
The study of animal life.

Zoometry
The comparative measurements of the parts of the animals.

Zooming

In computer graphics, causing an object to appear smaller or larger by moving the window and specifying various window sizes.

Zygote

A zygote or zygocyte, is the initial cell formed when two gamete cells are joined by means of sexual reproduction. In multicellular organisms, it is the earliest developmental stage of the embryo. In single-celled organisms, the zygote divides to produce offspring, usually through meiosis.

Zygotic induction

The lytic development of a prophage upon its transfer into a recipient cell which lacks the same prophage. Because the recipient cell does not contain the repressor protein required for maintance of lysogeny, expression of the genes required for lytic growth occurs as soon as the phage enters the recipient.

Appendix –I
The Greek Alphabet

Letters	Name
A	alpha
B	beta
	gamma
	delta
E	epsilon
Z	zeta
H	eta
	theta
I	iota
K	kappa
	lambda
M	mu

Letters	Name
N	nu
	xi
O	omicron
	Pi
P	rho
	sigma
T	tau
Y	upsilon
	phi
X	Chi
	psi
	omega

Fundamental Constants

Constant	Symbol	Value in SI units
acceleration of free fall	g	$9.806\ 65$ m s^{-2}
Avogadro constant	L, N_A	$6.022\ 141\ 79(30) \times 10^{23}$ mol^{-1}
Boltzmann constant	$k = R/N_A$	$1.380\ 6504(24) \times 10^{-23}$ J K^{-1}
electric constant	ε_0	$8.854\ 187\ 817 \times 10^{-12}$ F m^{-1}
electronic charge	e	$1.602\ 176\ 487(40) \times 10^{-19}$ C
electronic rest mass	m_e	$9.109\ 382\ 15(45) \times 10^{-31}$ kg
Faraday constant	F	$9.648\ 3399(24) \times 10^4$ C mol^{-1}
gas constant	R	$8.314\ 472(15)$ J K^{-1} mol^{-1}
gravitational constant	G	$6.674\ 28(67) \times 10^{-11}$ m^3 kg^{-1} s^{-2}
Loschmidt's constant	N_L	$2.686\ 7774(47) \times 10^{25}$ m^{-3}
magnetic constant	μ_0	$4\pi \times 10^{-7}$ H m^{-1}
neutron rest mass	m_n	$1.674\ 927\ 211(84) \times 10^{-27}$ kg
Planck constant	h	$6.626\ 068\ 96(33) \times 10^{-34}$ J s
proton rest mass	m_p	$1.672\ 621\ 637(83) \times 10^{-27}$ kg
speed of light	c	$2.997\ 924\ 58 \times 10^8$ m s^{-1}
Stefan-Boltzmann constant		$5.670\ 400(40) \times 10^{-8}$ Wm^{-2} K^{-4}

SI Units

Base and dimensionless SI units

Physical quantity	Name	Symbol
Length	metre	m
mass	kilogram	kg
time	second	s
electric current	ampere	A
thermodynamic temperature	Kelvin	K
luminous intensity	candela	cd
amount of substance	mole	mol
*plane angle	radian	rad
*solid angle	steradian	sr

*dimensionless units

Derived SI units with special names

Physical quantity	Name of SI unit	Symbol of SI unit
frequency	hertz	Hz
energy	joule	J
force	newton	N
power	watt	W
pressure	pascal	Pa
electric charge	coulomb	C
electric potential difference	volt	V
electric resistance	ohm	
electric conductance	Siemens	S
electric capacitance	farad	F
magnetic flux	weber	Wb
inductance	henry	H
magnetic flux density (magnetic induction)	tesla	T
luminous flux	lumen	lm
illuminance	lux	lx
absorbed dose	gray	Gy
activity	becquercl	Bq
dose equivalent	sievert	Sv

Decimal multiples and submultiples to be used with SI units

Submultiple	Prefix	Symbol	Multiple	Prefix	Symbol
10^{-1}	deci	d	10	deca	da
10^{-2}	centi	c	10^2	hecto	h
10^{-3}	milli	m	10^3	kilo	k
10^{-6}	micro		10^6	mega	M
10^{-9}	nano	n	10^9	giga	G
10^{-12}	pico	p	10^{12}	tera	T
10^{-15}	femto	f	10^{15}	peta	P
10^{-18}	atto	a	10^{18}	exa	E
10^{-21}	zepto	z	10^{21}	zetta	Z
10^{-24}	yocto	y	10^{24}	yotta	Y

Conversion of units to SI units

From	To	Multiply by
in	m	2.54×10^{-2}
ft	m	0.3048
sq.in	m^2	6.4516×10^{-4}
sq.ft	m^2	9.2903×10^{-2}
cu.in	m^3	1.63871×10^{-5}
cu.ft	m^3	2.83168×10^{-2}
l(itre)	m^3	10^{-3}
gal(lon)	l(itre)	4.546 09
miles/hr	$m\ s^{-1}$	0.477 04
km/hr	$m\ s^{-1}$	0.277 78
lb	kg	0.453 592
$g cm^{-3}$	$kg\ m^{-3}$	10^3
lb/in^3	$kg\ m^{-3}$	$2.767\ 99 \times 10^4$
dyne	N	10^5
poundal	N	0.138 255
lbf	N	4.448 22
mmHg	Pa	133.322
atmosphere	Pa	$1.013\ 25 \times 10^5$
hp	W	745.7
erg	J	10^{-7}
eV	J	$1.602\ 10 \times 10^{-19}$
kW h	J	3.6×10^6
cal	J	4.1868

Appendix – II
The Electromagnetic Spectrum

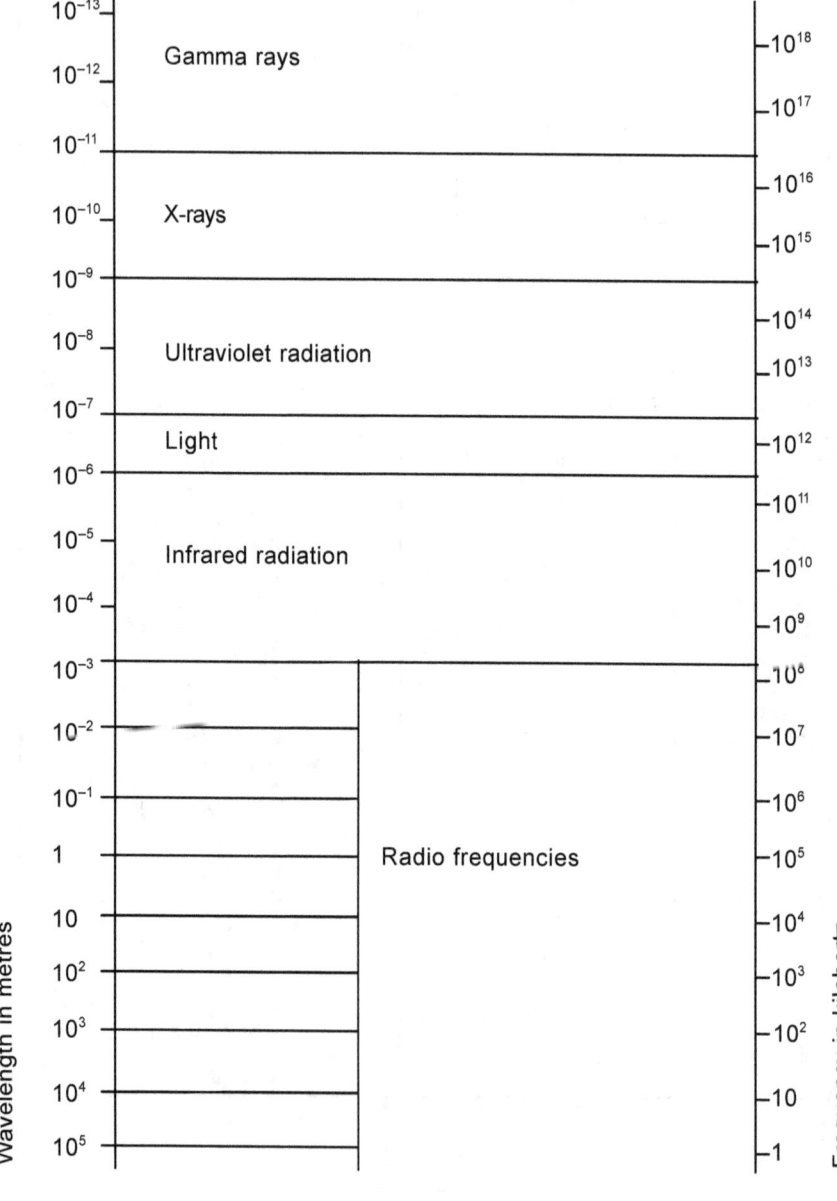

Appendix – III
The Periodic Table

Appendix – IV
The Chemical Elements

Element	Symb	a.n.	r.a.m.	Element	Symb	a.n.	r.a.m.
actinium	Ac	89	227*	iold	Au	79	196.967
aluminium	Al	13	26.98	lafhium	Hf	72	178.49
americium	Am	95	243*	lassium	Hs	108	265*
antimony	Sb	51	121.75	lelium	He	2	4.0026
argon	Ar	18	39.948	holmium	Ho	67	164.93
arsenic	As	33	74.92	hydrogen	H	1	1.008
astatine	At	85	210*	indium	In	49	114.82
barium	Ba	56	137.34	iodine	I	53	126.9045
berkelium	Bk	97	247*	iridium	Ir	77	192.20
beryllium	Be	4	9.012	iron	Fe	26	55.847
bismuth	Bi	83	208.98	krypton	Kr	36	83.80
bohrium	Bh	107	262*	lanthanum	La	57	138.91
boron	B	5	10.81	lawrencium	Lr	103	256*
bromine	Br	35	79.909	lead	Ph	82	207.19
cadmium	Cd	48	112.41	lithium	Li	3	6.939
caesium	Cs	55	132.905	lutetium	Lu	71	174.97
calcium	Ca	20	40.08	magnesium	Mg	12	24.305
californium	Cf	98	251*	manganese	Mn	25	54.94
carbon	C	6	12.011	meitnerium	Mt	109	266*
cerium	Ce	58	140.12	mendelevium	Md	101	258*
chlorine	Cl	17	35.453	mercury	Hg	80	200.59
chromium	Cr	24	52.00	molybdenum	Mo	42	95.94
cobalt	Co	27	58.933	neodymium	Nd	60	144.24
copper	Cu	29	63.546	neon	Ne	10	20.179
curium	Cm	96	247*	neptunium	Np	93	237.0482
darmstadtium	Ds	110	271*	nickel	Ni	28	58.70
dubnium	Db	105	262*	niobium	Nb	41	92.91
dysprosium	Dy	66	162.50	nitrogen	N	7	14.0007
einsteinium	Hs	99	254'	nobelium	No	102	254*
erbium	Er	68	167.26	osmium	Os	76	190.2
europium	Eu	63	151.96	oxygen	O	8	15.9994
fermium	Fm	100	257*	palladium	Pd	46	106.4
iluorine	F	9	18.9984	phosphorus	P	15	30.9738
"rancium	Ft	87	223*	platinum	Pi	78	195.09
gadolinium	Gd	64	157.25	plutonium	Pu	94	244*
gallium	Ga	31	69.72	polonium	Po	84	210'
germanium	Ge	32	72.59	potassium	K	19	39.098

R.a.m values with asterisk denote mass number of the most stable known isotope

Element	Symb	a.n.	r.a.m.	Element	Symb	a.n.	r.a.m.
praseodymium	Pr	59	140.91	technetium	Tc	43	98*
promethium	Pm	61	145	tellurium	Te	52	127.60
protactinium	Pa	91	231.036	terbium	Tb	65	158.92
radium	Ra	88	226.0254	thallium	Tl	81	204.39
radon	Rn	86	222*	thorium	Th	90	232.038
rhenium	Re	75	186.2	thulium	Tm	69	168.934
rhodium	Rh	45	102.9	tin	Sn	50	118.69
roentgenium	R8	111	272*	titanium	Ti	22	47.9
rubidium	Rb	37	85.47	tungsten	W	74	183.85
ruthenium	Ru	44	101.07	ununbium	Uub	112	285*
rutherfordiiim	Rf	104	261*	ununtrium	Uut	113	284*
samarium	Sm	62	150.35	ununquadium	Uuq	114	289^s
scandium	Sc	21	44.956	ununpentium	Uup	115	288"
seaborgium	Sg	106	263*	ununhexium	Uuh	116	292'
selenium	Se	34	78.96	uranium	U	92	238.03
silicon	Si	14	28.086	vanadium	V	23	50.94
silver	Ag	47	107.87	xenon	Xe	54	131.30
sodium	Na	11	22.9898	ytterbium	Vb	70	173.04
strontium	Sr	38	87.62	yttrium	V	39	88.905
sulphur	S	16	32.06	zinc	Zn	30	65.38
tantalum	Ta	73	180.948	zirconium	Zr	40	91.22

Appendix – V
Simplified Classification of the Animal Kingdom

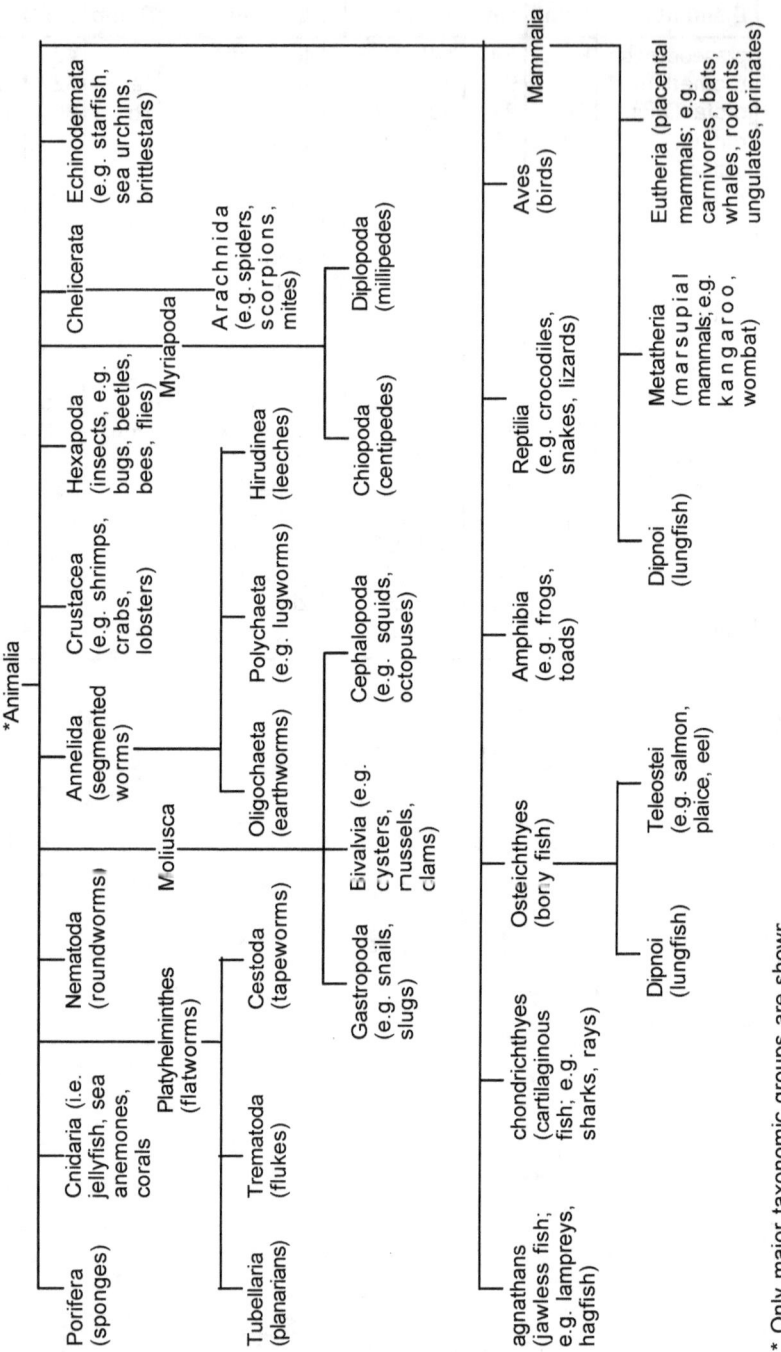

* Only major taxonomic groups are shown

Simplified Classification of Land Plants

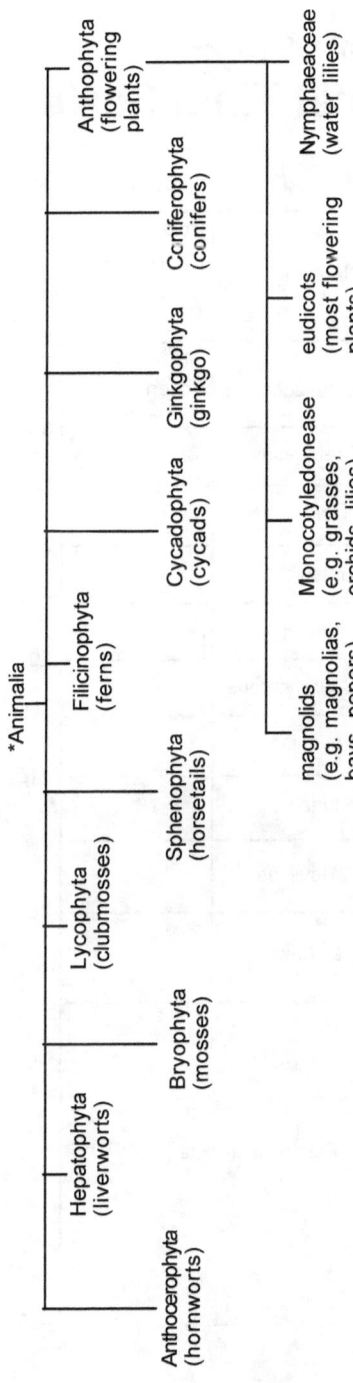

* Extinct and mostly extinct groups are excluded

Appendix – VI
Geological Time Scale

millions of Years ago	Eon	Era	Period	Epoch	Millions of years ago
	Phanerozoic	Cenozoic	Neogene	Holocene Pleistocene Pliocene Miocene	23
			Palaeogene	Oligocene Eocene Palaeocene	65
		Mesozoic	Cretaceous		145
			Jurassic		200
			Triassic		251
		Phaeozoic	Permian		299
			Carboniferous		359
			Devonian		416
			Silurian		444
			Ordovician		488
			Cambrian		
542	Proterozoic		Precambrian time		542
2500	Archaean				
3600	Hadean				
4500					4500

Appendix – VII
Model Organisms and their Genomes

Scientific name	Description/ common name	Type of organism	Genome size (Mb)	Haploid no. of chromosomes	No. of genes	Website
Escherichia coli/K-12	nonpathogenic reference strain of E. coli	eubacterium	4.6	1	4576	http://ecocyc.org/
Dictyostelium discoideum		amoebozoan cellular slime mould	34	6	13 600*	http://dictybase.org/
Saccharomyces cerevisiae	budding yeast used in baking and brewing	fungus	12.1	16	6600*	www.yeastgenome.org/
Neurospora crassa	red bread mould	fungus	40*	7	9820*	www.broad.mit.edu/annotation/genome/neurospora/
Zea mays	maize (corn)	monocotyledonous flowering plant of the grass family	2000-3000*	10 (including supernumerary (B) chromosomes)	7	www.maizegdb.org/
Arabidopsis thaliana	thale cress	dicotyledonous flowering plant of the mustard family	125	5	27 873	www.arabidopsis.org/
Caenorhabditis elegans		nematode	97	6 autosomes + X sex chromosome	19 500*	www.sanger.ac.uk/Projects/C_elegans/
Drosophila melanogaster	fruit fly	dipteran insect	16.5	3 autosomes + X and Y sex chromosomes	15 185	http://flybase.bio.indiana.edu/
Danio rerio	zebrafish	teleost fish	1762	25	19 059*	http://zfin.org/cgi-bin/webdriver?Mlval=aa-ZDB_home.apg

Scientific name	Description/ common name	Type of organism	Genome size (Mb)	Haploid no. of chromosomes	No. of genes	Website
Gallus domesticus	chicken	bird	1050	38 autosome + Z and W sex chromosomes	13 000*	http://ensembl.bioinfo.helsink.fi/Gallus_gallus/index.html
Mus musculus	laboratory mouse	mammal	2632	19 autosomes + X and Y sex chromosomes	20 000*	http://www.informatics.jax.org/
Homo sapiens	human	mammal	3000	22 autosomes + X and Y sex chromosomes	20 000-	www.ncbi.nlm.nih.org/genome/guide/human/

* Approximate or estimated value(s).

Appendix – VIII
Major Mass Extinctions of Species

Extinction event(s)	Date (millions of year ago)	Organisms most affected	Estimate of percentage of species made extinct	Cause(s)
Late Cambrian (series)	c. 488	trilobites, brachiopods, conodonts (primitive toothed vertebrates), ?soft-bodied arthropods	?	?change in sea level
Late Ordovician	c. 444	echinoderms, brachiopods, trilobites, ostracods, nautiloids	70-85	glaciation and fall in sea levels
Late Devonian (series)	c. 360	cephalopods, corals, brachiopods, bryozoans, echinoderms, trilobites, ammonites, agnathans, armoured fishes	70-83	?global cooling and reduced oxygen levels in deeper waters
Late Permian (Permo-Triassic; PTr)	251	corals, crinoids, ammonites, brachiopods, bryozoans, trilobites, land plants, insects, terrestrial vertebrates	<95	?volcanic activity with consequent global warming and changes in marine environment
Late Triassic	200	brachiopods, ammonites, bivalve and cephalopod molluscs, marine reptiles, conodonts, labyrinthodonts (primitive amphibians), insects	80	?climatic changes due to continental drift
Cretaceous-Tertiary (K-T)	65	dinosaurs, flying reptiles, ammonites, fish, brachiopods, planktonic organisms, plants	75-85	?meteorite collision (Alvarez event)

Appendix – IX
Nobel Prizes in Physics

Year	Name of prizewinner (s)	Nature of work or discovery
1901	Wilhelm Conrad Rontgen (1845-1923) German	Discovery of X-rays
1902	Hendrik Lorentz (1853-1928) Dutch Pieter Zeeman (1865-1943) Dutch	Discovery and explanation of the Zeeman effect
1903	Antoine Henri Becquerel (1852-1908) French Pierre Curie (1859-1906) French Marie Curie (1867-1934) Polish-French	Discovery of spontaneous radioactivity Work on radioactivity
1904	John William Strutt (Lord Rayleigh) (1842-1919) British	Discovery of argon
1905	Philipp Eduard Anton von Lenard (1862-1947) German	Work on cathode rays
1906	J. J. Thomson (1856-1940) British	Work on cathode rays (discovery of the electron)
1907	Albert Abraham Michelson (1852-1931) US	The Michelson-Morley experiment
1908	Gabriel Lippmann (1845-1921) French	Invention of a form of colour photography
1909	Guglielmo Marconi (1874-1937) Italian Karl Ferdinand Braun (1850-1918) German	Development of wireless telegraphy
1910	Johannes Diderikvan der Waals (1837-1923) Dutch	Work on the equation of state for gases and liquids
1911	Wilhelm Wien (1864-1928) German	Discoveries of the laws of radiation of heat
1912	NilsGustafDalen (1869-1937) Swedish	Invention of automatic valves used in lighthouses and buoys
1913	Heike Kamerlingh-Onnes (1853-1926) Dutch	Investigations in low-temperature physics
1914	Max von Laue (1879-1960) German	Discovery of X-ray diffraction by crystals
1915	William Henry Bragg (1862-1942) Australi an-British William Lawrence Bragg (1890-1971) Australian-British	Work on X-ray crystallography
1917	Charles Glover Barkla (1877-1944) British	Work on X-ray spectroscopy
1918	Max Planck (1858-1947) German	Discovery of energy quanta
1919	Johannes Stark (1874-1957) German	The splitting of spectral lines in electric fields

Year	Name of prizewinner (s)	Nature of work or discovery
1920	Charles Edouard Guillaume (1861-1938) Swiss	Research on nickel-steel alloys, used in the standard metre
1921	Albert Einstein (1879-1955) German-Swiss	Services to theoretical physics, especially the photoelectric effect
1922	Niels Bohr (1885-1962) Danish	Work on the structure of atoms and atomic spectra
1923	RobertAndrews Millikan (1868-1953) US	Work on the electron charge and on the photoelectric effect
1924	Manne Siegbahn (1886-1978) Swedish	Research in X-ray spectroscopy
1925	James Franck (1882-1964) German Gustav Hertz (1887-1975) German	Studies of collisions of electrons with atoms
1926	Jean Baptiste Perrin (1870-1942) French	Work on colloids and sedimentation equilibrium
1927	Arthur Holly Compton (1892-1962) US	Discovery of the Compton effect
1928	Charles Thomson Rees Wilson (1869-1959) British	Invention of the cloud chamber
	Owen Willans Richardson (1879-1959) British	Work on thermionic emission
1929	Prince Louis-Victor Pierre Raymond de Broglie (1892-1987) French	Discovery of the wave nature of electrons
1930	Chandrasekhara Venkata Raman (1888-1970) Indian	Discovery of the Raman effect
1932	Werner Heisenberg (1901-1976) German	Work on quantum mechanics
1933	Erwin Schrodinger (1887-1961) Austrian Paul Dirac (1902-1984) British	Work on quantum mechanics and atomic theory
1935	James Chadwick (1891-1974) British	Discovery of the neutron
1936	Victor Francis Hess (1883-1964) Austrian	Discovery of cosmic radiation
	Carl David Anderson (1905-1991) US	Discovery of the positron
1937	Clinton Joseph Davisson (1881-1958) US George Paget Thomson (1892-1975) British	Discovery of electron diffraction by crystals
1938	Enrico Fermi (1901-1954) Italian	Discovery of new radioactive elements and of nuclear reactions produced by slow neutrons
1939	Ernest Lawrence (1901-1958) US	Invention of the cyclotron and its use in making artificial elements

Year	Name of prizewinner (s)	Nature of work or discovery
1943	Otto Stern (1888-1969) German	Work on molecular beams and the proton magnetic momenl
1944	Isidor Isaac Rabi (1898-1988) US	Work on nuclear magnetic resonance
1945	Wolfgang Pauli (1900-1958) Austrian	Discovery of the exclusion principle
1946	Percy Williams Bridgman (1882-1961) US	Work on physics at high pressure
1947	Edward Victor Appleton (1892-1965) British	Investigations or'the physics of the upper atmosphere; discovery of the Appleton layer
1948	Patrick Maynard Stuart Blackett (1897-1974) British	Development of the Wilson cloud chamber, used in nuclear physics and cosmic radiation studies
1949	Hideki Yukawa (1907-1981) Japanese	Theoretical prediction of the existence of mesons
1950	Cecil Frank Powell (1903-1969) British	The photographic method of studying nuclear processes; discovery of the pi meson (pion)
1951	John Douglas Cockcroft (1897-1967) British Ernest Thomas Sinton Walton (1903-1995)Irish	Pioneering work on the transmutation of atomic nuclei by accelerated particles
1952	Felix Bloch (1905-1983) Swiss Edward Mills Purcell (1912-1997) US	Development of new techniques in nuclear magnetic resonance measurements
1953	FritsZernike (1888-1966) Dutch	Work on the phase-contrast; method; invention of the phase-contrast microscope
1954	Max Born (1882-1970) German-British	Fundamental research in quantum mechanics, especially the statistical interpretation of the wave function
	WaltherBothe (1891-1957) German	Invention of the coincidence method to study cosmic radiation
1955	Willis Eugene Lamb (1913-2008) US	Work on the hydrogen spectrum and discovery of the Lamb shift
	Polykarp Kusch (1911-1993) US	Precision determination of the electron magnetic moment
1956	William Bradford Shockley (1910-1989) US JohnBardeen (1908-1991) US Walter Houser Brattain (1902-1987) US	Research on semiconductors and the discovers of the transistor

Year	Name of prizewinner (s)	Nature of work or discovery
1957	Chen Ning Yang (1922-) Chinese Tsung-Dao Lee (1926-) US	Investigations of the parity laws in particle physics
1958	Pavel Alekseyevich Cherenkov (1904-1990) Il'ya Frank (1908-1990) Soviet Igor Yevgenyevich Tamm (1895-1971) Soviet	Work on the discovery and interpretation of Cherenkov radiation
1959	Emilio Gino Segre (1905-1989) US Owen Chamberlain (1920-2006) US	Discovery of the antiproton
1960	Donald Arthur GJaser (1926-) US	Invention of the bubble chamber
1961	Robert Hofstadter (1915-1990) US Ludwig Mo'ssbauer (1929-) German	Studies of nuclear structure Gamma-ray absorption and discovery of the Mdssbauer effect
1962	Lev Davidovich Landau (1908-1968) Soviet	Theoretical work on condensed matter physics, especially liquid helium
1963	Eugene Paul Wigner (1902-1995) Hungarian-US	Theoretical work on nuclear and particle physics, especially using symmetry principles
	Maria Goeppert-Mayer (1906-1972) US I- Hans D. Jensen (1907-1973) German	Discoveries concerning nuclear shell structure
1964	Charles Hard Townes (1915-) US Nicolay Gennadiyevich Basov (1922-2001) Soviet Aleksandr Prokhorov (1916-2002) Soviet	Fundamental work in quantum electronics leading to oscillators and amplifiers based on the maser-laser principle
1965	Sin-Itiro Tomonaga (1906-1979) Japanese Julian Schwinger (1918-1994) US Richard Phillips Feynman (1918-1988) US	Fundamental work in quantum electrodynamics
1966	Alfred Kastler (1902-1984) French	Discovery and development of optical methods for studying Hertzian resonances)
1967	Hans Albrecht Bethe (1906-2005) US	Theory of nuclear reactions especially energy production in stars
1968	Luis Walter Alvarez (1911-1988) US	Contributions to particle physics, in particular the discovery of resonance states
1969	Murray Gell-Mann (1929-) US	Discoveries concerning the classification of elementary particles and their interactions

Year	Name of prizewinner (s)	Nature of work or discovery
1970	Hannes Olof Gosta Alfven (1908-1995) Swedish	Fundamental work in rnagnetohydrodynamics
	Louis Eugene Felix Neel (1904-2000) French	Discoveries concerning antiferromagnetism and ferrimagnetism
1971	Dennis Gabor (1900-1979) British	Invention and development of holography
1972	John Rardeen (1908-1991) US Leon Neil Cooper (1930-) US John Robert Schrieffer (1931-) US	For their jointly developed theory of superconductivity (the BCS theory)
1973	Leo Esaki (1925-) Japanese Ivar Giaever (1929-) Norwegian-US	Discoveries regarding tunnelling phenomena in superconductors
	Brian David Josephson (1940-) British	Theoretical predictions connected with the Josephson effect
1974	Martin Ryle (1918-1984) British	The aperture synthesis technique in radio astronomy
	Antony Hewish (1924-) British	The discovery of pulsars
1975	Aage Niels Bohr (1922-) Danish Ben Roy Mottelson (1926-) Danish Leo James Rainwater (1917-1986) US	Theory of the nucleus (the liquid-drop model)
1976	Burton Richter (1931-) US Samuel Chao Chung Ting (1936-) US	Discovery of the J/ particle
1977	PhilipWarrenAnderson(1923-) US Nevill Francis Mott (1905-1996) British John Hasbrouck van Vleck (1899-1980) US	Fundamental theoretical work on magnetic and disordered systems
1078	Pyoti Loonidovich Kapitsa (1894-1984) Soviet	Work on low-temperature physics
	Arno Allan Penzias (1933-) US Robert Woodrow Wilson (1936-) US	Discovery of cosmic microwave background radiation
1979	Sheldon Lee Glashow (1932-) US Abdus Salam (1926-1996) Pakistani Steven Weinberg (1933-) US	Theory of the unified weak and electromagnetic interactions
1980	James Watson Cronin (1931-) US Val Logsdon Fitch (1923-) US	Discovery of CP violation in the decay of neutral K-mesons
1981	Nicolaas Bloemhergen (1920-) US Arthur Leonard Schawlow (1921-1999) US	Development of laser spectroscopy
	Kai Manne Borje Siegbahn (1918-2007) Swedish	Development of electron spectroscopy

Year	Name of prizewinner (s)	Nature of work or discovery
1982	Kenneth G. Wilson (1936-) US	Theory of critical phenomena in connection with phase transitions
1983	Subrahmanyan Chandrasekhar (1910-1995) Indian	Theoretical studies concerning the structure and evolution of stars (the Chandrasekhar limit)
	William Alfred Fowler (1911-1995) US	Studies of the nuclear reactions of importance in the formation of the chemical elements
1984	Carlo Rubbia (1934-) Italian Simon van der Meer (1925-) Dutch	Work at CEBN leading to the discovery of the W and Z particles.
1985	Klaus von Klitzing (1943-) German	Discovery of the quantum Hall effect
1986	Ernst Ruska (1906-1988 (German	Work in electron optics and the design of the first electron microscope
	Gerd Binnig (1947-) German Heinrich Rohrer (1933-) Swiss	Design of the scanning tunnelling microscope
1987	Johannes Georg Bednorz (1950-) German Karl Alexander Miiller (1927-) Swiss	Discovery of superconductivity in ceramic materials (high-temperature superconductivity)
1988	Leon Max Lederman (1922-) US Melvin Schwartz (1932-2006) US Jack Steinberger (1921-) US	The neutrino beam method and the discovery of the muon neutrino
1989	Norman Foster Ramsey (1915-) US	Invention of the separated oscillatory fields method and its use in the hydrogen maser and other atomic clocks
	Hans Georg Dehmelt (1922-) US Wolfgang Paul (1913-1933) German	Development of the ion-trap technique
1990	Jerome I. Friedman (1930-) US Henry Way Kendall (1926-1999) US Richard E. Taylor (1929-) Canadian	Investigations of deep inelastic scattering of electrons on protons and bound neutrons
1991	Pierre-Gilles de Gennes (1932-2007) French	Work on order phenomena, in particular in liquid crystals and polymers
1992	Georges Charpak (1924-) French	Invention and development of particle detectors, in particular the multiwire proportional chamber
1993	Russell Alan Hulse (1950-) US Joseph Hooton Taylor Jr. (1941-) US	Discovery of a binary pulsar and its use to demonstrate gravitational waves
1994	Bertram Brockhouse (1918-2003) Canadian	Work on neutron spectroscopy

Year	Name of prizewinner (s)	Nature of work or discovery
	Clifford Glenwood Shull (1915-2001) US	Work on neutron scattering techniques
1995	Martin Lews Perl (1927-) US	Discovery of the tau lepton and contributions to lepton physics
	Frederick Reines (1918-1998) US	Detection of the neutrino and contributions to lepton physics
1996	David Morris Lee (1931-) US Robert Coleman Richardson (1937-) US Douglas D. Osheroff (1945-) US	Discovery of superfluidity in helium-3
1997	Steven Chu (1948- JUS Claude Cohen-Tannoudji (1933-) French William Daniel Phillips (1948-) US	Development of laser techniques to trap atoms and produce low temperatures
1998	Robert B. Laughlin (1950-) US Horst Ludwig Stormer (1949-) German Daniel Chee Tsui (1939-) US	Discovery of a new type of quantum fluid with fractionally charged excitations
1999	Gerardus't Hooft (1946-) Dutch Martinus J.G. Veltman (1931-) Dutch	Quantum theory of electroweak interactions
2000	ZhoreslvanovichAlferov(1930-) Russian Herbert Kroemer (1928-) German Jack St. Ciair Kilby (1923-2005) US	Developing semiconductor heterostructures Invention of the integrated circuit
2001	Eric Allin Cornell (1961-) US Wolfgang Ketterie (1957-) German Carl Edwin Wieman (1951-) US	Work on Bose-Einstein condensation
2002	Raymond Davis Jr. (1914-2006) US Masatoshi Koshiba (1926-) Japanese	The detection of cosmic neutrinos
	Riccardo Giacconi (1931-) US	The discovery of cosmic X-ray sources
2003	Alexei Alexeevich Abrikosov (1928-) Russian Vitaly Lazarevich Ginzburg (1916-) Russian Anthony James Leggett (1938-) British	Pioneering contributions to the theory of superconductors and superfluids
2004	David J. Gross (1941-) US H. David Politzer (1949-) US Frank Wilczek (1951-) US	Discovery of asymptotic freedom in the theory of the strong interaction
2005	Roy J. Glauber (1925- JUS	Work on the quantum theory of optical coherence

Year	Name of prizewinner (s)	Nature of work or discovery
2006	John L. Hall (1934-) US Theodor W. Hansch (1941-) German	Work on laser spectroscopy (the optical frequency comb technique)
	John C. Mather (1946-) US George F. Smoot (1945-) US	Work on the cosmic microwave background radiation (COBE)
2007	Albert Fert (1938-) French Peter Grunberg (1939-) German	Discovery of giant magneloresistance
2008	Yoichiro Nambu (1921-) US	Discovery of the mechanism of spontaneous broken symmetry
	Makoto Kobayashi (1944-) Japanese Toshihide Maskawa (1940-) Japanese	Discovery of the origin of then broken symmetry predicting at least three families of quarks
2009	Charles Kuen Kao (1933-) China	Transmission of light in fibres for optical communication
	Willard S. Boyle (1924 -) Canada George E. Smith (1930 -) US	Invention of imaging semiconductor circuit - the CCD sensor
2010	Andre Geim (1958 -) Russia Konstantin Novoselov (1974 -) Russia	Two-dimensional material graphene
2011	Saul Perlmutter (1959 -) US Brian P. Schmidt (1967 -) US Adam G. Riess (1969 -) US	Expansion of Universe through observations of supernovae

Nobel Prizes in Chemistry

Year	Name of prizewinner (s)	Nature of work or discovery
1901	Jacobus Henricus Van't Hoff (1852-1911) Dutch	Discovery of the laws of chemical dynamics and osmotic pressure in solutions
1902	Hermann Emil Fischer (1852-1919) German	Work on sugar and purine syntheses
1903	Svante August Arrhenius (1859-1927) Swedish	The electrolytic theory of dissociation
1904	Sir William Ramsay (1852-1916) British	Discovery of the inert gaseous elements in air and the determination of their place in the periodic system
1905	Johann Friedrich Wilhelm Adolf Von Baeyer (1835-1917) German	Advancement of organic chemistry and the chemical industry through work on organic dyes and hydroaromatic compounds
1906	Henri Moissan (1852-1907) French	Investigation and isolation of the element fluorine, and for his electric furnace
1907	Eduard Buchner (1860-1917) German	Biochemical researches and the discovery of cell-free fermentation
1908	Lord Ernest Rutherford (1871-1937) New Zealand-British	Investigations into the disintegration of the elements and the chemistry of radioactive substances
1909	Wilhelm Ostwald (1853-1932) Latvian-German	Work on catalysis and investigations into the fundamental principles governing chemical equilibria and rates of reaction
1910	Otto Wallacfi (1847-1931) German	Pioneering work in the field of alicyclic compounds
1911	Marie Curie (1867-1934) Polish-born French	Discovery of the elements radium and polonium, the isolation of radium, and the study of this element
1912	Victor Grignard (1871-1935) French Paul Sabatier (1854-1941) French	Discovery of the Grignard reagent Method of hydrogenating organic compounds in the presence of finely divided metals
1913	Alfred Werner (1866-1919) German-born Swiss	Work on the linkage of atoms in molecules, especially in inorganic chemistry

Year	Name of prizewinner (s)	Nature of work or discovery
1914	Theodore William Richards (1868-1928) US	Accurate determinations of the atomic weights of many chemical elements
1915	Richard Martin Willstatter (1872-1942) German	Work on plant pigments, especially chlorophyll
1918	Fritz Haber (1868-1934) German	The synthesis of ammonia from its elements
1920	Walther Hermann Nernst (1864-1941) German	Work in thermochemistry
1921	Frederick Soddy (1877-1956) British	Work on the chemistry of radioactive substances and investigations into the origin and nature of isotopes
1922	Francis William Aston (1877-1945) British	Discovery, by means of his mass spectrograph, of isotopes in a large number of nonradioactive elements
1923	Fritz Pregl (1869-1930) Austrian	Invention of the method of microanalysis of organic substances
1925	Richard Adolf Zsigmondy (1865-1929) Austrian-German	Demonstration of the heterogenous nature of colloid solutions and for the methods developed to study them
1926	Theodor Svedberg (1884-1971) Swedish	Work on disperse systems
1927	Heinrich Otto Wieland (1877-1957) German	Investigations of the constitution of the bile acids and related substances
1928	Adolf Otto Reinhold Windaus (1876-1959) German	Work on the constitution of the sterols and their connection with the vitamins
1929	Sir Arthur Harden (1865-1940) British Hans Karl August Simon Von Euler-Chelpin (1873-1964) German-Swedish	Investigations on the fermentation of sugar and fermentative enzymes
1930	Hans Fischer (1881-1945) German	Work on the constitution of haemin and chlorophyll, especially the synthesis of haemin
1931	Carl Bosch (1874-1940) German Friedrich Bergius (1884-1949) German	Contributions to the invention and development of chemical high pressure methods
1932	Irving Langmuir (1881-1957) US	Discoveries and investigations in surface chemistry

Year	Name of prizewinner (s)	Nature of work or discovery
1934	Harold Clayton Urey (1893-1981) US	Discovery of heavy hydrogen (deuterium)
1935	Frederic Joliot (1900-1958) French Irene Joliot-Curie (1897-1956) French	Synthesis of new radioactive elements
1936	Petrus (Peter) Josephus Wilhelmus Debye (1884-1966) Dutch	Contributions to our knowledge of molecular structure through investigations on dipole moments and on the diffraction of X-rays and electrons in gases
1937	Sir Walter Norman Haworth (1883-1950) British	Investigation of carbohydrates and vitamin C
	Paul Karrer (1889-1971) Russian-Swiss	Investigations on carotenoids, flavins, and vitamins A and B2
1938	Richard Kuhn (1900-1967) Austrian-born German	Work on carotenoids and vitamins (declined the award because of political pressure but later received the diploma and the medal)
1939	Adolf Friedrich Johann Butenandt (1903-1995) German	Work on sex hormones
1939	Leopold (Lavoslav) Stephen Ruzicka (1887-1976) Croatian-Swiss	Work on polymethylenes and higher terpenes
1943	George De Hevesy (1885-1966) Hungarian-born Swedish	Work on the use of isotopes as tracers in the study of chemical processes
1944	Otto Hahn (1879-1968) German	Discovery of the fission of heavy nuclei
1945	Artturi Ilmari Virtanen (1895-1973) Finnish	Research and inventions in agricultural and nutrition chemistry, especially for a fodder-preservation method
1946	James Batcheller Sumner 7-1955) US	Discovery that enzymes can be crystallized
	John Howard Northrop (1891-1987) US Wendell Meredith Stanley US (1904-1971)	Preparation of enzymes and virus proteins in a pure form
1947	Sir Robert Robinson (1886-1975) British	Investigations on plant products of biological importance, especially the alkaloids
1948	Arne Wilhelm Kaurin Tiselius (1902-1971) Swedish	Work on electrophoresis and adsorption analysis, especially discoveries concerning the complex nature of the serum proteins

Year	Name of prizewinner (s)	Nature of work or discovery
1949	William Francis Giauque (1895-1982) US	Contributions to the field of chemical thermodynamics, particularly the behaviour of substances at very low temperatures
1950	Otto Paul Hermann Diels (1876-1954) German Kurt Alder (1902 1968) German	Discovery and development of the diene synthesis (the Diels-Alder reaction)
1951	Edwin Mattison McMillan (1907-1991) US Glenn Theodore Seaborg (1912-1999) US	Work on the chemistry of the transuranium elements
1952	Archer John Porter Martin (1910-2002) British Richard Laurence Millington Synge (1914-1994) British	Invention of the technique of partition chromatography
1953	Hermann Staudinger (1881-1965) German	Discoveries in the field of macromolecular chemistry
1954	Linus Carl Pauling (1901-1994) US	Work on the nature of the chemical bond and its application to the elucidation of the structure of complex substances
1955	Vincent Du Vigneaud (1901-1978) US	Work on biochemically important sulphur compounds, especially for the first synthesis of a polypeptide hormone
1956	Sir Cyril Norman Hinsheiwood (1897-1967) British Nikolay Nikolaevich Semenov (1896-1986) Soviet	Studies of the mechanism of chemical reactions
1957	Lord Alexander R. Todd (1907-1997) British	Work on nucleotides and nucleotide coenzymes
1958	Frederick Sanger (1918-) British	Work on the structure of proteins, especially insulin
1959	Jaroslav Heyrovsky (1890-1967) Czech	Discovery and development of polarography
1960	Willard Frank Libby (1908-1980) US	Discovery and development of the technique of carbon-14 dating
1961	Melvrn Calvin (1911-) US	Work on carbon dioxide assimilation in plants
1962	Max Ferdinand Perutz (1914-2002) Austrian-British Sir John Cowdery Kendrew (1917-1997) British	Studies of the structures of globular proteins

Year	Name of prizewinner (s)	Nature of work or discovery
1963	Karl Ziegler (1898-1973) German Giulio Natta (1903-1979) Italian	Discoveries concerning the chemistry and technology of high polymers
1964	Dorothy Crowfoot Hodgkin (1910-1994) British	Determinations by X-ray techniques of the structures of important biochemical substances
1965	Robert Burns Woodward (1917-1979) US	Achievements in the art of organic synthesis
1966	Roberts. Mulliken (1896-1986) US	Work concerning chemical bonds and the electronic structure of molecules using molecular orbital theory
1967	Manfred Eigen (1927-) German Ronald George Wreyford Norrish (1897-1978) British Lord George Porter (1920-2002) British	Studies of extremely fast chemical reactions, effected by disturbing the equlibrium by means of very short pulses of energy
1968	Lars Onsager (1903-1976) Norwegian	Discovery of sugar nucleotides and their role in the biosynthesis of carbohydrates
1969	Sir Derek H. R. Barton (1918-1998) Odd Hassel (1897-1981) Norwegian	Development of the concept of conformation and its application in chemistry
1970	Luis F. Leioir (1906-1987) Argentinian	Discovery of sugar nucleotides and theri orla in the biosynthesis of carbohydrates
1971	Gerhard Herzberg (1904-1999) German-Canadian	Work on the electronic stucture and geometry of molecules and free radicals
1972	Christian B. Anfinsen (1916-1995) US	Work on ribonuclease, especially the connection between the amino acid sequence and the active conformation
	Stanford Moore (1913-1982) US William H. Stein (1911-1980) US	Contribution to the understanding of the connection between chemical structure and catalytic activity of the active centre of the ribonuclease molecule
1973	Ernst Otto Fischer (1918-2007) German Sir Geoffrey Wilkinson (1921-1996) British	Pioneering work, performed independently, on the chemistry of the sandwich compounds

Year	Name of prizewinner (s)	Nature of work or discovery
1974	Paul J. Fiory (1910-1985) US	Theoretical and experimental work on the physical chemistry of macromolecules
1975	Sir John Warcup Cornforth (1917-) Australian-British	Work on the stereochemistry of enzyme-catalysed reactions
1975	Vladimir Prelog (1906-1998) Bosnian-Swiss	Work on the stereochemistry of organic molecules and reactions
1976	William N. Lipscomb (1919- JUS	Studies on the structure of boranes, illuminating problems of chemical bonding
1977	Ilya Prigogine (1917-2003) Russian-Belgian	Contributions to non-equilibrium thermodynamics, particularly the theory of dissipative structures
1978	Peter D. Mitchell (1920-1992) British	Formulation of the chemiosmotic theory
1979	Herbert C. Brown (1912-2004) British-US GeorgWittig (1897-1987) German	Development of the use of boron- and phosphorus-containing compounds, respectively, into important reagents in organic synthesis
1980	Paul Berg (1926-) US	Fundamental studies of the biochemistry of nucleic acids, with particular regard to recombinant DNA
	Walter Gilbert (1932-) US Frederick Sanger (1918-) British	Contributions concerning the determination of base sequences in nucleic acids
1981	Kenichi Fukui (1918-1998) Japanese Roald Hoffmann (1937-) Polish-US	Theories, developed independently, concerning the course of chemical reactions (frontier-orbital theory and the Woodward-Hoffmann rules)
1982	Sir Aaron Klug (1926-) Lithuanian-British	Development of crystallographic electron microscopy and the structural elucidation of biologically important nucleic acid-protein complexes
1983	Henry Taube (1915-2005) Canadisn-US	Work on the mechanisms of electron-transfer reactions, especially in metal complexes
1984	Robert Bruce Merrifield (1921-2006) US	Development of methodology for chemical synthesis on a solid matrix

Year	Name of prizewinner (s)	Nature of work or discovery
1985	Herbert A. Hauptman (1917-) US Jerome Karle (1918-) US	Development of direct methods for the determination of crystal structures
1986	Dudley R. Herschbach (1932-) US Yuan T. Lee (1936-) Taiwanese John C. Polanyi (1929-) Canadian	Research on the dynamics of chemical elementary processes
1987	Donald J. Cram (1919-2001) US Jean-Marie Lehn (1939-) French Charles J. Pedersen (1904-1989) Norwegian	Development and use of molecules with structure-specific interactions of high selectivity (crown ethers and cryptands)
1988	Johann Deisenhofer(1943-) German Robert Huber (1937-) German Hartmut Michel (1948-) German	Determination of the three-dimensional structure of a photosynthetic reaction centre
1989	Sidney Altman (1939-) Canadian-US Thomas R. Cech (1947-) US	Discovery of the catalytic properties of RNA
1990	Elias James Corey (1928-) US	Development of the theory and methodology of organic synthesis (retrosynthetic analysis)
1991	Richard R. Ernst (1933-) Swiss	Development of high resolution nuclear magnetic resonance (NMR) spectroscopy
1992	Rudolph A. Marcus (1923-) Canadian-US	Work on electron-transfer reactions in chemical systems
1993	Kary B. Mullis (1944-) US Michael Smith (1932-2000) British-Canadian	Discovery of the polymerase chain reaction Work on oiigonudeotide-based site-directed mutagenesis and its use for protein studies
1994	George A Olah (1927-) Hungarian-US	Work on carbocation chemistry
1995	Paul Crutzen (1933-) Dutch Mario J.Molina (1943-) Mexican-US F. Sherwood Rowland (1927-) US	Work in atmospheric chemistry, particularly the formation and decomposition of ozone
1996	Robert F. Curl (1933-) US Sir Harold W. Kroto (1939-) British Richard Smalley (1943-2005) US	Discovery of fullerenes
1997	Paul D. Boyer (1918-) US John E.Walker (1941-) British JensC. Skou(1918-) Danish	Elucidation of the mechanism underlying the synthesis of ATP Discovery of an ion-transporting enzyme, Na^+,K^+-ATPase
1998	Walter Kohn (1923-) Austrian-US John A. Pople (1925-2004) British	Development of density-functional theory Development of computational methods in quantum chemistry

Year	Name of prizewinner (s)	Nature of work or discovery
1999	Ahmed H. Zewail (1946-) Egyptian	Studies of the transition states of chemical reactions using femtosecond spectroscopy
2000	Alan J. Heeger (1936-) US Alan G. MacDiarmid (1927-2007) New Zealand-US Hideki Shirakawa (1936-) Japanese	Discovery and development of conductive polymers
2001	Williams. Knowles (1917-) US Ryoji Noyori (1938-) Japanese K. Barry Sharpless (1941-) US	Work on chirally catalysed hydrogenation reactions Work on chirally catalysed oxidation reactions
2002	John B. Fenn (1917-) US Koichi Tanaka (1959-) Japanese Kurt Wuthrich (1938-) Swiss	Development of ionization methods for mass spectrometric analyses of biological macromolecules Development of NMR spectroscopy for determining the structure of biological macromolecules in solution
2003	Peter Agre (1949-) US Roderick MacKinnon (1956-) US	Discovery of water channels in cell membranes Structural and mechanistic studies of ion channels in cell membranes
2004	Aaron Ciechanover (1947-) Israeli Avram Hershko (1937-) Hungarian-Israeli Irwin Rose (1926-) US	Discovery of ubiquitin-mediated protein degradation
2005	Yves Chauvin (1930-) French Robert H. Grubbs (1942-) US Richard R. Schrock (1945-) US	Development of the metathesis method in organic synthesis
2006	Roger D. Kornberg (1947-) US	Studies of the molecular basis of eukaryotic transcription
2007	Gerhard Ertl (1936-) German	Studies of chemical processes on solid surfaces
2008	Osamu Shimomura (1928 -) Japan Martin Chalfie (1947 -) US Roger Y. Tsien (1952 -) US	Green fluorescent protein, GFP
2009	Venkatraman Ramakrishnan (1952 -) India Thomas A. Steitz (1940 -) US Ada E. Yonath (1939 -) Israel	Structure and function of the ribosome
2010	Richard F. Heck (1931 -) US Ei-ichi Negishi (1935 -) China Akira Suzuki (1930 -) Japan	Palladium-catalyzed couplings in organic synthesis
2011	Dan Shechtman (1941 -) Israel	Discovery of quasi crystals

Nobel Prizes in Biology

Year	Nobel prize	Name of prizewinners)	Nationality	Nature of work or discovery
1901	Physiology or Medicine	Emrl Adolf von Behring (1854-1917)	German	Developed a diphtheria antitoxin based on serum derived from immune individuals
1902	Physiology or Medicine	Ronald Ross (1857-1932)	British	Established that malaria parasites are transmitted by mosquitoes
1904	Physiology or Medicine	Ivan Petrovich Pavlov (1849-1936)	Russian	Investigated importance of sight and smell of food in stimulating the digestive system
1905	Physiology or Medicine	Robert Koch (1843-1910)	German	Discovered the bacterium responsible for tuberculosis
1906	Physiology or Medicine	Camillo Golgi (1843-1926)	Italian	Identified fundamental aspects of nervous system organization
		Santiago Ramon y Cajal (1852-1934)	Spanish	
1907	Physiology or Medicine	Charles Louis Alphonse Laveran (1845-1922)	French	Identified the protozoan responsible for malaria
1908	Physiology or Medicine	Ilya Ilyich Mechnikov (1845-1916)	Russian	Discovered phagocytosis
		Paul Ehrlich (1954-1915)	German	Studied antisera and immunity
1909	Physiology or Medicine	Emil Theodor Kocher (1841-1917)	Swiss	Studied the physiology, pathology, and surgery of the thyroid gland
1910	Physiology or Medicine	Albrecht Kossel (1853-1927)	German	Identified the chemical nature of cell components, particularly proteins and nucleic acids
1913	Physiology or Medicine	Charles Robert Richet (1850-1935)	French	Discovered anaphylaxis
1914	Physiology or Medicine	Robert Barany (1876-1936)	Austro-Hungarian	Investigated the physiology of the inner ear and devised the Barany test for diagnosing disease of the vestibular apparatus
1915	Chemistry	Richard Martin Willstatter (1872-1942)	German	Determined key aspects of chemical nature of chlorophyll and other plant pigments

Year	Nobel prize	Name of prizewinners)	Nationality	Nature of work or discovery
1919	Physiology or Medicine	Jules Bordet (1870-1961)	Belgian	Discovered the immune component alexin, later called complement
1920	Physiology or Medicine	Schack August Steenberg Krogh (1874-1949)	Danish	Discovered physiological mechanism controlling capillary diameter in the blood vascular system
1922	Physiology or Medicine	Archibald Vivian Hill (1886-1977)	British	Discovered that heat produced following muscle contraction indicated oxygen consumption
		Otto Fritz Meyerhof (1884-1951)	German	Showed that lactic acid produced by contracting muscles was subsequently converted to glycogen by aerobic reactions
1923	Physiology or Medicine	Frederick Grant Banting (1891-1941)	Canadian	Discovered insulin
		John James Richard Macleod (1876-1935)	Canadian	
1927	Chemistry	Heinrich Otto Wieland (1877-1957)	German	Characterized the nature of bile acids
1928	Chemistry	Adolf Otto Reinhold Windhaus (1876-1959	German	Identified key aspects of sterol chemistry and link with vitamin D
1929	Physiology or Medicine	Christiaan Eijkman (1858-1930)	Dutch	Identified cure for beriberi
		Frederick Gowland Hopkins (1861-1947)	British	Discovered vitamins
1930	Physiology or Medicine	Karl Landsteiner (1868-1943)	Austrian	Discovered the ABO system of human blood groups
1930	Chemistry	Hans Fischer (1881-1945)	German	Determined the chemical nature of haem
1931	Physiology or Medicine	Otto Heinrich Warburg (1883-1970)	German	Identified the enzymes involved in cell respiration
1932	Physiology or Medicine	Charles Scott Shernngton (1857-1952)	British	Studied nervous control and integration of muscle reflexes

Year	Nobel prize	Name of prizewinners)	Nationality	Nature of work or discovery
1933	Physiology or Medicine	Edgar Douglas Adrian (1889-1977)	British	Investigated principles of nervous signalling based on impulse frequency
		Thomas Hunt Morgan (1866-1945)	US	Established chromosomes as the physical basis of genetic linkage
1935	Physiology or Medicine	Hans Spemann (1869-1941)	German	Discovered an embryonic organizer
1936	Physiology or Medicine	Henry Hallett Dale (1875-1968)	British	Discovered that acetylcholine is a chemical transmitter of nerve signals
		Otto Loewi (1873-1961)	Austrian	
1937	Physiology or Medicine	Albert von Szent-Gyorgyi (1893-1936)	Hungarian	Discovered fundamental components of cellular respiration
		Walter Norman Haworth (1883-1950)	UK	Discovered ring structures of sugars and synthesized vitamin C (ascorbic acid)
		Paul Karrer (1889-1971)	Swiss	Determined the structure of carotene and synthesized vitamins A and B2 (riboflavin)
1938	Physiology or Medicine	Corneille Jean Francois Heymans (1892-1968)	Belgian	Determined the role of the carotid sinus in regulating heart rate and blood pressure
1938	Chemistry	Richard Kuhn (1900-67)	German	Determined the structures of vitamins A and B2 and synthesized vitamin Bs (pyridoxine)
1943	Physiology or Medicine	Henrik Carl Peter Dam (1895-1976)	Danish	Discovered and characterized vitamin K
		Edward Adelbert Doisy (1893-1986)	US	
1944	Physiology or Medicine	Joseph Erlanger (1874-1965)	US	Identified different classes of nerve fibres according to their conducting velocity
		Herbert Spencer Gasser (1888-1963)	US	
1945	Physiology or Medicine	Alexander Fleming (1881-1955)	British	Discovered, isolated, and purified penicillin
		Ernst Boris Chain (1906-79)	British	
		Howard Walter Florey (1898-1968)	Australian	

Year	Nobel prize	Name of prizewinners)	Nationality	Nature of work or discovery
1946	Physiology or Medicine	Hermann Joseph Muller (1890-1967)	US	Discovered that X-rays cause a high rate of mutations
1947	Physiology or Medicine	Carl Ferdinand Cori (1896-1984)	US	Discovered how glycogen is broken down and resynthesized
		Gerty Theresa Cori (1896-1957)	US	
		Bernardo Alberto Houssay (1887-1971)	Argentina	Studied the effects of pituitary hormones on blood glucose
1948	Chemistry	Arne Wilhelm Kaurin Tiselius (1902-71)	Swedish	Developed electrophoresis as a technique for separating proteins and confirmed the existence of different classes of serum proteins
1950	Physiology or Medicine	Edward Calvin Kendall (1885-1972)	US	Identified the structure and biological effects of the adrenocortical hormones
		Tadeus Reichstein (1897-1996)	Swiss	
		Philip Showalter Hench (1896-1965)	US US	
1953	Physiology or Medicine	Hans Adolf Krebs (1900-81)	British	Discovered the citric acid cycle (Krebs cycle)
		Fritz Albert Lipmann (1899-1986)	US	Discovered coenzyme A and established its importance in intermediary metabolism
1955	Physiology or Medicine	Axel Hugo TheodorTheorell (1903-82)	Swedish	Established mechanism of action of oxidative enzymes
1955	Chemistry	Vincent du Vigneaud (1901-78)	US	Synthesized the hormone oxytocin
1957	Chemistry	Alexander R. Todd (1907-97)	British	Synthesized the purine and pyrimidine bases of nucleic acids and also various coenzymes, including FAD, ADP, and ATP
1958	Physiology or Medicine	George Wells Beadle (1903-89)	US	Formulated the one gene-one enzyme hypothesis (now known as the one gene-one polypeptide hypothesis)
		Edward Lawrie Tatum (1909-75)	us	

Year	Nobel prize	Name of prizewinners)	Nationality	Nature of work or discovery
		Joshua Lederberg (1925-)	US	Discovered genetic recombination and conjugation in bacteria
1958	Chemistry	Frederick Sanger (1918-)	British	Determined the amino acid sequence of bovine insulin
1959	Physiology or Medicine	Severo Ochoa (1905-93)	US	Discovered enzymes that catalyse the formation of RNA and DNA from their respective nucleotides
		Arthur Kornberg (1918-2007)	US	
1960	Physiology or Medicine	Frank Macfarlane Burnet (1899-1985)	Australian	Discovered acquired immunological tolerance
		Peter Brian Medawar (1915-87)	British	
1961	Physiology or Medicine	Georg von Bekesy (1899-1972)	US	Established the physical mechanism of hearing within the cochlea of the inner ear
1961	Chemistry	Melvin Calvin (1911-97)	US	Determined the reactions of carbon assimilation during photosynthesis (the Calvin cycle)
1962	Physiology or Medicine	Francis Harry Compton Crick (1916-2004)	British	Discovered the chemical structure of DNA and its significance for the transfer of genetic information
		James Dewey Watson (1928-)	US	
		Maurice Hugh Frederick Wilkins (1916-2004)	New Zealand-British	
1962	Chemistry	Max Ferdinand Perutz (1914-2002)	British	Determined the structure of the protein myoglobin using X-ray crystallography
		John Cowdery Kendrew (1917-97)	British	
1963	Physiology or Medicine	John Carew Eccles (1903-97)	Australian	Discovered how ionic movements are intrinsic to nerve cell excitability
		Alan Lloyd Hodgkin (1914-98;	British	
		Andrew Fielding Huxley (1917-)	British	
1964	Physiology or Medicine	Konrad Bloch (1912-2000)	US	Discovered crucial steps in cholesterol synthesis

Year	Nobel prize	Name of prizewinners)	Nationality	Nature of work or discovery
1965	Physiology or Medicine	Feodor Lynen (1911-79)	German	Identified key role of coenzyme A in fatty acid metabolism
		Francois Jacob (1920-)	French	Formulated the operon model of gene regulation
		Jacques Monod (1910-76)	French	
		Andre Lwoff (1902-94)	French	Determined the mechanism by which bacterial cells infected with bacteriophages undergo lysogeny
1966	Physiology or Medicine	Peyton Rous (1879-1970)	US	Discovered that certain viruses can cause cancer in animals
1967	Physiology or Medicine	Ragnar Granit (1900-91)	Swedish	Discovered fundamental aspects of the neurophysiology of vision
		Haldan Keffer Hartline (1903-83)	US	
		George Wald (1906-97)	US	
1968	Physiology or Medicine	Robert W. Holley (1922-93)	US	Elucidated the genetic code and its role in protein synthesis
		Har Gobind Khorana(1922-)	US	
		Marshall W. Nirenberg (1927-2010)	US	
1969	Physiology or Medicine	Alfred D. Hershey (1908-97)	US	Established that DNA is the genetic material of bacteriophages
		Max Delbruck (1906-81)	US	Demonstrated genetic recombination between viruses
		Salvador E. Luria (1912-91)	US	
1970	Physiology or Medicine	Bernard Katz (1911-2003)	British	Discovered the nature of certain neurotransmitters and the mechanism of their storage, release, and inactivation at synapses
		Ulf von Euler (1905-83)	Swedish	
		Julius Axelrod (1912-2004)	US	
1970	Chemistry	Luis F. Leioir (1906-87)	Argentinian	Discovered the role of sugar nudeotides in glycogen synthesis
1971	Physiology or Medicine	Earl W. Sutherland (1915-74)	US	Discovered cyclic adenosine monophosphate and demonst-

Year	Nobel prize	Name of prizewinners)	Nationality	Nature of work or discovery
1972	Physiology or Medicine	Gerald M. Edelman (1929-)	US	rated its importance as a second messenger in cell signalling Determined the chemical structure of antibodies
		Rodney R. Porter (1917-85)	British	
1972	Chemistry	Christian B. Anfinsen (1916-95)	US	Established that amino acid sequence alone determines the biological activity of enzymes
		Stanford Moore (1913-82)	US	Identified the chemical groups contributing to the active site of the enzyme ribonuclease
		William H. Stein (1911-80)	US	
1973	Physiology or Medicine	Karl von Frisch (1886-1982)	German	Demonstrated certain basic aspects of individual and social behaviour in animals under natural conditions
		Konrad Lorenz (1903-89)	Austrian	
		Nikolaas Tinbergen (1907-88)	British	
1974	Physiology or Medicine	Albert Claude (1899-1983)	Belgian	Discovered certain cell components, including lysosomes and ribosomes
		Christian de Duve (1917-)	Belgian	
		George E. Palade (1912-2008)	US	
1975	Physiology or Medicine	David Baltimore (1938-)	US	Discovered the role of the enzyme reverse transcriptase during infection by RNA viruses
		Howard Martin Temin (1934-94)	US	
		Renato Dulbecco (1914-)	US	Established the concept of virus-induced transformation of normal cells into cancer cells
1977	Physiology or Medicine	Roger Guillemin (1924-)	US	Discovered peptide hormones in the brain
		Andrew V. Schally (1926-)	US	
		Rosalyn Yalow (1921-)	US	Developed radioimmunoassay for peptide hormones
1978	Physiology or Medicine	Werner Arber (1929-)	Swiss	Discovered restriction enzymes and their applications in molecular genetics
		Daniel Nathans (1928-99)	US	
		Hamilton O. Smith (1931-)	US	

Year	Nobel prize	Name of prizewinners)	Nationality	Nature of work or discovery
1978	Chemistry	Peter D. Mitchell (1920-92)	British	Formulated the cherniosrnotic theory of biochemical energy transfer
1979	Physiology or Medicine	Alan M. Cormack (1924-98)	US	Developed computerized tomography
		Godfrey N. Hounsfield (1919-2004)	British	
1980	Chemistry	Paul Berg (1926-)	US	Pioneered recombinant DNA techniques
		Walter Gilbert (1932-)	US	Developed techniques form sequencing nucleic acids
		Frederick Sanger (1918-)	British	
1980	Physiology or Medicine	Baruj Benacerraf (1920-)	US	Determined the genetic basis of histocornpatibility antigens on body cells and their significance in immune mechanisms and tissue transplantation
		Jean Dausset (1916-2009)	French	
		George D. Snell (1903-96)	US	
1981	Physiology or Medicine	Roger W. Sperry (1913-94)	US	Identified the main functional specializations of right and left cerebral hemispheres
		David H. Hubel (1926-)	US	Made key insights into the structural and functional organization of the visual cortex
		Torsten N. Wiesel (1924-)	Swedish	
1982	Physiology or Medicine	Sune K. Bergstrom (1916-2004)	Swedish	Discovered key aspects of the nature, metabolism, and biological actions of prostaglandins and related substances
		Bengt I. Sarnuelsson (1934-)	Swedish	
		John R. Vane (1927-2004)	British	
1982	Chemistry	Aaron Klug (1926-)	British	Developed crystaliographic electron microscopy to determine the structure of protein-nucleic acid complexes
1983	Physiology or Medicine	Barbara McClintock (1902-92)	US	Discovered mobile genetic elements (transposens)
1984	Physiology or Medicine	Niels K. Jerne (1911-94)	Danish	Developed theories explaining antibody specificity and diversity

Year	Nobel prize	Name of prizewinners)	Nationality	Nature of work or discovery
1985	Physiology or Medicine	Georges J. F. Kohler (1946-95) Cesar Milstein (1927-2002) Michael S. Brown (1941-) Joseph L. Goldstein (1940-)	German Argentine-British US US	Described the hybridoma technique for producing monoclonal antibodies Described the importance in cholesterol metabolism of cell surface receptors for low-density lipoproteins
1986	Physiology or Medicine	Stanley Cohen (1922-) Rita Levi-Montalcini (1909-)	US Italian-US	Discovered, respectively, epidermal growth factor and nerve growth factor
1987	Physiology or Medicine	Susumu Tonegawa (1933-)	Japanese	Demonstrated how genetic recombination in immune cells produces the diversity of antigen receptors and antibodies
1988	Chemistry	Johann Deisenhofer (1943-) Robert Huber (1937-) Hartmut Michel (1948-)	German German German	Determined the three-dimensional structure of a photosynthetic reaction centre
1989	Physiology or Medicine	J. Michael Bishop (1936-) Harold E. Varmus (1939-)	US US	Discovered that viral oncogenes are derived from normal cellular genes
1989	Chemistry	Sidney Altman (1939-) Thomas R. Cech (1947-)	Canadian-US US	Discovered the catalytic properties of RNA
1991	Physiology or Medicine	Erwin Neher (1944-) Bert Sakmann (1942-)	German German	Studied the operation of single ion channels in cell membranes
1992	Physiology or Medicine	Edmond H. Fischer (1920-) Edwin G. Krebs H918-)	Swiss-US US	Discovered the importance of protein phosphorylation as a regulatory mechanism for cellular functions
1993	Physiology or Medicine	Richard J- Roberts (1943-) Phillip A. Sharp (1944-)	British US	Discovered 'split genes', consisting of exons and intervening noncoding introns

Year	Nobel prize	Name of prizewinners)	Nationality	Nature of work or discovery
1993	Chemistry	Kary B. Mullis (1944-)	US	Invented the polymerase chain reaction technique
		Michael Smith (1932-2000)	Canadian	Developed the technique of site-directed mutagenesis
1994	Physiology or Medicine	Alfred G. Gilman (1941-)	US	Discovered G proteins and their role in cell signalling
		Martin Rodbell (1925-98)	US	
1995	Physiology or Medicine	Edward B. Lewis (1918-2004)	us	Identified the genes that control the development of Drosophila embryos
		Christiane Nusslein Volhard(1942-)	German	
		Eric F. Wieschaus (1947-)	US	
1995	Chemistry	Paul J. Crutzen (1933-)	Dutch	Made fundamental contributions to understanding of ozone chemistry and the threat posed to the ozone layer by human-derived chemicals
		Mario J. Molina (1943-)	US	
		F. Sherwood Rowland (1927-)	US	
1996	Physiology or Medicine	Peter C. Doherty (1940-)	Australian	Discovered the mechanism by which cytotoxic T cells recognize virus-infected cells
		Rolf M. Zinkernagel (1944-)	Swiss	
1997	Physiology or Medicine	Stanley B. Prusiner (1942-)	US	Discovered prions
	Chemistry	Paul D. Boyer (1918-)	US	Determined the structure and mechanism of ATP synthetase
		John E. Walker (1941-)	British	
		Jens C. Skou (1918-)	Danish	Discovered sodium/potassium ATPase (the sodium pump) in cell membranes
1998	Physiology or Medicine	Robert F. Furchgott (1916-2009)	US	Discovered that nitric oxide is a key signalling molecule in the cardiovascular system
		Louis J. Ignarro (1942-)	US	
		Ferid Murad (1936-)	US	
1999	Physiology or Medicine	Gunter Blobel (1936-)	US	Formulated the signal hypothesis whereby proteins are tagged with peptide 'address labels' to specify their destination within the cell

Year	Nobel prize	Name of prizewinners)	Nationality	Nature of work or discovery
2000	Physiology or Medicine	Arvid Carlsson (1923-)	Swedish	Demonstrated the mechanism of action of dopamine as a neurotransmitter in the brain
		Paul Greengard (1925-)	US	
		Eric R. Kandel (1929-)	US	Discovered how changes in nerve synapses are the basis of learning and memory
2001	Physiology or Medicine	Leland H. Hartwell (1939-)	US	Identified key genes and proteins involved in regulating the cell cycle
		R. Timothy Hunt (1943-)	British	
		Paul M. Nurse (1949-)	British	
2002	Physiology or Medicine	Sydney Brenner (1927-)	British	Identified crucial genes that regulate organ development and programmed cell death (apoptosis)
		H. Robert Horvitz (1947-)	US	
		John E. Sulston (1942-)	British	
2003	Chemistry	Peter Agre (1949-)	US	Discovered water channels in cell membranes
		Roderick MacKinnon (1956-)	US	Determined the spatial conformation of the potassium ion channel
2004	Physiology or Medicine	Richard Axel (1946-)	us	Discovered the family of genes encoding olfactory receptors and how olfactory signals are received by the brain
		Linda B. Buck (1947-)	us	
2004	Chemistry	Aaron Ciechanover (1947-)	Israeli	Discovered the process of ubiquitin-mediated protein degradation in living cells
		Avram Hershko (1937-)	Israeli	
		Irwin Rose (1926-)	US	
2006	Physiology or Medicine	Andrew Z. Fire (1959-)	us	Discovered RNA interference
		Craig C. Mello (1960-)	us	
2006	Chemistry	Roger D. Kornberg (1947-)	us	Determined the molecular basis of transcription in eukaryotic cells

Year	Nobel prize	Name of prizewinners)	Nationality	Nature of work or discovery
2007	Physiology or Medicine	Mario R. Capecchi (1937-)	US	Developed the technique of using embryonic stem cells to create mouse strains carrying targeted gene modifications
		Martin J. Evans (1941-)	British	
		Oliver Smithies (1925-)	US	
2008	Physiology or Medicine	Harald zur Hausen (1936 -)	Germany	Human papilloma viruses causing cervical cancer
		Françoise Barré-Sinoussi (1947 -)	France	Human immunodeficiency virus
		Luc Montagnier (1932 -)	France	
2009	Physiology or Medicine	Elizabeth H. Blackburn (1948 -)	Australia	Protection of chromosomes by telomeres and enzyme telomerase
		Carol W. Greider (1961 -)	US	
		Jack W. Szostak (1952 -)	UK	
2010	Physiology or Medicine	Robert G. Edwards (1925 -)	UK	Development of invitro fertilization
2011	Physiology or Medicine	Bruce A. Beutler (1957 -)	US	Activation of innate immunity
		Jules A. Hoffmann (1941 -)	Luxembourg	
		Ralph M. Steinman (1943 - 2011)	Canada	Dendritic cell and its role in adaptive immunity

Note: The physiology or medicine prizewinners listed above have been selected for their contributions to biology; they do not represent an exhaustive list of prizewinners

Popular Science

Author: Vikas Khatri
Format: Paperback
Language: English
Pages: 160
Price: ` 110

Experiments are an inseparable part of any scientific study or Research. In this book, the author has tried to simplify science to the readers, particularly the school-going students through easy and interesting experiments. All the experiments given in the book are based on some scientific phenomena, such as atmospheric pressure, high and low temperatures, boiling, freezing and melting points of solids, liquids and gases, gravitational force, magnetism, electricity, solubility of substances, etc. Thus, read and carry out each of these fun-filled experiment in your homes or schools under the supervision and guidance of your teachers, parents or elders.

Author: Dr. C.L. Garg & Dr. Amit Garg
Format: Paperback
Language: English
Pages: 120
Price: ` 140

81 Classroom projects on: Physics, Chemistry, Biology & Electronics for Sec. & Sr. Sec. Students. Science projects and models play a pivotal role in inculcating scientific temper in young minds and in harnessing their skills. Students of classes 10 th, 11th & 12 th have to work on such projects and these carry much weight in the overall performance.
All these aspects have been considered during the compilation of the projects and models. This book will also be an ideal choice for parents interested in enhancing scientific temper of their children and for hobbyists.

Author: A.H. Hashmi
Format: Paperback
Language: English
Pages: 206
Price: ` 495

Complete science homework compen-dium for children aged 8 to 16. Through Short paragraphs and great pictures the book explains all about, Environment, Transport, Energy, Communi-cation, Electricity & Magnetism, Light & Sound, Chemistry, Universe, Earth, Animal & Plants, Human Body and others in 17 sections! Guaranteed to build scientific temper in children to excel in studies! Equally useful for parents and guardians to understand and explain to the youngsters the different areas of scientific world in which we live. Competitive exam candidates will also be greatly benefitted in getting a short and crisp answer to their inquisitiveness.
A must have book for every home!

English Related

Author: Califord Sawhney
Format: Paperback
Language: English
Pages: 230
Price: ` 88

We can not ignore the complexities of the English language which sometimes perplex a reader or even a scholar. *Improve your Word Power* by Clifford Sawhney simplifies all these complexities by providing answers to the nagging grammatical queries, syntax, style, choice of words, spellings, etc. This book serves as a complete guide that elaborately explains the usages of nouns, adjectives, adverbs, phrases, proverbs and so on.
Hence, it will undoubtedly serve as a bible for both the lovers and wizards of English language.

Author: Archana Mathur
Format: Paperback
Language: English
Pages: 148
Price: ` 120

- The book offers practical advice for writing proper and attractive prose.
- It will help improve one's communication ability and skill.
- The topics cover Common Errors, Confusing set of Figures of Speech, Foreign Words and Phrases and various aspects of Grammar and Syntax.
- The entries have adequate and appropriate examples.
- The topics are arranged alphabetically for easy reference.

This work is a contribution to various aspects of writing correct and good English, focusing on the requirements of the Indian writers.

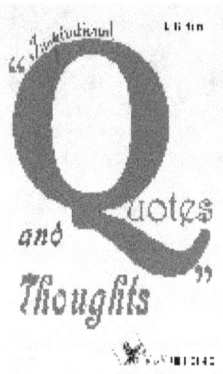

Author: G.C. Beri
Format: Paperback
Language: English
Pages: 132
Price: ` 96

This book contains as many as 460 inspiring quotes classified in well defined 19 groups. This classification itself indicates that all major aspects in human life have been covered.

Even a cursory reading of some quotes will convince the reader that in a small space it presents a mine of wisdom that will always be inspiring.

To one who is passing through some major difficulties and as a result feeling depressed and confused, this book *'Inspirational Quotes and Thoughts'* would bring him out of that disturbed mental state. It will instil in him confidence, inspiration as well as positive outlook that are needed for success and happiness in life.

Quiz Books

Author: Manasvi Vohra
Format: Paperback
Language: English
Pages: 144
Price: ` 110

The study of environment is a must for us as we are an integral part of the environment. It includes composite physical and biological sciences including subjects, such as Ecology, Botany, Zoology, Physics, Chemistry, Soil Science, Geography, etc. Hence, in order to understand and learn more about the environment in which we live in and to find answers to all our queries regarding the mysteries that surround us, *Environment Quiz Book* is an ideal one.
The book includes several interesting and simple:
• Questions & Answers
• MCQs
• Fill in the Blanks
• Crossword
• Word Search
• True & False

Author: Rajeev Garg & Amit Garg
Format: Paperback
Language: English
Pages: 192
Price: ` 96

That is what your child will find in this A to Z Quiz Series – brilliant books brimming with the latest information and simple explanations of fascinating facts and feats about our constantly evolving world. Designed to boost your child's knowledge base, each page comes alive with new facts in an engrossing form of short Questions and Answers with explanatory illustrations, all of which makes it easy to read, easy to follow and easy to remember.
Each book covers a subject comprehensively. Students, parents and teachers would find these books helpful in boosting the knowledge level of children. These books come in handy for quiz contests, competitive exams, admission tests, career development etc.

Author: Gladys Ambat
Format: Paperback
Language: English
Pages: 256
Price: ` 120

Quiz blitzkrieg are brain fitness fundas of a unique kind! The thrill to win or lose gaming session of a quiz programme can give you an optimum level of mental fitness and alertness. You simply bubble over with the sheer joy of challenge. The book is a lively presentation for all youngsters and a pleasant leisure companion for the elders. The veteran author has put together over 4000 exciting quizzes and interesting brain-teasers to get all keyed up. While you race through every page – you could find yourself sitting on the edge of the chair. The book covers:
• Quiz Medley & Quickies
• Palindromes & Proverbs
• Villains in History & Fiction

Campus to Corporate

Author: V. Rajesh
Format: Paperback
Language: English
Pages: 104
Price: ` 120

Author: Prof. Shrikant Prasoon
Format: Paperback
Language: English
Pages: 200
Price: ` 135

Author: Bibhu Prasad Mishra
Format: Paperback
Language: English
Pages: 233
Price: ` 150

It is easy to skip a question during an exam if it is *"Out of Syllabus"* but what do you do if you are faced with a situation in life for which you were not given any inputs? Can you run away from the situation using the *"Out of Syllabus"* excuse? Career is one area where one is expected to know and manage situations. After all a person is paid a salary to be able to handle things and deliver results. The reality is that most people get a lot of academic and conceptual inputs relating to one's career choice but very little practical inputs on how to effectively use the academic learning.

Group Discussions (GD) are commonly used to assess several personality aspects of candidates during various entrance tests and as a part of selection process for various jobs. This book can be a game changer for most students, since even most technically sound and brilliant students often falter at GD.
This comprehensive guide book helps you clear the fog surrounding GD and its step-by-step instructions will make you a winner in GD.
This book includes:
• Insight into: Need of GD, Do's & Don'ts in GD, Body Language & Public Speaking, Skills & Ability required in GD, and so on
• Important GD topics, How to gather Information for GD, Reading & Practice for GD

The book *'Preparing for a Winning Interview'* is divided into two sections. The first section deals with the preparations, research and understanding various facets of the interview and its procedure.
The second section contains understanding and learning specific job skills in everchanging and challenging corporate environment; the role of an employee and the need to be prepared beforehand to fit in different organisation by meeting tough corporate tasks, and by coping with the changing works, conditions and milieu.
The book covers all the core areas of interview process, delicacies in work environment, intricacies of challenging spheres, the need of sustainbility, and presents ready and easy solutions.

Student Development

Author: Abhishek Thakore
Format: Paperback
Language: English
Pages: 142
Price: ` 110

Success today depends a lot on one's academic achievements. And to excel in studies, you don't have to be just an intelligent or brilliant student — but also one who knows how to manage studies and time. In fact, even a mediocre or a below-average student can perform exceedingly well by following a scientific system.
The Portrait of a Super Student now brings you an innovative system, specifically designed for super achievement. From simple, practical and timetested tips on how to manage time, controlling temptation, scheduling time and work, relaxing techniques to diet control, speed reading, building vocabulary, improving presentation, discussing studies.

Author: B.K. Narayan & Preeti Narayan
Format: Paperback
Language: English
Pages: 133
Price: ` 150

251 Study Secrets from the Diary of a Top Achiever provides you easy methods and tricks to achieve success in studies—without stress and tension. This unique 'quick help' book for students explains with all the topics that are important for your study success. Here are some of the topics:
- Confidence
- Motivation
- Choosing Career
- Fixing Goal in Mind
- Increasing Brainpower
- Programme to Succeed
- Concentration

This book is written in short, concise form so that you can read fast, learn quickly, and use instantly! If you need more help visit: www.mindpowerguide.biz

Author: Prem P. Bhalla
Format: Paperback
Language: English
Pages: 143
Price: ` 80

Exams play a major role in the lives of not just students, but adults too. Although youngsters are taught a variety of subjects to equip them for adult life, no school teaches them how to excel in exams. Most learn through trial and error. Others remain clueless about how to excel in exams. This crucial information if learnt can ensure that even those with average IQ excel in exams.
This book contains simple and practical tips and guidelines on how to tap your full potential and give off your best during exams. An invaluable guide for everyone due to appear in exams. It is equally useful for parents who wish to ensure their children do well and secure maximum marks.

www.ingramcontent.com/pod-product-compliance
Lightning Source LLC
Chambersburg PA
CBHW050329230426
43663CB00010B/1791